parrots
and related birds

t.f.h.

henry j. bates
and
robert l. busenbark

THIRD EDITION

edited and expanded by dr. matthew m. vriends

All black and white photos by Louise van der Meid except for those specifically credited otherwise in their captions and for the following: Dr. G. Allen: 187, 482; Dr. Herbert R. Axelrod: 351; Manolo Guevara: 194; Harry V. Lacey: 191; 455; Three Lions: 103; 106; 127; 207; Fred B. Mudditt: 403; 458; Horst Mueller: 1; 274; 461; 464; 467; 468; Carl Naether: 398; 479; John Rammel: 474.

All color photos are by Louise van der Meid except for those that are specifically credited otherwise in their captions and for the following: Horst Mueller: 321; 328; 333; 340; 352; 356; 361; 364; 372; 373; 376; 381; Harry V. Lacey: 129; 132; 133; 136; 137; 140; 141; 145; 148; 149; 152; 153; 160; 348; 349.

ISBN 0-87666-967-4

Distributed in the U.S.A. by T.F.H. Publications, Inc., 211 West Sylvania Avenue, P.O. Box 27, Neptune City, N.J. 07753; in England by T.F.H. (Gt. Britain) Ltd., 13 Nutley Lane, Reigate, Surrey; in Canada to the book store and library trade by Clarke, Irwin & Company, Clarwin House, 791 St. Clair Avenue West, Toronto 10, Ontario; in Canada to the pet trade by Rolf C. Hagen Ltd., 3225 Sartelon Street, Montreal 382, Quebec: in Southeast Asia by Y.W. Ong, 9 Lorong 36 Geylang, Singapore 14; in Australia and the south Pacific by Pet Import Pty. Ltd., P.O. Box 149, Brookvale 2100, N.S.W., Australia. Published by T.F.H. Publications, Inc. Ltd., The British Crown Colony of Hong Kong.

PREFACE

It is the purpose of this book to introduce people in all walks of life and with all ranges of interests to the wondrous parrot family. The beginner in the hobby will find much that will be useful in making decisions as to what birds and equipment he should buy for a start. The experienced aviculturist will find data on many birds which are rare and on which published information is at best limited and obscure. Housing, general care, breeding, genetics, hybridizing, diseases, disorders, taming, talking, and feeding are all covered in this book. The number of individual species and their characteristics and requirements are widely covered. There are more pictures in color and in black and white than in any other single volume in this price range devoted exclusively to parrots in Aviculture.

In writing of the various birds of the parrot family, much needless repetition has been avoided by listing several general characteristics for each genus. Further repetition has been avoided by describing the best known member of any species which is subdivided into various subspecies. Since there are only slight differences separating most subspecies, we felt it would be even more succinct to point out those differences rather than to give an entire description in which the differences might become lost in the reading.

There are too many rules set down by too many people in the bird world. One authority insists that birds be fed one diet, while another equally important authority will prescribe a different feeding routine. Aviaries and cages are the bases of many disagreements among novices, experienced aviculturists, and noted authorities. Because one person has greater success with one diet or one type of aviary, he naturally assumes that this success will extend to everyone who follows his example. One successful method of taming or teaching a bird to talk does not preclude success with another method.

There are many ways of accomplishing the same end result. Just as there are personality differences in every human being, so, too, there are no two birds which are alike. Every time someone lays down a rule on the care, feeding, or taming of birds he will find a bird which insists on breaking it. The more rigid the rule, the more numerous the exceptions.

Therefore, please bear in mind that, although this book covers many detailed points in bird care, there are other methods which are also successful. In many cases alternative methods are outlined. The writers are not attempting to state clear-cut and concise rules which must be followed. Through several years of experience, in which nearly every conceivable problem has arisen, we have learned more from the exceptions than from the rules. This is the spirit which we hope to impart to our readers.

In addition, the writers have drawn upon the experiences, observations, and study of other serious-minded bird fanciers who have contributed much to the scope of this volume.

ACKNOWLEDGMENTS

This book was made possible because the writers and all those who helped had a desire to share their experiences, knowledge, and enjoyment with other people.

Louise Van der Meid photographed all the birds illustrated in this book, and it was a long, arduous task. Dorothy Speed, whose fine collection is well represented in the illustrations, furnished helpful information on an ideal diet for parrot-like birds. Mrs. Speed's birds also have been the basis for many personal experiences with rare and unusual birds. The writers value highly their close and long-standing friendship with Mrs. Speed and would like to acknowledge her assistance.

Other friendships have contributed much to this work. Jerome Buteyn gladly opened his aviaries to allow us to obtain many of the photographs in this book. Jack Thropp, the curator of the birds at the Jerome Buteyn Ranch in San Luis Rey, assisted us with some of the uncooperative birds and helped with some of the finer points of identification.

Harold Rudkin, at his ranch in Fillmore, assisted us in photographing one of his beautiful pairs of Grand Eclectus Parrots. Kenneth Wyatt in Torrance opened his excellent aviaries to us for pictures of the Red Rosellas, Bourkes, Elegants, and Redrump Parrakeets, also some of the rare birds belong to Herb Melvin.

Dr. M. Dale Arvey, from the Department of Biological Sciences at Long Beach State College, Long Beach, California, helped on the chapter on Diseases and Ailments. Dr. Arvey's laboratory experience and technical background, coupled with a keen interest in aviculture, have aided invaluably in this chapter.

Many of the birds were photographed at the Palos Verdes Bird Farm.

HANK BATES
BOB BUSENBARK

Walteria, California.

NOTES AND INFORMATION ON THE SECOND EDITION

Since the first edition of this book appeared in 1959, we have had many additional experiences with birds of the parrot family. Also, we have received letters from readers in nearly every one of the United States as well as readers in many countries abroad—from Norway to Ceylon, from Switzerland to Australia and New Zealand. Many of the letters, of course, concern the companion volume to this book, *Finches and Softbilled Birds;* and many letters have to do with both books.

We have, since 1959, been able to travel rather extensively not only within the United States but also to several European countries and to many countries in the Orient always looking for zoos, birds, and people interested in birds. We have found our books and booklets—seven to date—in places which seemed surprising to us. To find our books being used or offered for sale in Holland, England, the Philippines, Japan, Singapore, Bangkok, Penang, and other faraway places is a gratifying experience. To receive letters offering additional useful material or contrasting avicultural management in the different countries is always a pleasure.

Every letter which reached us has been answered to the best of our ability even though the time available for each answer becomes limited as the number of letters increases. Many of the letters and long distance telephone calls with many of the problems had already been answered satisfactorily in the various books; but, when a cherished pet is in trouble, the worried owner may not read quite far enough or often seeks more specific information for his particular problem which is often a little different, frequently exceptional, and sometimes unanswerable. One of the many memorable exceptional telephone calls came from a man in the Bahamas wanting to know how far a macaw could fly. His pet had flown out to sea. After it was recovered, he sent us very extensive newspaper coverage complete with pictures of the adventurous bird and the happy reunion.

More than ever, we have become convinced through the letters, the growing friendships, the personal contacts in our travels, and the many visitors who have come to the Palos Verdes Bird Farm, that the people who are interested in birds, whether as individual pet owners or as full-fledged aviculturists, are indeed very nice people. Many people, for the sake of other birds, are happy to share their findings.

Among the most important additions in this second edition are the detailed diets used in handfeeding baby birds of various species. These diets and experiences are presented by the people who have developed them over long periods of successful use. Included are many small details and suggestions which may seem inconsequential but which become very important if the outcome is to be really successful. The writers would like especially to extend their appreciation to Mrs. Velma Hart, Mr. Kenneth Wyatt, and Mr. Ralph Small for their notable contributions which the writers have reported in this second edition.

Experiments in diet improvements usually proceed slowly because everyone is reluctant to digress too much all at once for fear of causing harm to the birds. Only in states of emergency does one resort to drastic measures, and sometimes the findings become valuable to all bird fanciers if reported. For the most part aviculturists are not scientists. Major discoveries have often come about as the result of many trials and errors as well as small but progressive one-step-at-a time experiments. Fads and many persistent erroneous beliefs which almost amount to superstitions have often hampered progress along with the slow acceptance of new ideas. Real progress in aviculture has nevertheless been accomplished at an ever increasing pace, and a good share of that progress can be attributed to the many people who share their experiences.

Identification of various species has accounted for a good many of the letters which we have received on the first edition. An additional chapter has been added to expand descriptions of many species, to fill in several gaps, and to correct a few errors. Part of this task was solved by the opportunity extended by Charles O'Brien to examine museum skins in the American Museum of Natural History in New York City which has the largest collection of bird skins in the world. Also helpful in this task have been visits to zoos in various parts of the United States and in many countries abroad.

Though the writers have photographed birds in zoos and private collections wherever possible in their travels and have used the photographs for additional material, few of the photographs are suitable for reproduction. With the exception of the marvelous bird house at the Milwaukee Zoo and some aviaries in the San Diego Zoo, most zoos were not meant for photographers. Many have backgrounds which are distracting or cluttered. Lighting is too often insufficient for anything but time exposures or flash bulbs. The birds seldom pose for time exposures, and flash bulbs can cause undue fright. Another drawback in photographing birds is the difficulty in focusing out the wire mesh of aviaries or cages. Except in rare instances, it is not possible to remove birds belonging to zoos or even private aviaries into cages or enclosures which provide satisfactory lighting and backgrounds for photography. Several of the new pictures added to this book are therefore extraordinary because all the needed requirements have been supplied for excellent portrait photography. The ideal avicultural book would show photographic representations of each genus and of many of the variable species, but this is not possible at this time. Such a task would require years of traveling and amassing perhaps thousands of photographs from all parts of the world for the best pictorial representations.

In the meantime, the knowledge continues to accrue; and the exceptions to the rules continue to increase. The variations in management and diet required by different climates as well as differences in foods available in different parts of the world show the ingenuity and resourcefulness of bird fanciers as well as the adaptability of the birds.

In many countries, sunflower seed is not available; and so substitutes must be found. Several seeds not available in the United States are used very successfully instead of several seeds which we in this country consider basic. Fruits are also variable in many parts of the world not only in cost and general distribution but seasonally as well. Thus the low cost and easy access of highly nutritious papaya to be found in Thailand, the Philippines, Hawaii, and similar areas are unobtainable or too costly in most countries of the world. Mr. Gust. Gjessing, owner of the northernmost aviary of the world in Drammen, Norway, states that fruits are generally too expensive in his area though he does feed plenty of apples and, in season, wild blueberries and raspberries. Other fruits and vegetables are largely ignored because the birds have never become accustomed to them. Green food is available only in the summer. As a substitute, Mr. Gjessing adds algae flour (made from dehydrated ocean plants from the

Arctic Ocean) for additional minerals and vitamins C and B^{12}. A cod liver oil by-product furnishes supplemental amounts of vitamins A and D. His birds also eat the bark which they enjoy stripping from branches supplied every week whenever possible.

Imagine the climate variations which require differences in housing. Tropical and subtropical areas require minimum shelters from the temperature standpoint. Even the warm tropic rains can be utilized by the birds. Their love for bathing in rainfall produces the very best plumage to be seen anywhere. In hot, dry weather we have frequently had to resort to a garden sprinkler on top of aviaries to bring temperatures down to safe levels. Mr. Gjessing in Norway must maintain thermostatically controlled heating devices during the prolonged winter to keep the temperature up to six or seven degrees above zero. In one letter he stated "All the birds are outside today as it is very fine and sunny air, and the temperature is eight degrees above zero" (presumably centigrade).

In many areas of the world due to cold weather, the birds in zoos or in private collections must be housed in totally enclosed heated buildings during winters. Too many of the birds of the parrot family under these circumstances are not given satisfactory bathing facilities or sufficient humidity to prevent the skin from becoming dry and itchy. As a result many fine specimens are be-draggled and badly feather plucked by the time good outside weather again becomes available. Frequent spraying of water helps in preventing these problems if caught before the feather plucking becomes a firmly entrenched bad habit.

HENRY J. BATES
ROBERT L. BUSENBARK
Torrance (Walteria)
California

A NOTE ABOUT THE THIRD EDITION

This third edition differs from the previous editions by, in addition to having more and newer photos, having a more up to date nomenclature, although the scientific classification of parrots is still under constant revision, resulting in the fact that names that are correct today may change by tomorrow.

Additional material also has been added as far as photographs, feeding schemes and such are concerned.

In the text itself only minor modifications and updatings have been made. The major difference between the text of this third edition and that of the second edition is that it is arranged differently. All of the material which had appeared as Chapter 19 under the heading "ADDITIONAL DESCRIPTIONS AND DATA ON THE SPECIES" in the second edition has now been incorporated into the various chapters dealing with the individual groups of parrots. This makes the information easier for the reader to find and absorb, as it is now not necessary to refer to separate sections in the text for all information applicable to a given species.

I hope that the book will now give even more pleasure to those interested in the fascinating and all-absorbing hobby that is called Aviculture.

Neptune, New Jersey
June, 1978

Dr. Matthew M. Vriends

Contents

Chapter 1- INTRODUCTION TO PARROTS IN AVICUL-
TURE. 11
Introduction and generalized information, including
history of aviculture, scope and values of the hobby,
and hints to the novice who wants to keep parrots.

Chapter 2- FEEDING. 15
This chapter presents general dietary requirements
for all members of the parrot family, starting with
the simple diet of the budgie and working on up to
the more complicated diets. It also contains a diet
which we consider to be the very finest and most
perfect ever offered to a bird in captivity. It was
evolved by Dorothy Speed, a sincere student of
aviculture who has studied and experimented most
carefully.

Chapter 3- AVIARIES AND EQUIPMENT 24
Includes recommendations for every piece of equipment needed in an aviary and dimensions and construction suggestions for aviaries of all different
kinds of parrot-like birds.

Chapter 4- TAMING. 41
Includes different methods of taming and reasons for
each. This chapter can be used as a handy manual
for taming any species of parrot-like bird.

Chapter 5- TALKING. 54
This chapter lists the various techniques of teaching
parrots how to talk and explains why some are successful and why some are not.

Chapter 6- THE CAGED HOUSEHOLD PET. 61
Lists changes in diet, maintenance, and other factors
differing in the care of the pet bird from an aviary.

Chapter 7- GENETICS AND HYBRIDIZING........... 70
These interesting subjects are usually treated in a
manner which is either hazy or so highly technical
that thay are not understandable. They are covered
from a scientific view-point but in a layman's
language.

Chapter 8- DISEASES............................. 79
Modern treatment with wonder drugs has not yet
been properly recorded in any book on birds. There
are also many obscure disorders which are baffling
and difficult to treat. This chapter is the result of
much personal interest and experience in collabora-
tion with Dr. Dale Arvey, of the Department of
Biological Sciences at Long Beach State College,
whose laboratory experience is very extensive
because of a personal interest.

Chapter 9- THE PARROT FAMILY.................... 98
Scientific data and classifications which have always
been overlooked or particularly misused with frequent errors in previous publications, but which are
interesting and useful in understanding the status of
each family. Explains use and meaning of scientific
names.

Chapter 10-THREE UNUSUAL SUBFAMILIES......... 107
Strigopinae, Netsorinae, and Micropsittinae. Three
Subfamilies which are interesting but of no great
concern in aviculture due to rarity and, in some
cases, due to difficulty in maintenance.

Chapter 11-LORIES, LORIKEETS, AND CLOSELY
RELATED BIRDS........................ 112
Subfamily: Loriinae. One of the most interesting,
most entertaining, and most numerous of all parrot
groups. The members are nectar feeders rather than
seedeaters.

Chapter 12-COCKATOOS................................ 159
Subfamily: Cacatuinae. Contains all genera of the
subfamily, including Cockatiels. Members of this
family have fanciful crests and unusual coloration.

Chapter 13-MACAWS AND CONURES................ 199
Includes all genera of two very unusual and
somewhat similar South American groups.

Chapter 14-PARROTS.................................. 275
Includes all varieties from Africa, South America,
Australia, New Zealand, New Guinea, the Philip-
pines, and the South Pacific Islands.

Chapter 15-PARRAKEETS............................. 375
Includes species from all over the world.

Chapter 16-LOVE BIRDS AND PARROTLETS........... 457

Chapter 17-HANGING PARROTS AND GUAIABERO..... 471

Chapter 18-ADDITIONAL DATA ON SEX DETERMINA-
TION, BREEDING AND HAND FEEDING.... 475

APPENDIX................................. 513

SELECTED BIBLIOGRAPHY............... 515

INDEX..................................... 517

PHOTO INDEX........................... 541

I

INTRODUCTION TO PARROTS IN AVICULTURE

The hobby of keeping birds is called Aviculture, a term embracing all varieties of birds. The aviculturist is interested in maintaining conditions and proper food conducive to the good health and long life of his birds. In most cases he is interested in breeding these birds and has performed the very worthwhile service of preventing the extinction of several varieties of beautiful birds whose natural habitats have been destroyed by the encroachment of civilization.

The ornithologist has contributed much to the world's knowledge of birds in their natural habitat, their particular uses and values to man, their individual habits, and much more. Aviculturists, drawing heavily upon the ornithologists' contributions, have compiled a further store of first-hand knowledge of birds in captivity under unnatural or semi-natural conditions. Public zoos, which keep birds, usually have an aviculturist as a curator of birds.

Of all the birds of the world, it is the parrot family that offers the most versatility. Parrots become the tamest pets, bear the widest assortment of colors and patterns, display every conceivable personality trait, range in price from one to many thousands of dollars per specimen, and vary in size from the small Budgerigar to the large Macaw. On top of all that, they are easily cared for and can talk back to you.

EXOTIC COLORS

There is something exotic about most members of the parrot family. Artists, designers, and decorators who work with tropical motifs generally add parrots to their fabrics, wallpapers, or pictures. And there is no reason to use artistic license and distortions of line and color because there is nothing fancier than the birds themselves.

Every conceivable color combination has been tried by Mother Nature in adorning the parrot family. A few years ago the color combination of rose and grey was high fashion news in interior decoration. It was the last word in elegance and gracious living. But nowhere was it more beautifully epitomized than it has been all along in the Rose Breasted Cockatoo.

11

Soft muted tones, exquisite shadings, accent colors, or brilliant, violent reds, yellows, greens, purples or blues—they are all well represented in the parrot family.

MYRIAD SHAPES

A variation in shape is also characteristic of the parrot family. Shapely birds are adorned with fanciful, movable crests or long tapering, graceful tails. Some are ordinary. Many are exotic. All have beauty.

The exotic color combinations and the many beautiful shapes are undoubtedly two very good reasons for keeping parrots as pets. This is true whether the bird fancier keeps one bird as a pet in his household or whether he has an extensive array of aviaries housing a multitude of different parrots gathered from around the world.

NATURAL HABITATS

Parrots are found mostly in tropical climates all around the world. South and Central America are particularly rich in parrot life. Africa and India contribute some very popular members of this family. China and other Oriental countries have many varieties. The Philippine Islands have some very choice parrots which are seldom seen in this country. Many of the South Pacific Islands boast a wide range of parrot types. However, it is Australia that provides the largest selection of the world's really exotic parrots. From Australia come the Budgerigar and Cockatiel, the world's most popular and easily bred parrot-like birds. Most of the world's family of Cockatoos and a majority of the species of large parrakeets are native to Australia, New Guinea and New Zealand.

EARLIEST PARROT FANCIERS

During the days of the Roman Empire, parrots zoomed to popularity as pets. The ancient Romans were partial to members of the Ringneck Parrakeet family. These were regarded as a novelty or toy because they could imitate the human voice. Also, because they were high priced luxuries, they soon denoted a certain high station in life. The parrots of ancient times, and even as late as the eighteenth century, were commensurate with the mink coat in milady's closet today. In those days, parrots were housed usually in elaborate and expensive cages.

Because of the ignorance of their owners, parrots were often abused and maltreated. If a parrot did not speak when spoken to, it would be punished. The method used to teach a bird to talk was to crack him over the skull while repeating the word to be learned. This brutal method of teaching persisted for a long period in history. Apart from being ineffective, it probably accounted for some of the high mortality rate.

Gradually, the more intelligent and humane bird fanciers among the aristocracy developed into true aviculturists. Some accrued vast collections of exotic birds and were successful in breeding many varieties. Also gradually, came the day when people of more modest means could afford to own pet birds.

The hobby of keeping and breeding birds of all kinds has attracted more universal interest in Europe than in America. A friend, recently travelling in Europe, reports that just about everyone has birds. "They may be fine birds or ordinary, but they are there. Even if there isn't a crust of bread in the house, there will be the much cherished pet bird."

REWARDS OF AVICULTURE

Bird fanciers have done their work well. There is no better proof that birds in captivity are well cared for and happy than the fact that they happily settle down to the job of rearing a family. They lose their fear of man, have no natural enemies with which to contend, and have their food and water provided without the natural job of procurement. It is no wonder that birds in captivity, which are well cared for, usually live longer and are in better condition than birds in the wild.

The word "captivity" is actually not good usage because it indicates that the birds are being kept prisoners against their will. The word "domesticity" is far more preferable and descriptive because the birds are obviously very happy in their domesticated state. Through continued use, therefore, "captivity" has gradually acquired the connotation of domesticity.

The rewards for the hobbyist are manyfold. Though the investment can range from a very modest pittance to many thousands of dollars, the enjoyment, relaxation, and companionship derived from a single pet bird quickly repay the original cost and upkeep. A bird fancier also benefits from the study and observation of the birds in his collection. If the goal is breeding, he will have surplus stock which he can sell or trade for new stock which will help to subsidize his hobby.

Although some people manage their bird collections in such a manner that they actually earn a surplus above investment and maintenance, it is unwise to go into the bird hobby with the object of earning money.

BEGINNERS' PITFALLS

Inasmuch as the hobby of Aviculture is so fascinating and so vast, even if confined to members of the parrot family, it might be well to add a word of caution here.

Many people rub their eyes in amazement when they see a good collection of birds for the first time. The decision soon follows to join the hobby as quickly as possible. Seemingly trying to make up for lost time, the new convert begins the mad race. As soon as he purchases his first birds, he sets a goal for another pair and then another. The sweet joys of yearning for a certain bird are surpassed only by the joys of possession itself. So many

13

birds are purchased and crowded together that little is accomplished along the lines of breeding the cherished birds.

Before long, the new convert is so shackled with the task of caring for his birds that he has little time left for observation and study. He has bought birds as quickly as he could afford them—sometimes even sooner. Soon he decides the entire venture was a mistake, that it is too much work, and that it is too expensive. All the while, it was his own impatience that destroyed his enthusiasm.

The word of caution is this: "Take it easy! Do not go in too deeply!" The rewards are much greater and longer lasting if you will follow this advice.

PARROT FANCIERS' PRIMER

The first experience in keeping parrot-like birds is usually the possession of a Budgerigar, the most reasonably priced and most widely available member of the family. There are three good reasons for owning a budgie. It is a charming and affectionate pet; it is easily bred and is most fascinating when rearing a family; because of its penchant for mutations it provides opportunities for the study of genetics.

Fresh from this triumph, the bird fancier meets the Cockatiel, equally enchanting as a pet and still reasonably easy to breed. A little more expensive and less available than the budgie, the Cockatiel becomes the next goal— and a very worthwhile goal it is, for the Cockatiel is one of the most charming and persistently affectionate birds in the world.

Perhaps the next step for the budding aviculturist is the addition of Love Birds, those colorful comics from Africa. Then comes the ownership of a Petz' Conure (popularly called Half Moon Parrot) or even a full sized parrot— usually one from the Amazon family.

With increasing visits to zoos, pet shops, or bird farms, the bird enthusiast one day sees a lovely pair of Ringneck Parrakeets or maybe a pair of Redrump Parrakeets. Here is the turning point. If the enthusiasm is great enough, either of these birds, or both, will change the bird fancier into an aviculturist. The purchase of Redrumps or Ringnecks is usually the result of a certain amount of study and preparation and a great amount of yearning. If the decision to make the purchase is reached, the object will in nearly all cases be that of rearing enough youngsters to pay for the next pair of birds.

These steps mark some of the most delightful and memorable experiences of any bird fancier's life. The pride of owning a beautiful living creature can only be matched by the pride of achievement when the first egg hatches from a bird in captivity. And what a day of exhilaration when the baby bird leaves the nest box! It is no wonder that bird keeping is a popular hobby. The real wonder is that there are some people for whom Aviculture, and especially parrots in Aviculture, is a tightly closed book.

14

2

FEEDING

For the most part, parrots are vegetarians, which means their foods consist of various seeds, fruits, and vegetables. However, the diet of many in the wild state includes insects which inhabit some foods.

SIMPLE DIET

In captivity, parrots are easily fed and will remain in excellent condition on a relatively simple diet. The fact that a diet is simple does not mean that nutrition need not be all-inclusive. Starting out a bird on a proper diet is very important because birds are creatures of habit and are reluctant to change, especially from a bad habit. New foods are often accepted with difficulty and only after many types of subterfuge have been employed.

All birds which are given nourishing diets are able to build up stamina and a reserve buffer against the onslaught of illnesses. Since many troubles stem directly from insufficient diets, it is wise to be certain that your birds are properly fed at all times.

The diet of any bird is much more effectively administered if it can be kept simple and at the same time nutritionally adequate. He who feeds complicated diets to birds starts off with good intentions but usually ends up with sporadic efforts.

TABLE SNACKS

It is unwise to allow your bird, regardless of its type, to snack from your table. Birds which are allowed to do so develop fondnesses for such harmful foods as mashed potatoes, bacon, eggs, sweets, and many others that cause various troubles.

BASIC DIET REQUIREMENTS

The basic requirements of birds, as with all animals, are proteins, carbohydrates, vitamins, fats, and minerals of many different kinds, including a host of minute quantities of the so-called "trace minerals".

The only changes in diet from aviary birds to individual pet birds is the curtailing of fattening foods. Since parrots in confinement become

15

somewhat lazy and are quite content with captivity, care must be taken to see they do not become sluggish and overly fat. The best remedy for this is to see that oats are not fed overabundantly and to force exercise upon the bird. A caged bird should be released from his cage and allowed flying time each week, even if he has to be prodded into it.

REFUSAL TO EAT

If for some reason a parrot goes off its food, there will be severe results in a very short time. Loss of body weight and stamina mean a further lack of interest in food, and the bird may quickly die. To combat such an occurrence, the bird should be offered practically anything it will eat. Bread, peanut butter, fruit, seeds, and vegetables would all help. If necessary, continue offering food from the hand. As long as a bird will eat, more than half the battle is won.

HAND FEEDING

If it is necessary to hand feed a baby parrakeet, Love Bird, Cockatiel, or larger parrot, ground millet seed and pablum, supplemented with liquid vitamins, are helpful. The bird will soon learn to eat from a spoon.

BASIC DIET OF BUDGERIGAR

Since its diet is the simplest of all, we will start with the budgie and work upwards.

The basic diet of the Budgerigar consists of parrakeet or love bird mix, health grit, cuttlebone, greenfood, water, and some sort of dietary supplement.

PARRAKEET MIX

The personal preference of the writers narrows the parrakeet mix down to a simple one which is still nutritionally all-inclusive. It contains large white millet, canary, and oat groats. No red millet is used. Percentages run 35% for canary, 10% for oats during breeding season and cold weather, dropping to 5% in hot weather, and 55% to 60% for white proso millet. The drop in oats means an increase in millet. An excellent alternative is to raise the canary percentage to that of white proso millet; but, since canary is high in protein, the percentage should never fall below 35%.

GRIT

The grit or gravel should be more than ordinary sand. It has the double purpose of grinding up the food and furnishing necessary minerals which are lacking in other feeds. The base should be crushed granite. Sand is worn smooth and is not a satisfactory grinding agent. Other minerals such as iron oxide, sulphur, salt, calcium, lime, phosphorus, and charcoal are added to a good health grit.

16

CUTTLEBONE

Cuttlebone provides calcium and salt and also helps keep the beak trim. However, many birds of the parrot family are inordinately fond of chewing and destroy a cuttlebone as quickly as it is offered them. On the market now are harder and longer lasting cuttlebone blocks composed of powdered cuttlebone and a hardening agent. Some have added Vitamin B-12 and minerals.

If a bird refuses to eat either cuttlebone or cuttlebone block, a simple method of enticement is to scrape a few lines across the cuttlebone surface with a nail or fingernail file.

GREENFOOD

Greenfood is available in a wide variety, but carrot tops and dandelion are the richest in food value. Lettuce is not very nourishing, and, except for constant availability, there is no point in feeding it. Any greens coming from a source other than the home garden should be thoroughly washed. Insecticides may still be on the leaves and prove fatal to the birds.

Velma Hart hand-feeding a baby Mexican Double Yellow Head Parrot. Within a few weeks this ungainly baby became a beautiful and exceptionally tame full-sized parrot.

On the pet market now are different kinds of dehydrated greens which are very nourishing and quite inexpensive. They may be bought in small packets or in packages up to five pounds and have the great advantage of convenience. It is the daily feeding of greens that most people overlook. With dehydrated greens, which can be mixed with other foods or fed separately, the task of feeding is simplified.

WATER

Water should be clean and cool. Every open water dish should be thoroughly cleaned every day. A sponge is helpful in the application of "elbow grease" to scrub out water containers. Scum and algae in water containers invite infections from many insidious bacterial and protozoan organisms, including the dreaded amoebic dysentery. Metal water containers are to be avoided, due to corrosion and the resultant cleaning difficulties.

DIETARY SUPPLEMENT

A dietary supplement is helpful to the individual pet bird or to an aviary of birds. This should be one of the commercial mixtures prepared for this purpose or one of the liquid vitamin preparations which is soluble in drinking water. Care should be taken to select one in which the vitamins will not evaporate quickly. Many liquid preparations are not designed to be exposed to open air and sunshine; and, as a result, they are effective for only a short time. Powdered brewers' yeast sprinkled on seed is also a very effective supplement to the bird's diet.

DIET OF COCKATIELS AND OTHER SMALL PARROTS

The diet of the Cockatiel, Love Bird, Lineolated Parrakeet, and many other parrot family birds of similar size, is exactly the same as that of the budgie, except for the addition of sunflower seed. Sunflower seed is a very rich food. It has oils, fats, and proteins in abundance; and, also, it has a slight narcotic effect which is good for most birds.

DIET OF CONURES AND LARGER PARRAKEETS

The next step up the ladder of parrot family birds brings us to Conures and larger parrakeets. Consequently, we add another food requirement: fresh fruits and vegetables. A variety of these is recommended. Limitations are somewhat harmful. The overabundance of any one item to the exclusion of all others upsets the nutritional pattern. Suggested foods at this level are apple, orange, banana, grapes or soaked raisins, peaches, apricots, fresh corn on the cob, green peas, carrots, celery and similar foodstuffs.

The writers avoid avocado for parrot family birds but feed it to birds of the softbill family. Unfortunately, we have accepted the word of an article read a long time ago warning of the dangers of avocado. We have been very loath to try experiments which might prove the truthfulness of this article. It is just such a feeling as this that has given rise to many unproven ideas and legendary beliefs in the bird world.

DIET OF LARGER PARROTS

For larger parrot family birds, such as Amazon Parrots, Cockatoos, and Macaws, the only addition to the diet is some larger grains such as scratch feed, pigeon feed, and some seeds such as pumpkin and peanuts. Most pet shops carry parrot mixes which contain all these seeds and some red hot peppers as well. By the time this level is reached, it is truly a well-rounded diet. It includes the budgie's diet and every food item introduced with each new size of bird. To top it all, many parrots enjoy a little raw meat or even a few mealworms occasionally.

HEMP SEED

Hemp seed is used for many birds, including canaries, finches, and parrot-like birds. Hemp seed is actually the seed from the marijuana plant, unfortunately a source of drug addiction.

Many years ago, hemp seed, which lay untouched in the bottoms of dirty bird cages, was thrown out into gardens for wild birds when cages

Baby parrots quickly take to spoon-feeding and must be fed at frequent intervals. Though time-consuming, this is a very worth-while task. Hand-fed babies become the very best of pets.

19

were cleaned. If the wild birds did not consume it, the seed often grew into a very pretty plant. Because of its attractive leaf, its growth was encouraged by naive housewives who knew nothing of its dread potential or its true identity.

Eventually laws were passed which required sterilization of the seed before it could be imported into the United States. The sterilization process removed most of the danger of the pretty plants, but it also removed some of the food value. In fact, if the hemp seed lay in storage for a long time, it even built up some factors that were detrimental to birds. Then, too, sterilization did not completely solve the problem of sprouting seed.

California passed a law which prohibited completely the sale of hemp seed as a feed. This law prompted some bird fanciers to become indignant and to argue that the State was unfair to innocent parties because of the sociological problems arising from marijuana users. There is little need for such a feeling.

The actual food content of hemp seed is identical with that of sunflower seed. Wherever hemp seed is useful, sunflower seed will be equally useful. The only difference is that for small birds sunflower seed must be hulled. However, the cost of hulled sunflower seed and hemp seed is approximately the same. If the use for hemp seed is completely erased, the world will be a better place for all of us, including birds.

PROBLEM OF WEBBY SEED

The problem of webby seed often arises to plague the bird fancier. This is caused by a little moth which lays its eggs in seed, usually in summer. When the eggs hatch, a tiny caterpillar emerges to feed upon the seed. Later it spins its tiny cocoon to go into the period of dormancy before it becomes a moth. Despite freshness of seed, the moth will be present. Stocks of feed should be kept low during the summer. If the birds will eat the caterpillars, and they often do, they will add a little very nourishing animal protein to their diet.

Seed must be alive to be nourishing; and, in order to live, it must breathe just like any other living plant or animal. To check the food value of seed, plant a sample every now and then to see if it grows.

PEANUT BUTTER

A very little known foodstuff is peanut butter. Extremely nourishing and rich in natural oils, peanut butter offers food value found nowhere else. It improves plumage, keeps a bird in excellent physical condition, and is available to everyone.

The writers have made it a practice to encourage young parrots to become fond of peanut butter. The usual procedure is to spread it lightly upon bread at first and to increase the amounts until peanut butter alone is the desired

Dorothy Speed has an excellent collection of birds and does an excellent job of caring for them. Mrs. Speed prepares a selection of fruits and vegetables for each aviary.

goal for the parrot. We have had young Spectacle Amazons particularly become so fond of peanut butter that the introduction of a jar with peanut butter meant no let up until the jar was cleaned of every trace. For sickly birds and baby birds, we consider it a must. This is in addition to the other items of diet, of course.

NOURISHING TREATS

There are also many different kinds of treats offered on the pet market. Some of these are very nourishing and will enlarge the scope of the diet. Certain seeds, such as niger and flax, add sheen to the plumage. Some seeds, such as oats, are too fattening and should be fed sparingly. Spray millet is an excellent treat because it is not fattening and because it offers entertainment for the birds.

As a rule, it is best to limit treats for the birds to one-fourth the amount of parrakeet mix consumed. An overly fat bird may be put on a diet of a very high percentage of plain canary with white proso millet; but no oats, and lots of greenfood.

FRUITS AND VEGETABLES

Some budgies, Cockatiels, and Love Birds develop a taste for various fruits and vegetables. Although this is an exception, it is a good habit to

21

encourage. Larger parrot family birds take readily to such items on the avian menu and flourish. There is no reason why the smaller birds should not do likewise. Most, however, will refuse.

MRS. SPEED'S DIET

Now the writers would like to detail the various items in the diet offered to the birds of Dorothy Speed, of Fresno, California. Mrs. Speed has spent much time in ferreting out the different requirements of birds and finding a food which fills each requirement. She has proven the effectiveness of her dietary education by maintaining her birds in prime condition, despite severe heat in summer and freezing weather in winter, during which her birds remain in outdoor aviaries with no change whatever against seasonal fluctuations. Moreover, she has successfully hand-reared several parrots from tiny chicks to fledgling size. On several occasions, she has cleared up severe conditions which seemed hopelessly incurable through her knowledge of diet and loving care.

Mrs. Speed's diet for her birds consists of many different items, each item fulfilling a different purpose. Sunflower is one basic item, which is balanced by a mixture of small seeds consisting of four parts large canary, four parts oat groats, four parts fine cracked corn, two parts large white proso millet, and one part rape seed. A generous portion of safflower is offered because of its beneficial similarity to niger. Mrs. Speed says safflower is non-fattening, helps to break colds, cure diarrhea, and prevent conditions resembling old age which the relaxed life of captivity often creates in young birds.

One tablespoon of a top protein, small dog kibble, is added along with an equal portion of a high quality grade of turkey mash pellets. Ingredients in this food help strengthen quill structure, prevent dead in shell and slipped tendons, promote fertility, and increase iridescence of feather structure.

Additional nourishment is offered by feeding a half teaspoon of dry yeast in pellet or baker's form and one tablespoon of wheat germ. Two raw peanuts and one walnut are given daily. One quarter red apple, one-eighth orange, and two small slices of banana are offered each day. Other fruits are offered in season, and pomegranates are especially relished by Mrs. Speed's birds.

In addition to fruit, Mrs. Speed feeds at least one green and one yellow vegetable each day. Examples are corn on the cob, various types of squash, carrots and beets (including the tops), cabbage, kale, and other vegetables.

Eucalyptus seed and leaves are offered while still green. Fresh supplies of branches for chewing replace old ones as soon as they are used up.

Health grit and oyster shells round out the diet.

Using a pushcart, Mrs. Speed can easily feed a variety of foodstuffs with one stop for each aviary. The cart is pushed down a safety aisle so that entry into aviaries may be accomplished without fear of having birds escape.

Once a month Mrs. Speed substitutes for water a solution of one teaspoon of baking soda to one quart of water brought to a boil and cooled. The purpose is to sweeten the crop and to clean out the bird's system.

Proof of the effectiveness of this diet lies in the condition of Mrs. Speed's birds, many of which are pictured in the illustrations of this book.

The diet for baby parrots used by Mrs. Speed for the first two weeks consists of a mixture of one-third raw egg yolk, one teaspoon pablum, white corn flour such as is used in making tortillas, and one teaspoon wheat germ. All of this is moistened with hot water.

After two weeks the egg yolk is eliminated, and the white corn flour is increased. Wheat meal is added. This mixture is used for four weeks, after which a teaspoon of ground sunflower and a teaspoon of ground dog kibble are added. As the bird increases in size, the texture of the ingredients is thickened, and further ingredients of the mature bird's diet are gradually added until the bird is self-feeding on a mature diet.

3

AVIARIES AND EQUIPMENT

This chapter is not written with the idea of establishing rigid rules for the beginner to follow. Instead, the purpose is to record examples and styles of aviary construction and usable equipment that have proven successful under many different conditions. Another purpose is to discourage the use of unsightly and inefficient structures that detract from the birds. In all suggestions, there is room for individual preference and even for improvement.

UNPLANNED AVIARIES

It is quite common for beginners to buy a bird first and then to figure out where to put it. Although this is the usual practice, it is definitely not the best. Usually such unplanned arrangements look like sections of a shanty-town which is ready for bulldozers. The writers have been in aviaries where it was necessary to open ten doors and pass through nine aviaries in order to get into a particular flight. In one such aviary, it was necessary to step over a 20-inch railing at one door and duck 2 feet to get through the next door. It was the same all the way down the line, with no two doors alike in shape, size or location. Some of the shelters were constructed from piano boxes and anything that happened to be at hand. Unfortunately, this monstrous type of aviary is the rule rather than the exception.

PLANNED AVIARIES

Practical aviaries are those in which there is simplicity and uniformity of design and the need for a minimum of upkeep. A large range of aviaries should be easily accessible for rapid cleaning, feeding, and watering, with as little disturbance as possible for the sake of the birds. Since mites are a nuisance and a health menace for birds, as many nooks and crevices as possible should be avoided.

Simplicity of design is a must for parrot aviaries. The aviaries for finches and softbills can be beautiful affairs because it is possible to landscape them with plenty of shrubs and bushes and because there are many species that will live together in complete harmony. For parrots, the case is just the opposite. Except for Budgerigars and Love Birds, it is wise to keep each

Attractive and durable aviaries at the Southern California ranch of Jerome Buteyn are beautifully landscaped. These aviaries house various cockatoos and macaws. Note the pet Lear's Macaw on top of the flight in the foreground. Playful as puppies, two of these rare specimens are kept at liberty on Mr. Buteyn's ranch. They never wander from the aviaries.

pair separately and not waste time trying to plant or landscape an aviary. It will be to no avail.

In planning aviaries for parrots several important factors must be considered: safety doors, location, size of aviary, type and size of wire mesh, size of shelter, materials for shelter and framework, and type of floor.

SAFETY DOOR

If the overall aviary is to be divided into a number of flights, a wired-in

Tall flights offer ample exercise for even the largest members of the parrot family. Metal pipe framework is attractive and provides adequate defense against chewing.

aisle should be built so that all doors are easily accessible. This provides a safety door to prevent birds from escaping and obviates the necessity of entering any but the desired aviary. If the aviary is not to be divided, there should still be a safety door to prevent escape. A safety door is two doors with a sort of vestibule separating them. It is well worth the little added expense.

LOCATION

The location usually cannot be changed. One must use what space is available. Therefore, it is of the utmost importance that the aviary be designed to give protection from prevailing cold winter winds. It should be placed in a sheltered spot, even though this means obscuring easy vision or placing it in an awkward position. It is far better to rearrange the rest of the garden than to cause suffering among the birds.

SIZE

The size of the aviary would naturally depend upon the type of birds to be housed and whether the ultimate goal is for breeding or merely for display. If for display purposes only, such as a zoo would ordinarily require, the size need only be a good comfortable space that will allow for enough exercise to keep the birds in good condition. If for breeding, then there are certain desirable factors to keep in mind.

Budgerigars will breed in anything ranging in size from a small cage on up. Cockatiels should have more room for plenty of exercise if the parents are to be in prime condition for breeding. As a rule it would be wise to have flight space of 10 feet or more. The larger the flight, the better. Elegant Parrakeets, small Conures, Lineolated Parrakeets, and birds of similar size will successfully breed and thrive in aviaries of this size. Love Birds, like Budgerigars, will breed in almost any size aviary or large cage. A moderate size aviary is even better than a large aviary provided the birds are not overcrowded.

For all larger parrakeets, the best results are obtained with flights longer than 16 feet; 20 or more feet would be even more desirable. A height of

Aviaries built for Rosellas, Polyteline parrakeets and other similar sized parrakeets. Though the framework is wood, there has been no destructive chewing.

Wire attached to the inside of this nest box failed to discourage the Leadbeater Cockatoos who were using it. They discovered the lower part of their box was not wired on the outside, and they happily proceeded to destroy it.

8 or 9 feet should be allowed. Many are constructed up to 15 feet in height. Width can be restricted to 4 or 5 feet, depending on the size of the bird.

Cockatoos and full-sized parrots will thrive better in wider aviaries, with a length of 20 or more feet. Macaws, because of their size, will require aviaries of greater dimensions in all directions.

The dimensions of all the above aviaries provide the best chances for success. However, successful results can be achieved in smaller aviaries. For example, it has been brought to the attention of the writers that Macaws have successfully bred in a cage. Val Clear, in Indiana, has the young Macaws to prove it.

WIRE MESH

The wire mesh to cover the aviaries for parrot family birds should be strong enough to withstand the onslaught of powerful beaks. The larger the bird, the stronger the mesh required. If at all possible, the mesh should be fine enough to prevent the entrance of mice, rats, or even sparrows to save on feed bills. If necessary, a smaller mesh on the outside and a larger and stronger mesh on the inside should halt the invaders.

At any cost, it would be advisable to separate adjoining aviaries with double layers of mesh of adequate strength and enough space between the layers to prevent close contact of neighboring species. This precaution will prevent the playful destruction or disfigurement of young and naive birds by birds in neighboring aviaries.

There are several types of wire mesh available. The type most widely in use is hexagonal in shape. If the mesh is one-half inch, it is called aviary netting, and is available in many pet shops. For most birds this size is ideal; but, for parrot family birds, its use is limited to Budgerigars, Cockatiels, and some of the larger parrakeets. Love Birds and larger members are very adept at making the holes in the mesh much larger.

Also available in hexagonal shape is one-inch and two-inch mesh in correspondingly greater strengths. The large mesh is recommended for large parrots and Macaws, but it has the disadvantage of allowing the entrance of sparrows, mice, rats, and snakes. A 2-foot strip of metal surrounding the outside areas of the aviary will help in keeping out snakes, mice, and rats, but will have no effect on the sparrows.

Another type of netting that is becoming widely popular is welded wire

Aviaries built by Kenneth Wyatt housing Redrump, Bourke's, and Elegant Parrakeets. These species breed freely even with small Australian finches.

Jack Thropp, Curator of Birds on the Buteyn Bird Ranch, uses feeding stations designed to offer protection from rain. These are used in the large parrot flights where shelters are very small. An added advantage is that these stations can be placed away from nest boxes so that breeding birds need not be disturbed.

Jack Thropp in an aviary containing a breeding pair of Scarlet Macaws. The large box on the ground is typical of nest boxes used for large Macaws. Mr. Thropp keeps a wary eye on these breeding Macaws because their friendly manner changes to one of savage resentment at any intrusion during the breeding season. Though some large parrots do not resent intrusion during breeding seasons, most of them do.

fabric. The mesh is rectangular in shape and gives a very neat appearance. Since it is very strong wire, it is suitable even in the smaller mesh for most parrot-like birds. Even Macaws have difficulty in getting a good beak hold to destroy the wire.

This mesh comes in one-half by one inch size and one by two inch size. The larger size is often called turkey wire, but then so are some other types of mesh. Macaws can get a good beak hold on the larger size and can bend the wires. The welded wire fabric is easier to work with when constructing the aviary because there is no need to stretch the wire to prevent sagging, as is advisable with aviary netting. Its greater strength has one disadvantage: If a frightened bird, or a newly introduced bird, dashes against the wire, it may be injured since there is very little "give" to the wire. A tragedy can be averted if leafy branches are placed against the wired end of a long flight until newly introduced birds become accustomed to the dimensions of their new home.

SHELTERS

The sizes of the shelters need not be in proportion to the length of the aviary. All that is necessary is adequate shelter for the birds without over-crowding. Since most of the larger parrakeets, and certainly all of the large parrots, Cockatoos, and Macaws should be housed one pair per aviary, it follows that the shelter need not be large.

A metal garbage can makes a good nest box because the birds cannot destroy it. This one for Cockatoos can be used where the summer heat is not a dangerous factor.

CONSTRUCTION MATERIALS

Most members of the parrot family are very fond of chewing wood. The bigger the bird, the more it chews. For this reason, the most successful results in aviary construction are obtained by using materials that cannot be destroyed or defaced. The framework over which the wire is stretched can be made of pipe. The shelter can be made of a standard concrete mixture which is applied like stucco over strong wire mesh. Stucco is not sturdy enough.

Another suitable material for shelters is corrugated metal. Of course, the decision to use this type of material must be dependent on weather factors. If the climate is noted for extremely hot summers, the heat from the metal might be harmful to the birds.

Wooden framework for the wire and wooden shelters are still the most popular construction materials, and they are quite satisfactory. Some parrots do not cause too much destruction by chewing; and, if one does show signs of becoming really destructive, it is a simple matter to line the inside of the shelter and the framework with sheet metal or strong wire mesh.

The fact that a parrot will happily chew itself out of house and home does not mean that it is trying to escape. Parrots in captivity are well contented and do not miss the wild native habitat in the least. Chewing is good exercise and good entertainment, but it is exasperating to the bird fancier. If additional wood for chewing is provided, parrots may not be quite so destructive to their aviaries.

A simple homemade nest box for Cockatiels. Since there is no hollowed-out bottom, this box has a thick layer of shavings forming a central collecting place for the eggs. A flat bottom would result in eggs rolling into corners and being neglected.

A nursery for a baby parrot improvised by Velma Hart. Mrs. Hart succeeded in hand-rearing this baby Mexican Double Yellow Head to maturity.

FLOOR

The floor can be made of concrete or natural soil. The concrete floor is sanitary and easily cleaned; the natural soil floor is inexpensive. If concrete floors are not desired, it would be wise to build the aviaries on a concrete foundation that reaches at least eighteen inches below the earth's surface. This feature will prevent such pests as mice and rats from entering the aviary. There are other pests, which plague certain areas, whose entrance

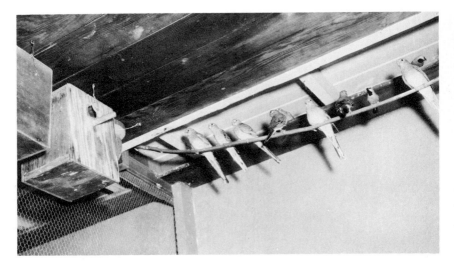

Redrump Parrakeets and Australian Finches in an aviary. Nest boxes suitable for Red-rumps are shown at the left.

will be blocked by this type of foundation. Snakes, rats, mice, and other varmints can contaminate food, frighten parents off their nests, destroy chicks and eggs, and even kill grown birds. All this, as well as the inordinate amount of feed consumed by rats and mice, can be avoided by this type of construction.

PERCHES

The furnishings for the parrot aviary include perches, feeders, waterers, and nest boxes. There are so many different styles of equipment available that not much can be said in this section which will not give rise to many exceptions. However, a few suggestions may be helpful.

Perches must fit the feet of the birds and must be neither too large nor too small if the birds are to be comfortable. The ideal perch is one in which the birds' toes cover all but one-fourth the circumference. Also, it is advisable to have perches of different sizes so that the grip exerted by the birds need not always be the same. This will allow some relaxation for the birds.

Authorities do not agree upon what constitutes the ideal perch. Some prefer round perches, such as dowels. Others prefer oval perches set diagonally. Still others prefer square perches with the corners only slightly rounded. Most will agree that natural branches are excellent.

Many bird fanciers think they are providing additional pleasure for their birds if they place many perches at all levels throughout the aviary. In so doing they clutter the flight area and prevent their birds from getting adequate exercise. For the best breeding results, two perches are sufficient in most cases. One should be in the shelter and the other at the far end of the flight.

The perches should be placed far enough from walls to prevent needless soiling from their droppings. Also, it is very important to avoid loose or wobbly perches or swings because a slip or shift may harm breeding birds during mating and result in infertile eggs.

FEEDERS

Many styles of feeders are available to the bird fancier. Open pans or dishes are popular, even though many birds take pleasure in scattering seed from open feeders. The resulting waste is needlessly expensive.

Also available in most pet shops are wooden or metal feeders, with storage capacity, which allow a limited amount of feed to be exposed to the birds. These feeders require less frequent replacement of food and prevent seed hulls from dropping back in. Wooden feeders are not wholeheartedly recommended because parrot-like birds are sometimes fond of reducing them to splinters.

When selecting feeders of this style, it is important to know beforehand if they are adaptable for sunflower seed as well as for the small seeds.

Although the Redrump Parrakeet is considered pugnacious by many bird fanciers, the ones owned by Kenneth Wyatt breed regularly in an aviary containing a variety of Australian finches.

WATERERS

Water containers should be made of crockery, pottery or glass. Metal is objectionable because of rust or other deterioration. Aluminum is useful for a time but eventually becomes pitted. Deterioration of any type hinders proper cleaning. Metal water containers have another disadvantage in that there is the possibility of a reaction against additives such as medicine of any type or liquid vitamins.

The gravity type of waterer is very successful for budgies, Cockatiels, and other smaller parrot family birds. This device consists of an inverted bottle with rubber stopper and glass or metal tube. When a bird touches the end of the tube with its beak it gets a drop of water that is replaced in the bottle by a bubble of air travelling up the tube. As long as the beak or tongue is held against the tube, drops of water will come from the tube.

This watering device is successful because most birds are inquisitive, and, if there is a crowd, they will play "follow the leader." However, daily care must be taken to make certain the water is feeding properly. Some birds playfully stuff seed or other material into the tube. If too much sunshine hits the tube, algae and scum will collect on the glass and allow the water to drain. Tubes must be cleaned often with a small brush. On the whole, this enclosed waterer keeps the water cleaner and is better for feeding liquid vitamins in the water because there is less evaporation.

A metal oil drum converted into a nest box for such inveterate chewers as Bare Eyed Cockatoos is safe except in warm climates. Ventilation should be provided to prevent overheating.

Nest box for Lories and Lorikeets. The wired bottom is covered by another layer of smaller mesh wire which is covered by a layer of charcoal to absorb the liquid droppings of these birds.

NEST BOXES

The size and style of nest boxes naturally depends upon the variety of bird. In the wild state, parrot-like birds usually dig holes in trees and tunnel downward. Decaying logs and large limbs are acceptable for most parrots but are not readily available.

The budgie box is well known and probably needs no description. However, it may be well to record its average dimensions: six and one-half inches square by nine inches high. Also, since no nesting material is used, there should be a saucer-like bottom to keep the eggs from rolling into corners where the hen might neglect them. The entrance hole should be about two inches in diameter and a small perch, which extends both inside and outside the box, should be inserted just below the entrance. This same box is suitable for Lineolated Parrakeets, Love Birds, and birds of similar size.

For Cockatiels, most Conures, and birds of similar size, the box must be larger. An average size would be nine by nine inches square by fifteen inches high. The hollowed-out bottom is also necessary, and the hole should be about three inches in diameter.

Nest boxes for larger parrakeets, such as Ringnecks and Rosellas, should

A very practical nest box for many species of parrot-like birds. The entrance is reinforced by metal to discourage chewing.

Nest box for Cockatiels, conures, and many similar-sized parrakeets. This one is occupied by Jiggs, one of the favorite pets of the authors.

be larger. The most popular type of nest is the grandfather clock style, which is from twelve to eighteen inches square and up to three feet deep. The entrance hole is about four inches in diameter. The perch below the entrance should be of greater diameter than the ones used for Budgerigars or Cockatiels but need not extend inside the box. Because of its depth, there should be wire mesh, preferably welded wire fabric or hardware cloth, extended from the entrance hole to the bottom on the inside of the box. If at all possible, the mesh should stand out from the wall of the box one-fourth inch to allow for a good beak and foothold to climb out. Since there is no certainty of the depth in which the birds wish to nest, it would be quite possible for young birds to become trapped in deep boxes if it were not for this mesh.

The box is then filled up to the entrance hole with pine shavings. When the birds come into breeding condition, they remove shavings to the desired depth. A pile of shavings below the nest box is usually a good indication that the birds should be disturbed as little as possible and that there should be no peeking into the nest box.

For larger parrots such as Amazons and Cockatoos, the nest boxes must be formidable affairs of considerable size. Often a large barrel cut in half is excellent. The enclosed smaller end becomes the top; a suitable bottom should be fastened securely. If the birds try to remodel the box, wire mesh or metal should be fastened at least around the six-inch entrance hole. The

A large barrel makes an excellent nest box even for Moluccan Cockatoos. A precautionary measure to prevent this condition would be a layer of wire attached to the inside as well as the outside.

A choice of nest boxes is always desirable. For these Alexander Ringnecks, Dorothy Speed provided a tree trunk and a grandfather clock type of nest box. The inside of this nest box is wired to allow parents and young to climb to the entrance.

writer has seen metal garbage cans in successful use, but the weather conditions were ideal with no chance of overheating the chicks or brooding hens.

Macaws will nest on the ground with a long, low box as a cover. The box should be about five or six feet long, three or four feet wide, and about two feet high. The entrance hole should be large enough for the birds to enter with ease.

For Lories, because of the highly liquid nature of their droppings, the writers use a box as spacious as a Cockatiel box except that it is longer and not quite as high. The most important difference is that the bottom is a layer of one-eighth inch hardware cloth covered with a layer of pea-sized charcoals. Charcoal has a tendency to absorb and to sweeten the inevitable soilage.

4

TAMING

Taming a bird of the parrot family is a simple task if a few rules are followed. The basic rules are the same whether the bird is a parrakeet, Love Bird, Cockatiel, full-sized parrot, or Macaw. The only difference is in the birds themselves, which means that some are easier to tame than others. The budgie and the Cockatiel are the two easiest.

First of all, start the taming process with a young bird between six and ten weeks old. Regardless of sex, a budgie of this age, for instance, can be tamed in one hour.

Secondly, a bird to be tamed and taught to talk should be alone. Once the bird is tamed and taught to talk it may be kept with another young, tame bird. The older bird will teach the younger bird to talk.

It is true that the older bird will not learn new words as easily as it did when it was alone. However, the writer knows of a Cockatiel and a budgie who have lived together for over five years. Both are tame and both talk, but no new words had been acquired for nearly four years. Suddenly, the budgie began picking up new words with no training whatever. This unusual and unexpected behavior completely mystified everyone. No one yet has discovered the reason for all the new words and phrases.

WING CLIPPING AS A TRAINING AID

Some people refuse to have the wing clipped because they feel it is cruel to the bird. While an unclipped bird can be tamed, it is true that much more perseverance is necessary. The best way to tame a bird with an unclipped wing is to keep it in its cage until it has become thoroughly familiar with the hand of one person before it comes out. Otherwise, the teacher will waste valuable training time retrieving the bird from inaccessible places and frightening it to the point where taming might become impossible.

It is not cruel to clip a bird's wing. Having tried all different methods of taming, the writers always return to the one in which the primaries on one side are clipped.

There are several wing clipping patterns. Some experts prefer clipping all the primary flight feathers on each wing so that the bird will not be off balance either in appearance or in flight. Others prefer leaving the last

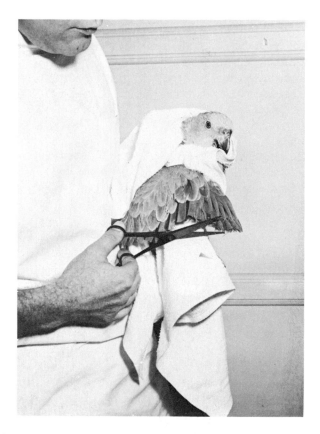

The task of clipping wings usually calls for some sort of restraint. A towel thrown over the bird helps to get the proper grip and to prevent biting. Parrots of this size are very strong and should be handled in this manner only by an experienced person.

three flight feathers on each wing and trimming both primary and secondary flight feathers. When the wings are folded, there is no visible indication that there has been any clipping whatever.

The pattern of wing clipping preferred by the writers is to clip all the primary flight feathers on one wing. No feathers should be clipped closer than the primary coverts to allow some room if a quill should become split. If a quill should split down into the feather follicle, an ingrown feather may be the result. The primary coverts are a row of feathers which overlap the flight feathers near the base of the wing.

When one wing is clipped, the bird settles down better and gives up trying to fly. The reason is that it aims for one direction but flies in a curve missing the desired goal entirely. Opponents to this method dislike the unbalanced appearance and the curved flight.

THE BUDGIE'S FIRST HOUR OF TAMING

While this technique is outlined for budgies, it is essentially the same for all other birds.

Some authorities say to wait two weeks until the bird becomes oriented to new surroundings before starting training. To wait two weeks to train any young bird smaller than a full-fledged parrot is a big mistake. It is just two weeks of wasted time that results in a diminished return as far as the resultant tameness is concerned.

Get busy right away. The first hour is all important. In its bewildered state from lack of orientation the bird can easily be liberated of any fear of man it may be developing through association with other birds. The bird is completely receptive to training.

Some exceptionally tame parrots will submit to any type of handling. Clipping the wings of these birds is a simple job.

A tame adult Yellow Naped Amazon on the left and tame Mexican Double Yellow Head on the right. Note the caution between these newly introduced individuals. They are familiar with humans but not other birds.

Take the bird out of the cage and hold it low so that when it flies it will not hit the floor too hard. In about twenty minutes it will learn that it can no longer fly and will stop trying.

While it is on the floor surround it from below with outstretched fingers on both hands and lift up. The bird has to come up with the fingers. It may stay only a moment, but continue the routine until the bird sits on the index finger facing you. Let it sit for awhile to become used to the finger. Then, using the index finger on the other hand, nudge the bird on the chest slightly enough so that it becomes unbalanced. Instinctively the bird will climb up on the finger. As soon as it becomes settled, repeat this process, which gives the effect of climbing a ladder.

When the bird flies off, start from the beginning and work all the way through. Fast, jerky, or hesitant movements should be avoided. Talking softly to the bird throughout this procedure has a calming effect.

It is best if one person spends this first hour with the bird to avoid distractions and unnecessary confusion. This person should not be afraid of a bird bite. Flinching from a possible bite is very bad. When a bird opens its beak and leans towards an outstretched finger, it is doing so because it uses the beak in climbing and is merely trying to be certain that its next perch will be firm. If the finger is quickly withdrawn, the effect will be one of teasing the bird. Any bird that is teased will invariably bite in a short while, and the older it grows, the harder the bite becomes. Similarly, any bird which is picked up bodily is likely to become a biter if this practice is continued.

After the budgie is finger tamed, it should be allowed the experience of losing its fear of other people by being handled by them. It should become familiar with perching on shoulders. If at all possible, someone should try to rub its head and the back of its neck. Many birds do not like this, but they should be given the opportunity of deciding for themselves.

TAMING COCKATIELS

The procedure for taming a baby Cockatiel is the same as for the budgie. Cockatiels are the sweetest birds in the world and just about the easiest to tame. A young bird up to fourteen weeks of age is the best, and can be tamed, regardless of sex, in about an hour.

In just about every book on birds there are suggestions for hand feeding baby Cockatiels to insure tameness. This is about the most unnecessary job in the world, because baby Cockatiels just seem to beg to be tamed. Countless times the writers have taken just a few minutes to show a new Cockatiel owner how to tame his bird. During those few minutes the job is done. From then on, it is a matter of companionship to strengthen the union between bird and human.

Many people fear a Cockatiel's bite, but a baby Cockatiel's beak is

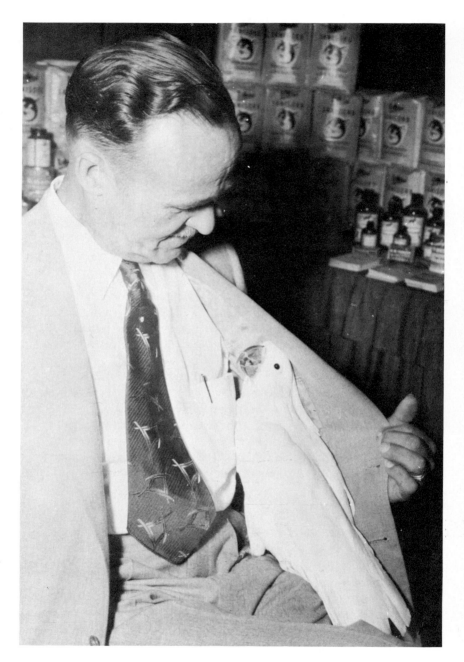

Carl Bochert and his devoted pet Greater Sulphur Crested Cockatoo, "Cookie". This picture demonstrates the devotion shown by some Cockatoos toward their owners.

softer than an adult's beak and cannot inflict a serious wound. Flinching from an expected bite can bring very bad results in time. If a baby bites, it is because it is afraid. To release the bite, bring a finger rapidly, but gently, up under the chin of the bird. There is no need to inflict punishment upon the bird. Flicking the bird's beak is a mistake which may lead to an habitual resentment and a chronic biting habit. Calmness and gentleness on the part of the trainer will bring the best results in a very short time.

The bond of affection a Cockatiel holds for its owner is one of the strongest shown by any pet. It very likely surpasses anything in the bird world. If the writers were suddenly denied the pleasure of all their birds and pets except one, they would unhesitatingly choose a Cockatiel to be that one pet.

TAMING LOVE BIRDS

The same technique is used in taming a Love Bird, but it takes more work. The extra work is worth it, though, because a tame Love Bird is exceptionally talented, especially when it comes to learning tricks.

It is most important to start with a very young bird that has been out of the nest for a week and has been weaned. In fact, much more could be accomplished if people who hand-feed Cockatiels would spend their time hand-feeding baby Love Birds. They hand-feed very easily and make the most delightful pets right from the beginning.

If your Love Bird is not hand-fed, be prepared to spend more time in taming. Use the same procedure as with the budgie, but be exceptionally patient. If the bird bites, use a tight-fitting glove. It takes more composure to tame a biting bird as well as a lot more mercurochrome, but the person who has perseverance will be well rewarded.

It is the Love Bird that was used most often in trained bird acts on the stage because of its ability to learn tightrope walking, pushing baby carriages, and many other tricks.

TAMING LARGER PARROTS

For all other members of the parrot family, the wisest course to follow in taming is to use a little more time in approaching the bird. Because of the formidable beaks, which increase in leverage power as they increase in size, it is important that trainer and trainee be in just the right mood for maximum success.

Suppose that you are a novice bird fancier and have a desire to own a talking parrot. In a nearby pet shop you see a pretty parrot and decide that this is the bird you have been wanting. To make it more difficult, let us suppose that this reasonably young parrot has never been trained and has about as much experience with humans as you have with birds. This situation is just about as basic as you can get.

The parrot must be manhandled by the pet shop proprietor while getting its wings clipped and the toenails trimmed. This is to make it easier for you, but the bird takes the manhandling a little differently. Its response is one of fear. Your response to the parrot is one of fear also because you have heard stories about the amazing power of a parrot's bite. You do not wish to lose a finger or to experience the pain which attends such a bite. Now is the time to build up your courage and convince yourself that you are going to be the boss. Convince yourself also that if it is necessary to receive a bite to tame your bird the end result will be well worth it. And really, a parrot's bite is not nearly so bad as all those tales. The only reason a young parrot will attempt to bite is that it is afraid. Remove the need for fear, and it will gladly reciprocate.

Approach your bird slowly and carefully at first. Offer it food from your fingers, especially some little item it particularly likes. Talk softly to reassure the bird. In a very short time, it will refrain from rearing back in paralyzed fright.

In a short time, hold a perch up to its chest. In most cases, the bird will step upon the perch, using its beak in the climbing process. Understand that the beak did not go down to the perch to bite. Instead, it went down to hold the perch firm so that the bird could ascertain the safety of climbing up onto it.

After a few attempts at this routine with the perch, use your other hand to distract the bird's attention and to edge it over onto the hand that is holding the perch. This is quite a painless operation; please do not show any fear. The bird will notice fear on your part, and you will lose whatever progress you have made. By now the parrot has come to realize that the gentleness and kindness you have shown are not a threat to it. Once it is on your hand half the battle is won. Both you and the bird have learned a great deal.

Remove the perch as inconspicuously as possible. This is accomplished by talking softly and distracting the bird's attention while doing so. It will not even realize that it is perched upon a human hand unless you move. As soon as you can, move about the room with the bird still perched on your hand. The bewilderment shown by the bird is all to your advantage. It will soon see that it is perched on your hand with no harm to it. Spend as much time as possible this first time. Offer the bird food from your other hand. Talk softly all the time. When it is time to return the bird to its cage most of the battle of taming will have been won. Building up your own courage is the greatest part of that battle.

The second time you handle the bird should be in the same manner as the first, but after that do away with the perch. Continued use of the perch will result in a stick-trained bird. A stick-trained bird is not desirable because an obstacle is always between you and it. Offer your hand

Two exceptionally tame and talented Petz' or Half Moon Conures. These birds put themselves to bed and cover themselves up, put pennies in a bank, push a baby carriage, and do many other tricks.

as a perch. You will be delighted by the confident manner in which it is accepted.

From then on the whole affair is a wonderful companionship between you and your bird. Let it use your shoulder as a perch and do not be afraid that your ears will suffer disfigurement.

Should the bird bite, use the same method of combating a Cockatiel's bite. A turn of the wrist towards you will pull your finger out of the way. At the same time bring another finger up under the parrot's chin to deflect the bird's aim. It is useful to know that the bird will find considerable difficulty in getting a bite-hold if you present a rounded wrist with fingers and hand turned under as far as possible.

The association is firm by now. You love the parrot, and it loves you. Try to scratch the bird's head. It will most likely love it.

PARROT INDIVIDUALISM

Parrots are extreme individualists. The relationship between bird and human is harmonious to the extent that training techniques are adapted to meet the strong individual needs of each pet.

Some parrots detest men and at the same time lavish their affection upon any woman who happens to be near. Some are the opposite. Some will

Tommy, the Greater Sulphur Crested Cockatoo owned by the writers, is bilingual, speaking both German and English. Tommy is a very reliable television performer. When the bright klieg lights are turned on, Tommy assumes the center of attention with his comic antics.

Jiggs, this Petz' or Half Moon Conure owned by the writers, is remarkably intelligent and a good pet although not so erudite as this picture may indicate.

prefer just one person to love and may develop a vicious jealousy of anyone offering competition. Also, some parrots will express hatred for one person and affection for all others. But, remember that birds are individualists like any other person or animal. There are no two alike, and it is impossible to predict any outcomes.

Many amusing stories can be told about the extreme individualism of parrots. A lady, feeling that her husband had wanted a parrot long enough, decided to give him a Half Moon Conure for Christmas. The reason for the delay had been her great fear of birds. The writers sold her a very tame, overly friendly, talking Half Moon, with which she surprised her husband.

The real surprise came later. The Half Moon formed a deep, possessive attachment for the lady and was very unhappy if it could not be on her shoulder all the time. As its affection grew for its unwilling mistress, the Half Moon developed an extreme animosity towards everyone who came into the house. Its jealousy was especially directed against the unfortunate husband to whom it had been given.

Although this incident has caused considerable merriment among friends and family, the lady has completely overcome her fear of birds and recently came in to buy another bird for her husband.

Often the slightest change in a person's appearance can result in a complete change of a bird's attitude toward that person. About ten years ago some friends of the writers became the owners of a magnificent Sulphur

Crested Cockatoo named Tommy. Naturally Tommy was the recipient of considerable admiration from all visitors, and he was vain enough to enjoy every moment of it. He would dance in circles, throw his crest forward, and use every trick to attract attention. He had a particularly flirtatious movement of his head which invited you to "come on in." Tommy enjoyed being held, and he was particularly happy when sitting on anyone's shoulder. He would nuzzle up to anyone and would frequently bestow kisses upon a total stranger.

One day, however, one of the writers wore glasses for the first time while visiting Tommy. Tommy contemplated this change for quite some time and then suddenly reached up and bit him on the lip. From that day forward, Tommy refused to become friendly with him. Even though Tommy came into the possession of the writers five years ago, there has been no change in his attitude. Despite every trick in the book, Tommy holds himself disdainfully aloof from this writer. To everyone else he extends the most cordial of welcomes and displays the same effusiveness as before.

BREEDING

Many members of the parrot family have successfully been reared in captivity. Some, in fact, do not seem to know when to stop. Most, however, are slow and give the idea that they are possibly uncooperative.

It is impossible to predict which species will breed and which will not. Some bird fanciers have almost fantastic success with many birds which have the reputation for being impossible to breed, but often they cannot rear birds which are the easiest for most people.

Much of the success in breeding comes from proper diet, proper aviaries, and suitable equipment. Two other factors require a great deal of consideration.

One factor is the isolation of each pair. There are several species that get along reasonably well with other birds, but the best successes are always with those birds which are housed one pair per aviary.

The second factor is patience. Isolation also means for inquisitive owners to keep their noses out of the nest boxes of breeding birds. Some of the greatest disappointments have come about because upset hens deserted their nests after being disturbed by overly anxious and overly inquisitive humans.

For most birds of the parrot family, springtime is breeding time. Preparation of nest boxes and more attention to the diet with an eye towards conditioning for breeding assume great importance during this time. Some bird fanciers feed wheat germ oil during this time to insure greater fertility of eggs.

Since most birds of the parrot family come from tropical climates, there is often a necessity for moisture or humidity to keep eggshells from

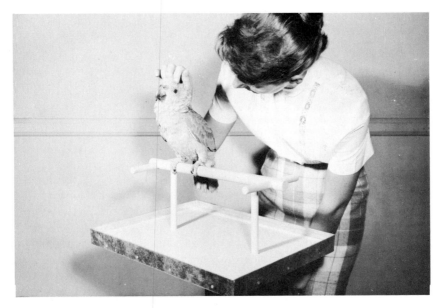

Most pet parrots will enjoy being rubbed on the nape of the neck and under the chin if started as young as this Yellow Naped Amazon.

becoming too hard. Eggshells which are too hard present a great obstacle for chicks trying to peck their way out at hatching time. Except in the case of Love Birds, the best way of providing moisture is to soak some of the shavings or other nesting material in water several weeks before they are put in the breeding pens. If covered with dry nesting material, the loss of moisture is very slow.

Most Australian birds, such as the various parrakeets, parrots, and cockatoos, are good breeders. The large family of Ringneck Parrakeets has some prolific breeders. South American parrot-like birds are poorer or slower breeders.

So many members of the parrot family have very long lives and do not seem to be in any particularly great hurry to fulfill the natural instinct for reproduction. The bird fancier must assume the familiar attitude of patience if he wishes success.

In the chapters covering the individual genera and species, mention is made of individual birds that are good breeders and of changes or modifications that will help to assure greater success.

5

TALKING

A talking bird is a mimic and not a reasoning power. It will learn to imitate words and phrases and, in some cases, will go as far as word associations. For example, a good trainer can elicit a certain response by using a particular phrase or question. He may say to a parrot, "How are you today?" and have the parrot respond with, "Just fine, thank you." The teaching of conditioned responses is a difficult job. More will be explained about this later.

There is much entertainment in listening to a talented talking bird, but it is rather a bore to have a bird which endlessly says just one word or phrase. The writers are much more interested in tame and companionable birds than in most talking birds simply because of the limited voice training so many receive.

It is quite true that many birds have a limited ability when it comes to talking, and it is also true that others have almost unlimited ability at picking up new words and phrases. The most dependable varieties for remarkably large vocabularies are the budgie, Yellow Naped Amazon, Panama, and African Grey. Many people will class the Mexican Double Yellow Head in this category; but, because of reservations mentioned in the section covering this species, the writers do not.

To class all other parrot family birds as poor or non-talking birds would be a great mistake. Many individuals make excellent talkers and surpass some of those in the most exalted category.

Most of the limitations attached to a parrot's vocabulary can be directly traced to its trainer. Most people who are successful in teaching their birds a few words stop when this is accomplished. They hurdle the most difficult part and then stop training altogether. Very few people ever continue the training lessons beyond this stage. It is seldom indeed that the full potential of a good talking parrot has been tapped.

Many good parrots prove this by picking up snatches of conversation quickly and haphazardly. The writers have had many parrots which carried on long telephone conversations beginning naturally with "Hello" and lapsing into long garbled sounds and pauses with frequent "yes" or "no" and "Oh, my" highlights. These birds were obviously imitating previous owners who spent considerable time on the telephone.

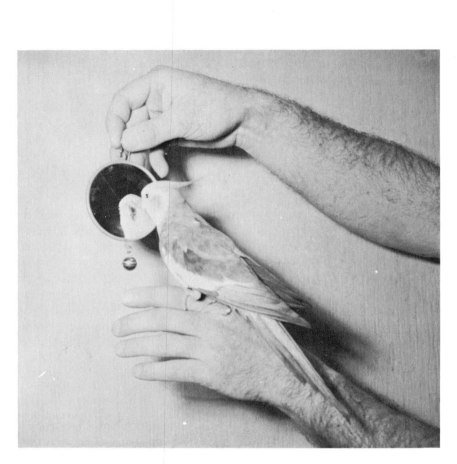

This Cockatiel, named Butch, likes mirrors. He was never allowed to see mirrors until he learned to talk. His education, therefore, was not retarded by his excessive vanity. Butch is one of the most favored pets at the Palos Verdes Bird Farm.

THE PARROT VOICE

The voice of any parrot family bird is by nature loud and sharp. There is very little musical quality in it, even though there are a few notable exceptions. The voice of the popular Mynah is closer to a human's voice than that of a parrot. Parrots' voices, however, are clearly audible and have a considerable range.

The talking voice is far more pleasant than the harsh wild calls. The talking voice of the budgie is rather small, high pitched, and a bit squeaky. Many people refuse to call it a talking voice because they expect a human's resonance. The uninitiated must listen carefully before he knows that the bird is actually talking.

A Cockatiel's voice is a little clearer, but it is still high pitched. The Half Moon's voice is clear, slightly lower pitched, but squeaky in most cases.

Generally speaking, the talking voice of any parrot family bird increases in clarity with a corresponding increase in size of species. In parrots especially, there is a wide range of voice inflection. Many parrots speak in more than one voice. The writers have a Scarlet Macaw which speaks in a man's deep calm voice and also in the high-pitched excitable voices of children replete with delighted squeals and laughter. Many Amazon Parrots are reasonably adept at imitating the household soprano; and the writers have owned one Yellow Naped Amazon which, when everything became quiet, sang hymns in a monotonous contralto.

Some birds of the parrot family are equipped with such harsh natural calls that the average person would rather they not be kept nearby. Since there are so many lovely different species from which to choose, it is best to avoid birds with unusually harsh voices.

TRAINING RECORDS

There are several methods used in teaching a bird to talk. As long as the training is on a consistent level and the trainer has perseverance, all methods will work. It is the haphazard and inconsistent application of a method that produces ineffectiveness—not the method itself.

The easiest way to teach a bird to talk is to buy a bird training record and use it on an automatic record-changing phonograph. In this manner, the trainer can leave the house to escape the monotony of hearing one short phrase repeated over and over again. This teaching aid often shortens the time before the first words are learned.

There are some excellent training records on the market which, though devised mainly for parrakeets, are usable for any type of talking bird. The best records have one or two simple phrases on each side spoken in a clear and concise feminine voice. The words are spoken slowly, with an inflection, for each phrase, that remains constant throughout the lesson. The idea is to play one side only until the bird learns the lesson, and then start the lesson on the other side. After that, the owner himself should pick up the training by repeating the phrases often enough so that the bird responds to the human voice rather than the machine's.

There is at least one set of training records that contains eight different lessons. Each lesson becomes progressively a little more difficult and a little more complicated; and yet, the bird learns easily.

This is an excellent method of training, so long as each lesson is thoroughly learned and is in everyday usage before proceeding to the next. After learning each lesson, the bird should be given a review of everything it has learned previously so that it will not forget. Also, the trainer must transfer the bird's response to the record to the voice of the human by direct participation in the lessons.

No one can be certain whether this bird is taking his talking lessons seriously or whether he is fascinated by the spinning disc. At any rate, records are useful aids in teaching parrots to talk if the owner is too busy to accomplish the task.

It is quite possible that the phrases on training records do not appeal to the bird owner. It still is easier to use a record to get the bird started on its linguistic education. With the efforts of the bird owner directed towards the transfer of learning from the phonograph to the human, the third and fourth lessons are quickly taught regardless of the medium used.

Several records on the market are useless. These show no repetition and contain everything from nursery rhymes to complete recitations of the Gettysburg Address. There are some lengthy recordings of a parrakeet's voice saying many different things. These are useful in proving to humans that a parrakeet can talk, but they are of little value in teaching other birds.

DAILY LESSON ROUTINE

If records are not used as training aids, it is wise to set up a daily routine for the bird and the trainer. The daily routine should not be less than twenty minutes of concerted effort on the part of the trainer devoted exclusively to the bird at the same hour each day. Although it is not necessary, the bird would learn faster if two twenty-minute periods could be given to training each day.

Some people prefer early morning training, while others prefer late evening training; the time does not really matter as long as the lessons are given at the same hour daily. The trainer should choose that part of the day that is most quiet and free of distractions.

The chosen lesson should be simple and should be repeated slowly during the training period. The trainer should use the same voice tones throughout.

Clear enunciation is necessary if the bird is to learn properly. The best human voice for training is that of a child or a woman. If a man's voice is used, the result will be a coarser, less understandable voice in the bird. Ordinarily, a child lacks perseverance to carry the job through; but there are some notable exceptions. That leaves the job mostly to the housewife, who usually has more than enough to occupy her day.

This daily routine must continue for a long time before results are evident and before the bird learns what is expected. If the trainer is persistent in her efforts, there will come a day when the bird will repeat her words. At first they may sound garbled and indistinct, but the bird will perfect them in a few days.

The first indication that the bird will talk will be a sound different from its natural voice. Any difference in tonal quality coming from the bird should be added impetus to the trainer. Lessons can be given more frequently to accelerate the results.

After the first word or phrase is successfully taught, it should be brought into frequent usage by the bird. This can only be done by further repetition on the part of the trainer. The words should be repeated often and at many intervals during the day and evening. The bird will soon learn that it is expected to say its new words under all circumstances and on command.

When this is accomplished, try another simple word or phrase, preferably one that will work in well with the first word or phrase. Follow the same routine as before. The bird will learn faster than before. From this point on, the lessons should be continued but should be more varied. Frequent reviews will help in retaining previous learning while the vocabulary is being expanded.

THE CONDITIONED RESPONSE

After a dozen or so words have been learned, the bird will connect phrases and words which were not previously together. In some cases, the bird does a bit of transferring and rearranging in its phraseology. Now is the time to start with conditioned responses.

Suppose you wish a bird to answer a question or respond in a given manner to a certain remark. Let us say that you wish to ask, "How are you today?" and have the bird answer, "Just fine, thank you."

The first step is to follow a rigid training procedure in teaching the bird to say, "Just fine, thank you." You should say nothing else during these lessons. The manner in which you start the lesson and the time of day should never vary.

When the bird learns to say the desired phrase, the lesson should be continued until the bird has built up a conditioned response. This means that as soon as you approach the cage at that particular time of day, the parrot automatically realizes it is expected to say, "Just fine, thank you."

After you are sure of the parrot's response, you should approach the cage at training time with the question, "How are you today?" Its response will be automatic, "Just fine, thank you."

The trained response must then be transferred to the question rather than the time of day and manner of approach. This is done through practice. It should be tried at other intervals during the day and night to make certain that the proper transfer of learning has been made. Care must be taken that the bird does not learn to ask the question as well as give the answer. If it does, some of the charm is lost.

Other conditioned responses can be taught, but the trainer should not be unhappy if the bird makes a few errors. Eventually, the bird will learn the question and will say, "How are you today?" The trainer should invariably reply, "Just fine, thank you." The bird may sometimes transfer an incorrect response. The writers know four very well-trained Mynah birds that have been taught conditioned responses. One bird was taught to say, "How are you today?" Another was taught to respond with, "Just fine, thank you." The third bird was taught to say, "What's your name?" The fourth bird was taught to respond in a charmingly bewildered manner with, "I don't know." Through close association, it was not long before the birds were picking up each other's responses and questions. The results were highly entertaining, providing amusement for many people for hours on end.

CHOICE OF TRAINING TECHNIQUES

There is much contradictory information published regarding the teaching of birds. Actually, nearly all of the different techniques are correct and workable. Each person must choose his own most convenient technique.

Some people prefer to cover their birds' cages to avoid outside distractions and allow full concentration on the trainer's voice. In many cases this method has proved highly satisfactory. In others, the bird goes to sleep. It is a good idea, however, to remove the mirrors which adorn the cages of most small parrot-like birds. The bird will not concentrate on learning when it is distracted with the opportunity of chatting with its likeness. After the bird is a good talker, the mirrors may be returned.

Some experts say the bird should be perched on the index finger facing the trainer's mouth. In this manner, full concentration on the part of the bird can be expected when the trainer speaks the words of the lesson. If all other conditions in the house are ideal, this may easily be the best method.

To save time and to make the job of training less monotonous, some housewives perform household chores during training periods. If a housewife is adept at concentrating on serious teaching and serious dishwashing at the same time, this method may be highly successful. However, rustling sounds and running water may present distractions to the bird. If the bird learns at all well, it may talk only while the kitchen faucet is running.

Others suggest that, in order to talk, a bird, regardless of species, should have its tongue split. This is one of the most stupid and most cruel suggestions ever made. No bird, whether it is a crow, raven, Mynah, or parrot, should ever have any surgery performed in an effort to increase its talking ability. If the reader should ever see a sign or anything in print which advocates this outrage, he should vigorously protest. Even if surgery could help in teaching a bird to talk, man does not have to stoop so low to obtain such a means of flattery.

We suggest again that you select your own most convenient training technique. We also wish to emphasize that, when choosing your bird, you make certain it is young and friendly from the start.

An adult bird, whether from an aviary with no previous training or trapped in the wild, is called a "broncho" due to the difficulty in breaking it to the human hand. Although the writers have tamed many bronchos, there is always a certain lack of companionship between human and bird. Most bronchos never talk; and, despite the most adamant efforts, the majority refuse to become tame and confiding.

6

THE CAGED HOUSEHOLD PET

Since there are so many companionable and affectionate birds available, there is no reason for any household to be a prison for a bird. Instead, a bird should consider the entire household as its own particular universe. It should be allowed a certain amount of freedom from the cage to exercise and to feel that the world is its oyster. The bird that remains confined for its entire life to a small cage is usually a sad bird.

EXERCISE

Exercise is extremely important for any bird. When a bird gets outside its cage, its first act is usually to stretch its wings, get a firm foothold, and then flap its wings rapidly and violently for a few moments. If the bird is a small member of the parrot family, and if the wing is unclipped, it may fly around the room a few times. Since parrots in captivity have a tendency to become lazy, they usually do not attempt to fly about a house and often must be prodded into taking exercise of some sort.

PLAYPENS AND PERCHING STATIONS

In addition to its cage, the household pet should have a playpen or perch available somewhere outside the cage. Unclipped smaller parrot-like birds prefer about three or four playpens or perching stations interspersed throughout the house. They can be conditioned to stay within a confined area by acquainting them with the various locations while their wings are still clipped. If food or a favorite toy is kept on the stations, the bird will soon regard them with enjoyment and will fly to the perches when the wing grows out. There are many selections of playpens at nominal prices in every pet shop.

If the wing is to remain clipped at all times, the stations can be grouped together more closely, with connecting ladders to the cage. More distant stations may be set up also, but it is important that they be furnished with food and water so that the bird will not go hungry if it happens to be feeding time and there is no one around to carry it back to the cage.

For larger parrots, there are some very attractive and well-built stands on the market. Because of their heavy duty construction, some of these are a little expensive; but they are well worth the price because of their durability. There are plenty of modestly priced playpens and ring perches available. Remember its favorite pastime of chewing when you are buying stands or playpens for a parrot. It is best in the long run to avoid items that will be easily destroyed.

TOYS

Visit your local pet shop and select a few toys for your bird. You will find a selection to suit any type of bird at reasonable prices. Toys are useful because they provide entertainment as well as necessary exercise. Do not be chagrined if your bird destroys its toys. Remember that you are buying entertainment for your bird, and the cost is very small.

DIET

The diet of the household pet is basically the same as outlined in the chapter on feeding. However, it will be well to remember that the household pet is greatly curtailed in activity compared to an aviary bird and cannot spend much time in the sun. Therefore, the dietary supplement is important to the bird. There should be an ample supply of Vitamin D to compensate for the lack of sunshine. Most dietary supplements fulfill this requirement.

The following series of pictures shows various examples of cages, play-pens, and toys suitable for the pet parrot.

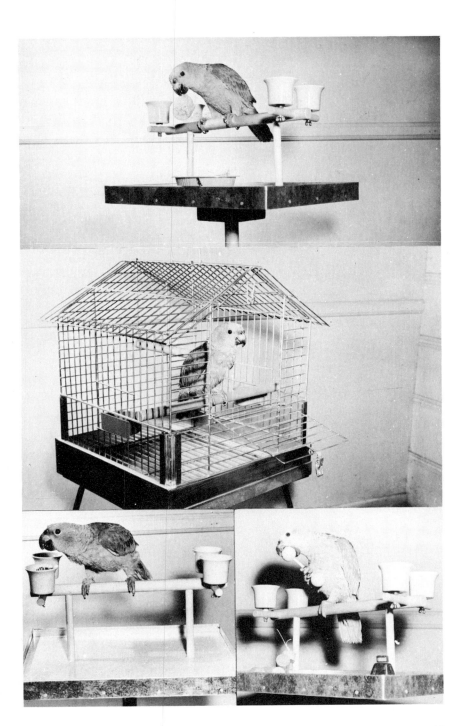

Since birds have a very poorly developed sense of smell, there is no problem in introducing a liquid dietary supplement. However, many birds object to a difference in the texture of their foods, and some even avoid a color change in food or water. Any changes should be made gradually.

The reduced activity of a household pet means that fattening foods should be avoided or fed sparingly. In an aviary, the bird would burn up its excess energy in flight or in rearing a family; but the household pet stores it up as fat. The fat and sluggish bird has a shorter life expectancy than a lithe and active bird.

If your bird shows signs of becoming fat and sluggish, it is a simple matter to put him on a diet. Eliminate all foods you know to be fattening. Change the parrakeet or Love Bird mix to equal parts of canary and millet and eliminate oat groats. Be a little more generous with the dietary supplement and be certain that it is a good supplement. In a reducing diet, the supplement should be one of the liquid vitamin preparations mentioned in the chapter on feeding. Add more greens and fresh fruits to the diet. Though fattening, sunflower seed cannot be successfully eliminated from a parrot's diet.

SPRAYS

In an aviary, both sunshine and rain help to give a bird its glossy sheen. When it rains, providing it is a soft, warm rain, most parrot-like birds love to spread their wings, fan their tails, and raise the body feathers to catch every drop. Especially thrilling is the fast movement of the bird's head which tries to reach any spot the rain missed and to rub moisture from the head into the dry places.

In the case of the household pet, there is no rain available; but there are some excellent sprays that fulfill the requirement even better because most of them also kill mites. A spray of this nature should be used at least once a week on all birds except Cockatiels and Cockatoos. Because of the nature of their feathers, which slough off a chalky powder, anything with an oil base would be harmful. Plain water is best on these birds.

BATHING

A bath is an important part of a bird's daily routine. Unfortunately, most members of the parrot family must learn to bathe. They do not come by it naturally. As mentioned before, most parrots bathe when it rains, and some roll around on wet grass. The conditioned response is again helpful in their training.

For those birds that like to roll on wet grass, place wet greens in the bath dish each morning. Gradually, over a period of time, add a little water to the bath dish and slowly cut down the amount of greens. Before the bird realizes what has happened, it is taking a regular bath. Once learned, the bath becomes a highly enjoyable part of the bird's routine.

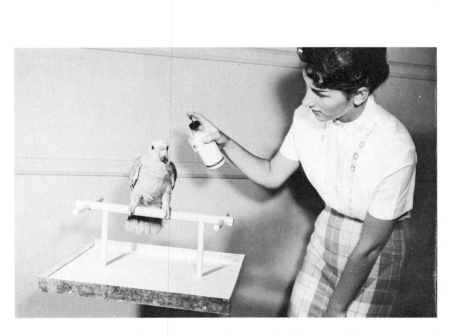

All parrots enjoy baths if they are properly oriented while young. There are several excellent commercial spray baths which kill mites and give gloss to plumage.

BIRD BATHS

For small birds of the parrot family, there are several bird baths on the market that have mirrored bottoms. The same conditioned response method works out here. The bird sits in the bath dish looking at himself in the mirror. Over a period of time a little water is added. Once there is enough water, the bird will take a bath. Filling up the bath dish right from the start will frighten the bird away.

For birds whose bath consists of falling rain in the wild state, the training process is virtually the same. Most pet shops carry little sprayers to use on birds. Spray your bird at a set time each morning, and make sure it is on a large bath dish during the spraying. Each day spray a little more than the day before until the bird is getting as much water from the bath dish as from the spray. The spray may eventually be discontinued, provided the bird will start the bath without it. Some birds refuse to look at the bath until they have some spray.

BATHING HABITS

Since bathing is a conditioned response in most parrot-like birds, many different bathing habits are formed. Some birds will bathe only by ducking their heads in the drinking water and rubbing the moisture over the rest of their bodies. This indicates good bathing habits were not taught when the bird was most responsive to learning.

Some people teach their birds to bathe in the kitchen sink under running water. This is a most dangerous habit for a bird that is allowed its freedom most of the time, because one day it might just fly under the faucet when the hot water is running. The bird may be severely burned or even killed by the shock.

DRAFTS

The household pet will remain very hardy if a few precautions are observed. Remember that the bird in your home is protected from all adverse weather conditions and has no resistance built up to withstand sudden temperature drops. In most cases, the undercoat of downy feathers is far less insulating for a household bird than for an aviary bird. Its owner, therefore, should take reasonable precautions to protect it from drafts at all times.

A household pet should never be placed in or near a window. In such a location it will not derive benefit from the sunshine nor will it be protected from drafts. Even a sealed window usually admits some draft that can endanger the bird, and sunshine coming through a window causes a continual moult that is equally dangerous. The draft hazard can produce colds, asthma, and pneumonia; and the continual moult saps the strength of the bird.

Many people prefer to cover their bird's cage at night. A cover restricts possible drafts and helps the bird get needed rest during late family gatherings. It also keeps the bird quiet.

If the bird owner decides to cover the bird at night, he must be consistent. The bird, having further temperature insulation provided, will in time lose some of its natural insulation. If the cover is forgotten, the bird might catch cold. If the decision is made to discontinue the practice, it should be done in summer so that, when the bird moults, it will produce a heavier layer of downy feathers for further insulation.

SUNSHINE

If you prefer to give your bird some sunshine out of doors each day, the cage should be placed in a protected location so that drafts will not occur. Also, the bird should be placed in such a location that it can move out of the sunshine if it should get too warm. Overheating and too much sunshine can also be harmful. Should you be interested in putting your cage and bird in the sunshine each day, it would be best to start in late spring or early summer.

This same rule applies to acclimating the bird to an outdoor aviary for the winter. Start slowly and build up the time for outdoor living. By the time moulting season arrives, the bird's hardiness will have improved immeasurably. If it is to live full time in an outdoor aviary, then it should spend summer nights outdoors. If not, the cage should be brought inside

Pet birds are perfect gifts for most people. The Half Moon or Petz' Conure shown here is one of the most popular of all parrots.

before sundown. When the moulting season is finished, the bird will have grown an undercoating of downy feathers to permit its wintering out of doors.

MOULTING

Birds should moult once each year, generally over the last six weeks of summer. In this period the bird replaces old feathers with new ones. It assumes a somewhat shaggy, pincushion appearance due to the many pin-feathers.

This rule holds true for many birds of the parrot family, but there are some variations. Many parrots seem to moult more slowly and, correspondingly, will start earlier. There is a common belief in a seven-year moulting cycle in larger parrots. For seven years, each successive moult is supposed to be heavier than the previous one. Then the moult becomes mild for the eighth and the cycle begins again. The writers have never verified the truth of this interesting idea.

Often a bird will moult out of season. If it is outdoors all the time and is suddenly brought indoors, the sudden temperature change induces the out-of-season moult; climatic variations bring on an out-of-season moult. There is no cause for alarm unless the moult is continual; if it is, the reason

This excellent birdroom houses several pet parrots. All cages are uniform in size and are placed on tables built especially to size for each cage. The tables are on coasters for easy movement when cleaning the floor. The height of the tables is perfect for easy cleaning of cages. An exercise stand gives each bird a chance to do any extra playing while its cage is being cleaned.

should be determined and corrected. During the moulting season, extra attention should be given to the diet to be sure the replacement of feathers does not prove overtaxing to the bird. Dietary supplements take on an added significance during the moulting season.

RED MITES

One very frequent problem with small caged birds is red mites. Most of the trouble begins with owners who do not understand the dangerous threat of these pests. Since mites are a recurring nuisance, their threat to the health of the bird should not be underestimated.

The presence of mites is easily noted if one knows what to look for. They are tiny red creatures which hide in nooks and crevices during the day and creep out to feed upon the bird's blood at night. A heavy infestation, if unchecked, can reduce a bird to a miserable, debilitated state in a short time. Favorite hiding places are the notches in perches, cuttlebone crevices and holders, hidden areas in the cage, and even in nearby drapery folds. An easy manner of detection is to place a white flannel cloth over the cage at night and check it in the middle of the night. The redness of the mites can be seen quite clearly against the white flannel.

Several worthwhile preparations are in your pet shop to aid in combating mites. For aviaries, a non-injurious spray is best. This type of spray is also good for a caged bird if used once a week during hot weather when mites are at their worst. There are also several handy little mite-killing gadgets that one need merely hang on the cage; a vaporizing agent is constantly at work against the mites. The useful span of these gadgets varies from five weeks to three months.

There are many other ways of getting rid of mites; but, since they entail considerable effort, the task is likely to be postponed too often to prove effective. Some sprays require that the bird, food, and water be removed before using. Various eradicating agents such as axle grease, kerosene, tobacco stems, and sheep dip have been used; they do the job well enough but are messy and present some danger to the birds.

It is unwise to pamper your bird to the point that it becomes like a hothouse flower; for, if you do, it will become easy prey to many illnesses. On the other hand, your pet deserves your good judgment in the exercise of your responsibility to keep it healthy and happy.

7

GENETICS AND HYBRIDIZING

Once in a while a new mutation occurs on the avicultural scene that causes considerable interest among bird fanciers. Because it is different and because it is rare, a new mutation usually brings a high selling price.

Mutations occur in every type of living plant or animal and are caused ordinarily by a weakness or a chemical change in genes. A mutation may be caused by a tangling of chromosomes during the synaptic phase or by chromosomal aberrations.

The usual result of a mutation is a change in color. This is the characteristic with which we are most concerned in this work.

LETHAL FACTORS

Not all mutations are desirable. In some types of mutations there are "lethal factors" at work. The best illustration of this is in the *dominant white factor* of the canary. If this factor is present in the homozygous state, i.e , if it is "double factored," the bird cannot survive because of a lethal reaction caused by the two similar genes. The bird either dies in the shell or just after hatching. Therefore, we know that every living white canary is heterozygous for color or carries one factor for white and one for yellow. Since the white is dominant, the yellow is masked. Mating two white canaries to each other automatically gives an overall percentage of twenty-five percent dead chicks. White to yellow is the best mating because the two colors are evenly divided in the offspring and there are no dead babies.

To date there are no mutant lethal factors known in the parrot family but they could always crop up. The presence of lethal factors has been suspected in a few instances.

WILD MUTATIONS

Many of the species of birds came into being as a result of mutations. There are many subspecies and closely related species existing about which there can be no doubt. When mutations occur in the wild state, it is nothing short of a miracle if the mutant survives. To go ahead and create a subspecies is even more miraculous.

Because of nature's system of checks and balances and her severe law of "survival of the fittest," it is understandable that only the plants and

A very rare lutino parrot of the genus Amazona. The forehead is a beautiful shade of pinkish-red. The eyes are pink and the rest of the coloring is a rich golden yellow.

animals nearest to perfection and most efficient in the struggle for existence could have survived the competition. These are nature's finest creations. If a mutation is not efficient, the mutant must perish. If a mutation is efficient, a new race may evolve.

Because of this rigorous ordeal to produce the strongest and most perfect races, most of the mutations are recessive or weak in character. That is to say, the original type is dominant or stronger. With this pattern of dominance and recessiveness, most of the mutations are absorbed or hidden by the dominant wild type. Doubtless, there are numerous mutations in all living things which have been in existence for untold years with no visible outward indication. They remain unknown because they are recessive to the original stronger wild type which masks their presence.

Albinos have long been known in nearly every form of life. Popularly, they are called "sports." But they are actually mutations. There is a mistaken belief that an albino suddenly comes into being; in actuality, the mutation may have occurred several generations previously. In birds of the parrot family, an albino is sex linked. That means the mutation occurred on the pair of chromosomes which is responsible for the sex of the individual. The particular nature of the sex chromosomes prevents an albino factor from being hidden too long.

When a visible mutation occurs in the wild state, there are several factors against its survival. First of all, the mutant may be avoided by birds of its own species and have no chance to reproduce its new variation. Secondly, because it is different, it will be more readily noticed by all predators or other enemies and will most likely be their prime target. If the mutant does have a chance to mate with another bird, it will probably be masked by the dominant nature of the wild variety. Only by chance mating with another bird carrying the presumable recessive factor will there be any opportunity for recreating the new variation.

MUTATIONS IN CAPTIVITY

In captivity, the mutation process is better controlled. If a mutation becomes visible, the bird fancier interested in genetics immediately maps out plans for different test matings to determine the nature of the mutation and where it fits into the general pattern. He then fervently hopes the parents will cast another mutant of opposite sex to help insure continuation of the new variety. If not, he hopes the birds will cooperate in the test mating program.

The Budgerigar has the record for the greatest number of mutations. By applied use of genetical knowledge and successful breeding practices, budgies are now available in a wide range of attractive colors, patterns, and combinations. It is becoming quite difficult to keep track of all the possible combinations of the different varieties. There has been a great deal of progress in establishing color variations within the last thirty-five to forty years. Prior to this period the only available color was the original green variety. To prove that the original green is still the strongest, one need only place one bird of each mutation, equalizing the sexes of course, in an aviary and let the birds go to nest. In a few years, the original normal green will be the only color of the descendants.

The pattern of mutations set by the budgie can be used as a guide in expected mutations of other species of parrot-like birds. Some mutations have occurred and have been successfully established. Others will follow.

The oldest color aberrations in the budgie follow Mendel's laws of inheritance and are called, simply enough, normals. The dominant color variety is the original or "wild" green.

The first recorded instance of a mutation, recalled by the writers, was found long ago in a description of a flock of wild budgies in which there was a yellow bird. We tried in vain to trace the source in which this statement was found, especially since we wanted to be certain whether the mutation was a normal yellow or a lutino. Presumably, however, it was a normal yellow, for that is the first color variation recorded in captivity. This color variety was devoid of the normal amount of dark pigment in the plumage except for a slight amount which gave the bird a chartreuse shade.

The next successful mutation was one in which every trace of yellow was removed. This is the cyanistic phase which results in a blue and white bird. Both mutations, so far, are recessive to green. Crossing the blue bird with the yellow bird presents us with all normal green babies so far as appearance is concerned. However, hidden under the dominant green are the recessive blue and yellow.

When a bird carries more than one color factor, it is said to be "split." In other words, the progeny were green split blue and green split yellow. The scientific term for this is *heterozygous*. If both color factors are the same the bird is *homozygous*.

It was only a matter of time before the fourth member of this quadrangle appeared. This mutation was called normal white; in appearance it was a pastel blue. Genetically, it is recessive to the other three types. It occurred because of the union of the chromosome which eliminated the yellow with the one which eliminated the dark pigment.

Other mutations followed, but the purpose of this chapter is to show similarities of mutation patterns between budgies and other birds. To try to include all the mutations of the budgie and fit them into their proper places we would have to cover much more ground than this one chapter allows.

The next mutation with which we are concerned is albinism. There are two color phases of this mutation. The yellow is called a lutino, and the white is called albino. The only difference between the two is that one is basically a green bird, and the other is basically a blue bird. The albinistic mutation masks these other colors. Since most original colors are green, it is not surprising that the first albinistic factor to appear was the lutino. Lutinos are always beautiful with an overall very rich, smooth yellow body and pink eyes. The albino is pure white with pink eyes.

As explained above, the albinistic mutation is sex linked. Because the mutation occurs on that part of the chromosome which is missing in the female, there need be only one factor present for the bird to show that factor. Indeed, a female cannot be "split" for any sex-linked factor. The male, however, must have both factors present before he will be either albino or lutino in appearance. The male can be "split" for the factor. Because of this, it is usually the female which appears first and numbers predominantly thereafter.

The last mutation factor which concerns us is the *pied factor* which has made its appearance in the Love Bird and in the budgie families, as well as in many other forms of bird life.

The pied factor is not a stable one. There are several different pied factors in budgies, each of which follows a different pattern of inheritance.

Most mutations of other members of the parrot family, either in captivity or in the wild state, follow the pattern set by budgies; but as yet, they have not completed the pattern. It would not be incorrect to say that the above mutations would be the most probable expectations in future generations regardless of species of parrot family bird.

To date there are several mutations which are becoming established. In most species the mutants are lutinos. In existence now are lutino Indian Ringneck Parrakeets, Nyassaland Love Birds, and several species of Amazon Parrots. Ringneck Parrakeets and Nyassaland Love Birds are established as definite color varieties; but none of the lutino Amazon Parrots have, to date, been successful in breeding.

The cyanistic phase, or blue mutations, are rare; but they are slowly becoming available in Indian Ringneck Parrakeets. In America, the blue phase is well established in Masked Love Birds. Exceptionally rare are blue Princess Alexandra Parrakeets found in Europe.

Whenever the two mutations for lutino and blue phases occur, there is a race to produce an albino. The first bird breeder to succeed will have a far more valuable and rare bird on his hands, but the writers are not quite certain as to what else he will gain. Personally, the writers are not the least interested in removing nature's original colors or the lovely mutant lutino to replace them with a flat white albino.

Pied mutations are present in Peach Faced Love Birds. The one man who seems to have had the good fortune to have the mutation originate in his aviaries was the late Herman Ebert, of Arcadia, California. Mr. Ebert made no pretense of being a geneticist, but he knew he had something. He carefully saved all progeny which showed the pied factor as well as the parents of the progeny.

His goal was to produce a yellow Love Bird with the rosecolored face. Since the pied factor is an undependable and not always an attractive mutation, he never quite succeeded.

After Mr. Ebert's untimely death, the birds containing the pied factor passed into the capable hands of geneticist Wayne Cotta. It was in Mr. Cotta's aviaries that the writers saw the rare, completely rosecolored Peach Faced Love Bird. They have never seen or heard of another.

Cinnamon coloring is another mutation which may attain prominence

74

in the future. Within a period of two months the writers have received information of a cinnamon mutation in several parrot-like birds. One was in a Yellow Naped Amazon Parrot. David West became the owner of a cinnamoncolored Lineolated Parrakeet. The writers have become the owners of two young Mexican Double Yellow Heads which have apricot coloring, in place of yellow, on the heads and a cinnamon bronze color suffused with green coloring. The red shoulders are a diluted shade of the normal red in other Mexican Double Yellow Heads. In appearance the two birds seem to be a pair; but, since both are quite young, several years will have to elapse before an attempt at breeding can be made.

MODIFIERS

In addition to mutations, there are modifiers in the genes which affect many characteristics of birds.

In numerous varieties of birds there are "geographical races" that show slight variations from the norm. These slight variations are caused by modifications which, because of geographical isolation, are built up into a homozygous condition in all the birds of the particular species coming from the given area. Many of these go unnoted in the field of aviculture. Examples are legion. The African Grey Parrot exhibits some of these modifications in the depth of the red coloring on the tail and possibly in the shading of grey on the body. None of these slight variations have resulted in any subspecies of the African Grey. The Cockatiel has many modifiers which have resulted in several slight color variations, but none are ranked as subspecies. Certain modifications show up in the extent of yellow coloring that seems far more prevalent in some birds. There are many Cockatiels, particularly females, that possess yellow wing patches instead of white. The greyness also shows considerable variation.

Great disunification in the depth of the rose coloring is apparent in Rose Breasted Cockatoos. It is believed that concentration of modifiers has built up these changes and has evolved individual races.

There are many other examples of modifiers in the wild state, but let us look at the domesticated budgie to get a clearer picture of modifiers.

There is a vast difference between the American Exhibition Budgie and the English Exhibition Budgie. Heads are larger, necklace spots are larger, the entire body is larger, and everything about the bird is well proportioned in the ideal English Exhibition Budgie. The introduction of the "English strain" in America has been the source of many bitter controversies in American bird shows because English stock nearly always wins over American birds.

The English Exhibition Budgie is basically the same bird as the original Australian wild budgie and the American Exhibition Budgie. There are vast differences in appearance, however, that have been brought about by skilled concentration on modifiers in the selective breeding programs of English fanciers.

In America, there is a world of difference between the Exhibition Budgie and the average pet. Again, this is brought about by concentrating on the modifiers.

The picture of the ideal show bird is the starting point. Slowly, those who are striving for the ideal accomplish the desired changes through rigid selective breeding, inbreeding, and line breeding.

INBREEDING

Inbreeding is usually the mating of brother and sister.

The term inbreeding is often maligned as signifying the increase of inherent weaknesses; but, in building up a definite strain, it is an invaluable technique which cannot be overlooked. Inbreeding is the surest way of concentrating those modifiers which bring about the desired results. There are no champion strains of livestock that have not resorted to inbreeding.

However, the technique is a slippery one. Not all modifiers are good and the concentration of bad modifiers is even more quickly entrenched than the concentration of good ones. Rigid, almost ruthless, selection of strongest and best individuals for inbreeding is of the greatest necessity. Minute attention to the smallest detail is of great importance. Culling out even the slightest imperfections is a must.

Misapplication and lack of knowledge of this technique quickly deteriorates the strain and strengthens the belief that inbreeding is to be avoided.

SELECTIVE BREEDING

Selective breeding refers to the careful selection of birds possessing desired qualities which are to be strengthened.

LINE BREEDING

Line breeding refers to the technique of mating related birds that exhibit the desired characteristics. Line breeding is usually the mating of cousins, or mother to son, or father to daughter.

Line breeding can be carried on for generations before it is necessary to introduce totally unrelated blood lines in order to insure stamina. The introduction of unrelated blood lines is referred to by the term of "outcrossing." It is also used in reference to mating for colors. For instance, a strain of lutinos may gradually deteriorate without the occasional outcrossing to the sturdier normal green. Inbreeding often requires more frequent outcrosses than line breeding.

All line breeding, selective breeding, and especially inbreeding, should be on an individual pair basis rather than colony breeding.

The writers once built up a strain of budgies specializing in normal sky blues, normal cobalts, and normal mauves. Concentrating on line breeding, the strain was built up for several generations to the point that the original pair of birds was in some way related to every member of the strain. The constancy of modifiers showed up in similarities in disposition, ease of taming, adeptness for talking, richer shades of coloring, increased size, better proportions, and larger necklace spots. It was also curious that when we entered the aviaries housing members of this strain, the birds were quick to fly to us to see what little treats we were bringing them. If the treat was green food, the budgies would swarm all over us. Naturally, some of these traits, such as familiarity and lack of fear, were acquired through the example set by the original hen and her first offspring, all of whom were tame. However, we like to think that these traits were inherited.

HYBRIDS

Hybrids are the result of a cross mating between two species. In almost all instances, a hybrid is a last resort. Individual species ordinarily have no desire to depart from their own kind for reproduction. For this reason most hybrids are somewhat difficult to produce. A lack of similarity in the chromosomal structure of the parents means that the eggs produced would be infertile. Many hybrids are mules, which means they are incapable of reproduction. In order to be capable of reproduction, a hybrid must come from parents which have highly similar genetical makeup.

A lady once asked us very enthusiastically if we had a Brazilian Crested Cardinal for sale. We replied that we had several at the time. She said, "Good. I'll take a male. I'm going right home to mate it with my female parrakeet so that I can get red-crested budgies. I just know they will sell."

In that short statement, the lady stressed her ignorance of genetics and hybridization. No matter how long or how hard she tried, she could never be successful with such a project. She might just as well have attempted to mate a dog to a cat.

Different species of Love Birds will cross, but a Love Bird will not mate with a Conure or a budgie. If a hybrid is desired by the bird fancier, it is usually because of an interest in experimentation or an attempt to gain offspring from two solitary birds that lack mates. A good rule to follow in attempting a cross is to be certain the birds are of the same genus. The first part of their Latin names should be the same. This does not mean that it would be impossible to mate birds of different genera; it means that success is more likely if the genus is the same.

Very often a solitary bird will show great affection for a bird totally unlike its own kind and will stimulate the bird fancier's thoughts to the possibility of a cross. If such is the case, the bird fancier is usually heading

Hybrid Cockatoo: Rose Breasted × Greater Sulphur Crested. Note the grey of the Rose Breasted intermingled with the white of the Sulphur Crested. This rare hybrid is owned by Herb Melvin.

down a blind alley. For the most part, hybrids are not desirable. The offspring are usually not as attractive as either of the parents, although there are a few notable exceptions. One of the most outstanding exceptions is the truly beautiful result of a cross-mating between two species of Rosella Parrakeets: Brown's X Yellow Rosella. On the other hand, Love Bird hybrids and numerous others are quite unattractive.

8

DISEASES AND AILMENTS

Birds, it seems, are susceptible to almost as many disorders as are humans. Many veterinarians in recent years have taken a special interest in birds. This required a considerable amount of extra study and practical experience on their part, for the course in veterinary medicine includes very little on birds. A veterinarian experienced with birds has the advantage over the "Doctor of Experience" because of his scientific background in pathology, anatomy, medications, surgical techniques, and the many other studies on life functions.

A person who has a knowledge of birds plus a keen eye can quickly tell the condition of a bird. A healthy bird has bright eyes, sleek plumage, and an alert demeanor. An unhealthy bird has dull eyes, puffed or lusterless plumage, and an apathetic manner. Half the battle in curing a bird of any illness is the recognition of the above danger signals and the application of first aid until proper diagnosis can be made.

FIRST AID

First aid consists of setting up the ailing bird in a hospital cage, applying heat, and making certain that the bird continues to eat. In almost all cases, first aid will help prolong the bird's life and give it a fighting chance. There are sound and important reasons for first aid.

The application of heat helps to maintain the bird's normal body temperature of 104° to 108° Fahrenheit. Without this help, the bird becomes more listless and stops eating. When it stops eating, it loses ground very rapidly and has no interest in living. Heat and interest in food are the two greatest hopes for recovery, since the metabolic rate in birds is extremely high.

A hospital cage can be any type of convenient structure which is suitable for the bird. Perches should be removed, and open feed dishes should be placed on the floor of the cage. An insulating cloth of light color should cover three sides and the top of the cage to help hold the heat. To provide the heat, a 25-watt bulb could be suspended in the cage by means of an extension cord or a heating pad could be placed under the cage. Care should be taken to arrange the bulb so that it does not burn the cloth cover; or, if the heating pad is used, a cover over the pad will prevent soiling.

Of course, the ideal would be to have a specially constructed hospital cage with thermostatically controlled heat. There are now some on the market. Saving the life of one bird more than repays the cost of such a cage.

The front of the cage is left open to prevent obstruction of the view. This is a psychological aid for the bird. If the bird is a pet, the sight of its owner provides a lift which helps it to maintain an interest in life. If it is an aviary bird, another psychological aid is to put its mate in with it, providing the disease is not contagious. The solicitude of a bird for a sick mate is often very touching. This can be most readily noted in Cockatiels. The writers have more than once seen a dead Cockatiel with its mate still trying to revive it. Removing the dead bird is a shattering experience for the mate, and there is a prolonged period of grieving. During illness, a Cockatiel benefits psychologically from the presence of its mate more than perhaps any other bird.

PREVENTION

First of all the prevention of diseases and disorders is far more practical than any cure. Protection against drafts is of primary importance and is far more simple than treating a cold which may develop into fatal complications. An adequate diet will prevent a majority of deficiency disorders which erupt in a variety of obscure, mysterious conditions and which are particularly obstinate to treatment. Exercise keeps the bird in excellent condition and helps to build up resistance to common weaknesses and illnesses. Cleanliness of food, water, and aviaries is of extreme importance. Many times in this chapter the reader will meet up with the advice "clean up and disinfect." This advice cannot be overstressed. In fact, concentrated precautionary measures as indicated above will be adequate safeguards against at least ninety percent of all illnesses.

In addition to heeding the dietary suggestions listed in the chapter on feeding, particular attention to certain foods will be helpful in speeding a recovery and getting a bird to regain strength lost during the illness.

The use of dietary supplements during recovery cannot be overstressed. In addition to the various fruits and the usual supplement, the writers prescribe greater amounts of peanut butter, an increase of vitamin concentrates, and two or three drops per day of Super D Concentrated cod liver oil. The amount given depends upon the size of the bird.

USEFUL MEDICATIONS

There are several medications which a bird collector should keep on hand at all times for emergencies as well as for common, easily treated disorders.

Hydrogen Peroxide is an invaluable aid. It is a mild disinfectant and coagulates the blood.

Iron Sulfate (popularly called Monsel's salts) is useful in coagulating blood.

Yellow Oxide of Mercury (ophthalmic style) in a 2% strength is the most beneficial eye ointment obtainable. Results are almost unbelievable in nearly all types of eye disorders.

Wonder Drugs or Antibiotics which are extremely useful are aureomycin, terramycin, achromycin, sulfamethazine, and penicillin.

Of these, aureomycin, terramycin, and sulfamethazine are available in pet shops and give specific directions as to strengths to be used. In some, directions are given only for canaries and parrakeets. The dosage for large birds could be tripled or quadrupled, but it should be coupled with the knowledge that larger birds will drink more liquids than a small bird and, therefore, will gain far more benefit from a single pill than will small birds.

Penicillin and achromycin are not available in pet shops and cannot be obtained without a prescription. They should not be administered except on the advice of a veterinarian. Overdoses could prove harmful, and under-doses are usually ineffective. Penicillin is generally useless in any form other than by injection into the blood stream. Since it is a very thick substance, injection is very difficult and impossible except on a large parrot-like bird. On the other hand, achromycin is easy to administer and is highly effective for many disorders. Its results often surpass that of the other wonder drugs.

In the absence of specific directions, the dosage of wonder drugs for a standard sized parrot such as the Amazon would be the same as for an infant child. Adjustments up or down can be made for other sizes of birds.

In treating birds for an illness, the writers prefer to administer first aid and one of the antibiotics as per instructions because antibiotics are specific aids for many diseases. Of course, not all disorders can be helped by antibiotics, and for these there are other appropriate medications.

Unfortunately, the use of antibiotics has often gone too far and it is common practice to suggest an antibiotic as a cure-all for practically every type of illness. The reader should be warned that overuse of antibiotics kills the vitally necessary good bacteria as well as those which are harmful.

There are many gaps in the understanding of bird disorders and diseases. Symptoms vary with individuals, and treatments often bring different results. In many cases, infection and the resultant debility of the bird opens the avenue for additional infections which complicate matters. If one treatment fails, another should be tried.

BACTERIAL INFECTIONS

Infections from bacteria and viruses are generally difficult to pinpoint without the aid of experienced laboratory personnel. Symptoms of many such diseases are nearly identical. Most are highly contagious and can result in widespread epidemics. In extensive aviaries with numerous birds, it would be a very wise precaution if all new birds could be put in an isolation cage or aviary for at least thirty days' observation before being placed with other birds.

Some examples of avian bacterial diseases are staphylococcosis, streptococcosis, typhoid, paratyphoid (or salmonellosis), pullorum, and fowl cholera (or pasteurellosis). These are in addition to specific diseases, which are discussed below.

Virus diseases that affect birds are bronchitis, bird pox, newcastle's disease, leukosis. Many new ones are being discovered regularly with the increased interest in laboratory research.

The treatment is questionable in most of these diseases and recovery is doubtful. Antibiotics such as sulfas and mycins are sometimes helpful and should be used. Unfortunately, even if the infected bird recovers, there is always the danger of its remaining a carrier.

Prevention is far easier than the cure.   Clean up and disinfect.

COLDS

A cold in birds is caused by a virus just as it is caused by a virus in humans, though it is not transmissible to humans.

Some symptoms are about the same as in humans: runny nose, sneezing, listlessness, difficulty in breathing, lack of appetite, occasionally watery eyes, and ruffled feathers. Some of the symptoms resembling colds are actually certain molds affecting the mouth. If unattended, a cold may result in a continuing weakness that will lead to the development of many other infections, especially pneumonia.

Treatment consists of isolation first because the cold virus is airborne and will spread. Apply heat of 80° to 85° and an inhalant to keep nasal passages clear. Careful attention to diet is necessary to be certain that the bird continues to eat. Aureomycin sometimes helps but is not always effective.

PNEUMONIA

This infection can be caused by a number of bacteria that get a foothold because of too much heat or too much cold. It often develops during the aftereffects of a prolonged cold. The lungs become spongy and watery due to excess fluids in the lungs. In advanced cases the exudate becomes cheesy.

Babies are generally able to recover from pneumonia, but they frequently become stunted and susceptible to various ailments.

Treatment is the same as for a cold, with the mandatory addition of an antibiotic such as aureomycin, terramycin or achromycin.

TUBERCULOSIS

True tuberculosis in parrots is rare, but many other disorders are diagnosed as tuberculosis. Since "going light" is one of the symptoms of tuberculosis, many other diseases with this symptom are superficially diagnosed as avian tuberculosis.

Avian tuberculosis is caused by a different organism, *Mycobacterium avium*, than mammalian tuberculosis; and so, there is no real need for worry about transmission of the disease to humans.

PSITTACOSIS

This disease has two technical names; one that causes needless headlines and another that has been relegated to obscurity for so long it is now seldom used. The causative filterable virus is *Miyagawanella psittaci.*

The name that causes the needless headlines is Psittacosis, popularly termed Parrot Fever. The other is Ornithosis. If the virus which causes this illness were confined to the psittacine, or parrot order of birds, the term psittacosis would be correct. Actually, however, the virus has been found in all birds, and the name Ornithosis is, therefore, more appropriate.

The disease was first discovered in a parrot late in the 1920's. The fact that it was transmissible to humans and could cause death resulted in sensational headlines in newspapers all over the world. It was a bright period for journalists, but it was an unpleasant one for bird fanciers. Importations on all· parrot-like birds were prohibited and are still controlled by stringent regulations. For a long period, it was illegal to transport any parrot-like bird across a state border. Only a few states now prohibit interstate traffic in psittacine birds.

The disease is caused by virus and very closely resembles pneumonia. Since isolation of different viruses was unknown until recent years, it is understandable that many cases of human pneumonia were termed parrot fever whenever the patients had had some contact with a parrot-type bird. Even now there is strong popular suspicion that virus disease results from contact of any sort with a psittacine bird.

The study of medicine has made great strides since the war. Viruses can be isolated, studied, and many can be controlled. These include the ones for ornithosis and pneumonia. Aureomycin, terramycin, and achromycin are all effective against the ornithosis virus.

The wonder drugs have erased the necessity for import restrictions. Prohibition causes high prices and encourages smuggling; this also increases the incidence of the disease instead of eliminating its danger.

Symptoms, while sometimes resembling those of a severe cold or pneumonia, are more aggravated. They are inconstant; and, therefore, an accurate diagnosis cannot be made by observing the bird. Qualified diagnostic centers are few, but they can be located through state health departments. A blood specimen is necessary for a positive diagnosis. In large birds, it is possible to get a blood specimen without too much damage to the bird. Unfortunately, in order to obtain a sufficient blood sample from a smaller bird it would have to be put to death.

Let us emphasize the great rarity of ornithosis. If your bird becomes ill, do not jump to the conclusion that it has the disease. If it came from a reputable source, has been kept clean, and has been fed a nourishing diet, chances of its ever contracting the disease are minute indeed.

PROTOZOAN DISEASES

Protozoa are single-celled animals. Many of these attack birds and cause various illnesses and diseases, ranging from coccidiosis to a form of amoebic dysentery. Fortunately, they seldom become a real problem. Cleanliness is the best preventative measure.

COCCIDIOSIS (*Coccidia*)

This is mainly a hot weather disease that affects the intestine. It is caused by a minute protozoan. Fortunately it is rare in aviaries and practically non-existent in individual household pets. Coccidiosis is common to poultry and may spread to an aviary through visitations of wild English Sparrows. When it does strike, it can become epidemic in proportions; birds become weak, emaciated, sometimes have bloody diarrhea, and finally die.

We know of only one sure treatment for coccidiosis, but it is so drastic and so dangerous that we will not prescribe it for fear it will be improperly used. Various antibiotics have been used, but none can be considered completely successful.

Since coccidiosis is spread by droppings containing oocysts, or egg-like bodies, again we say the best prevention is to clean up and disinfect.

SWOLLEN OIL GLAND

The oil gland is located at the base of the tail on the upper side. Its purpose is to secrete oil which the birds use in preening their feathers. Occasionally, the gland opening becomes clogged and results in an inflammation caused by a backlog of oil; it resembles a tumor. It is a simple task to remove the clogged material with a toothpick or matchstick, applying pressure gently until the backlog has exuded from the gland.

Occasionally, however, there is a tumor in the oil gland. If there is an open sore, any bleeding, or if the material does not squeeze easily from the gland, a malignant tumor can be suspected; and a veterinary should be consulted.

TUMORS AND CANCER

Tumors are common in some birds, especially in budgies and old parrots. Many are benign fatty tumors (or lipomas) and can be removed by surgery. The best surgeon in all cases would be a veterinarian who has the experience, education, and equipment to perform the operation.

Fatty tumors occur most often on the chest, but they can be found elsewhere on the body. When on wings they appear to be quite painful to the bird. Often they grow so large that the bird cannot adequately fold its wings. Again a veterinarian should be consulted for proper removal.

Many tumors are cancerous and offer no hope of a cure. Some are easily detected. Others are internal and almost defy detection. Whenever a tumor is located in the area of vital organs, there is danger of cancer. Brain tumors caused by head injuries can cause distended eyes and sometimes blindness.

ABSCESSES

Abscesses are often confused with tumors because of their firmness. Removal by means of surgery and the application of an antibiotic to prevent reinfection is the only necessary treatment. Some abscesses are caused by bacterial agents such as *Sphaerophorous* and *Micrococcus*.

SINUS

Often there are tumor-like nodules above the eye or on the top of a bird's head. While some of these could be actual tumors, the majority are caused by impacted sinus conditions. The material forming the nodule, yellow and cheese-like, consists of deposits of thickened mucus that have collected behind clogged sinus passages.

The ideal way to remove these deposits is to open the passages and promote a slow drainage so as not to damage the delicate tissues. Sometimes, however, these conditions develop so rapidly that the nodules are very hard before they are noticed. In such cases, proper drainage cannot be encouraged; using first slight massage, minor surgery can remove the deposits by inflicting a small wound into the nodule with a pin-prick or a slight scratch. Within two or three days a scab will have formed over the small wound. Much of the cheese-like material will cling to the scab when it is removed. The rest can be removed by slight massage towards the opening. Care must be taken to remove all the material from the passages to prevent the condition from recurring. Usually there is no bleeding whatever. The opening should be cleansed with an extremely mild disinfectant.

There are, however, disadvantages to this type of treatment. The delicate tissues of the sinus passages may become injured beyond repair, and there is no assurance that the condition will not recur. If it does recur, the same treatment must be repeated. All told, the disadvantages seem to be outweighed by the advantage of alleviating the bird's distress. The writers have performed this operation may times because of the prevalence of avian sinus conditions in coastal areas. Seldom has there been a fatality either during or after such an operation.

Sinus troubles are usually brought on as an aftermath of a cold and are low grade infections. They may manifest themselves in other ways. Puffiness of sacs under the eyes and swollen or tear-filled eyes are frequent symptoms. Sometimes the eyes are closed as a result of exudates. The customary treatment employed by the writers in these cases is to apply an ophthalmic style of yellow oxide of mercury ointment as used for humans. A generous application for three or four days along with a mild vapor rub on the nostrils clears up the condition very well. Aureomycin ointment in ophthalmic style has been used in place of the mercury oxide ointment with good success. Boric acid ointments have also been used but with slower and less exacting results.

ASTHMA

Asthma is also a low grade infection brought on as an aftermath of a cold. Treatment may be necessary for a period of six months. A wheezy rattling and difficulty in breathing are symptoms. If it can be ascertained that the bird has recently had a cold, one can be reasonably sure of asthma. There are several other highly contagious diseases which display similar symptoms; and so, care should be taken to be certain the diagnosis is correct.

The surest (however slow) method of treatment is to isolate the bird and to administer a suitable inhalant for about an hour every day. There are some good inhalants on the market for birds. Some are strong enough to do the job but not so strong as to cause irritations to tender membranes. The best method of administering the inhalant is to employ an electric vaporizer. This is easiest and most effective. A dry, arid, and warm environment would be helpful. Antibiotics tried by these authors have not proven effective, and prolonged use of antibiotics is not advisable.

MOLDS

Fungi attack birds in various ways and create many deadly illnesses. Birds become infected by these fungus molds in different manners. Some are airborne. Some are introduced by dirty water, rotting seeds, moldy foodstuffs, perpetual dampness in hidden corners, and filth.

Cleanliness and disinfectants will prevent infection from most molds. Treatment of the various molds depends upon the parts affected and the extent of infection.

Symptoms vary according to type of mold and affected organ. A watery, mushy body is usually caused by molds which draw the water out of the rest of the body.

Some symptoms, which are the same as for colds, are caused by molds that affect the mouth.

Most molds cause unthriftiness. Those infecting the digestive tract usually cause diarrhea which results in pasted vents.

Treatments are not always successful. Some antibiotics are effective. Bluestone, in a weak diluted form, works on several types of molds. Prevention is far easier and more successful than treatment. The easiest rule is to clean up and disinfect.

EXTERNAL MOLDS

External molds can be treated by cleaning the infected part with a mild detergent or a disinfectant soap, followed by a mild astringent. Keep the bird in a very warm room. Dirty seed can spread a mold that causes watery eyes.

INTERNAL MOLDS

If the internal mold infection affects the digestive tract, a primary rule to follow is to clean out the digestive tract with a good laxative.

Various antibiotics are effective in the treatment of molds. There are molds that affect the mouth, crop, gizzard, and the entire digestive tract. One of these, called Thrush (*Candida albicans*), is reasonably common.

ASPERGILLOSIS (*Aspergillus fumagatus*)

This infection is caused by a fungus spore that attacks the lungs and air sacs. Sometimes it is called "air sac infection," but often it is referred to as "mold pneumonia." It causes cheesy exudates to accumulate in the various cavities and produces difficult breathing, weakness, poor appetite, and frequent neck stretching in the sick bird. Half-grown birds are easily affected.

Although this mold is generally airborne and is often spread in this manner, it can also be introduced in moldy foodstuffs, especially bread.

There is no sure cure for this infection although research is being done to find one. Prevention is far easier than a cure.

SOUR CROP

Sometimes the crop becomes sour through simple digestive upsets. When this happens a teaspoon of baking soda in a quart of water will sweeten the crop in a couple of days.

The most serious cause of sour crop is a mold that breaks down the rubbery walls of the crop, making them thin and flabby.

MOUTH CANKER

Few maladies are as painful to birds as mouth canker. A prolonged case can result in emaciation and even death; because it becomes so painful, the bird stops eating.

This disorder is usually dietary in character and is more often found in budgies and other parrakeets. It is noticeable because of an irritation around the bird's beak. A smaller whisker-like appendage often grows at the corners of the mouth, eventually dropping off and being replaced by another.

Treatment is simple, but it requires patience. The affected corners of the mouth should be painted with merthiolate or mercurochrome every day until the condition disappears. In prolonged cases, the method of treatment may produce a slight blistered effect. Treatment should be postponed for a few days in these instances, even though the blistered effect seems to cause no harm. Usually, the condition disappears before this point is reached.

ENTERITIS—BACTERIAL AND PROTOZOAN

Overcrowded, dirty quarters is the usual cause of this deadly disease. Symptoms are diarrhea, loss of weight, listlessness, weakness, and rapid death. Since it spreads rapidly, affected individuals should be isolated and treated with aureomycin or a remedy containing sulfamethazine. Constant temperatures of 80° to 85° should be maintained.

Correct diet, roomier and sterilized quarters, and clean food and water receptacles will eliminate this problem in aviaries.

DIARRHEA—BACTERIAL AND PROTOZOAN

This condition of loose droppings is a symptom of many other illnesses and is rarely a disorder in itself.

There are many types of laxatives available, but some are harsh. In our experience with our own birds, we have obtained the best results by using two tablespoons of black strap molasses in one quart of distilled water. We suggest the use of this mixture instead of water for two days. If the condition is unchanged after five days, the treatment should be repeated.

In addition to cleansing the digestive tract of the bird, the high carbohydrate content of molasses gives quick food value that is easily absorbed.

Caution: Never give a laxative for any type of internal bleeding or bloody diarrhea. Bloody diarrhea can be caused by an internal injury, certain types of pneumonia, coccidiosis, and other dangerous organisms. In such cases a laxative could aggravate the condition.

GOING LIGHT

This term refers to a symptom rather than a disease in itself. For many years it has been applied to most cases in which the diagnostician could not pinpoint the true ailment. Therefore, a great many disorders have been grouped under this one term.

Whenever a bird loses weight, it is said to be "going light." The reason for loss of weight is an exceptionally high metabolic rate and a constant need for replenishing the used up energy. When a bird becomes ill, it often lacks appetite and refuses to eat a suitable amount of food; it then uses up its own flesh for nourishment, resulting in a rapid loss of weight.

Look for other indications of specific ailments before ending the diagnosis with the term "going light."

CONSTIPATION

This is a minor disorder which can be the result of many causes such as heavy infestation of mites, worms, and colds. The clogged digestive tract must be cleared by means of a suitable laxative. In appearance the droppings may even look as if the bird had diarrhea, but they will be white in color. Whitish droppings are urates devoid of fecal matter. See *Diarrhea* for proper remedy.

REGURGITATION

Bringing up foods can be traced to various causes. The first and most frequent cause is a desire to mate. Most birds bring up food to feed their mates. In the absence of a mate, a bird will choose an object or person upon which to bestow its affectionate regurgitation. Although an unpleasant habit, it is not serious and will pass.

The more serious causes will result in trouble if unattended. Constant regurgitation may denote an illness and is usually brought on by one of several crop disorders such as molds, sour crop, or crop impaction.

There are additional minor and also rarer causes. These include foreign particles that irritate the crop, poison, or indigestion.

Regurgitating is also one symptom of a cold. It is a method of eliminating mucus.

BOTULISUM OR LIMBERNECK (*Clostridium botulinus*)

This deadly infectious poison is responsible for a condition called "limberneck." It is a form of paralysis that starts in the neck and eventually creeps over the bird's entire body.

The cause is an organism present in dirty water and rotting food, and the type of general uncleanliness that attracts flies. Little can be done for the infected bird, but prevention is simple: clean up and disinfect.

MISCELLANEOUS

Several disorders occur for which there is no known cure. Some are conditions frequently associated with old age in birds, such as arteriosclerosis or hardening of the arteries, arthritis, liver and kidney diseases, and gout. Although incurable, these disorders can be prevented by proper diet.

SHOCK AND HEART ATTACKS

Heart attacks cannot be cured in birds. Often the first attack is fatal. If it isn't, even the slightest fright or sudden disturbance can bring on another. Proper diet and exercise are good measures of prevention.

Shock can kill a bird very quickly. In many instances, shock is almost identical in symptomatic behavior to heart failure. It can occur as the result of an injury or during treatment when a sick bird must be handled. It can also occur during surgery when the work is too extensive. Nothing can be done to prevent this except to plan treatments and surgery so that they can be extended over a longer period of time.

EGG BINDING

This problem can be very serious, usually causing rapid death if un-attended. Fortunately, it is easily relieved if quickly detected.

Symptoms are puffiness, lack of vitality, extreme weakness, and a straining motion in attempting to expel the egg. Close examination will usually reveal the location of the egg in a bulge near the vent.

Treatment consists of placing the bird in a very warm (80° to 85°) hospital cage and putting, with an eye-dropper, a few drops of slightly warmed mineral oil or olive oil in the vent. In most cases, the egg will be laid safely within a few hours. In stubborn cases, slight pressure above the egg will assist in its expulsion. Extreme care should be exercised so as not to break the egg. After the egg is expelled, the bird quickly recovers and is back to normal; but it should not be given nesting facilities again for several months.

The writers do not believe in giving oils orally. Mineral oil coats the intestine and prevents absorption of certain food materials. Also, trying to extract the contents of the eggs with a hypodermic syringe and getting the bird to expel the crushed shell has proven unsatisfactory in most cases. Delicate membranes in the oviduct would be seriously damaged.

Egg binding is an unnecessary ailment in nearly all cases. Proper diet and plenty of exercise will prevent nearly all such disorders.

RUPTURED EGG SAC

Occasionally, the task of laying an egg becomes difficult, and a portion of the oviduct is expelled along with the egg. When this happens, the egg dangles from the vent and is covered by a thin membrane with prominent blood vessels.

Treatment is simple but somewhat delicate. The membrane should not be touched with dry fingers, cotton, or instruments. A mild, slightly warmed saline solution should be available for moistening anything that comes in contact with the membrane. The opening of the membrane must be stretched enough to force the egg through. In severe cases, the egg can be broken and the shell removed carefully so that the membrane will not be scratched or damaged.

After the egg has been removed, the membrane should be returned gently inside the vent. A warm, wet, blunt eye-dropper is helpful here. Usually the membrane will contract and place itself in its proper position once it has been returned to the vent.

SOFT SHELLED EGGS

This problem is almost always the result of inadequate calcium in the diet. Several weeks before nest boxes are added for the birds, additional calcium and lime should be added to the diet. Oyster shell and cuttlebone are the main sources for these ingredients. Cod liver oil is necessary for the proper absorption of calcium.

FEATHER PLUCKING

When a bird starts to pluck its own feathers, it is usually because of one of two reasons: a dietary deficiency or an acquired vice. The chapter on diet lists treatments for a deficiency, but in this case the addition of some animal protein in the form of raw meat may also be helpful.

If feather plucking is an acquired vice, many tricks can be used to break it. Usually the habit is formed through boredom. Additional freedom, more attention, or new toys may prove to be good distractions. Whatever the cause, perseverance and psychology must be used to ferret out and eradicate it.

OVERGROWN BEAKS

This is one of the commonest disorders in pet budgies and a not too uncommon disorder in aging parrots. The writers have found that the ratio of household pet birds with overgrown beaks is much greater than that of aviary birds. Granting that the individual pet owner is more likely to come to us for help on this problem than the collector, who will himself perform the task of trimming beaks, we still hold to this ratio because of specific observations made in our own and many other aviaries. Seldom, we have ·noted, does this problem arise in aviaries unless there is an actual beak deformity.

There are two main types of overgrown beaks especially noticeable in budgies. One type is a long slender overgrowth that seems to be of normal texture. The other is a coarse soft overgrowth. Each should be treated in different ways.

The normal-textured overgrowth is apparently due to lack of chewing exercise. If the bird can be induced to chew on some of the beak pacifiers available on the market, this problem can be eliminated.

The coarse soft overgrowth appears to be caused by a dietary deficiency, mainly lack of calcium and trace minerals. Ironically, an overabundance of calcium can create the same basic problem.

Once this second type of overgrowth begins, it is nearly impossible to curtail. A corrected diet, beak conditioners, and aviary freedom all fail to bring about a recovery.

Just about the only recourse is to trim the beak to normal length, and not less, at regular intervals. In small birds, trimming the beak is a simple routine matter. Many types of clippers are suitable. In some cases, the vein in the beak grows right along with the overgrowth. Therefore, it is best to trim small pieces at a time so as not to cut deep into the blood vein. After the desired length has been reached, the sides of the overgrowth should be trimmed and shaped into a normal pointed beak.

In large parrots, the beak-trimming job is far more difficult because of the necessity of restraining the bird. If the overgrowth is long and slender, the aptest tool is one of the better types of dog toenail clippers available in pet shops. This same tool is excellent for trimming parrots' toenails. If the overgrowth will not fit into the toenail clippers, the sides should be trimmed until it does.

There are other tools that will doubtless fill the need but we have found nothing else that will give the necessary leverage or that will not slip. Scissors are useless in performing this task.

Should the vein in the beak become cut, apply Monsel's Salt (iron sulfate), or Hydrogen Peroxide to coagulate the blood.

Parrots are often brought to us with the mistaken idea that beaks should be trimmed because a new beak growth has begun. The older growth will appear to be uneven and shorter than the new growth. This is a natural occurrence and shows that the bird has had proper opportunities to chew. Eventually the older jagged parts will slough off. It is unwise to clip such a new growth unless it has gone beyond the normal length.

OVERGROWN TOENAILS

Frequently all species of parrot-like birds grow long toenails that need

The job of trimming the sharp toenails of strong parrots is difficult. It should only be attempted by experienced people since a slight shift may cause too deep a cut and result in bleeding. The grip around the neck exerts just enough pressure to control the bird and not enough to cause harm. The most satisfactory tool is the toenail clippers made for dogs.

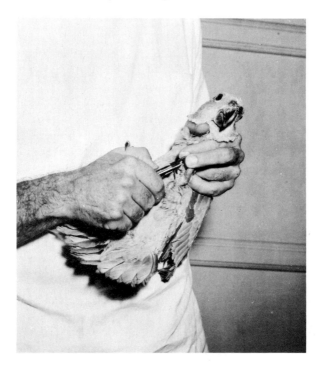

clipping at regular intervals. This is mainly a problem of household pets, but it also often occurs to aviary birds.

Small birds' toenails should be trimmed with ordinary fingernail cutters and large birds' with dog toenail cutters. Trim to a length approximating the normal length or just slightly longer. Occasionally, the blood vein in the toenail grows in much the same manner as the vein in the beak. It is wise, therefore, not to clip too much from the toenails at a time. If bleeding should occur, apply Monsel's salts or hydrogen peroxide.

EYE CATARACTS

Little can be done to cure this condition once it occurs. Its cause can usually be traced to an inadequate diet over a prolonged period. Prevention is much the easiest course. In some cases, improvement of diet brings about a partial recovery.

FRENCH MOULT

The presence of French Moult is indicated by the constant loss and replacement of flight feathers on the wing and the long tail feathers. Birds affected usually cannot fly and are very irregular in appearance. The constant replacement of feathers saps the bird of a tremendous amount of vitality and thereby weakens it. In most cases, the ailing bird will not live a normal life span.

Bitter controversies have raged over the cause and cure of French Moult. Mostly the disorder has affected budgies, but also some Cockatiels and Love Birds. Staunch arguments are brought forth attributing the cause to be a dietary deficiency on the one side and to a tiny mite which invades the feather follicle at an early age on the other side. Not wishing to stand on either side of this battle, we would like to report our successful methods of prevention: spraying often and thoroughly to kill mites and feeding an all-inclusive diet.

BUMBLEFOOT

This is a painful disorder found frequently in budgies. Cheesy substances collect in deposits on feet or legs and seem to exert a great pressure. In many cases the bird is unable to bend its toes or grasp a perch. The cause is normally poor diet with too many rich foodstuffs.

Treatment consists of eliminating these substances by cutting a small incision lengthwise and pressing the substances outwards through the incision. Apply a strong astringent (not iodine) frequently.

If the bird is severely affected, treat only one or two masses at a time. The extreme pain may put the bird in shock and could cause death.

PARASITIC WORMS

There are several types of internal parasitic worms that are seldom detected. In cases of chronic unthriftiness where other remedies and safeguards fail, worms should be suspected.

Cropworms are almost microscopic and look like fibers pointed on both ends. They give a toxic slough. Fortunately, they are not prevalent.

Spiral worms affect the proventriculus. They are very prolific with an average production of 10,000 eggs within the life span of twenty-eight days.

Globular fatworms also attack the proventriculus, embedding themselves in the glands, forty all told, that are within it. This is a very deadly worm; it takes only a few to kill the affected bird. Symptoms are unthriftiness and "going light."

A wire-worm affects the gizzard.

EYE WORM

This is a slender, white worm less than one-fourth of an inch long that infests the inner angle of the eye.

TAPEWORMS

There are two types of tapeworms that infest birds. One settles in the intestine and duodenal loop. The other, called the microscopic tapeworm, imbeds itself in the base of the villi. Its puncturing action injects toxic poisons into the digestive organism and leaves the bird in an unthrifty appearance.

Tapeworms require an intermediate host. Treatment is difficult, uncertain, and dangerous. In the case of round worms, such as the above varieties, it consists of a piperazine product or a total intake of less than half of one percent of nicotine sulphate in the food. For other tapeworms, a total intake of half of one percent of Kamala powder in dry foods over a period of five days is effective. The treatment should be discontinued for twenty days and then repeated for five more days. A laxative should be administered to flush the digestive tract following treatment.

The dosage of these medicines requires the most meticulous measuring and proportioning. The treatments for worms, therefore, are seldom used. It is much easier to maintain cleanliness, the best method of prevention.

RED MITES

These little creatures, pinpoint in size, are prevalent wherever there are birds. As a rule, the single pets attacked are usually small birds such as canaries, finches, or budgies. In aviaries, red mites particularly attack nestlings and brooding hens, often causing so much irritation that hens leave the nest.

These mites are red because they are filled with the blood of their victims. In really heavy infestations, mites can drain enough vitality from the birds to cause death.

In the case of caged birds detection can most easily be made at night. Cover the cage with white flannel cloth and check it during the night. If mites are present, they can more easily be noticed against the white background.

In aviaries, mites can be detected by probing in hidden corners, in wall cracks, behind nest boxes, and similar areas.

Eradication of mites requires perseverance more than anything else. During the warmer seasons, aviaries and cages should be sprayed once each week. There are many sprays now available at pet stores. Those that can be used without removing food, water, or birds are the ones recommended. The spray should be fine enough to penetrate crevices or holes.

FEATHER MITES AND QUILL MITES

These mites can do considerable damage to plumage of birds, but, fortunately, they are not widespread. They should be suspected if the plumage appears to be chewed up and there is no other reasonable explanation.

Treatment consists of spraying the bird with a mild, harmless insecticide. To be certain of its safety and effectiveness, buy one of the mite sprays labeled "for direct use" on birds.

SCALY LEG MITES

These mites occasionally become a problem by causing the scales on a bird's legs to become prominently abnormal in appearance and sometimes inflamed.

Treatment consists of applying a mite-killing oil or salve which smothers the mites and softens the scales. There are also several home remedies, but we prefer those on the market prepared expressly for this purpose.

MANGE MITES

A certain mange mite (there are many) affects some birds, particularly budgies and larger parrakeets. It spreads slowly and has a deteriorating effect on beaks, ceres, and surrounding facial area. This has long been a serious problem to budgie fanciers.

Recently two qualified men, Robert Wichmann and Douglas J. Vincent, Jr., have reported extensively on this disorder (*All Pets Magazine*, August, 1958). They state that an effective cure has been found in the use of the drug, EURAX. Application should be administered by a veterinarian.

BROKEN LEGS AND WINGS

Broken legs are common in small birds, such as parrakeets, but rare in larger birds. If it is a simple fracture, there is no danger to the bird. Since a fracture will usually heal within a week or ten days, the writers never bother with splints and difficult paraphenalia that are a source of irritation to the bird and of questionable benefit. The bird will favor the leg and not try to use it.

All perches except one close to the floor should be removed. Open food and water dishes should be placed on the floor of the cage. The cage should be covered to discourage climbing. The bird will use its wing and beak as aids in moving from place to place. Recovery is amazingly fast. If the bone knits improperly, there will always be a lump or bend in the leg; but this causes no apparent discomfort to the bird.

More serious fractures in which the bone is completely severed and, in many cases, extended from the skin, will probably result in a loss of the leg. If the individual situation really warrants it, the leg should be amputated and disinfected with hydrogen peroxide.

If there is a chance of saving the leg with a splint, then it will be worth the effort. Splints can be made with sufficiently large feather quills, or plastic molded into a suitable shape, or even from scotch tape. The reader must realize that a splint will be an irritation to the bird; and, if it is too tightly bound, it will hinder circulation.

Broken wings are treated the same as a simple fracture of the leg. By letting them droop naturally, there is a better chance of recovery.

Badly torn and bleeding wings usually result in severe shock and death. If a brace is necessary, the wing should be carefully folded in a natural position and very gently, somewhat loosely, held by a sling fashioned in any manner necessary to hold the wing in place. Most wing slings are of questionable benefit and will certainly direct more of the bird's attention to the wound. Picking and struggling with the sling will be seriously detrimental.

Most of the dangers of broken legs and wings can be avoided by the removal of anything that will entangle or ensnare the bird. Loose strings, hanging wires, nets left behind in aviaries, sharp or close areas on cages, a spool of thread or yarn, even a lady's hairnet, can all entangle a bird so hopelessly that in the ensuing desperation it will seriously injure itself.

HEAD INJURIES

Most head injuries are caused by the bird dashing headlong, in blind fright, into a wall or taut wire netting. In an injury of this type, the neck is sometimes broken. This kills the birds almost instantly. More often, there is a short period of immobility when the bird seems to be in a coma or a state of paralysis. In some cases, the bird seems to recover quickly and shows no further sign of injury.

This is not the end of the injury, however. The writers have checked many mysterious deaths and numerous unexplainable paralytic conditions in birds and have traced them back to head injuries as the only possible external causes. Often there will be a period of blindness that leaves the bird in a state of nervous bewilderment, the bird constantly turning its head, and flinching from even the slightest sound. The eyes will appear distended as if there were an internal growth or tumor pressing them outward. The condition will often pass and sight be restored, but, except for first aid, there it not much that is possible in the way of effective treatment.

The writers have never conducted clinical tests to ascertain the validity of these suppositions, but the numbers of similar case histories lend credence to their theory.

PUTTING TO SLEEP

Sometimes all efforts to bring about the recovery of a sick bird fail. If the bird is in pain, or is likely to be a carrier of infection, or is obviously going to die, it is far more humane to put it to sleep than to prolong its suffering. There are several methods of accomplishing this task; but the one which seems the least drastic and least painful is to put the patient in a paper bag and hold its opening tight around a car exhaust. In less than a minute the carbon monoxide will have asphyxiated the bird.

SUMMARY

Throughout this chapter are to be found examples of hopeless or difficult diseases. Research is now being carried on as never before and will doubtless lend a clear understanding to many of the bird diseases that are still beclouded. An encouraging sign is the awakening of some of the poultry pharmaceutical houses to the problems of pet birds. The past research spent on poultry, and the vast benefit to that industry, is a good indication of future aid to the field of Aviculture.

As mentioned before, almost ninety per cent of all disorders and diseases can be prevented by proper diet and cleanliness. Often it is too late when the neglect of these two basic principles brings on infection. Success or failure with birds hinges upon the application of these two basic principles more than anything else.

9

THE PARROT FAMILY

Technically speaking, any member of the Parrot Family is a parrot. Speaking less broadly, but more correctly, the Order of Parrots is divided into many different categories and many different kinds of birds. The Order of Parrots is called *Psittaciformes*, and all members have certain general characteristics. For example, all parrots have similar hooked bills and peculiar mallet-shaped tongues. Most hooked bills can exert great force, useful in obtaining food or as a weapon against enemies. Most parrots have strong, heavy legs and feet, useful in climbing through trees in search of food. In this respect, the bill also aids in climbing. All parrots are mainly vegetarian. They have harsh natural voices and the ability for mimicry.

The technical term for Parrot Family is *Psittacidae*. This huge family is broken down into six subfamilies of which three are relatively unimportant from an avicultural standpoint.

Subfamilies are divided into genera, the singular form for which is *genus*. Each genus has certain clearly defined characteristics which separate it from other genera. The members of each genus show a close relationship to each other. In some cases, the genus is subdivided into a further category called *subgenus*. Although the subgenus is given a definite name, it is not included in the specific name of the bird. Members of the subgenus have further peculiar characteristics which separate them from other members of the genus.

The next subdivision is the *species*. In many birds, the species name is the end of the complicated structure of nomenclature, but there are several divisions in some species which are called *subspecies*. The differences that divide species into subspecies can be geographical habitat, size, or pattern and color variations. In some instances, there is a wide variation in color among subspecies, but this is the exception rather than the rule.

All scientific names are in Latin, are written in italics, and are of universal usage. Popular names often lead to confusion. Many birds may have the same popular name, but the full scientific name is never duplicated. Genera names can refer to characteristics of the genus. The names of species and subspecies frequently denote characteristics, habitat, or person for whom named. In many works the name of the ornithologist who first discovered and named the species follows the scientific name. The writers have dispensed with this

Thick Billed Parrots are very rare in aviculture. Beautiful in red and green, the yellow underwing coverts add a bright flash during flight. This is the only parrot which sometimes ranges northward from Mexico into the United States.

formality. The scientific names and regroupings of all birds in this book conform to James Lee Peters' *Check List of Birds of the World*.

It seems quite likely, though, that a major overhaul is forthcoming in the classifications within the Order of Psittaciformes. Volume III of Peters' *Check List of Birds of the World*, which includes the psittaciform birds, was published in 1937. Since then intensive work on behavior and evolutionary development has been accomplished and suggested regroupings have followed these studies. Among the several scientists who have contributed significantly to these studies are William C. Dilger, K. Immelmann, and J. LeGay Brereton.

While working on bird skins at the American Museum of Natural History in New York City, one of the writers had the opportunity to meet and to talk with Dr. Brereton, who was at that time at Cornell's Department of Ornithology while on sabbatical from his home base at the University of New England, New South Wales, Australia. Dr. Brereton in subsequent correspondence gave us some very interesting scientific papers which support reclassifications. Most of the generic and species names of Peters are retained, and so few actual scientific names are changed. Superfamily status helps in the main divisions, and family status is substituted for the subfamily status given by Peters. The main regroupings considerably change some of the previously accepted relationships. Two other major changes which do affect identification for the aviculturist are the changes in the generic names from *Kakatoe* (certain cockatoos) to *Cacatua* and *Lorius* (Eclectus Parrots) to *Eclectus*. A further change is the scientific separation from *Platycercus* of all those birds which Peters lists as the species *barnardius*, lifting them as before to the generic rank of *Barnardius*. The names used in this text will remain as presented by Peters with the understanding that in the future major ornithological changes may be forthcoming.

In working with the skins of birds at the American Museum of Natural History, the writers continued with their previous practice of measuring birds from the crown to the tip of the tail, which is contrary to the ornithological practice of measuring from the tip of the beak to the tip of the tail. Measuring bird skins is not always accurate, partly because of the manner in which they are prepared and possible shrinkage. However, working with the skins in the largest collection in the world helped to strike a good average, because there are so many examples of each of those species and subspecies represented in the collection.

A frequent practice in avicultural literature is to eliminate the second or species name if the bird is a subspecies. For example, Swainson's Blue Mountain Lorikeet is most frequently listed as *Trichoglossus moluccanus* rather than *Trichoglossus haemeatodus moluccanus*. Forsten's Lorikeet is usually listed as *Trichoglossus forsteni* rather than *Trichoglossus haematodus forsteni*. However, it is the opinion of the writers that the use of all three names is not only more correct, but it also helps to show the close relationship between these two subspecies. In writing descriptions of the birds, a lot of needless wordage has been eliminated merely by pointing out the differences between the subspecies. This practice has been followed consistently throughout. Of the three parts of the name for Swainson's Blue Mountain Lorikeet, *Trichoglossus* is the generic name; *haematodus* is the species name; and *moluccanus* is the subspecies name.

All members of the Parrot Family have been included, even in those instances where no description or popular name was available. Some members of the Parrot Family are not good aviary subjects, and some are not available. These members are included in this book because of the eventual possibility of their availability and because of the continually improving techniques in the proper maintenance and care of birds in captivity.

Another point in which confusion often arises is the frequent and indiscriminate usage of the words *parrot* and *parrakeet* or *lory* and *lorikeet*. The terms *parrakeet* and *lorikeet* generally apply to long-tailed slender birds; *parrot* and *lory* apply to short-tailed birds. Size has very little to do with these categories. There are many parrakeets larger than some parrots and many lorikeets larger than some lories. The practice of calling parrakeets by the designation parrots and lorikeets by the term lories is mainly a holdover from early ornithological practices.

For the sake of clarity and better understanding of the Order of Parrots, an outline is given showing subfamilies, genera, and subgenera.

ORDER: Psittaciformes
    Family: Psittacidae
        Subfamily: Strigopinae (Owl Parrots)
           Genus: *Strigops*
        Subfamily: Nestorinae (Kea Parrots)
           Genus: *Nestor*
        Subfamily: Loriinae (Lories, Lorikeets and similar birds)
           Genus: *Chalcopsitta*
                Eos
                Trichoglossus
                Psitteuteles
                Pseudeos
                Domicella
                Phigys
                Vini
                Glossopsitta
                Charmosyna
                Oreopsittacus
                Neopsittacus
                Psittaculirostris
                Opopsitta
                Lathamus (Parrakeet with Lorikeet-like characteristics)
        Subfamily: Micropsittinae (Pigmy Parrots)
           Genus: *Micropsitta*
        Subfamily: Kakatoeinae (Cockatoos)

Genus: *Prosciger*
      Calyptorhynchus
Subgenus: *Zanda*
          Calyptorhynchus
Genus: *Callocephalon*
      Cacatua
Subgenus: *Cacatua*
          Lophochroa
          Ducorpsius
          Licmetis
          Eolophus
Genus: *Nymphicus* (Cockatiel)
Subfamily: Psittacinae (Macaws, Conures, Parrots, Parrakeets and all other members of the Parrot Family)
Genera: *Anodorhynchus* (Macaws)
      Ara (Macaws)
      Aratinga (Conures)
      Nandayus (Conures)
      Leptosittaca (Parrot with similarities to Conures)
      Conuropsis (Extinct)
      Rhynchopsitta (Parrot with similarities to Conures and Macaws)
      Cyanoliseus (Conures)
      Ognorhynchus (Conures)
      Pyrrhura (Conures)
      Microsittace (Conures)
      Enicognathus
      Myiopsitta (Parrakeets)
      Amoropsittaca (Small Parrakeet)
      Psilopsiagon (Parrakeets)
      Bolborhynchus (Parrakeets)
      Forpus (Parrotlets)
      Brotogeris (Parrakeets)
      Nannopsittaca (Small type of Parrot)
      Touit (Small type of Parrots)
      Pionites (Caiques)
      Pionopsitta (Parrots)
      Hapalopsittaca
      Gypopsitta (Parrots)
      Graydidascalus (Parrot)
      Pionus (Parrots)

Blue and Gold Macaws are among the largest and showiest of the South American parrot-like birds. They all have some aptitude for speech and frequently become very tame and affectionate. All species have loud and raucous voices, but they can be controlled to a certain extent.

Amazona (Parrots)
Deroptyus (Parrot)
Triclaria (Parrots)
Poicephalus (Parrots)
Psittacus (Parrots)
Coracopsis (Parrots)
Psittrichas (Parrots)
Eclectus (Parrots)
Geoffroyus (Parrots)
Prioniurus (Parrakeets)
Tanygnathus (Parrots)
Mascarinus (Extinct)
Psittacula (Parrakeets)
Polytelis (Parrakeets)

Subgenus: *Polytelis* (Parrakeets)
      Spathopterus (Parrakeets)

Genus: *Aprosmictus* (Parrakeets)
Alisterus (Parrakeets)
Prosopeia (Parrakeets or Musk Parrots)
Psittacella (Parrakeets)
Bolbopsittacus (Guaiabero)
Psittinus (Parrot)
Agapornis (Love Birds)
Loriculus (Hanging Parrots)
Platycercus (Parrakeets)
Purpureicephalus (Parrakeets)
Northiella (Parrakeets)
Psephotus (Parrakeets)
Neophema (Parrakeets)
Eunymphicus (Parrakeets)
Cyanoramphus (Parrakeets)
Melopsittacus (Budgerigar)
Pezoporus (Parrakeets)

There are several members of the Parrot Family which are extinct. There seemed to be no point in covering them in this book, but mention has been made within the proper genus of those which are extinct. The main purpose has been to warn of the possible fate of other birds who may soon be on the path to extinction. In two instances, entire genera are extinct: *Mascarinus* (sometime after 1834) and *Conuropsis*. The latter is the Carolina Conure, which was the only member of the Parrot Family native to the United States.

The Carolina Parrakeet, *Conuropsis carolinensis,* the only American parrot-like bird, is now extinct. New York Zoological Society photo.

The extinction of the Carolina Conure was brought about by ceaseless slaughter waged by farmers who considered the bird a pest. Since the Carolina Conure was plentiful, aviculturists apparently did not bother to breed this bird (the last known bird died in 1918 at the Cincinnati Zoo). Fortunately, today's aviculturists are not so lax and have definitely saved several species from becoming extinct.

The Kakapo resembles an owl and is the only member of its genus. It runs more than it flies, and in short is one of the strangest birds in the parrot family.

Note: *centimeter measurements provided after the scientific names in the accounts of individual species and subspecies discussed in Chapters 9 through 17 are based on Forshaw's* Parrots of the World *(T.F.H. Publications) and represent currently accepted* average *lengths. Lengths given in inches in the discussions proper were based on a different measurement system and therefore can to a certain extent conflict with the centimeter measurements.*

THREE UNUSUAL SUBFAMILIES
Strigopinae, Nestorinae, and Micropsittinae

Subfamily: Strigopinae

Genus: *Strigops*

OWL PARROT OR KAKAPO *(Strigops habroptilus) (64 cm)*.

A vanishing race is the mysterious Owl Parrot of New Zealand. It is a night parrot and resembles an owl more than it does a parrot. The predominant coloring is green, which helped to reduce its numbers because its feathers were used as adornment in native tribal dress. Another reason for its decline has been the introduction of unnatural enemies.

The Kakapo is a short, stocky parrot with a small outstretched hooked bill and with a tail approximating one-third its length. It runs more often than it flies.

The vegetarian diet consists of fruits, nuts, berries, green shoots, roots, seeds, grass and insects. It is the only member of its genus and there is one record of a life in captivity (the last bird died in February 1968. - New Zealand Wildlife Service).

Subfamily: Nestorinae

Genus: *Nestor*

Members of this subfamily are very rare and but seldom seen. They have brushlike tongues and live principally on nectar, but they add insects and insect larvae to the diet as well. One, the Kea, is considered a serious problem bird in New Zealand. The basic colorings are dull olive with only a little decorative relief to embellish the color schemes.

KAKA OR BROWN PARROT *(Nestor meridionalis) (45 cm)*.

The very rare Kaka, or Brown Parrot, of New Zealand is basically olive brown in color with a grey crown and a dull, purplish-red abdomen. There is also red on the tail and red with a tinge of yellow on the back of the neck.

Previously abundant, the Kaka was used extensively as a feathered adornment by natives and was later slaughtered by civilized sportsmen who had nothing better to do.

The diet consists mainly of insects, insect larvae and nectar.

The race *Nestor meridionalis septentrionalis* is more extensive on North Island, while the first-mentioned is confined to New Zealand, South Island and Steward Island of New Guinea *(N.m. meridionalis)*.

The controversial Kea Parrot is not particularly attractive, but it has a fascinating personality and a legendary reputation.

KEA PARROT *(Nestor notabilis) (48 cm).*

Though lacking a glamorous appearance, the Kea has a reputation as legendary as it is controversial. Its range is confined to the perpetually snowcapped mountainous areas of New Zealand, where it has gained an incredible reputation as a sheep killer. Keas really do attack sheep, but only when the sheep are trapped in the snow or are injured. They are certainly not an important predator.

As mentioned before, the Kea is not attractive. Basically, its color pattern is rather dull and cluttered. The main coloring is an olive green with brownish-red markings. The extensive rump area is a dull reddish tone, the underwings are yellowish, mottled with dark markings, and a reddish coloring appears near the base of the wings. There is some blue in the flights.

The bill is of a curious shape. Instead of a tucked-in bill of normal proportions, it is a long and slender outstretched affair, indicating a tendency towards digging for roots, grubs, and bulbs. The tongue is brushlike, indicating that nectar is part of the normal diet.

The personality of the Kea is undoubtedly highly interesting, and all owners of the species in captivity take great pride in this ownership. Keas have been bred in captivity at the San Diego Zoo and in Europe.

The fourth member of the genus, *Nestor productus,* is extinct (sometime after 1851).

Subfamily: Micropsittinae
Genus: *Micropsitta*

PIGMY PARROTS

There are six species and thirteen subspecies of the group of minute Pigmy Parrots. The total size among the different species varies from three to three and a half inches including tails which vary from one-half to three-fourths of an inch. This is smaller than many of the different groups of popular finches. All are slender and shapely with tiny, trim beaks and small, squared tails. Pronounced indentations occur on the sides of the upper mandible near the tip. All are pretty with a predominant color of green and various accent colors. Sexes of most seem to be very similar, but some females show less extensive color variations. However, these differences may also be due to maturity factors. The various species range in the general vicinities of the Solomon Islands, New Guinea, the Papuan Islands, and many surrounding islands.

Pigmy Parrots are the smallest parrots in the world, and they have not yet been kept successfully in captivity. They are sometimes called Woodpecker Parrots because of their sharp and precise hopping mannerisms in clambering around trees, and their short, pointed tail feathers are strong enough to give support while the birds cling to the sides of trees. They dig their nests in termitaries, and they are apparently gregarious enough that the parents do not mind sharing their quarters with even adult offspring. Youngsters seem reluctant to leave home.

The diet is not yet known, but the basic items are presumed to be fungi. Stan Bergman of Sweden wrote a very interesting account of his personal experiences with these mysterious little parrots in New Guinea. This article appeared in the November-December, 1960, issue of the *Avicultural Magazine*. In this article, Mr. Bergman was able to keep a nestling alive for sixty-four hours; but his mixture of milk, sugar, mashed paw paw, and wheat flour did not agree with the bird's system.

The writers feel that someday a suitable diet may be discovered. Those experimenting with such an unknown diet would probably do best if they started with the simplest, purest, and most digestible elements. Milk is apparently too harsh for the delicate digestive system and should be avoided. Honey and water supplemented with vitamins, minerals, and proteins would probably be a good base; and mild, easily digested fruit, preferably varieties native to the birds' natural habitat, could be added to the nectar base. The main difficulty would be in supplying the proper fungi and the necessary enzymes. There are so many different types of fungi that selection and percentages of amounts given would be a very perplexing problem. This, of course, should only be attempted by a scientist who knows what he is doing. Doubtless, the fungi ingested by these birds aids in their digestion. It is assumed that the birds would pay no attention to fruit until a satisfactory nectar and fungus diet is first established. It is doubtful if these birds would ever include seeds in their diet, but they might gain a fondness for tender buds of leaves and flowers.

Considerable experimental work will be necessary before a satisfactory diet could be devised. The above suggestions may or may not solve the problem, but at least provide an approach to a possible solution. Above all, the main concept is to provide simple basic ingredients. These are the ones least likely to set off harmful reactions which the bird cannot survive.

The Mountain Pigmy Parrot or Red-Breasted Pigmy Parrot, *Micropsitta bruijnii*, with four subspecies, is from New Guinea. It has a dull buffish-orange cap covering the forehead and crown as well as on a low-slung large cheek patch. Here the pale buff shades into orange on the lower extremities. The rest of the head coloring is a brilliant cobalt blue to the nape and the sides of the neck. Upperparts and sides are bright green with black spangles on the inner parts of the scapulars. A broad swath of red-orange extends from the chest through the underside of the tail in a concentration that is the brightest on the lower abdomen. This is one of the larger Pigmies totaling three and a half inches including the three-fourths inch squared tail (9 cm).

Finsch's Pigmy Parrot, *Micropsitta finschii,* with five subspecies, is from the Solomon Islands and the Bismarck Archipelago. It is all green with a bright concentration of blue on the crown and a trace of red on the center of the abdomen. The size and shape is almost the same as in the above species.

Key's Pigmy Parrot, *Micropsitta keinensis,* with three subspecies, is from southern and western New Guinea, and the western Papuan, the Kei and Aru Islands. It is also the same size and shape as the above two species. It has an irregular crown patch of dull yellow, a dark brown face, and black scapular spangles adding only slight variation to the dominant green. The subspecies *chloroxantha* from New Guinea, Onin Penisula, West Irian and the Western Papuan Islands adds an irregular bright reddish patch on the abdomen. It is called the Red Bellied Pigmy Parrot.

Micropsitta geelvinkiana with its two subspecies inhabits islands in Geelvink Bay. It has a larger more massive head, a brown face, and blue on the crown. Bright blue also occurs on the upper tail feathers, and an irregular orange-yellow variation appears on the abdomen and lower chest. The black scapular spangles add a further variation from the predominant green. One race is called Misori's Pigmy Parrot, and the other is called Geelvink's Pigmy Parrot.

The Lesser Pigmy Parrot, *Micropsitta pusio pusio* from the Bismark Archipelago and south-eastern and north New Guinea, is the smallest of the genus totalling only three inches including a half inch tail. This subspecies has a bright and vivid cobalt blue patch, elliptical in shape, down the center of the crown. The rest of the head, including the lower nape and forehead, is a dull buff shade with a rust-orange tinted eyebrow. The underparts are pale dull green, and the rest of the coloring is green as in all the other species. The subspecies *beccarii* from New Guinea, called Beccari's Pigmy Parrot, has dull and pale brownish facial areas extending up to the sides of the crown. Blue on the head extends from the forehead through the crown. All the other subspecies from New Guinea and the Louisade Archipelago have the same basic green with paler underparts, but there are some variations such as duller crown patches, duller facial areas, and less orange on the eyebrows (8.5 cm).

Meek's Pigmy Parrot, *Micropsitta meeki* from the Admiralty Islands, is three and a half inches long including a tail of three-fourths of an inch. The head is dull brownish variably mottled in dusty-dark to pale buffish shades. The dull greenish-yellow underparts which extend through the abdomen are irregularly marked with dull, dusty tips on the feathers. The lower abdomen and ventral areas are bright green. The very similar subspecies *proxima* is from St. Matthias and Squally Islands.

11

LORIES, LORIKEETS,
AND CLOSELY RELATED BIRDS

Subfamily: Loriinae

Altogether, there are fifteen genera in the subfamily Loriinae. Members are widely varied in size and color. They range from some of the least attractive to many of the most spectacularly brilliant and beautiful birds in the world.

The two common characteristics are diet, which consists of fruits and nectar, and the strange brushlike tongue, which is used to gather up the nectar. Lories and lorikeets have tongues which enable them to lap up nectar in much the same manner as a cat laps up milk.

Lories are hardy and take very kindly to captivity.

The diet of lories and lorikeets in captivity is simple. The writers feed a mixture of a special nectar syrup diluted with water. Honey could be used instead. Evaporated milk is added to the mixture. In addition, fruits and pound cake are offered.

Although some lories eat occasional sunflower seeds, the author never offers seeds of any type to any member of the subfamily. For several months in the past year, one of the commercial brands of mynah bird pellets have been offered to a pair of Swainson's Blue Mountain Lorikeets. They disdainfully refused to have anything to do with this foreign food for a long time, and so it was discontinued. One day some of this food was accidentally put in the aviary with the lorikeets, and they attacked it in a suprisingly vigorous manner. It was as if they had been denied one of their greatest pleasures for most of their lives and were going to make up for lost time.

Since most of the diet of lories and lorikeets is liquid, the droppings follow the same pattern. In a cage, lories can easily and quickly soil their plumage. In a spacious aviary, however, they keep themselves in immaculate condition. They bathe frequently and spend a lot of time vainly preening their feathers.

A further indication of their vanity, as well as their comical and affectionate personalities, is in their elaborate and amusing poses. Sharp, exaggerated movements and lavish affection highlight the activities of these birds in their playful moods.

There are many members in the exuberant Lory subfamily, nearly all of them exceptionally fascinating and entertaining birds. However, they should not be mixed with other birds; they have a habit of teaming up, catching other birds in unaware moments, and murdering them.

Genus: *Chalcopsitta*

The members of the genus *Chalcopsitta* are medium in size and have proportionately longer squared tails than those of the genus *Eos*. Other major differences between the two genera are the naked base of the lower mandible in the genus *Chalcopsitta* and the black bill.

The basic colors are dull reds, blacks, and greens. The habitats are New Guinea and surrounding islands. Except for the brilliant Cardinal Lory, all members of this genus are rather unattractive and lacking in well-defined patterns. There is no sexual dimorphism.

BLACK LORY *(Chalcopsitta atra atra)(32 cm)*.

The very rare Black Lory comes from the islands of Salwati and Batenta and the opposite coastal areas of New Guinea.

The predominant black coloring is highlighted by a purplish gloss and red markings on the thighs and at the base of the tail. The rest of the tail has a dull yellow-olive tinge.

Like other members of the genus, it is medium in size: thirteen and a half inches, including a five-inch tail.

BERNSTEIN'S LORY *(Chalcopsitta atra bernsteini)*

This is a subspecies of the Black Lory inhabiting Misol. The thighs are black instead of red. The size is the same.

RED QUILLED OR RAJA LORY *(Chalcopsitta atra insignis)*

The Raja Lory inhabits Amperbon Island in Geelvink Bay and reaches into the region around MacCleur Gulf.

It is eleven inches in length, including a tail slightly less than five inches.

Basically, this Lory is black with a purplish gloss. There are paler streaks on the neck and head which show occasional reddish tinges. The forehead is dull red. Traces of red surround the bill and extend into the throat. Other traces of dull red appear on the chest and especially on the thighs. The underwings are mostly reddish with black markings. The vent has some red. The tail is reddish at the base, changing to yellow on the outer parts.

A second race, *Chalcopsitta insignis spectabilis,* has been proposed; but it is not known whether it is a definite subspecies or a hybrid between the Raja and the Red Fronted Lory.

RED FRONTED LORY OR YELLOW STREAKED LORY *(Chalcopsitta sintillata sintillata) (31 cm).*

This large-bodied Lory is ten and a half inches long with a three and a half inch tail.

The beak is black, as is most of the head except for a red forehead and loreal area. The black shades into a metallic green over all of the bird, but it is brightest on the back and rump. The green breast has feathers with orange streaked centers. This same pattern is repeated at the lower end of the neck. The thighs are red, and there is some red in the tail. The underwing coverts are red.

The Red Fronted Lory is native to the head of Geelvink Bay and the southern coast of New Guinea.

A subspecies, *Chalcopsitta sintillata chloroptera,* has green underwing coverts and comes from the south-eastern coast of New Guinea. The orange streaks are missing on the breast and back.

Another subspecies, *Chalcopsitta sintillata rubrifrons,* comes from the Aru Islands and has more extensive red areas on the forehead and loreal area. This subspecies is more accurately called the Red Fronted Lory.

DUYVENBODE'S LORY *(Chalcopsitta duivenbodei) (31 cm).*

Duyvenbode's Lory comes from the northern coast of western New Guinea.

The main coloring is a deep dusky olive. The black bill is encircled by a dull yellowish ring that is especially prominent around the lower mandible. There are dull orange striations on the chest and on the thighs and paler striations on the nape and back. The rump is a slate color.

Two other races occur: *Chalcopsitta duivenbodei duivenbodei* from the western part of the Mandated Territory of New Guinea and *Chalcopsitta duivenbodei syringanuchalis* from the north-eastern coast of New Guinea.

CARDINAL LORY *Chalcopsitta cardinalis) (31 cm).*

The well-known Cardinal Lory is twelve inches long, including the medium-long tail.

It is brilliant red except for the black feet and black margin surrounding the bill. The eye ring is black. The wings and tail are a darker red with perhaps a tinge of brown.

The Cardinal Lory is abundant and noisy in its native habitat of the Solomon Islands. It is a delightful aviary inhabitant and has an amusing display.

114

Genus: *Eos*

Members of the genus *Eos* are about the same size as those of the genus *Chalcopsitta* but have shorter tails. The bills are red to orange, and the wing colors are predominantly red. All are much more attractive than the members of *Chalcopsitta*.

BLACK WINGED or BLUE CHEEKED LORY *(Eos cyanogenia) (30 cm)*.

The Black Winged Lory's wings are its focal point. The interior parts of the wing feathers are red and the outer parts are black; the effect is that of a beautiful, irregular pattern. The rest of the coloring is subordinate to the wing pattern except for a bright purple which flares out and backward from the loreal region, around the eyes, and back to the nape. The overall color is a dull wine red brighter on the cheeks and lower abdomen. The thighs are black.

Shaped like most of the genus, this bird is nine inches long, including the three-inch tail.

The habitat is the island of Biak and other islands in Geelvink Bay.

BLUE STREAKED LORY *(Eos reticulata) (31 cm)*

The Blue Streaked Lory comes from the Tenimber Islands and is very rare in captivity.

The beak is orange-red, and the basic plumage is red with a great deal of black in the wings and broad tail. Behind the eye is a wide, deep blue band dropping down into the side of the neck. The mantle is dark with pale blue streaks, and the rump is red with dark areas in which paler blue stripes are centered. The chest is mottled with dark areas. A fine line of blue frames the upper mandible. The black in the wings and tail is very irregular. Black also surrounds the eyes. The pale blue streaks on the mantle are intensely glossy, and the basic red is brilliant.

VIOLET NECKED LORY *(Eos squamata) (27 cm)*.

The Violet Necked Lory is an ostentatious mixture of purple and deep red. The bill is black. Salmon red is found on the forehead, throat, and below the eye. The red breast feathers have purple tips. The wings have a dull bronze-green gloss over the red which is repeated in the tail. The underwing coverts are red. The rump is dark blue. Large red spots are found near the base of the quills; from them is derived the popular name of Red Quilled Lory (a misleading name because a member of the genus *Chalcopsitta* is popularly called Red Quilled Lory). The underside of the tail is a dull red at the base, shading to yellow on the major portions. The main highlight is the violet collar.

The Violet Necked Lory (subspecies *squamata*) is eight and a half inches including the four inch tail. The beak is orange-horn instead of black as previously described. A rich shade of purplish-maroon occurs on the crown, nape, mantle, and on a collar surrounding the neck and expanding on the throat which gives the bird its popular name. The same shade occurs on a large abdominal area, but it is darker. The red is brilliant, and the black and red in the flights are irregular but bright. There are several variations in individuals. The subspecies *obiensis*, slightly larger in body and shorter in tail, shows more brilliant red. The collar is more violet and noticeably thinner with no expansion in any area as in the above.

The four races of the Violet Necked Lory are as follows:—

Eos squamata squamata is called Wallace's Lory and is from the Western Papuan Islands, Schildpad Islands, on Gebe, Waigeu, Batanta and Misool. The only appreciable difference is the thinness of the violet collar.

Eos squamata riciniata is the Violet Necked Lory of the northern Moluccas.

Eos squamata obiensis is a race restricted to the Isle of Obi in the Moluccas.

Eos squamata atrocaerulea is called Edward's Lory and is from Maju Island. The abdomen is marked by a large purplish area, and the wings have fewer black markings.

BLUE TAILED LORY *(Eos histrio) (31 cm)*.

Also called the Red and Blue Lory, the Blue Tailed Lory has blue on the crown extending down into the eyes and covering the back. The blue is interrupted by a broad red patch on the nape. More blue covers the chest. The wings are marked with black, rather similar to those of the Black Winged Lory. The upper tail is dull blue while the rest of the bird is red.

The total length of the Blue Tailed Lory is nine and a half inches including the tail of four and a half to five inches. The blue on the crown extends down past the eyes in a broad line and covers the back, interrupted by a broad red patch on the nape. The blue chestband is also wide, and a blue bar also crosses the lower abdomen. The underside of the tail is mostly dull red with black accents. The tail is black and red like the wings instead of blue which perhaps makes the popular name of Red and Blue Lory more appropriate than the Blue Tailed Lory. The forehead is bright red, and the rump is maroon. The subspecies *talautensis* has less black on the wings and far more solid red. The red is also more extensive on the forehead and less broad on the nape.

Three races exist of this rare species:—

Eos histrio histrio from the Great Sangi and Siao Islands, described above.

Eos histrio talautensis from the Talaud Islands, which differs only in the amount of black markings in the wings.

Eos histrio challengeri from the Nenusa Islands, which differs only in the far less extensive blue coloring of the chest.

RED LORY or MOLUCCAN LORY *(Eos bornea) (31 cm)*.

The Red Lory is a rarity in avicultural circles. It is lighter in color and larger than the Cardinal Lory. Blue occurs on the vent and occasionally in the chest. The edges of the wings are rather blackish. Four races exist:-

Eos bornea bornea from Amboina and Saparua.
Eos bornea cyanonothus from Buru.
Eos bornea rothschildi from Ceram.
Eos bornea bernsteini from the Kai Islands.

The four races of the brilliant Red Lory differ slightly in size and shading. Blue occurs on the vent, undertail coverts, only rarely in the chest, and on the center of the back. The race *bornea* is ten and three-fourths inches long including the tail of four and three-fourths inches. The subspecies *rothschildi* is nearly identical to *bornea*. The race *bernsteini* is slightly smaller and slightly less bright in red shading. The fourth race, *cyanonothus,* is nine and a half inches long including the four inch tail and is darker and duller in red shading, almost maroon on the back and chest. More blue occurs on the back.

CERAM LORY or BLUE EARED LORY *(Eos semilarvata) (24 cm)*.

The Ceram Lory is another lory which has no real standing in the avicultural field because of its great rarity and unavailability. It is confined to the middle of Ceram and has a bluish cheek patch extending from the bill.

The Ceram Lory is brilliant red with a bright blue abdomen. The back and wings have a darker shade of read, nearly maroon. The bluish cheek patch extending from the lower mandible tapers off on the sides of the neck. The flights are black and red, and the tail is a dull mixture of both colors.

A questionable species is *Eos goodfellowi*, which resembles the Ceram Lory and may be related. It is confined to the Isle of Obi.

Genus: *Trichoglossus*

Members of the genus *Trichoglossus* are large lorikeets and are often referred to as lories. However, all have long pointed tails and are true lorikeets, even though there are many true lories that are much smaller.

This is a popular and colorful genus and includes several of the most readily available species.

PERFECT LORIKEET *(Trichoglossus euteles) (25 cm)*.

The Perfect Lorikeet is sometimes called the Plain Lory, a name that describes it well. The horn-colored bill and yellow bar on the underside of the wing are practically the only variations from the basic green coloring. The yellow underside of the wing is bordered with a blackish shade on the tips. The head has a yellowish-olive tinge, and the underparts are paler than the upperparts.

The Perfect Lorikeet is from the lesser Sunda Islands. It is about eight and a half inches in length, including the slightly longer than four-inch tail.

ORNATE LORY *(Trichoglossus ornatus) (25 cm)*

The Ornate Lory is green except for the cap and undersides down to the abdomen. The purplish-blue cap has an irregular shape. It covers the entire head and surrounds the eyes, flaring backwards and interrupting the cap-like pattern. Cheeks and throat are red. The chest and a small area behind the cap on the neck are red with green scales on the tips of the feathers.

The Ornate Lory is from the Celebes and adjacent islands.

The size of the Ornate Lory is seven and three-fourths inches including the tail of slightly more than three inches. Some of the scales on the tips of the feathers behind the cap are green and some are black. A bright yellow patch follows the black patch on the side of the neck.

SCALY BREASTED LORIKEET *(Trichoglossus chlorolepidotus) (21 cm).*

A basically green lorikeet of eight inches, the Scaly Breasted has a narrow three-inch tail. The beak is orange. Yellow slips through on the green shoulders, and red emerges through the green on the throat. The breast is yellow with green-bordered feathers, giving it a scaly appearance. The under-wings are red.

The habitat is north Queensland, south to the Illawarra district (N.S.W.).

RED LORY or RED LORIKEET *(Trichoglossus rubiginosus) (24 cm)*

The nine-inch Red or Cherry Red Lorikeet is native to Ponape in the eastern Caroline Islands.

It is basically a deep maroon red with dull olive wings. The olive tail has yellowish tips on the upperside and is yellowish on the underside. Bluish-black bars, which are lacking in pattern, mark the underparts. The bill is orange.

The Red Lorikeet is nine and a half inches long, including the four-inch tail. The body is heavier, and the tail is shorter than most species in this genus. The chest has slight black scallops on the edges of the feathers, and the duller wings have blackish edges on many feathers.

Many other members are subspecies of the species *Trichoglossus haematodus* and show a very basic similarity in pattern and coloring.

SWAINSON'S BLUE MOUNTAIN LORIKEET or LORY *(Trichoglossus haematodus moluccanus) (26 cm).*

The most readily available member of the subfamily, Swainson's Blue Mountain Lory or Rainbow Lorikeet, is also one of the loveliest. It is the best breeder of all Lories in captivity and, in the wild state, is found abundantly in eastern Australia, Tasmania, Kangaroo Island and Eyre Peninsula.

In size, this large Lorikeet is eleven and a half inches, including the long pointed tail of five inches.

The beak is orange, contrasting with a brilliant deep violet-blue head. It has a pale green collar. The wings, back, rump, and tail are green. The full large area of the chest is basically brilliant red with an irregular mixture of yellow, which gives it the loveliest effect. The lower part of the chest shades into a deeper rich violet-blue. This is accomplished by the combination of blue tips on the red feathers, the blue graduated till the feathers are all blue in appearance. The thighs are green, and the underside of the tail is olive green with some yellow. The underwings are red at the shoulders and black on the remaining area except for an intermedial spot of yellow.

In addition to the outstanding array of colors, there is a bright luster which produces a glowing effect. A lovely bird indeed!

As if the appearances were not enough, Blue Mountains have personalities rivaling their color schemes. They are cheerful, comical, and provide endless amusement. They enjoy playing games with each other and often roll and tumble in the manner of puppies. They enjoy striking elaborate poses. They become affectionate and excellent pets.

Males have slightly larger heads and bills than the females. The young are less vivid in color, with a dull brownish bill.

In addition to Swainson's Blue Mountain Lorikeet, there are twenty other subspecies very much like it.

RED COLLARED LORIKEET *(Trichoglossus haematodus rubritorquis).*

This northern Austrialian bird is frequently called the Orange-Naped Lorikeet.

It is just as beautiful as the Blue Mountain Lorikeet and is similar in size and coloration. However, it has a paler head than the Blue Mountain Lory and a red-orange collar followed by a blue collar, instead of the pale green one. The rest of the plumage seems a little flatter and harder than the richly glowing Blue Mountain.

Sexes are alike, but the male has a larger head. Young birds have less brilliance in the plumage and a dull bill.

This bird's personality is very similar to that of the Blue Mountain Lorikeet.

FORSTEN'S LORIKEET or LORY *(Trichoglossus haematodus forsteni)*

Forsten's Lorikeet is just like the Swainson's Blue Mountain Lorikeet except that its violet blue head coloring continues beyond the yellowish-green nuchal collar. There is also a less extensive blue area on the abdomen. Forsten's Lorikeet is also smaller than the Blue Mountain variety, being only ten inches long. It is a good breeder and is available, but not as abundant as the Blue Mountain.

One subspecies, *Trichoglossus haematodus djampeanus,* is very similar to Forsten's Lorikeet. Its habitat is the Isle of Djampea (Flores Sea)

MITCHELL'S or RED BREASTED LORIKEET *(Trichoglossus haematodus mitchellii)*

The Red Breasted Lorikeet, another subspecies similar to the Blue Mountain, is found in Lombok and Bali.

It is eight inches in length, including the long tail. The orange bill sets off the dark blue-black head with the greenish tinge on the crown. The throat and cheeks are bluish. The nuchal collar is pale green like that of Swainson's Blue Mountain Lory. The wings are red and yellow, and the rest of the upperparts are green. The undersides of the wings are partly red with broad areas of black and yellow on the flight. The chest is bright red followed by dark blue on the abdomen. This area has blue and green on the sides. The rest of the underparts are a mixture of yellow and green.

Females are slightly duller in color with yellow mixing in the red chest.

MASSENA'S or COCONUT LORIKEET *(Trichoglossus haematodus massena)*

About ten inches in length, this lovely species from the New Hebrides Islands resembles Swainson's Blue Mountain Lorikeet in shape.

The bill is orange and the forehead, crown, and facial areas are blue, followed by a wide purple band and a pale green nuchal collar. The throat is deep purple, and the breast is red with narrow dark blue-black scaled edges like those of the Blue Mountain. The abdomen is green with a yellow mixture appearing further down, all upperparts behind the nuchal collar are bright green. A yellow bar occurs on the underside of the wing.

This hardy species is abundant in its wild habitat but rare in captivity. It is one of the many lorikeet species whose members are called Coconut Lories because they frequent groves of coconut trees.

BLUE FACED LORIKEET *(Trichoglossus haematodus intermedius)*

The Blue Faced Lorikeet (subspecies *intermedius*) is eight and a half inches long including the three and a half inch tail. Blue on the forehead and crown is followed by a dark violet on the hindcrown and a bright but light green nuchal collar. Remaining upperparts are vivid green. The red chest has scalloped blackish or bluish tips which are less broad than those of Rosenberg's Lorikeet.

EDWARD'S LORIKEET *(Trichoglossus haematodus capistratus)*

Edward's Lorikeet from Timor is much less colorful than most of the subspecies. The yellow chest shows slight traces of red, and the green abdomen shows traces of yellow. Eyebrows of green trail around the lower boundary of the cap. The race *fortis* has bright green above the eyebrows, on the lower crown, and on the lower part of the throat. The broad nuchal collar contains much yellow. The rest of the head is dark, rich blue; and remaining upperparts are bright green. The broad chest area is yellow with traces of orange and a few dark scalloped tips. The abdomen is dark green. Yellow and green are mingled on flanks, thighs, and undertail coverts. The length of nine and a half inches includes the tail of four and three-fourths inches. The race *flavotectus*, nine and three fourths inches including the four inch tail, is very similar to Edward's Lorikeet except the chest is of a flatter, somewhat less vivid shade.

Weber's Lorikeet (subspecies *weberi*) is overall green but with variations in shadings. The head is particularly rich in green with a pale green shade on the chest and nuchal collar. Back, wings, tail, and abdomen are dark green. The eight and a half inch length includes a three and three-fourths inch tail.

GREEN NAPED LORIKEET *(Trichoglossus haematodus haematodus)*

The wide habitat of the Green Naped Lorikeet includes western New Guinea, the western Kai Islands, Buru, Ceram, and Amboina.

The green collar is wider than but does not extend as far as the collar of the Blue Mountain. Also, the abdomen is mostly green.

DARK THROATED LORIKEET *(Trichoglossus haematodus nigrogularis)*

This species from the Aru Islands is like the Green Naped Lorikeet except for a paler overall coloring and a darker blue throat.

The Dark Throated Lorikeet (subspecies *nigrogularis,* sometimes listed as *caeruliceps*) has a blue head, a green nuchal collar, and slight black tips on the red chest feathers. There are also reddish-pink flecks on the mantle. The size is nine inches including the three and three-fourths inch tail. The Green Naped Lorikeet (subspecies *haematodus*), eight and a half inches including the tail of three and a half inches, has a wider but shorter collar of green and very prominent black scallops on the chest. The abdomen is mostly green with ex tensive yellow on the inner parts of the feathers on the flanks and ventral area. Several other species are very similar. Deplanch's Lorikeet (subspecies *deplanchii*) has a slightly darker throat, and the purple on the hindneck is less vivid. The size is nine and a half inches in length including the four inch tail. The race *micropteryx* has a tinge of burgundy on the lower back of the crown instead of purple and prominent scallops on the chest. The race *aberrans,* about half an inch shorter, is otherwise practically identical to *micropteryx.* The subspecies *flavicans,* called the Olive Green Lorikeet, is practically identical to the above two races but slightly larger at ten inches in length with its four and one-fourth inch tail. The burgundy on the hindcrown and the scallops on the chest are especially similar. The abdomen is green, red, and yellow. The race *nesophilus* has a duller shade of burgundy on the lower crown and less prominent scallops on the chest.

ROSENBERG'S LORIKEET *(Trichoglossus haematodus rosenbergii)*

From the Island of Biak comes Rosenberg's Lorikeet.

A fine border of red on the nape follows the blue head. The underside of the wings is red, and there is rather more blue on the red chest.

OLIVE GREEN LORIKEET *(Trichoglossus haematodus flavicans)*

The green upperparts of the Olive Green Lorikeet are paler and more olive in color. The blue of the abdomen is replaced with green, red, and yellow.

The habitat is Hermit Island and other neighboring islands of Manus.

BROOKS' LORIKEET *(Trichoglossus haematodus brooki)*

This subspecies is confined to Spirit Island in the Aru Islands. In the wild this bird lives in timber areas, mainly coastal. It is a very common, and also an extremely playful and likeable bird which prefers the flowering native trees, especially eucalypts, banksias, and melaleucas. The bird has a noisy screech and chatters unceasingly as it feeds. Birds in the air will hear others in the tree below and will drop in to join them.

KALAO COCONUT LORIKEET *(Trichoglossus haematodus stresemanni)*

From Kalao tua, this is also a common bird in timber and flowering trees. It is an aggressive bird and will chase other birds trying to feed in the same trees. They nest in high holes in trees, lining their nests with bits of bark or eucalyptus leaves. Both birds work in its preparation, and 2 to 4 eggs are laid.

122

BLUE HEAD COCONUT LORIKEET *(Trichoglossus haematodus caeruleiceps)*

This subspecies from southern New Guinea lives in blossoming trees and bushes. It is also very common. As with all lorikeets, the sexes are mainly alike, and these birds indulge in upside down gymnastic movements when feeding. Their nest, in a hollow, is usually high in the tree.

YELLOW AND GREEN LORIKEET *(Trichoglossus flavoviridis flavoviridis)*

The little Yellow and Green Lorikeet from the Sula Islands is mainly green with a greyish nape. The entire head and underparts down to the abdomen are yellowish scaled with green tips.

It is six and a half inches long, including the pointed tail of slightly more than three inches.

A subspecies, Meyer's Lorikeet *(Trichoglossus flavoviridis meyeri)*, has a definite chartreuse forehead and a tinge of brownish-olive on the nape. The tail and rump are brownish-olive above and yellowish on the underside. The undersides of the flights are black, and the underwing coverts are green. The beak is horn color.

Meyer's Lorikeet is from the Celebes Islands.

MRS. JOHNSTONE'S or MOUNT APO LORIKEET *(Trichoglossus johnstoniae) (20 cm)*

Mrs. Johnstone's Lorikeet is basically green with a yellow chest and green scaled outer margins. The green scales become smaller as they approach the abdomen. The yellow gradually is replaced by a dull yellow-green on the area of the vent and undertail coverts. The dominant variations occur on the head. Starting with the red bill, the face and forehead are red. As the red approaches the outer limits, it is restricted to the tips of the feathers, giving it red scales on a green base on the crown and on a yellow base at the sides of the face and throat. There is a considerable yellow area on the cheek and ear covert area. The narrow line of brownish-purple crosses the lores and surrounds the eyes, behind which it widens and extends backwards around the crown and meets at the other side on the nape of the neck. This meeting point of color is less distinct in the female.

This small lorikeet has a tapering pointed tail.

The habitat is Mindanao in the vicinity of Mount Apo of the Philippine Islands.

GOLDIE'S LORIKEET *(Trichoglossus goldiei) (19 cm)*.

Goldie's Lorikeet, a seven-inch species from the mountains of New

Guinea, lives at an altitude of between three thousand and eight thousand feet.

The bill is black, and the basic coloring is green. Color variations are in the purple head and red crown and in the streaked yellow of the neck, chest, and abdomen. It differs from the Varied or Red Crowned Lorikeet in that the bill is black rather than red.

Goldie's Lorikeet is rare in the United States but it has been bred. It is attractive but not as spectacular as many species of Lories.

RED CROWNED or VARIED LORIKEET *(Trichoglossus versicolor)*

The Red Crowned Lorikeet is a small bird of seven inches inhabiting the tropical area of northern Australia to the coast of northeast Queensland.

It has a red bill with red crown and forehead. The cheek patches are pale yellow, and the neck is bluish-green with gold streaks and flecks. The chest is a dull wine color with yellow streaks. The rest of the coloring is green, but the abdomen and neck are also streaked with yellow. A pronounced characteristic is a bare skin patch around the eyes. Females have a paler red on the crown. The young have duller colors and the red of the crown is replaced by green with a few red flecks.

The Red Crowned Lorikeet is rare in captivity, but it has been bred both in England and in Australia.

IRIS LORIKEET *(Trichoglossus iris) (20 cm)*

There are three races of this small Lorikeet which has a very limited range. The subspecies *iris* is seven and one-fourth inches long including the tail of two and three-fourths inches. A bright vermilion on the forehead and crown fades on the upper part of the crown and shades into green tinges on the hindcrown. A darker shade surrounds the eyes and nostrils, and a plum patch occurs on the ear behind the eye. A broad nuchal collar of pale green is followed by a narrow band of vivid green. Remaining upperparts and the sides of the neck, face, and throat are bright green. The chin is dull plum. Remaining underparts are green with darker and brighter green scales on the chest. The race *rubripileum,* six and three-fourths inches long including the tail of two and a half inches, is somewhat smaller than *iris* with a less bright shade of red extending smoothly and evenly down the nape to the nuchal collar. The race *wetterensis*, slightly larger than both the other races, is seven and a half inches with a three inch tail. Patterned like *rubripileum,* the red is brighter on the forehead and duller, shading to plum, on the crown and nape.

Genus: *Pseudeos*

DUSKY LORY *(Pseudeos fuscata) (25 cm).*

One of the least gaudy of the lories, the Dusky Lory deserves its name.

The overall coloring is a blackish-grey with a light horn-colored beak. A rust coloration slips through on the nape, crown, and throat. The abdomen is mostly a dull rust red.

This is a stocky bird of eight and a half to nine inches, including the three-inch broad tail.

The Dusky Lory comes from New Guinea and is confined to the Island of Salawati and on Japan Island.

Though one of the darkest and least colorful of all Lories, those color accents which the Dusky Lory does possess are very strong with a glowing intensity. Especially noticeable, for example, is the pale, frosty buffish-white on the rump. The underside is dull and cluttered with a broad blackish band with pale tips on many feathers across the upper chest and a narrower one across the lower chest. The red between these areas is more vivid and red-orange than on any other area. The thighs are also red, but this feature is variable in intensity. The sides and abdomen are black and a dull red on the inner webs of the flights remains mostly hidden. The reddish shades on the underside of the tail are very noticeable.

The White Rumped Lory (subspecies *incondita*) is generally brighter and the colors of red and black are more strongly contrasting. The rump has frosty white tips on the feathers, and the cap is a strong buffish shade.

Genus: *Lorius*

Members of the genus *Lorius* used to be grouped under the heading *Domicella* and are described as being the most typical of the large group of Lories and Lorikeets.

All have orange bills and a predominantly red pattern with black and green accent markings. In most species the undersides of the flights are yellow with broad outer margins of black.

The members of this genus are all very beautiful. Many are quite common in captivity. They are ideal aviary birds if they can be obtained.

CHATTERING LORY *(Lorius garrulus) (30 cm)*

A brilliant Lory from the Halmahera and Weda Islands, the Chattering Lory is ten to ten and a half inches including the broad three-inch tail.

The beak is dark horn color. The basic color is brilliant red with a darkish shoulder. There are a few lemon yellow streaks on the back, almost as if they had been applied by a paint brush. The green wings have a bronze tinge lighter at the shoulders and shading to a greenish-black on the flights. The tail is black from the halfway point to the tip. Underneath it is dull bronze.

This dazzling Lory is a perfect aviary bird and is a constant delight with its comical antics. It is also the most frequently available member of the genus.

YELLOW BACKED LORY *(Lorius garrulus flavopalliatus)*

The Yellow Backed Lory from Batjam and Obi is a duplicate of the Chattering Lory except that the lemon yellow streaks are far more extensive. It is also a delightful aviary bird, but it is not often obtainable.

PURPLE BELLIED or LOUISADE LORY *(Lorius hypoinochrous) (26 cm).*

The Purple Bellied has a simple color pattern: horn-colored bill, black cap, green wings and tail, and a red shading of the flights into a purplish tinge in the area of the abdomen. Most of the underside of the flights is yellow with a broad blackish margin at the outer tips. This mantle is a purplish shade, and the cere is unusually pale. The total length is eleven inches including the broad four inch tail. This is and extremely rare and attractive bird.

There are three subspecies:

Lorius hypoinochrous hypoinochrous from the Louisade Archipelago.

Lorius hypoinochrous rosseliana from Rossel Island in the Louisade Archipelago.

Lorius hypoinochrous devittatus from southeastern New Guinea and surrounding islands.

JOBI LORY *(Lorius lory jobiensis) (31 cm).*

Another great and rare beauty, this bird is sharply and attractively patterned in black, red, green, yellow, and blue.

This is a stocky Lory about nine inches long with a good sized head and a broad two and a half inch tail.

The beak is horn color. A large black cap covers the head down to the eyes and back to the nape. A narrow band of red on the nape separates a wide black collar near the shoulders. Another narrow red band separates the black shoulders. There is a narrow bright red "U" shaped area between the wings. The rump and thighs are red. The tail is blackish. The wings are green shading into black at the ends of the flights.

The cheeks, face, throat, and chest are brilliant red. The abdomen is black, and the vent is bright blue.

The habitat is the islands of Japen and Mios Nom.

A very similar subspecies is *Lorius lory cynauchen* from the Island of Biak. The blue is more extensive in the abdominal area.

BLACK CAPPED or TRI-COLORED LORY *(Lorius lory lory) (31 cm)*

Highly colorful, this lory is somewhat similar to the Jobi Lory but has a less precise pattern. It has the black cap followed on the neck by the narrow band of red which connects with the red of the underparts. The shoulder is

The Yellow Backed Lory and other Lories do best in birdrooms and outdoor aviaries with roomy and well-heated shelters. They are very intolerant towards other parrots but usually less vicious towards their own species. They are extremely active, climbing and bounding about. Single birds become affectionate and gentle towards their owner.

blue, followed by some red before reaching the all-red rump. The wings are green above and yellow underneath, with the outer half of the flights black.

All the throat, neck, and chest are red blending into black on the sides of the chest and abdomen. The black blends into a blue vent and blue thighs. The black color pattern of the sides of the chest and abdomen is quite irregular. The beak is horn color.

This rare bird is not as beautiful as the Jobi Lory. However, it is a fine beauty and well compensates for the trouble taken to find it.

Its habitat is New Guinea (western Papuan Islands and some islands in Geelvink Bay).

The remaining subspecies, all of which incidentally have green backs, will all be called Black Capped Lories by aviculturists.

Lorius lory erythrothorax, from the coastal areas of southeast New Guinea. This subspecies has a red chest with the blue confined to the abdomen.

Lorius lory somu, from southern New Guinea.

Lorius lory rubiensis from the southern coasts of New Guinea and the shores of Geelvink Bay. This species has blue confined to a broad band across the chest and extending downward into the abdomen.

Lorius lory salvadorii from northern New Guinea.

Lorius lory viridicrissalis from northern New Guinea has a pale and narrow band of red on the nape following the cap.

PURPLE NAPED LORY *(Lorius domicella) (28 cm)*.

The lower part of its black cap shades into a violet purple. The flights are green. The underwing coverts are blue followed by yellow flights with broad blackish margins. The rest of the coloring is red, darker on the back and upper-wing coverts. There is a trace of a yellowish collar on the undersides.

It is from Ceram and Amboina; introduced to Buru.

The very beautiful Purple Naped Lory is nine inches long including the broad three and one-fourth inch tail.

YELLOW COLLARED LORY *(Lorius chlorocercus) (28 cm)*.

Sometimes called the Yellow Bibbed or Green Tailed Lory, this Solomon Islands species is a large, ten and a half inch, short-tailed variety.

It inhabits lowland forests of the eastern Solomon Islands but seldom frequents coconut plantations, possibly because there are so many other Lories busily inhabiting these plantations.

The plumage is mostly red with the wings and latter half of the tail green. the undersides of the wing are red and blue, and the thighs are blue. There is a dominant and broad yellow band across the throat. The crown is black and there are black spots on the sides of the throat. The bill is bright red, and the feet are black. The underwings have a considerable amount of blue.

The Black-Masked Lovebird is very popular. This species is less pugnacious and somewhat quieter than the Peach-Faced. Black-Masked Lovebirds are easily bred.

Immature Swainson's Blue Mountain Lorikeets are friendly, alert, and active.

BLUE THIGHED LORY *(Lorius tibialis) (28 cm).*

The range of the Blue Thighed is unknown.

The basic coloring is red with a bluish-black cere and eye ring. The hint of the yellow collar is present as in the Purple Naped. A black band marks the outer area of the upperside of the tail. The uppersides of the wings are blue on the coverts and black on the flights with a large yellow area in the center of the flights. The thighs are blue.

The total length is eleven and a half inches with a broad tail of slightly less than four inches.

WHITE NECKED LORY *(Lorius albidinucha) (28 cm).*

The White Necked Lory is from the almost inaccessible island of New Britain. The size is nine inches including the broad three and one-half inch tail. Mostly a brilliant and smooth red, this species has equally brilliant and smooth contrasts. The extensive black cap is followed by a white patch which is nearly an inverted triangle except that the lower angle is rounded. The wings and tail are bright green.

Genus: *Phigys*

COLLARED LORY *(Phigys solitarius) (20 cm).*

The Collared or Solitary Lory of the larger Fiji Islands is the only member of its genus.

The bill and feet are orange. The crown and neck are deep purple or blackish. A bright double collar of green and red crosses the mantle. The rest of the upperparts are red with a deep purple on the rump. The underparts are bright red interrupted by green undertail coverts and deep purple on the abdomen.

The Collared Lory lives in flocks in flowering trees in the Fiji Islands. Like all members of the parrot family from these area, it is rare in captivity.

It is about eight inches long.

Genus: *Vini*

The five members of the genus *Vini* are shaped like other true Lories but are small. The average size is seven inches, including a two and a half inch tail. All are brilliant in coloration and are extremely rare.

BLUE CROWNED LORY *(Vini australis) (19 cm).*

Native to Samoa and Tonga Islands, Fotuna Island, and the Lau Archipelago, the small seven-inch Blue Crowned Lory is basically bright green.

The Scarlet or Red and Yellow Macaw is the most frequently seen of all Macaws and is possibly the most vivid in color.

The Jardine's Parrot is from Africa and very rare. It resembles the Amazon Parrots in shape but is much smaller.

Bright accents are a blue crown, a large red patch covering cheeks and throat, and another red patch on the center of the abdomen. Deep purple follows the red on the abdomen and there is some yellow on the rather short tail.

Also rare in captivity, the Blue Crowned lives in parties (6 - 12 and more) and feeds on flowers of the coconut tree.

KUHL'S RUFFED LORY or RUBY LORY *(Vini kuhlii) (19 cm).*

Kuhl's Ruffed Lory is richly colored in green, blue, and red. All the upperparts are green except for a broad patch of blue across the nape of the neck. The red on the underparts starts with the lores, runs through the eyes, surrounds the cheeks with an indentation, flares outwards again and encloses most of the abdomen. The completeness of the red pattern is interrupted by a large rich blue patch covering the abdomen, thighs and vent. The undertail coverts are green. The uppertail is mixed with green, red, and blue.

Kuhl's Lory is seven inches long, including the tail which is slightly over two and a half inches.

Their habitat is Rimitara and the Austral Islands, and they are very rare in captivity.

It might be mentioned that this beauty has a tinge of bronze on the back, pale green on the rump, and a hint of a green throat collar. The green cap on the crown has especially brilliant streaks. The total length is actually six and a half inches including the two-inch tail.

TAHITI BLUE LORY *(Vini peruviana) (18 cm).*

Extremely rare, the Tahiti Blue Lory inhabits the South Pacific islands of Society, Cook, and Tuamotu.

A true Lory, it is only seven and a half inches long, including a two and a half inch tail. The short tail is pointed, and the head feathers are rather enlongated.

It is deep, glossy, bright blue with a white area covering cheeks, throat, and bib. The bill and feet are yellow with a tinge of orange in the bill. Females have paler bills.

The Tahiti Blue Lory has been kept in captivity and has been bred by the Duke of Bedford.

ULTRAMARINE LORY or MARQUESAS BLUE LORY *(Vini ultramarina) (18.5 cm).*

The Ultramarine Lory inhabits the Marquesas Islands, is closely related to the Tahiti Blue Lory, and is slightly larger.

The beak is yellowish-tinged orange, lighter at the base. The head is a very rich metallic blue. The rest of the upperparts are lovely pale blue.

Underparts are white with a broad band of the same rich head coloring across the chest. Flecks of the same coloring appear on the white chest and abdomen. Females are slightly smaller.

Also extremely rare, the Ultramarine Lory has been successfully maintained and bred in captivity. The Lory sometimes shows a turquoise forehead patch on the rich metallic blue head. The rump is paler and more brilliant than the blue of the upperparts. The bluish-white tail is not lustrous. The total length is six and a half inches including the two inch tail.

STEPHEN'S LORY (Vini stepheni) (19 cm).

Stephen's Lory from Henderson Island is seven inches long including its three inch tail. All the upperparts are bright green, mostly uniform except for the paler rump and the yellowish tail. The color and pattern of the underparts resemble those of Kuhl's Lory, but they are often less precise or less uniform.

Genus: Glossopsitta

The three members of this genus are six to eight inches long and of slight build. The have small bills and pointed tails.

The predominant color variations appear on the head and all have an olive brown area on the mantle.

All are common in their native areas of southern and eastern Australia but are rare in captivity.

The diet in captivity would be the normal Lory diet minus seeds.

MUSK LORIKEET (Glossopsitta concinna) (22 cm).

Attractive but not strikingly beautiful, this little eight inch lorikeet is slender with a long narrow tail of three inches.

Predominantly green, the outstanding features are a wide red forehead band and red ear coverts. Bluish-green follows the red on the head, and a shoulder band completes the color variation on the body. The black beak is tipped with red.

Its native habitat is eastern and southeastern Australia and Tasmania and Kangaroo Island, where it is common. It is rare in captivity.

Females have less pronounced blue on the head. The young are duller and have dark brown bills.

PURPLE-CROWNED LORIKEET (Glossopsitta porphyrocephala) (15 cm).

Very common in the wild state in southern Australia, but rare in captivity, is the small and pretty Purple-Crowned Lorikeet.

The color pattern starts with a broad and variable red-orange frontal band followed by a deep purple crown. The ear coverts are yellow-orange. The area

The Red-Bellied Conure is quite rare in captivity. The bird is from southeastern Brazil and is the most typical species of the genus *Pyrrhura.*

The Yellow Cockatiel has yellow pigment at different concentrations; the genetics, however, is complicated by the seemingly high number of genes involved. The yellow was the first Cockatiel mutation to be established.

between the shoulders is olive brown. The rest of the upper parts are green; and, except for red underwing coverts, the underparts are light blue.

LITTLE LORIKEET *(Glossopsitta pusilla) (15 cm).*

This charming little Lorikeet is just slightly over six inches, including the two and a half inch pointed tail.

The basic coloring is green, lighter underneath. The black bill is very small. Red covers the forehead and an area extending down to the eyes, the sides of the face, and the throat. A buffy brown collar occurs just below the nape and above the shoulders. The ear coverts are very bright green.

The Little Lorikeet is also rare in captivity but rather common in its native areas of eastern and southeastern Australia and Tasmania.

Genus: *Charmosyna*

The Lorikeets of the genus *Charmosyna* are all smaller than those of the genus *Trichoglossus* and are delicate in appearance. Most of the species have two enlongated central tail feathers which add tremendously to the graceful and elegant form. Some are of exceedingly rich coloration and pattern making them easy candidates for the most beautiful birds in the world. The bills are small, quite delicately curved and pointed.

All members of this genus are very rare in captivity. Before restrictions, many were kept by aviculturists in Europe and proved to be easily maintained and not difficult to breed.

GREEN PALM LORIKEET *(Charmosyna palmarum) (17 cm).*

A small, long-tailed species of seven inches, the Green Palm Lorikeet inhabits the hills of New Hebrides, Santa Cruz, Duff, and Banks Islands. The entire coloring is green except for a trace of red on the chin, a tip of yellow on the tail, and an orange-yellow bill. The legs are like the bill, a bright orange.

The Green Palm Lorikeet is not likely to become a popular aviary subject because of its lack of variable colors.

MEEK'S LORIKEET *(Charmosyna meeki) (16 cm).*

Meek's Lorikeet of the mountainous areas of the Solomon Islands is six and a half inches long.

Mostly it is green, dark above and pale below. The crown has a bluish green spot, and the mantle has a glowing shade of pale brown. The underside of the tail is yellow. The bill is dark red, and the feet are orange.

Meek's Lorikeet is pretty, but it is not as lovely as most flamboyant lorikeets.

NEW CALEDONIAN LORIKEET *(Charmosyna diadema) (18 cm).*

A small Lorikeet from mountain forests of northern New Caledonia, the New Caledonian Lorikeet is supposed to inhabit tall flowerng trees. Little is known about this species. It is almost eight inches long, including the tail of three and a half inches.

Mostly it is green with a deep blue cap. The outer rim of the wings is blackish. The yellow bar on the underside of the wings is absent. There is also a small red patch near the vent. The green on the cheeks is pale, almost yellowish. The bill is orange-red; the feet are orange.

DUCHESS LORIKEET *(Charmosyna margarethae) (20 cm).*

From the Solomon Islands comes a well-proportioned, long-tailed Lorikeet of eight inches which is one of the most exquisitely beautiful of all the Parrots of the world. The Duchess Lorikeet is quiet and feeds in flowering trees in the mountains.

Try to picture a brilliant red bird with a wonderful pattern of trim and contrasting colors. The bill is reddish-orange. A black band extends backwards from the eyes to the back of the crown. The chest has a broad band of bright yellow bordered on both sides by a narrow band of bluish-black. The wings and back are dark green followed by a golden olive on the rump that is repeated on the underside of the tail. The feet are orange.

Sexes are distinguished by the colors on the sides of the rump: red for males and yellow for females.

Unfortunately, the Duchess Lorikeet is never available. Some day it may be available along with many other exotic birds which are not possible for aviculture now.

BLUE EARED LORIKEET, RED FLANKED LORIKEET or PLEAS-ING LORIKEET *(Charmosyna placentis) (17 cm).*

The Blue Eared Lorikeet is from New Guinea, the Aru Islands, and the western Papuan Islands.

The overall green is interrupted in the male by a large streaked blue ear patch and red on the cheeks, the lores, and throat. The sides and underwing coverts are red. The undersides of the flights are blackish with a broad yellow wing bar. The underside of the tail is red at the base followed by blue and ending in red. The female lacks the red markings and the blue ears. Only in the center part of the central feathers does red remain. The tail is tipped in yellow, and the large cheek patch has prominent streaks of lustrous yellow against a brownish background. The beak is red, and the underparts are dark and vivid green. The total length is five and three-fourths inches including the two inch tail which is usually somewhat shorter than the tail of the male.

This lutino Cockatiel is, by definition, sex-linked, which means that a male lutino must have had a lutino mother. But a lutino hen obtains her color wholly from her father. The mother's color is immaterial.

The Green Cheeked Amazon is extremely noisy but is certainly a pretty bird.

This lovely Lorikeet has five races: *intensior,* from the Moluccas; *pallidior,* from New Britain, New Ireland, New Hanover and other nearby islands; *subplacens,* called Sclater's Lorikeet, from Woodlark Island and eastern New Guinea; *ornata,* and *placentis,* from the southern Moluccas, Kai and Aru Islands and southern New Guinea.

Sclater's Lorikeet differs only in having a yellowish tinge on the crown and a deeper blue on the ears.

STELLA'S LORY or LORIKEET *(Charmosyna papou stellae) (42 cm).*

Stella's Lorikeet is a long, slender bird with a long tail and a small head. The dominant colors are red and green. Green covers the wings and also the tail in a slightly more olive shade. Red covers the underparts, back, sides of the face, throat, neck, rump, and upper tail coverts. There is some purple on the rump. The bill is orange. The forehead, crown, and nape are not red. First there is a cap of maroon covering forehead and nape, followed by a large black patch down to the lower end of the nape; a purple patch seems superimposed on the black of the nape. The male has two long and graceful central tail feathers of olive brown with yellow tips. The female lacks the extension and has a yellow back. The male has black thighs, red and green on the underside of the tail, and a dark reddish shade instead of maroon on the forehead and nape. The body is five inches long; the tail is four and a half to five inches long; and the two central extensions of the tail may reach an additional six inches. The race *goliathina* is very similar. The subspecies *wahnesi* has a broad yellow bar across the lower chest and bright red on the vent, center of the abdomen, and undertail coverts. The nominate race, *papou,* called the Papuan Lory, also has black thighs. A narrow purplish band occurs on the hind part of the crown followed by a black bar. The subspecies *papou* is almost more beautiful than Stella's Lory. The red is brighter and covers the head. Another black bar occurs on the lower portion of the neck. The purple abdominal band is absent. In its place is an inverted and filled-in V-shaped area of black. There is yellow on the wings and shoulder area. The underwing coverts are red, and the undersides of the flights are blackish. The tail extensions are brownish-orange tipped in yellow. The underside of the tail is a rich golden yellow.

Stella's Lorikeet is found in southeastern New Guinea.

WILHELMINA'S LORIKEET *(Charmosyna wilhelminae) (13 cm).*

Wilhelmina's Lorikeet comes from New Guinea and is slightly less than four inches in length.

142

It is mostly green but has attractive color variations. The bill is orange; and the underwings are red. There is a broad blue band behind the crown and on the rump. A reddish patch precedes the rump. Yellow streaks mark the chest: some red hidden in the tail, a dull shade of purplish-plum on the crown followed by blue streaks, a large bright reddish patch prededing the rump and a plum shade on the rump itself which is less bright than the crown.

The two long central tail feathers add grace and charm, and this is true of all the long tailed Lorikeets in this genus.

FAIR LORIKEET *(Charmosyna pulchella pulchella) (18 cm).*

The Fair Lorikeet, whose name is less spectacular than it should be, is from the mountainous areas of western New Guinea.

It is a very lovely species with a red head and underparts and green wings. The lower part of the crown and the nape are covered by a purplish patch. Yellowish green streaks appear on the chest and abdomen. A wide stripe of purple on the rump is flanked by red. The two long central tail feathers are red; the outer ones are red at the base, green in the center, and yellow at the tips.

There are two other subspecies: *bella* from the mountains of central and eastern New Guinea and *rothschildi* from the Cyclops Mountains in northern New Guinea.

ROTHSCHILD'S LORIKEET *(Charmosyna pulchella rothschildi) (18 cm).*

Rothschild's Lorikeet is a subspecies of the Fair Lorikeet which has two subspecies altogether. Both the nominate race, *pulchella,* and the race *bella* are alike and are six and a half inches long including the three and one-half inch tail. The stripe of purple on the rump is flanked by a dull yellowish shade instead of red. Rothschild's Lorikeet is slightly larger and has the red on the head extending back to the nape before the purplish patch begins. The center of the chest where the yellow streaks appear is greenish instead of red.

RED THROATED LORIKEET *(Charmosyna rubrigularis rubrigularis) (17 cm).*

The Red Throated Lorikeet from New Britain and New Ireland is slightly less than seven inches. In shape it is much like other members of genus and has long central tail feathers for added elegance.

The throat has red markings, and there are blue streaks on the sides. The thighs are red, and the beak and feet are orange. The two long central tail feathers are tipped in yellow. The blackish undersides of the flights have the yellow wing bar. The rest of the bird is green.

Senegal Parrots are small, stocky, short and square-tailed parrots from Africa. In Europe they are inexpensive and have a reputation for being charming pets and just about as docile as a parrot can be.

A subspecies is *Charmosyna rubrigularis krakari* from Dampier Island off the coast of Huon Peninsula, New Guinea.

RED MARKED LORIKEET *(Charmosyna rubronotata rubronotata (17 cm).*

The Red Marked Lorikeet inhabits Salawati and the Berau Peninsula. It is six and a half inches long with a tail of less than three inches.

The basic color is green with large blue ear patches, yellow tips on the tail, and red on the crown, rump, upperwings, and also on a large area on the sides and underwing coverts. The yellow bar on the undersides of the blackish flights is much reduced.

A subspecies, the Kordo Lorikeet *(Charmosyna rubronotata kordoana),* has a far deeper and less bright shade of red. It inhabits the island of Biak in Geelvink Bay.

JOSEPHINE'S LORIKEET *(Charmosyna josefinae) (24 cm).*

Charmosyna josefinae has three races: *josefinae* from the mountains of western New Guinea, *cyclopum* from the Cyclops mountains of northern New Guinea, and *sepikiana* from the mountains of the Sepik region of New Guinea.

This lovely species lacks the tail extensions but is otherwise just as beautiful as Stella's Lorikeet.

It has the purple patch at the base of the crown and nape followed by the wide black border. The center of the abdomen and thighs are purple. The wings are green, and there is some purple on the rump. The two central tail feathers are red tipped in yellow, and the outer tail feathers are green tipped in yellow. All other parts are bright red, including the neck and area above the rump. The bill is orange.

The size is slightly over nine inches, including the tail which is almost four inches long.

BURU LORIKEET *(Charmosyna toxopei) (16 cm).*

The Buru Lorikeet is all green with a pale throat. Its habitat is Buru.

YELLOW STREAKED LORY or MANY STRIATED LORIKEET
(Charmosyna multistrata) (18 cm).

Seven inches in length including the three inch tail, the Yellow Streaked Lorikeet is all green, darker above and traced with many fine lustrous streaks of pale greenish-yellow. This Lory is from the southern slopes of the Snow Mountains in New Guinea.

Genus: *Oreopsittacus*

ARFAK LORY *(Oreopsittacus arfake arfake) (15 cm).*

The Arfak Lorikeet is slightly less than six inches long with a long, broad tapering tail.

It is a very pretty bird and is mainly green. The cap on the forehead and crown is red, and the bill is black. A large patch of blue covers the face below the eyes. There are small pale streaks on the upperparts of the patch. Red is found on the side. The underwing coverts and the tips of the tail are red. Females lack the red crown and forehead.

This extremely rare Lory comes from the Arfak Mountains in northwestern New Guinea.

VICTORIA LORY *(Oreopsittacus arfaki grandis) (15 cm).*

The Victoria Lory is a subspecies which lacks the red striations on the side. The red is brighter in the crown and tail. Blue precedes the red in the tail, and the striations on the face are white.

The habitat is southeastern New Guinea.

One other subspecies occurs: *Oreopsittacus arfaki major* from the Weyland Mountains and the Snow Mountains in western central New Guinea.

Genus: *Opopsitta*

FIG PARROTS

Members of the genus *Opopsitta* are small and have short tails, large heads and bills. They have the size and shape of Love Birds and the personalities of Lories. They are extremely fascinating birds.

Their extensive range includes Australia, New Guinea, and the Papuan and other islands in that general area. All are very rare in captivity and are not common in the wild state. They feed on fruits and seeds and are often called Fig Parrots.

A color pattern similar in most, if not all, of the species consists of red tips on the inner wing feathers and yellow patches on the sides of the breast. The basic coloring is green.

BLACK CHEEKED FIG PARROT *(Opopsitta gulielmiterti) (13 cm).*

The species *Opopsitta guliemeterti* is differentiated from the species *Opopsitta diophthalma* by a dull blackish cheek.

There are only minor differences in the seven subspecies, such as black frontal markings. They are exceptionally rare in captivity.

The races are listed below:

The Quaker Parrakeet is one of the few species which builds a real nest, a gigantic affair with many nesting cavities, each housing a different pair.

Opposite:
The Bronze-winged Parrot is from the Andes of Colombia, Ecuador, and northwest Peru. The bird is unusually attractive.

Opopsitta gulielmiterti is from Salawati and the opposite coasts of the Vogelkop.

Opopsitta gulielmiterti melanogenia is from the Aru Islands.

Opopsitta gulielmiterti nigrifrons is from northern New Guinea.

Opopsitta gulielmiterti ramuensis is from northern New Guinea (Ramu River district).

Opopsitta gulielmiterti amabilis is from northeastern New Guinea.

Opopsitta gulielmiterti fuscifrons is from the foothills of the Snow Mountains and the Oranje Range.

Opopsitta gulielmiterti suavissima is from the southern coast of southwestern New Guinea.

DOUBLE EYED FIG PARROT *(Opopsitta diophthalma diophthalma)* *(14 cm).*

This western Papuan Islands species has red forehead and cheeks with orange blending in at the back of the crown. A narrow band of violet borders the back of the crown. Above the eyes is a semicircle of bright blue feathers. The bill is silvery grey shading to black on the tip.

The Double Eyed Fig Parrot is very rare in captivity, but it has proven itself to be an intelligent and suprisingly good pet.

MARSHALL'S LORILET *(Opopsitta diophthalma aruensis)*

There is a subspecies which is identical to *aruensis* except for the additional range of northern Queensland and Cape York Peninsula. This species has been named *Opopsitta diophthalma marshalli.* The habitat given by Peters is the Aru Islands and New Guinea. This very rare species has a reputation for never having been kept in captivity, but the writers cannot confirm this.

The male has a red forehead with a yellow band following. The cheek patches are red with blue below. The rest of the coloring is green. Females have tan colored cheeks instead of red.

RED BROWED or BLUE FACED LORILET *(Opopsitta diophthalma macleayana)*

Sometimes called Leadbeater's Lorilet, the Red Browed has an Australian range in northern Queensland.

It has a red patch on the forehead and red cheek patches. Blue covers the areas around the eyes and below the cheek patches. The rest of the coloring is green. Females lack the red facial area.

This species is also very rare in captivity.

150

BLUE BROWED or RED FACED LORILET *(Opopsitta diophthalma coxeni)*

The rare Blue Browed Lorilet is native to southern Queensland and northern New South Wales.

The beak is black, and the forehead and lower cheeks are blue. The ear coverts are red, and there are red flecks on the face. The rest of the coloring is green.

Other races of *Opopsitta diophthalma* are *Opopsitta diophthalma virago* from Fergusson and Goodenough Islands and *Opopsitta diophthalma inseparabilis* from Tagula Island in the Louisade Archipelago.

Another possible race which may not be valid is *Opopsitta diophthalma coccineifrons*, restricted to eastern New Guinea.

Genus: *Lathamus*

SWIFT PARRAKEET *(Lathamus discolor) (25 cm).*

A rare bird in captivity, the Swift Parrakeet is also called the Swift Lorikeet. It travels with Lorikeets in the wild state feeding on nectar. It is amazingly talented in its undulating flight and aptly deserves its name of Swift Parrakeet.

The basic coloring is green, but there is a red forehead and some red on the face bordered with yellow. Blue appears on the cheeks, crown, and outer rims of the wings. Red appears on the underwing coverts, undertail coverts, and sporadically on the chest. The tail is blue with a red suffusion. The shoulder bears a small patch of deep red.

Sexes are alike, but the female is duller and shows less red on the chest.

The bird is rather small and slighter than most parrakeets. The long pointed tail, long flight feathers, and small head enhance its slight appearance.

The Swift inhabits Tasmania, Southern Queensland, New South Wales, Victoria, and southeast Australia. It has the reputation of delicacy in captivity.

Swift Parrakeets (or Lorikeets) are eight and a half inches long including the pointed tail of four inches. In addition to the description the Swift Parrakeet has bright blue areas in the wings, dark red on the shoulders, and red near the beak and on the chin. In Professor Brereton's rearrangement mentioned in the beginning of this chapter, this species, which stands alone in its genus, would be placed in a large family of Australian Parrakeets called Platycercidae. The aviculturist, however, will still consider it as a Lorikeet because of its dietary requirements.

151

The Spectacled Parrot is an inexpensive and common parrot and is regarded as a rather poor substitute for a higher-priced Double Yellow Head Amazon, which really doesn't do justice to the Spectacled Parrot.

Opposite:
The Vinaceous Amazon inhabits southeastern Brazil. It sometimes becomes an affectionate pet and good talker.

Genus: *Neopsittacus*

MUSSCHENBROEK'S LORY *(Neopsittacus musschenbroekii) (23 cm).*

The nominate race of Musschenbroek's Lory is seven and a half inches including the three and a half inch rather broad tail. The other race, *major*, is slightly larger. This species is mostly dark green with a dull brownish shade on the lower crown and and nape. Pale streaks mark this area. The dark green background of the lores and cheeks is highlighted by bright pale green streaks. Red is hidden on the inner webs of the wing feathers, and the underside of the tail is dull yellowish. The chest and central abdominal areas are variable between red and green. Red scallops on the tips of the feathers are heavily concentrated in the upper center of the abdomen. The subspecies *musschenbroekii* is from the mountains of western New Guinea, and *major* is from the mountains of eastern New Guinea.

ALPINE LORIKEET *(Neopsittacus pullicauda) (18 cm).*

The Alpine Lorikeet from New Guinea is very much like Musschenbroek's Lory. The total length runs seven to seven and a half inches including the broad three inch tail. The chest and underparts are all red with green sides, and there are no pale streaks on the back of the neck although they are present on the cheeks and face. There are three races: *pullicauda* from the mountains of eastern New Guinea, *alpinus* (which is paler on the chest) from the mountains of western New Guinea, and *socialis* from the mountains of the Huon Peninsula and the Morobe district in eastern New Guinea.

Genus: *Psittaculirostris*

DESMAREST'S LORY *(Psittaculirostris desmarestii) (18 cm).*

Desmarest's Lory with its six subspecies inhabits New Guinea and three nearby islands. The size is a heavy-bodied six inches with a short pointed tail of one and one-half inches. Both the head and the black beak on this species are large, and it is a beautiful species. The nominate race, *desmarestii*, from northwestern New Guinea, has a bright red forehead shading into golden yellowish-orange on the crown and nape. Then a pale green collar follows which shades into dark green on all the remaining upperparts except for some bright blue in the flight feathers.

A bright blue spot occurs on the lower area of the lores and under the eyes. Green below the eyes, on the cheeks, and around the throat is bright but shows traces of olive on the lower sides of the neck. A bright bluish-green patch in the center of the lower neck extends slightly outwards to the sides. Some dull shades of plum are nearly hidden on the sides of the upper chest because the tips of the feathers in these areas are a shade of blue. The sides and underwing coverts are brilliant blue. The remaining underparts are green except for the dull slate on the underside of the tail.

The subspecies *cervicalis* from southeastern New Guinea is even more beautiful and slightly larger. The red on the forehead is less bright but more extensive. The shading on top of the head is like a golden rust, stopping abruptly at the back of the crown. The large cheek area is the same golden rust, somewhat variable, but also covering the lores, chin, and throat. Blue and green are absent, but wisps of turquoise and vivid rust-orange highlight the ear coverts. The nape starts with brilliant cobalt which shades gradually into deep turquoise down towards the mantle. A brilliant band of cobalt borders the lower throat area. The subspecies *godmani* from the southern slopes of the mountains of southern New Guinea is very similar to *cervicalis*.

The race *occidentalis* from the islands of Salawati and Batenta is six and three-fourths inches long including the tail of one and three-fourths inches. There is a heavy concentration of red on the forehead and slightly less of a concentration on the nape. Vivid turquoise-green occurs under the eyes; and the rest of the head, nape, and upper chest are golden rust followed by dull plum on the rest of the chest. There are also turquoise blue accents on the sides and undersides of the wings.

The subspecies *blythi* from the Isle of Misol has a brighter red on the forehead and brighter golden yellowish-orange all over the head to the nape and throat. There is no blue under the eyes. Deep plum appears on the sides of the chest, and bright blue occurs on the sides under the wings and on the underwing coverts.

SALVADOR'S LORY *(Psittaculirostris salvadorii) (19 cm)*

Both races of Salvador's Lory (*salvadorii* and *edwardsii*) are from the northern coast of New Guinea and are very similar in appearance. The nominate race is six and one-fourth inches long including the short pointed tail of one and one-half inches. A bright light green cap down to the eyes and nape is followed by dusky gray on the nape and deep blue-black on the lower part of the nape. The rest of the upperparts are dark green with red hidden in the flights and some blue exposed on the flights. A big bright yellow cheek patch highlights the facial areas with more vivid streaks of yellow below the eyes flaring to the rear sides of the neck. Tufts of turquoise-blue follow the yellow. The lores are dark followed by bright red below the lore, the lower cheek areas, and the throat and chin. A dark violet blue band crosses the chest and is much broader on the sides. A large patch of red starts on the center of the chest and covers half the sides tapering to a point in the center of the abdomen. The sides, remaining areas on the abdomen, and all other underparts are green. The female lacks the red on the chest below the violet-blue band.

The Chattering Lory, dazzling in color, is a perfect aviary bird and a constant delight with its comical antics.

Opposite, above:
The Brown or Meyer's Parrot is a well-known charming pet and just about as docile as a parrot can be. It has a very unusual and beautiful color pattern.

Opposite, below:
The Malabar Parrakeet is rare in its native habitat. They are good breeders in captivity.

157

The Rose Breasted Cockatoo loves a rain bath and should have regular opportunities for indulging in it. If it feels the need for a bath it will ruffle its feathers and spread its wings as the drops begin to fall.

COCKATOOS

Subfamily: Cacatuinae

Genera: *Probosciger, Calyptorhynchus, Callocephalon, Cacatua, Nymphicus.*

The Cockatoo family comprises more truly exotic species than any other parrot-like family. All are adorned with crests, some fanciful and recurved, others recumbent. They range in size from the small Timor Cockatoo, approximately twelve inches in length, to the very large Palm Cockatoo, measuring twenty-nine inches. In mentioning the Timor as being the smallest, the writers are excluding the Cockatiel, which really belongs in this family.

All Cockatoos are native to Australia and a wide range of South Pacific Islands extending even to the Philippine Islands. They are exceptionally intelligent, and many are great clowns. They seem more active than other parrots. Most are longer-lived than other members of the Parrot Order, especially the Greater Sulphur Crested Cockatoo, whose age has been known to surpass far more than a hundred years. Many are much freer breeders than most parrots of a comparable size. Diet and breeding facilities are described in their respective chapters.

Cockatoos are equally excellent as pets or as aviary inhabitants. They thrive in captivity and relish the attention of admiring humans. Inveterate chewers, they should be supplied with plenty of wood or branches for chewing exercise.

Cockatoos have a peculiar feather structure which constantly furnishes a powdery-like slough. This slough has a cleansing effect that maintains the chalky appearance of the White Cockatoos and helps to give the soft pastel effect of many others. Even the Cockatiel has this type of feather structure.

Cockatoos native to Australia are generally despised by farmers because of their extensive crop damage. Unfortunately for birds and many animals, it is a worldwide characteristic of mankind to move in on nature's carefully set balance, tear up natural habitats, destroy food supplies, and obliterate natural breeding haunts. When the displaced birds or animals substitute new-grown crops for natural foodstuffs which man has previously destroyed, there is widespread moaning and vicious retaliation by man, whose ingenious methods of slaughter have rendered more than one species extinct. In

The White Cockatoo comes from Indonesia and is rare in aviculture. It is well known for its loud screech.

Dark Green Normal. This mutation is one for depth of color. One dark factor has been added. This dark factor can affect the depth of color in all birds except the albino. In a blue bird, the addition of one dark factor gives the color of cobalt blue. The cinnamon mutation, mentioned later, is also present in this specimen.

The Moluccan Cockatoo is one of the best talkers. It needs a very large cage and daily exercise and freedom, but the affection provided by a full-tamed bird is touching!

America, the prime example is the disappearance of the Carolina Conure, which was the only parrot native to the United States.

Australia, the home of some of the world's most exotic birds, shows decreasing numbers of many species. Instead of the needless slaughter, it would be a far better plan to trap the damaging and despised Cockatoos for export to the world's bird markets.

Genus: *Probosciger*

PALM COCKATOO *(Probosciger aterrimus) (60 cm).*

Unusual is a very mild adjective to describe this very rare and very large black Cockatoo. The only examples the writers have seen of this incredible bird are on display at the San Diego Zoo, where the usual exclamation upon seeing them for the first time is the all-inclusive "WOW!"

The Palm Cockatoo is fearsome looking rather than beautiful. It is large, almost thirty inches long, and has a huge beak on an oversized head topped by an abundant crest of spiny looking feathers. The entire coloring is black with a powdery grey tinge. The only relief from the somber coloration is a naked patch of skin on the sides of the face starting at the corners of the beak and extending over a considerable portion of facial area. This patch of skin can change color according to the state of the bird's emotions. If it is cold or is not feeling well, the cheek area is bluish. It changes to pink in its normal state and to a deeper, richer shade if angry or excited.

With all its gruffness, the Palm Cockatoo seems to be awkwardly gentle and affectionate. It appears to be affecting a demeanor of daintiness that lends a comical air to its antics.

There are three races of this bird with only slight differences that have achieved the rank of subspecies. They are as follows:

Probosciger aterrimus goliath is from western and southern New Guinea.

Probosciger aterrimus stenolophus is from nothern New Guinea.

Probosciger aterrimus aterrimus is from the Cape York Peninsula area, the Aru Islands, Misool, and southern New Guinea.

Genus: *Calyptorhynchus*

BLACK COCKATOOS

The genus is divided into the subgenera *Zanda* and *Calyptorhynchus*.

There are four species of these large Cockatoos ranging in size from

Seafoam Opaline showing the blue factor, the pale factor, the Opaline factor, and the third type of Yellow-Faced factor. This also has one dark factor, giving it the cobalt blue shade.

This is the same bird except for the elimination of the one dark factor.
This changes the cobalt blue shade to the sky blue shade.

Banksian or Red Tailed Black Cockatoo, a very rare and very large species of Australian Cockatoo.

twenty-three to twenty-seven inches in length. All are basically black with many small yellowish spots. All are slender in appearance because of the long broad tail and full bushy crest which, although composed of smaller feathers, has a far greater number of feathers than is found in most Cockatoos. The tail has a broad color band which mainly separates the different species. All are rare and expensive in America.

These large birds are good fliers but give the impression that their size is unwieldy with a lumbering awkwardness. Their tremendous wingspread and hawk-like tail, which fans outward when flying, requires an aviary of considerable size. For the most part, they are unsuitable for cages; but a young Funereal Cockatoo in the Dorothy Speed collection was housed for several years in a very large cage and did very well in it. This Cockatoo became an extremely affectionate pet. Though amusingly awkward, it amiably submitted to a handling that few other birds would tolerate.

In the wild, these birds feed mainly on wood-boring grubs. Therefore, some live food should be given in captivity.

Sexual differences occur in all species of the genus. Adult males have black beaks and females have white horn-colored beaks. All females are appreciably lighter in color and show greater color variations. Immatures are like females. They mature over a period of four years, gradually becoming like the adults.

BANKSIAN COCKATOO *(Calyptorhynchus magnificus) (60 cm).*

Also called the Red Tailed Black Cockatoo, this is the largest of the genus. The main characteristic is the red tail band.

The male has a dull gloss on the all black upper parts and greyish tipped feathers on the chest. The red tail band is very deeply colored, and the beak is black.

The female has yellow spots on the upper parts and yellowish barring on the chest. The tail has more of an orange-red bar mixed with yellow, and the beak is light horn color.

Immature birds are like females. As they mature over a four-year period, the young cocks turn slowly like the males.

There are four races of this bird: *Calyptorhynchus magnificus magnificus, Calyptorhynchus magnificus macrorhynchus, Calyptorhynchus magnificus naso,* and *Calyptorhynchus magnificus samueli.*

GLOSSY BLACK COCKATOO *(Calyptorhynchus lathami) (40 cm).*

This is very similar to the Banksian Cockatoo except for the following differences: the male is slightly smaller and has a brownish shade on the head; females do not have the spots and bars on the body feathers.

One of the first mutations in budgies, called a Normal Blue because it follows Mendel's Law of Inheritance. The yellow coloring is entirely deleted. This one is called Sky Blue and has no "dark factor."

A young Lutino budgie exhibiting the richness of color that has made this variety popular. Photo by Horst Mueller.

This is a very rare bird in the wild state and has been in captivity only a few times. It is found in eastern Australia and on Kangaroo Island.

WHITE TAILED BLACK COCKATOO *(Calyptorhynchus baudinii)* *(67 cm)*.

Also called Baudin's Black Cockatoo, this twenty-three inch bird is the same as the Funereal Cockatoo, except that the cheek patch and tail band are white. It inhabits southeastern and southwestern Australia.

FUNEREAL COCKATOO *(Calyptorhynchus funereus) (67 cm)*.

Also called by the descriptive name of Yellow Tailed Black Cockatoo, this species is close to twenty-five inches in length.

The upper black portions have less gloss and a slight brownish tinge. Under parts have pale yellowish tips on the feathers. The yellow tail band is pale and freckled with dark spots. A futher distinguishing feature is a large lemon cheek patch of very fine hairlike feathers.

The female is slightly smaller with more pronounced yellow edgings.

Genus: *Callocephalon*

GANG-GANG COCKATOO *(Callocephalon fimbriatum) (34 cm)*.

An oddity of the Cockatoo group, the Gang-Gang is sometimes labeled the Red Crowned or Helmeted Cockatoo. Both these names would be more descriptive than the accepted one. Very rare and seldom seen in America, this species is also very expensive. The size is about fourteen inches.

The basic coloring is a soft shade of powdery grey. Each feather has a light margin at the tip which gives a scalloped effect. Tail and flights are a little darker. The entire head is a pleasing shade of scarlet and is topped by a crest that can best be described as flimsy; the feathers are very curly and loose looking and seem to be tumbling about the crown. The beak is grey and the eyes are a soft, friendly brown. Altogether, the Gang-Gang gives quite a startling and pleasing appearance.

Sexual differences are as follows: males have some of the lower abdominal feathers barred with orange, red, and white; in females the same areas are a duller shade of orange, and the white is green tinged. Females also lack the red of the head and have bolder markings.

Gang-Gangs are supposed to be bad feather pluckers and not too pleasant in a cage. The birds in Mrs. Speed's collection have been equally pleasant in cage or aviary, and there has never been the slightest sign of feather plucking. The writers believe that the reason for this excellence of condition is due to the extremely adequate diet, the same for the Gang-Gangs as for all her other birds.

Some ornithologists like to distinguish two subspecies of the Gang-Gang Cockatoo: *Callocephalon fimbriatum superior* from New South Wales, and *Callocephalon fimbriatum fimbriatum* of Victoria, King Island and Tasmania.

Genus: *Cacatua*

GREATER SULPHUR CRESTED COCKATOO   *(Cacatua galerita galerita) (50 cm).*

This is the most frequently seen and most popular of all the Australian Cockatoos. A large bird, twenty inches long, it has the highly desirable qualities of great beauty, intelligence, adaptability, hardiness, and long life. Its availability is fair and breeding results are satisfactory.

Snow white predominates in color. A bright sulphur-yellow flaring crest is the perfect accent. A slight tinge of yellow is found on the underside of the wings and tail. Feet and beak are black. Eyes in the male are deep brown, almost black; in the female a deep burgundy color.

Tommy, the Greater Sulphur Crested Cockatoo, quickly seizes any opportunity to attract attention by striking elaborate poses.

Pied Cobalt Opaline. The Pied factor is inconstant and irregular. This one is the Dutch Pied Factor which is mostly dominant. The Dutch Pied usually has clear feathers in the tail and flights and a clear patch on the back of the head.

172

Harlequins are more variable in pattern than Dutch Pieds. The character of the mutation is recessive to normal. This one is a young Cobalt Blue Harlequin. The striations on the crown extend through the forehead, indicating an immature bird.

These Cockatoos have an extensive wingspread and are good fliers. Extreme individualists, no two personalities are quite the same. Pets are usually so vain they will go to any lengths to attract attention in order to be admired. As a rule, they are exceptionally tame and affectionate.

As aviary birds, they are hardy and will stand almost any climate.

The only disadvantage to a Sulphur Crested Cockatoo is that many individuals like to exercise their voluminous vocal powers. Our Tommy blasts forth every evening about 5:00 P.M. for a period of about fifteen minutes.

BLUE EYED COCKATOO *(Cacatua galerita ophthalmica)* *(50 cm).*

The New Britain and New Ireland Cockatoo of nineteen inches resembles the Greater Sulphur Crested Cockatoo except that the crest feathers are somewhat broader. There is an area of blue skin around the eye.

TRITON COCKATOO *(Cacatua galerita triton) (50 cm).*

The Papuan Island form of the very rare Blue Eyed Cockatoo is called the Triton Cockatoo. It is eighteen inches long.

Three other subspecies of the Sulphur Crested Cockatoo occur over a large area of Australia and some Indonesian Islands. They are:

Cacatua galerita eleonora from the Aru Islands.

Cacatua galerita fitzroyi from northern Australia and Western Australia, east to the Gulf of Carpentaria.

Cacatua galerita trobiandi from eastern Australia.

LESSER SULPHUR CRESTED COCKATOO *(Cacatua sulphurea sulphurea) (33 cm).*

Approximately thirteen inches long, this bird is in nearly every respect a miniature Greater Sulphur Crested Cockatoo. The only noticeable difference is a faint yellowish tinge on the breast and cheek patch. The beak is larger in proportion to the rest of the size.

The Lesser Sulphur Crested is from the islands in the Flores and Java Seas, the Celebes and Buton, not as readily available as the Greater, but usually less expensive. It has sometimes made a very charming pet but usually is not as talented at talking as is the Greater. Each bird the writers have had seemed shy and reluctant to be tamed; but once it lost its fear of humans, it made up for its shyness.

These birds prefer aviaries to cages. Since they are diminutive in size, however, they are frequently referred to as "apartment-sized Cockatoos."

Lessers are as hardy as their larger cousins and should be fed the same diet. There are five subspecies of this bird which are listed below.

CITRON CRESTED COCKATOO *(Cacatua sulphurea citrinocristata)*

The beautiful Citron Crested from Sumba is very slightly larger than the Lesser Sulphur Crested and better looking. The Lesser looks a little more like a slender, gangling teen-ager by comparison. The only other difference is the Citron Crested's long, graceful, bright orange crest.

The Citron Crested is quite rare and seldom offered for sale. Usually it is considerably more expensive than the Lesser. The writers have had ony a few of these lovely birds in their possession and have spent considerable time in trying to tame them. The end result, for the same amount of effort, always seemed less satisfactory than with Lesser Sulphur Cresteds. The Citron Crested's interest in learning to talk also seems to be quite limited. As an aviary bird, it is very active and charming.

Citrons are equally hardy and should be fed the same diet as other Cockatoos. They have the same eye colorings which distinguish the sexes in other similar Cockatoos.

TIMOR COCKATOO *(Cacatua sulphurea parvula) (33 cm).*

Similar to Lesser Sulphur Crested Cockatos except that they are smaller, Timor Cockatoos have less yellow on the back of the head and cheek and practically no yellow on the chest or abdomen. They are very rare and probably the smallest of the Cockatoos. They have, nevertheless, been bred in captivity. Their habitat is Timor and Samoa.

Three other subspecies are restricted to certain islands and show only minor differences. They are:
Cacatua sulphurea djampeana.
Cacatua sulphurea abbotti.
Cacatua sulphurea occidentalis.

UMBRELLA CRESTED COCKATOO *(Cacatua alba) (46 cm).*

This close relative of the Moluccan Cockatoo is also known as the White Crested and Greater White Crested Cockatoo. It is about three inches shorter than the Moluccan and with a much smaller body. The feathers are less voluminous and lack any shade of pink. In fact, the only feather coloring other than white is a yellow tinge under the tail and under the wings. The beak is black.

The crest is again a modified recumbent type of crest more closely resembling that of the Moluccan. The feathers are long, broad, and pure white.

Though not as beautiful as many other varieties of Cockatoos, it is still very handsome and very rare.

Original wild type of budgie, called Normal Green.

Photo by Mervin F. Roberts

A Young Green Opaline Self. As this bird matures, the chest areas become darker.

MOLUCCAN COCKATOO *(Cacatua moluccensis) (52 cm).*

In Europe this bird is mainly called Salmon Crested Cockatoo and is also frequently called the Rose Crested Cockatoo. It is very rare and expensive in America, and it is very beautiful.

It is twenty inches long, but because the tail is short its body is larger than most Cockatoos of similar length. Most of its abundant feathers are much longer and broader than those of similar sized birds.

This gives the Moluccan a bushy appearance that borders on shagginess when the bird frequently ruffles its feathers for a good shaking.

The crest is very long with each feather quite broad and curved backward over the head. In this instance, it bears a similarity to the previously described recumbent type of crest. However, the Moluccan's crest is so abundant that it does not even sit tight when lowered. It makes the already large head appear even larger and the large beak more proportionate to the head.

The major coloring seems to be a beautiful salmon-pink struggling through a thick outer layer of white. On the breast, the pink gets through, leaving more of a soft uniform tinge over this area than on all others with the exception of the crest. On the crest, the vivid salmon pink of the inner feathers seeps out from the softly tinged pink of the outer feathers. When the crest is raised, there are vivid flashes of this rich coloring.

Under the tail, there is a tinge of yellow suffused with the pink.

The beak is black but looks as if grey powder had been dusted on it. Eyes in the male are black; in the female brownish burgundy.

In addition to its great beauty and slow dignified movements, the Moluccan makes a wonderful pet and a good talker. The only drawbacks are the powerful voice and destructive beak.

PHILIPPINE COCKATOO *(Cacatua haematuropygia haematuropygia) (31cm).*

This attractive and rare little Cockatoo, called the Red Vented Cockatoo, resembles the Bare Eyed Cockatoo, but has white naked skin about the eyes.

It is mainly white with vermilion pink on the undertail coverts, on the ear coverts, and under the small crest. There is yellow under the flight feathers and yellow mixed with vermilion under the tail.

POLILLO COCKATOO *(Cacatua haematuropygia mcgregori)*

This bird is the same as the above, but of a larger race. There is some question as to its validity as a subspecies. Some authorities classify the two birds separately while others deny a separation.

This subspecies inhabits the Philippine Islands, including Palawan.

The magnificent Leadbeater Cockatoo is easily one of the great beauties of the bird world. The crest is very bright and is a wonderful contrast to the lovely soft pink found on the rest of the bird.

LEADBEATER'S COCKATOO *(Cacatua leadbeateri) (35 cm).*

This is the third of the three top favorites of the Cockatoo group. It is a native of Australia, where it is also known as the Pink Cockatoo and as Major Mitchell's Cockatoo. It measures about fifteen inches in length.

A description of the Leadbeater is painfully inadequate. Words cannot lead to a visual image of its striking beauty. The back, wings, and tail are snow white. Underwing coverts, chest, abdomen, the entire neck and chin, and sides of the face are a subtle pink. The crowning glory of this soft-colored bird is the very full and large crest, white at the tips with three bands of bright coloring, yellow in the center and red on each side.

The Leadbeater is an ideal aviary bird, a good breeder, and occasionally it makes a good household pet. In America, the demand greatly exceeds the supply.

Albino. The Albino factor is sex-linked and recessive. It masks all other colors. There are three forms of Albino. The yellow is called "Lutino" and is a green albino. The white is called "Albino" and is a blue albino. The third form is the intermediate shade of yellow and is caused by the over-all yellow-faced factor. Some people call this the "Buttercup" but this name is incorrect.

The newest mutation is called Clearbody. It is shown here in its intermediate development. The Clearbody was brought about by the skilled use of modifiers which gradually eliminated the dark pigment but left the dark markings. Since this bird was photographed, the task of removing the green has been definitely accomplished. The world of budgie fanciers has a new and attractive color variety. Continued strengthening of modifiers will result in a tightly stabilized condition which resembles a clear-cut and precise mutation much like the Clearwing is today.

Diet and breeding facilities are described in chapters on feeding and on aviaries and equipment.

The objection to the Leadbeater, ridiculously slight in the opinion of the writers, is its ratchety voice which, in reality, is not as loud as that of several other cockatoos.

Two subspecies of this cockatoo are as follows:

Cacatua leadbeateri mollis from southwestern Australia.

Cacatua leadbeateri leadbeateri from New South Wales and Victoria.

DUCORP'S COCKATOO *(Cacatua ducorps)* *(31 cm)*.

Short crested, this eleven-inch Cockatoo is a rarity from the Solomon Islands. It is known as the Red Vented Cockatoo.

It has some orange markings, particularly at the base of the crest. Reddish feathers surround the vent. The white crest feathers are broad and are about two inches long at their greatest length. Mostly hidden are pinkish-orange traces at the base of the crest.

GOFFIN'S COCKATOO *(Cacatua goffini)* *(30.5 cm)*.

This rare Cockatoo is the same as Ducorp's except that it is slightly smaller and has a tinge of red on the cheeks.

It is eleven and a half inches including the three inch tail. This rare bird has a faint tinge of pinkish-red on the cheeks and sides of the face, particularly noticeable on the lores. The crest feathers are slightly shorter.

BARE EYED COCKATOO *(Cacatua sanguinea)* *(30 cm)*.

This seventeen-inch Australian Cockatoo is also called the Little Corella and is one of the most intelligent members of the Cockatoo group. The first member which the writers met was not duly impressive. The second member, however, made them scurry back to their research books in disbelief. Its favorite habit was to cling to the end of a four-foot rope swinging in a circular motion about the head of a human. This bird, which belonged to Jerome Buteyn, subsequently found its way into the Dorothy Speed collection and is still the same charming and intelligent bird nearly ten years later.

In appearance, the Bare Eyed Cockatoo is not outstanding. Basically, it is an all-white bird with a recumbent crest. The bill is whitish and there is a bluish naked skin patch lumped below the eye. Pale yellow is under the tail and under the wings. Reddish feathers form a slight patch under the eye and at the base of the crest feathers.

The Bare Eyed Cockatoo is a free breeder in captivity and is one of the extremely active comics in the Cockatoo family. The more mundane appearance is adequately compensated by its personality. The only disadvantages are the habitual chewing and raucous voice.

Bare Eyed Cockatoo, the least attractive of the Cockatoos but one of the most talented and intelligent of all psittacine birds.

Blue Opaline "Self." This is a combination of the Opaline factor, the Clearwing factor, and the Blue factor.

The second major mutation was the nearly complete elimination of dark (or blue) pigment giving a light yellow or chartreuse color. The fact that there were still traces of dark coloring present gave it the chartreuse shade. From this point, selective breeding resulted in eliminating the chartreuse shade to make a pure yellow or "Buttercup." With the advent of "rare" budgies, the true Buttercup was lost in the shuffle. The shade of Buttercup was brought about by the use of "modifiers" which are minor variations which can be firmly entrenched in the homozygous state. Modifiers are responsible also for size, type, size of necklace spots, and many other characteristics.

185

The bizarre Slender Billed Cockatoo is usually as intelligent as its cousin, the Bare Eyed Cockatoo.

SLENDER BILLED COCKATOO *(Cacatua tenuirostris tenuirostris)* *(38 cm).*

This bird approximates the Bare Eyed Cockatoo except that it has more red on the face and apears to have a grossly overgrown upper beak and an improperly angled lower mandible. The reason for this curiously shaped beak is the manner of obtaining foods. It grubs roots and bulbs from the earth. For this reason the Slender Bill's aviary would be best if the floor contained growing grases or turf for beneficial natural digging. Otherwise, frequent clipping of the beak might be necessary.

Slender Billed Cockatoos are affectionate and gentle and make good talkers. Thousands of visitors to the California ranch of Jerome Buteyn remember the familiar voice of the two Slender Billed Cockatoos pictured in this book saying "Cookie want a drink."

Because of the exaggerated proportions of this bird, it could hardly be termed beautiful. However, the personality more than compensates for its bizarre appearance.

There is also a western race of the Slender Bill called *Cacatua tenuirostris pastinator.* This bird has less red on the head.

Genus: *Eolophus*

ROSE BREASTED COCKATOO *(Eolophus roseicapillus) (35 cm).*

Also known as the Roseate Cockatoo and Galah, this, second in popularity of the Cockatoo family, is another of nature's most beautiful creations and is further proof that Australia is the habitat of some of the most beautiful birds in the world. They are about fifteen inches in length and have a light pink recumbent crest. The upper parts (back, wings, and tail feathers) are a soft shade of powdery grey. Face, breast, and abdomen are a lovely rose-pink with a powdery pastel effect.

A Rose Breasted Cockatoo, *Eolophus roseicapillus,* photographed in the wild.

Olive-green Opaline.

An interesting size comparison between a budgie (light Green) and a Red Factor Canary.

Harlequin budgies: The bird at left exhibits the effect of the Harlequin pattern on basic blue coloring; the bird at right shows the pied effect on basic green coloring. Photo by Horst Mueller.

This is the most abundant, lowest priced, and best breeder of the Cockatoo family. Due to import restrictions, the price in this country is about four times higher than it should be. In Australia, Rose Breasteds have frequently been slaughtered on a wide scale because of purported crop damage. The writers understand that there was a bounty placed on their heads at one time.

As pets, most authorities do not rate them highly. In America, however, they are usually extremely amusing and affectionate pets and are reasonably good talkers.

As aviary birds, they are excellent. Mischievous and aggressive, they should be by themselves. Their only drawbacks are their voices and fondness for chewing.

There are three subspecies of this bird inhabiting Australia. The main differences are deeper or lighter shadings. Their specific names are *Eolophus roseicapillus kuhli* and *Eolophus roseicapillus assimilis* and *Eolophus roseicapillus roseicapillus*. *E. e. roseicapillus* is far richer in shading than *E. e. kuhlii*.

Genus: *Nymphicus*

COCKATIEL *(Nymphicus hollandicus) (32 cm)*

This native of Australia is possibly the most popular pet of the parrot family except for the budgie. It well deserves this popularity, for there is no other bird which displays the gentleness and affection of the Cockatiel. If we were suddenly denied the pleasure of all our birds except one, we would unhesitatingly choose a Cockatiel to be that one pet. They become reasonably good talkers and whistlers, are excellent companions, are readily available, and are inexpensive.

In appearance, the Cockatiel is a long slender bird with an overall length of twelve inches, half of which is a long, tapering, pointed tail. Its head is topped by a long graceful crest which can be raised or lowered at will. The major portion of the bird is a soft grey color in both sexes. The wings have a prominent white band starting at the shoulders and extending across the secondary wing coverts.

Adult males have bright yellow in the face extending upwards into the crest. Each cheek is adorned with a bright orange circular patch about the size of a dime. The underparts of the tail are dark slate color.

Adult females and all immature young have only a slight tinge of yellow in the face and crest. Cheek patches are duller in color, and the tails show irregular yellow bars on the underside.

The Cockatiel has long been popular among bird-lovers by reason of its hardiness, prolificacy, gentle disposition and charm, although it is not exactly a silent bird . . . but there are many worse noises than its shrill "koerroe, kreeou."

Mauve Opaline showing a better wing pattern. The Opaline factor is variable and careful selective breeding must be carried out to improve the strain. With the knowledge of genetics, the budgie breeder automatically knows that this bird carries two factors for Opaline and two dark factors. The condition of the two "like" factors is termed "homozygous." If the bird should be split for another factor, it would be called "heterozygous."

Derbyan Parrakeet (genus: *Psittacula*). This very rare species is expensive. Females are much less colorful. The particular male obligingly gave the photographer a partially spread wing to show the paler portion. Owned by Dorothy Speed.

Birds forced into too-close contact because of the small size of their cage will be subjected to stresses that will affect their health and behavior.

Immature male Cockatiels begin to show patches of yellow on the face at the age of six months. It is a full year before the entire face is yellow. Another year elapses before full vividness of the coloring is attained. Until the age of six months, there is no completely accurate method of sexing Cockatiels. Bright cheek patches are believed by some to be males. Others prefer to use the pelvic bone test: close pelvic bones indicate males and bones separated by more than an eigth of an inch indicate females. In attempting to sex the birds, we can achieve a higher degree of accuracy by using both methods of identification and hoping for the best. Our score has held close to 75%.

The writers have reared hundreds of Cockatiels and consider them among the best of all easily reared birds. The best procedure is to let the birds make an attempt at nesting when they are a year old but not to expect real success until the birds are a full two years old. If the birds are successful the first year or on their first try, all well and good; but, if they are not successful, they should not be condemned.

A standard Cockatiel nest box as described in the chapter on Equipment and diet as described in the chapter on Feeding are used by the writers. Since Cockatiels are marvelous fliers, the largest flight possible is recommended,

Male (left) and female Cockatiel, showing the solid coloration of the underside of the male's tail feathers and the light areas on the female's tail feathers.

Grand Electus Parrots show striking color variations between the sexes. The predominantly green male is outshone by the more brilliant female. The vivid red and blue is contrasted by the deep maroon color in the wings. This pair is owned by Harold Rudkin.

White Crowned Parrot (genus: *Pionus*). This is an excellent photograph, showing the extent of white on the crown and throat. Owned by Jerome Buteyn.

even though they have successfully been reared in large breeding cages. Best success is attained if they are limited to one pair per flight. Since they will not harm even the smallest finches, the writers make it a point to keep a breeding pair in every possible flight whether it be with small finches, canaries, various kinds of doves, including the normally pugnacious Australian Crested Dove, and on up to Ringneck Parrakeets. Love Birds are not recommended as suitable aviary companions because of pugnacity towards baby Cockatiels. Sometimes even budgies have a tendency to deplume or scalp baby Cockatiels.

Colony breeding of Cockatiels (this means more than one pair per flight) is often successful but ordinarily slower than keeping a single pair per flight. There is a gregarious attitude which curtails interest in rearing progeny. Sometimes there are harmless arguments over nesting sites which also present a delaying action.

The Cockatiel is the only example of its genus and is said to be a connecting link between Cockatoos and parrakeets.

There is considerable variation in the colors of Cockatiels. The greys vary between light and dark, and some have an extensive yellow wash covering the entire body.

Several years ago, the writers fell into a discussion of Australia's beautiful birds with a lady from Australia. We emphasized that we thought the Cockatiel was the best pet to come from Australia. The lady insisted that a Quarrion bird made the best pet and said she had never heard of a Cockatiel. A little research showed that the Quarrion and Cockatiel were the same bird. "Quarrion" is a colloquial name of aboriginal origin.

No bird could be more highly recommended than a Cockatiel.

13

MACAWS AND CONURES

MACAWS

There are thirty species and subspecies of Macaws covering a range from Mexico to Paraguay and southern Brazil. Only a very few species are widely available. These species are distributed in three genera: *Anodorhynchus*, *Ara* and *Cyanopsitta*.

All Macaws have certain common characteristics: large beaks, long tails, and more or less bare facial areas. They are very hardy and long-lived. Some are among the largest and gaudiest members of the parrot tribe. Nearly all have ear-splitting voices at times. The natural call is harsh, grating, and unpleasant, but the talking voices show a remarkable range and are usually very soft. Ordinarily, Macaws are not credited with an exceptional talking ability. However, it has been our experience that most of the readily available species have an ability far beyond the limits reached by the average talking pet and are highly intelligent and playful.

Despite the forbidding, powerful beaks and large size, a young Macaw, properly handled, can turn into the gentlest of pets. We had a charming Blue and Gold once which seemed to enjoy being manhandled. He could be cradled upside down in anyone's arms or picked up bodily around the waist like an inanimate object. He also enjoyed gripping a finger inserted into his beak and being swung to and fro. Of course, this does not mean all Macaws can be so easily handled. Each one should be approached with care until its disposition becomes known.

Several species of Macaws have been reared in captivity. Suggestions for suitable aviaries and nest boxes are covered in the chapter on aviaries and equipment. Diet is covered in the chapter on Feeding. Breeding Macaws usually resent intrusion and can become vicious if disturbed.

Sexing Macaws is very difficult and can be deceptive. Males generally have larger, more masculine heads and broader beaks. In some cases males are larger than females.

The favorite pastime of Macaws is to chew anything which happens to be near. Since chewing is a very necessary exercise for their powerful beaks, it would be wise to give them plenty of wood scraps to use and to reinforce

Barraband Parakeet (genus: *Polytelis*). Owned by Dorothy Speed.

Blue or Mealy Rosella Parrakeet (genus: *Platycercus*). This is the least colorful member of the genus but it is still highly attractive and popular. This picture fails to show the faint tinges of blues and yellows on the lighter parts of this large parrakeet. Owned by Jerome Buteyn.

The richly colored blue Hyacinth Macaw has a deep gloss and a huge size. The bare skin area is yellow and is limited to an area surrounding the eyes and another surrounding the lower mandible.

Lear's Macaw is smaller than the Hyacinth and lacks the rich blue gloss. The dark blue coloring is quite dull. The larger bare facial area is a much paler shade of yellow than that found on the Hyacinth Macaw.

anything which should be preserved. Lignum Vitae, an extremely hard type of wood, is available in perches to fit standard parrot stands.

Pet Macaws are sometimes chained to a perch by means of a chain attached to the leg. Such treatment is not only inhumane but also dangerous for any type of bird. Sudden fright or accidental entangling may result in a twisted, badly injured leg. If the bird is a wanderer, clipped wings would be far better.

Larger Macaws are quite heavy and, for flying, need more room for a take-off than most birds their size. Since this requires quite an exertion, most Macaws in captivity much prefer to climb or walk about rather than fly. Pets usually are quite content to stay on a perch and seldom make an effort to move away.

Some of the Dwarf Macaws closely resemble some of the larger Conures. The bare facial area of the Macaw, which may sometimes be restricted to the loreal area between the eyes and the beak, is the main characteristic that differentiates the genus *Ara* (Macaws) from the genus *Aratinga* (Conures).

Genus: *Anodorhynchus*

HYACINTH MACAW *(Anodorhynchus hyacinthus) (100 cm.)*

This very hardy bird is the most magnificent of all the Macaws. It is about thirty-four inches long, has a massive and powerful black beak, black feet, and a larger body than any of the others. The overall color is a very rich and deep hyacinth blue showing considerable sheen in sunlight. The only other color is a bright yellow naked skin around the eye and the lower mandible.

A staggering value is placed upon these very rare birds. Seldom offered for sale, the asking price in the current market usually reaches close to $3,000.

GLAUCOUS MACAW *(Anodorhynchus glaucus) (72 cm).*

This is a very rare and smaller version of the Hyacinth and is approximately the same size as Lear's. It lacks the richness of plumage, being a dull slate blue in total coloring. The bill is black and the cheek patch yellow.

LEAR'S MACAW *(Anodorhynchus leari) (75 cm).*

This is a small version (slightly less than thirty inches) of the Hyacinth. Notable differences are the lack of luster to the blue and a different arrangement of the naked yellow areas on the head. The eye ring is present, but, instead of the narrow band framing the lower mandible, there is a circular cheek patch at the corners of the beak. The yellow is greatly faded. They are extremely hardy and playful rascals.

White Crowned Parrot (genus: *Pionus*). An excellent picture of a rare species showing the bronze in the wings and the variable nature of the deep, dusky blue. This specimen is owned by Jerome Buteyn.

Cockatiels

BLUE AND GOLD MACAW *(Ara ararauna)*, also called Blue and Yellow Macaw *(86 cm)*.

The Blue and Gold rivals the Scarlet in popularity, price, and availability. It is similar in size to the Scarlet, but it has a slightly shorter tail. The brilliant blue and golden yellow coloring is in perfect contrast to the beautiful scarlet. The upperside of the tail, wings, backside, and neck are rich, deep blue. Underparts are bright golden yellow. The underside of the tail is blue tinged with yellow. The crown is greenish tinged with blue. The beak and feet are black, and the large flesh white cheek patches are lined across the face with rows of tiny black feathers. A black bib-like collar frames the lower part of the face.

The Blue and Gold seems to be somewhat more alert and more intelligent than other species of Macaws. Certainly they are the most inquiring and mischievous. They are good talkers and speak in sharp, clear tones. Young are similar in coloring to adults but lack the rich sheen. Since the young play together in the rough and tumble manner of puppies, they often have frayed and broken tail feathers.

MILITARY MACAW *(Ara militaris) (70 cm)*.

This species has never achieved as much popularity as the Blue and Gold or the Scarlet, even though it is less expensive. It lacks the attractive coloring of the Scarlet and the Blue and Gold. The writers have never seen one whose personality matched the high level of the others.

The Military is similar in size to the Scarlet but has a shorter tail which gives it the appearance of being less well-proportioned.

The predominant color is dull, almost olive, green. The forehead is deep red; the beak is blackish; and the bare cheek patch is lined with tiny feathers like the Blue and Gold. The wings, especially the primary flight feathers, are deep, dull, bluish-red. The tail feathers are brownish-red on the upper surface and nearly olive-yellow underneath.

Three races of this bird occur: *Ara miltaris mexicana* from Mexico; *Ara militaris militaris* from the northwestern part of tropical South America; and *Ara militaris boliviana* from the tropical parts of Bolivia to the Argentine border.

GREEN WINGED MACAW *(Ara chloroptera) (90 cm)*.

This Macaw is often known as Maroon Macaw, Red and Green Macaw, or Red and Blue Macaw. If one name can be settled upon, it should be Green Winged, the literal translation of the name *chloroptera*.

The Blue and Gold Macaw is very popular, although protected by law. It is probably the best talker of its genus and becomes very attached to one person or one sex . . . but will bite strangers.

Barnard Parrakeet (genus: *Platycercus*). This is not a really good representation of a
Barnard. It was much more beautiful on a perch, but it refused to cooperate with the
photographer. Owned by Jerome Buteyn.

Elegant Parrakeets (in foreground) and Redrump Parrakeets (on wire mesh). The Elegant lacks brilliant colors, but it deserves its name. It has great charm, is easily bred, and is one of the most popular of Australian Parrakeets. Owned by Kenneth Wyatt.

It has a deeper shade of red than the Scarlet Macaw and dark green instead of yellow on the wings. The bare cheeks of the Scarlet are replaced by tiny deep red feathers lining the face. Flight feathers are blue, and tail feathers are a blue-tipped deep red. The beak is light on the upper mandible and black on the lower mandible.

It has a large head and beak and a stocky body. The tail is shorter than the Scarlet's, giving the bird a less well-proportioned appearance.

This species is no longer frequently available.

SCARLET MACAW *(Ara macao) (85 cm).*

Also called the Red and Yellow Macaw, this is the most frequently seen of all Macaws, and it is possibly the most vivid in color. It also is one of the least expensive, and it makes a fine pet.

Its overall length is approximately three feet, nearly half of which is a long tapering tail. The basic color is a brilliant overall scarlet which is slightly richer on the head. Bright yellow and blue appear abundantly on the wings. The rump is a pale blue. Th tail has a deeper shade of blue mixed with red. The large beak is whitish horn color on the upper mandible and black on the lower mandible. A large bare cheek patch is white flesh color. The colors of immature birds are less rich.

YELLOW NAPED MACAW *(Ara auricollis) (38 cm).*

Sixteen inches long and a native of Bolivia, this rare dwarf Macaw has the distinguishing feature of a yellow collar on the lower nape. The head is dark. The forehead is blackish, and the bare facial area is extensive. The crown and lower facial areas are dull green, and the body green is somewhat brighter. Blue occurs on the flight feathers, and the tail is bluish with dull red on the inner half. The underside of the tail is sooty greenish-yellow.

SEVERE MACAW *(Ara severa) (46 cm).*

This rare and unusual Macaw is one of the dwarf varieties and somewhat resembles the Military in miniature.

The total length is barely twenty inches.

The predominant color is dark green and is well marked by harmonious color accents. The crown has a bluish tinge; the forehead has a dark brown band at the base of the upper beak. The large white, bare cheek area has faint traces of the feather lines and is offset by the shiny black beak. The attractive blue of the crown is repeated in a richer shade in the flight feathers and is mixed with green on the upperside of the tail. Red predominates on the under-

The Military Macaw is very large and relatively inexpensive, but, since it is less vividly colored than the Blue and Yellow or the Scarlet Macaw, it has never attain-
. ed a great popularity in the United States.

Alexander Ringneck Parrakeet (genus: *Psittacula*). This is a huge parrakeet with a very long tail. If the long central tail feathers are missing, this bird looks ungainly and awkward because of the large head and bill. Note the large maroon wing patch. The wired portions help discourage playful chewing and ultimate destruction. Owned by Dorothy Speed.

Senegal Parrot, an unusually colored small parrot from Africa. This bird is owned by Dorothy Speed.

wing coverts and is mixed with brown on the underside of the tail and at the base on the upperside.

This bird is far better proportioned than the Military and is found far less frequently.

The few we have known seemed to have good dispositions and were fair talkers. One was particularly affectionate.

There are actually two races of this species which show only slight color variations. They are listed as *Ara severa severa* and *Ara severa castaneifrons*.

Of the two races of Severe Macaws, the race *castaneifrons* is slightly larger in body than the nominate race and has a brighter nape tinged with blue.

ILLIGER'S MACAW *(Ara maracana) (43 cm).*

There is a similarity between this Macaw and the Severe Macaw.

Of the fifteen inch length, the tail is seven and three-fourths inches.

The large beak is black. There is a red-orange crescent just above the nostrils followed by a blue-green head. The overall coloring is dull olive green. There are red tinges to the abdomen and bluish flights. The upper tail is reddish-brown shading to greenish and then to bluish at the tips. The underside of the tail is yellowish.

This bird looks something like a large Petz' Conure. Instead of orange on the forehead, the Macaw has a darker persimmon color.

RED BELLIED MACAW *(Ara manilata) (50 cm).*

The popular name of this bird is misleading because there is nothing more than the faintest tinge of orange in the olive coloring of the underparts. It should be called *Black Headed Macaw.*

The size of this very rare Macaw is fourteen and a half inches.

The bill is dark but lighter at the tips. The bare area of the face, more extensive than that of the Noble Macaw, extends around the eyes from the halfway point of the upper mandible to the halfway point of the lower mandible. The forehead is black and on the crown starts changing slowly to a bluish-green on the nape. The wings have bluish flights with black tips. The rest of the coloring is dull olive green, except the tail which has a dull reddish tinge on the upper side and a faint yellowish tinge to the underparts.

There are discrepancies between the description and the skins at the American Museum of Natural History. There is no black on the forehead, but there is dark red on the abdomen. The throat and chest are brownish olive-green, and the wings show dark blue in both bright and dull hues. The total length is sixteen inches of which the body totals seven and a half to eight inches.

NOBLE MACAW *(Ara nobilis nobilis) (30 cm).*

A fourteen-inch unpretentious Macaw, this smallest of the genus is a perfect replica of a larger Conure, the Blue Crowned Conure, *Aratinga acuticaudata acuticaudata,* from Brazil. The main difference is that the Conure lacks the bare facial area of the Macaw. In the Noble Macaw, the bare area is restricted to the region of lores and eyes.

The coloring is overall dull green with some red at the bend of the wing and extending around the rim for two inches. The underwings are red down to the end of the red rim showing from the upperside. The crown and forehead are of a bluish tinge, and the beak is black. The undersides of the five-inch tail have a dull yellowish tinge. The flight feathers are tinged with black.

A close relative is the *Ara nobilis longipennis.* The only appreciable difference is an overall length of fourteen inches, including a six and one-half inch tail. The beak is light on the upper mandible and black on the lower mandible.

Another subspecies is *Ara nobilis cumanensis.*

Noble Macaws are very similar to, but smaller than, some of the larger conures. The main difference is the bare skin area in the loreal region (between eyes and beak) of the Noble Macaw. Conures have bare eye rings.

King Parrakeet (genus: *Alisteris*). This large Australian Parrakeet is one of the most beautiful and majestic of all parrakeets. The female is much less colorful than the male. This particular picture shows the blue rump and the pale, but bright wing bar. This pair owned by Jerome Buteyn.

Yellow Cheeked Amazon. The amount of red identifies these as young birds because, as the birds grow older, the red creeps irregularly down into the cheeks. Owned by Jerome Buteyn.

Gaudy Macaws can attract as much attention with their voluble voices as they can with their violently brilliant colors.

COULON'S MACAW *(Ara coulini) (41 cm)*.

Coulon's Macaw is very similar to Illiger's Macaw, but it has no orange on the forehead. The blue on this area and the sides of the facial area are especially noticeable. The bare area on the face is grayish and is greatly reduced when compared to Illiger's. The tips on the beak are white.

RED CROWNED MACAW *(Ara rubrogenys) (60 cm)*.

The Red Fronted or Red Crowned Macaw from Bolivia has brilliant, fiery red-orange on the forehead and crown in a variable and uneven pattern. Bright orange occurs on the shoulders, scapulars, near the outer tips of the wings, and on the sides of the chest under the folded wings. The body is pale dull olive, and the flights are pale dull blue. The tail on the upperside is a dull greenish shade mixed with blue and yellowish and smoky gray on the underside. The thighs are reddish. The bare facial area is small with black feathered lines as in the Blue and Gold Macaw.

GREAT GREEN MACAW *(Ara ambigua) (85 cm)*.

The Great Green Macaw (subspecies *ambigua* from Nicaragua, Costa Rica, Panama, and western Colombia) is very much like the Military Macaw except for a few major differences. It is larger than the Military and has a tail

218

Ara chloroptera is known as the Red and Blue Macaw and as the Green Winged Macaw. These birds were imported as early as the end of the sixteenth century.

African Grey Parrot which is well known as one of the finest talking birds in the world. It is a popular favorite throughout the world, but it is rather expensive in the United States. Owned by Jerome Buteyn.

Male Grand Eclectus. The female is a brilliant red, maroon and blue bird with a black beak. This picture shows very clearly the furry type of feather covering most of the body. This bird is owned by Dorothy Speed.

fifteen inches long. It also has a paler shade of green with traces of brown on the chin and additional traces of brown scattered on the chest. .The head is much larger, and the beak is also larger than on the Military. The subspecies *guayaquilensis* from western Ecuador and possibly southwestern Colombia has a larger body and less brown on the chin.

WAGLER'S MACAW *(Arc caninde) (85 cm).*

Wagler's Macaw, little known and limited to Paraguay and northern Argentina, is very much like the Blue and Gold Macaw. It is regarded by some to be a southern race or perhaps an age stage of the Blue and Gold. There are significant differences, however. There is no greenish tinge on the forehead, but there is a broad green band on the throat instead of black. This green band surrounds the bare skin on the face. The bare facial area is smaller. The feathered lines on the face are more numerous on the lores and the upper part of the cheeks. and they are green in color. The total length is about thirty inches long including the nineteen-inch tail. It therefore is not a Dwarf Macaw.

Genus: *Cyanopsitta*

SPIX MACAW *(Cyanopsitta spixii) (56 cm).*

This very rare Macaw has the reputation of being intelligent and affectionate, with some talent for talking and no worse proclivity for screaming than Amazons.

These birds do quite well in large cages if left out for daily exercise. As to their ability to stand cold there seems to be little information.

A pair of Spix Macaws hatched a young one, but did not rear it. The cock fed the hen while she was sitting, and the pair were very spiteful to other birds.

Spix Macaws, when young, should be given bread and milk.

CONURES

Genus: *Aratinga*

Members of the genus *Aratinga* have a wide variation in color, size, and habitat. They range from Mexico southward through a large part of South America.

222

The Spix Macaw, *Cyanopsitta spixii*. Photo by New York Zoological Society.

Fischer's Love Bird, a highly colorful and popular member of the Love Bird Family. Several members are very plentiful and easily bred. Owned by Palos Verdes Bird Farm.

Red Vented or Blue Headed Parrot (*Pionus menstruus*). This is one of the smoothest and prettiest of the South American Parrots. The female has a smaller head and a less vivid blue. Owned by Dorothy Speed.

The main common characteristic of these birds is the long and slender shape, with a long tapering tail, large head, and large beak.

Conures are like Macaws in miniature. However, some of the large Conures are larger than some of the dwarf Macaws. The basic difference between the two genera lies in the size of the bare eye ring; it is much smaller in Conures. Macaws have some bare facial areas.

Conures of the genus *Aratinga* often become excellent and affectionate pets if tamed young. They are also fair talkers. Many are very common while others are very rare. Nearly all have tremendous voices and are not recommended for crowded localities.

BLUE CROWNED or SHARP TAILED CONURE *(Aratinga acuticaudata) (37 cm)*.

A large fourteen-inch Conure with a seven-inch tail, the Blue Crowned is a perfect replica of Noble's Macaw except that it is slightly larger and has no bare areas around the lores. The head has more blue, especially on the crown. The overall coloring is dull green with some reddish at the base of the undertail. The beak is dark greyish-black, lighter at the tips.

This is a very common Conure in captivity.

Its habitat is eastern Colombia, northern Venezuela, Uruguay and Argentina; also on Margarita Island.

Other races include *Aratinga acuticaudata haemorrhous* from eastern Brazil and *Aratinga acuticaudata neumanni* from Cochabamba, Santa Cruz and likely Tarija and Chuquisaca (Bolivia).

The subspecies *haemorrhous* is usually correctly called the Blue Crowned Conure, even though the blue is less extensive on the crown. It is also about an inch smaller than the other varieties.

QUEEN OF BAVARIA CONURE *(Aratinga guarouba) (34 cm)*.

The Queen of Bavaria Conure from northwestern Brazil is also called the Golden or Yellow Conure. It is one of the rarest, most expensive, and most striking of all Conures.

This species is an overall brilliant golden yellow with rich green flight feathers. The large bill is pinkish, and the eye is orange.

The length is slightly over fourteen inches. It is large and heavy bodied.

JANDAY CONURE *(Aratinga jandaya) (30 cm)*

The outstanding Janday Conure is one of the favorites in the large family of Conures. It is more expensive than most Conures in the United States, but is far less expensive than the majority of rare Parrakeets. The Janday is usually available and finds a ready market.

The vivid and vibrant beauty of the Janday is dimmed only by its loud

The Green Conure *(Aratinga h. holochlora)* is known for its harsh voice, but the bird is unusually intelligent and has a talent for talking. The female has a broader beak.

Finsch's Conure is an attractive red and green conure with red on the head almost restricted to the forehead. It is smaller than the Cherry Headed or Wagler's Conure.

Plumhead Parrakeet (genus: *Psittacula*). This lovely species is not too well represented in the photograph because the long central tail feathers are missing. This detracts from the usual appearance of graceful charm. The bright maroon wing patch shows very clearly. Females of this species have grey heads instead of plum-colored heads. **Owned by** Jerome Buteyn.

Rock Pebbler Parrakeet (genus: *Polytelis*). This is one of the loveliest and most graceful of the Australian Parrakeets. The long slender tail is mostly hidden in this picture. This pair is owned by Dorothy Speed.

and raucous voice, a disadvantage in some environments. A few have been tamed and have made fairly good talkers. However, they are good breeders and, therefore, few ever receive training.

The bird should be seen to be appreciated. The male is ten inches long, including the long tapering tail. The body is stocky and the head is large. The beak is shiny black. The head, neck, throat, and chest areas are golden yellow with a rich tint of red above the beak reaching out, encircling the eyes, and covering the ear coverts. There are other tinges of red highlighting the yellow areas and graduating to the solid deep red abdomen. The thighs and vent area are dull green with some red flecks. The underside of the tail is black. The upperside of the tail is olive green in the center shading to deep blue and black at the tips. The back and wings are bright green with some blue in the flights. The rump is green with some red seeping through. There is considerable variation in the vividness of the yellow and the extent of the red mixtures which can be attributed to diet and to age.

As a rule, females and immature birds have less red mixed in the facial and chest areas and have some green flecking in the chest.

Its native habitat is northeastern Brazil.

SUN CONURE or YELLOW CONURE *(Aratinga solstitialis) (30 cm)*

The Sun Conure is considerably more rare, and more highly coveted, than the Queen of Bavaria Conure. Coming from the Guianas, it is like the Janday in size.

The overall coloring is bright orange-yellow, except for the green wings and tail, which are green shading to blue on the outer sides and tips.

GREEN CONURE *(Aratinga holochlora) (32 cm)*

The unpretentious Green Conure, or Green Parrakeet as it is called by some, is ten to twelve inches long, including the long five- to five-and-a-half-inch pointed tail.

It has a large head and bill and is an overall bright green, paler on the undersides. Flecks of red occasionally appear on the chest.

It inhabits the foothills and mountains of eastern and southern Mexico.

The nominate race of the Green Conure *(holochlora)* also has a few flecks of red on the lower cheeks.

GREEN CONURE *(Aratinga holochlora strenua) (32 cm)*.

This Green Conure is eleven inches long including the tail of five and one-half inches which is smaller than the other all green Conure *(Aratinga leucophthalmus)*. The shade of green is also darker. The eye ring in *strenua* is a dark grayish shade, and the bare skin is rough in texture compared to the eye ring of *leucophthalmus*, which is white and more extensive.

The native range of this bird extends over the Pacific slopes of Mexico and Central America; some authorities consider it to be a full species, not a subspecies.

Other highly similar races include:

Aratinga holochlora brewsteri from Sonora, Sinaloa, and Chihuahua in Mexico.

Aratinga holochlora brevipes from Socorro Island off the west coast of Mexico. This species is ten and a half inches long, including a long and narrow tail of four and a half inches.

Aratinga holochlora holochlora from eastern and southern Mexico.

Aratinga holochlora rubritorquis, called Red Throated Conure. This is a more southerly subspecies with some red flecking on the face and a red band on the throat. It comes from eastern Guatemala, Salvador, Honduras and northern Nicaragua.

FINSCH'S CONURE *(Aratinga finschi) (28 cm)*

This is another green Conure with a red forehead, red at the bend of the wing, and a pale horn-colored bill. It is smaller than most of the others, being just a little over eleven inches. The habitat is tropical Central America.

RED FRONTED or WAGLER'S CONURE *(Aratinga wagleri) (36 cm)*.

The Red Fronted Conure from Colombia and northern coastal region of western Venezuela is another large, fourteen-inch species. It is all green, paler on the underparts and richer on the upperparts. The crown and forehead are red, and there are some red fleckings on the throat. The bill is a pale horn color.

There are four races:

Aratinga wagleri wagleri from north-western Venezuela and Colombia.

Aratinga wagleri transilis from the Paria Peninsula in northeast Venezuela.

Aratinga wagleri frontata from western Ecuador and western Peru.

Aratinga wagleri minor from north central Peru.

MITRED CONURE *(Aratinga mitrata) (38 cm)*.

The Mitred Conure is another red and green Conure. It has a red face and flecks on the neck and occasionally on the chest. The bill is whitish horn color.

The total length is fifteen inches and the habitat is the subtropic zone of central Peru and southward to central Bolivia and western Argentina.

A subspecies, *Aratinga mitrata alticola,* is limited to the temperate zone of central Peru in the region of Cuzco.

231

Hawk Headed Parrot (genus: *Deroptyus*). The profile shows the unusual coloring on the neck. Owned by Dorothy Speed.

Festive Amazon Parrot. The most noticeable feature is hidden when the wings are folded: The rump is a brilliant glossy red. Other than the rump, the dominant characteristics are the plum-colored band on the forehead followed by a powdery blue shade. Owned by Jerome Buteyn.

CHERRY HEADED CONURE or RED HEADED CONURE *(Aratinga erythrogenys) (33 cm).*

A large Conure of twelve to thirteen inches long, including a three and a half inch tail, the Cherry Headed Conure has a large head and a large horn-colored beak. The overall coloring is bright green with a red rim framing the wings and red covering the head halfway back on the crown and surrounding the eye and cheek area. The large eye ring is yellowish. There is also a trace of red on the thighs.

This species is quite attractive, but it is rare in the United States. Its former name was *Aratinga rubrolarvata* and was popularly called the Red Masked Conure.

GREEN CONURE *(Aratinga leucophthalamus) (32 cm).*

This Conure is thirteen to fourteen inches in length and has a large head and bill.

It is completely green except for a few flecks of red on the head and neck, red at the bend of the wing, and reddish underwing coverts. The bill is yellowish horn color, and the bare eye ring is whitish.

The bill of the female is said to be broader than that of the male.

The Green Conure is not frequently seen in the United States, and there is not much demand for it because of its unimaginative color scheme. This species, however, appears to be quite intelligent.

The natural habitat is a wide range of tropical South America, including the Guianas, Colombia, Bolivia, and Brazil. There are four subspecies.

The Ecuadorian All-Green Conure, subspecies *callogenys,* has extensive red on the lower face, chin, and throat also forming a narrow red collar on the lower nape. It inhabits the tropical zones of eastern Ecuador and northeastern Peru.

HAITIAN CONURE *(Aratinga chloroptera chloroptera)*

The Haitian Conure from the Island of Hispaniola, ten to eleven inches long including the tail of five and one-half inches, has red on the underwing coverts. It is less bright in green than Mauge's Conure.

MAUGE'S CONURE *(Aratinga chloroptera maugei) (32 cm)*

This species is similar to the Cuban Conure and is from Mona Island; now extinct.

CUBAN CONURE *(Aratinga euops) (26 cm).*

Also called the Red Speckled or Euops' Conure, the Cuban Conure inhabits Cuba and was formerly found on the Isle of Pines.

Left: Green Conure *(Aratinga leucocephalus)*. The largest of all-green Conures, this species has a vivid white eye ring. Flecks of red occasionally appear on the head and neck. Right: *Aratinga holochlora.*

Cherry Headed or Red Headed Conure is a shapely and attractive green Conure with red on the sides of the face as well as the top of the head.

Red Rosella Parrakeets (genus: *Platycercus*). One of the most popular and most brilliant members of the genus. The angle of this picture does not show the characteristic wing pattern which is typical of most members of the genus. Note the less brilliant and less precise coloring of the female. Owned by Kenneth Wyatt.

Hybrid Rosella Parrakeets (Yellow Rosella x Brown's Rosella). This is one of the exceptions to the rule that hybrids are not as attractive as either parent. The surprising outcome is the red on the chest of the female which is not only lacking in the male hybrid but is also lacking on both parents. Owned by Kenneth Wyatt.

Its length is slightly over ten inches, and its basic color is green.

There are red flecks on the sides of the head and at the bend of the wing with a solid red on the underwing coverts. The large bill is a whitish-horn color.

WEDDEL'S CONURE *(Aratinga weddellii) (28 cm)*

Weddel's Conure is twelve inches long, including the long tapering tail.

It is green, yellowish on the chest, and has a golden brown tinge on the back. The head is brown with paler edges to the feathers and a faint bluish tinge on the crown. The beak is horn colored. The flights are bluish. The tail and rump have a golden brown tinge.

The habitat of this rare species is the Amazonian drainage area in Ecuador, Peru, Bolivia, and western Brazil.

Aztec Conure, like the Half Moon or Petz' Conure in size and coloring. The Aztec has the orange on the head limited to a narrow band between the nostrils.

AZTEC or OLIVE THROATED CONURE *(Aratinga nana astec) (26 cm)*.
This ten and a half inch species, which includes the four and a half inch tail, resembles the Petz' Conure in shape and basic coloring except for the beak. The upper mandible is less broad and massive at the base. Both mandibles are of a horn color with some darker streaks. The eye ring is less pronounced and is whitish. The basic coloring is green with some blue in the flights. The undersides are a paler shade of olive green except for the duller olive tinge to the throat and chest. There are traces of small orange feathers between the nostrils. The undersides of the flight feathers are slate, and the rest of the underwing feathers are light green. The underside of the tail is dull olive-greenish with a tinge of yellow.

The habitat is the humid zone of the Caribbean slope of Mexico and Central America. In the United States it is common and is often sold as an immature Petz' Conure.

A second race, *Aratinga nana vicinalis,* inhabits northeastern Mexico in the central part of Tamaulipas.

JAMAICAN CONURE *(Aratinga nana) (26 cm)*.
This is a well known Conure that lives on the slopes of tropical Central America from Tamaulipas to western Panama. It is ten and a half inches long and is mostly green with a brownish throat and chest. The flights are bluish, and the abdomen is a shading of olive. The bill is a whitish horn color, the legs are grey.

PETZ' CONURE or HALFMOON CONURE *(Aratinga canicularis eburnirostrum) (24 cm)*
Nine and a half inches long, including a four-inch tail, the Halfmoon's basic coloring is green, darker on the upperparts and paler olive on the lower parts. The flights have some dark blue mixed in with the green. The Macawlike beak is a horn color on the upper mandible an black on the sides of the lower mandible. The large bare eye ring is yellowish. The forehead has a band of orange which becomes more extensive with age. The crown is dull blue.

The Halfmoon Conure from western Mexico is one of the most popular parrot-like pets in the United States. It is almost always sold as a "dwarf parrot" and is quite reasonable in cost.

Except for its noisy habits, the Halfmoon is an almost perfect pet. If the reader contemplates buying a Halfmoon, he should be certain that it is a young bird capable of being tamed or else one that is already tamed. An adult bird can be a formidable adversary if it does not wish to be tamed. Another race, *Aratinga canicularis canicularis,* inhabits the Pacific slopes of Central America. *Aratinga canicularis claroe* comes from Western Mexico.

Immature White Bellied Caique. As it matures the black will disappear from the crown and be replaced by a bright apricot-orange. The beak also will lose the dark coloring near the base. Owned by Palos Verdes Bird Farm.

Male Indian Ringneck Parrakeet (genus: *Psittacula*). This picture shows the characteristic frontal band, plum-colored bill, moustache and collar, and the long graceful tail. This is the most prevalent and inexpensive member of the genus. It is a good breeder, but young birds take two to three years to assume adult coloration. Owned by Palos Verdes Bird Farm.

GOLDEN HEADED CONURE *(Aratinga auricapilla aurifrons) (30 cm).*

This Conure is rare in the United States and resembles the Petz' or Half-moon Conure.

It inhabits southeastern Brazil and is ten and a half inches long, including the four and a half inch tail.

The only appreciable difference from Petz' Conure is a slightly larger head and a different arrangement of the orange on the forehead. Instead of a wide band of orange, there is a circular patch starting at the forehead and extending to the crown.

A second larger race, with very minor differences, is *Aratinga auricapilla auricapilla* from Bahia in eastern Brazil.

The race *auricapilla* is nine to ten inches long including the five inch tail, and the subspecies *aurifrons* from southeastern Brazil is about an inch longer. This species looks very much like a very dull Janday Conure. The beak is black. A red fringe on the forehead and lores surrounds the eyes. The crown is yellow, brighter and more extensive on the race *aurifrons*. Dark and dusky red is irregularly scattered on the abdomen and sides with a brighter flash on the underwing coverts. The chest is dull grayish-green. Upperparts are green with bright but dark blue on the wings and olive on the tail.

BROWN EARED CONURE *(Aratinga pertinax ocularis) (25 cm).*

Slightly over nine inches with a four-inch tail, this rather dull species is basically green, lighter on the undersides and darker on the uppersides. The crown and forehead have a bluish tinge. The sides of the face, cheeks, lores, and throat are brownish, each feather characterized by a dark outer margin and a dull yellowish tinge to the center. The bare eye ring is whitish, and the beak is dark. There is some blue in the flights.

The natural habitat is Panama on the Pacific side.

The Brown Eared Conure makes a nice little pet. It is not often available, perhaps the result of very little damand because of its dull coloration.

One in our collection has selected our favorite Petz' Conure for a mate and has laid eggs.

Peters lists eight subspecies of *Aratinga pertinax,* and one other race *(chrysogenys)* is also recognized. Popular names vary more than the slight variations in color, and none is very attractive. The subspecies most likely to become available to bird fanciers is *ocularis*. The minor difference in this race is the trace of orange concentrated under the eyes. Since all are much the same, only the differences not previously described will be mentioned here. The Brown Throated Conure (subspecies *aeruginosa*) has a tinge of orange on the abdomen as one of its most notable differences. This race from Colombia and Venezuela is also likely to become available from time to time. The race *margaritensis* has a whitish forehead, a bluish crown, and yellowish-orange in

242

the cheeks. The island race *tortugensis* also has orange-yellow on the cheeks and face as well as a pale but brighter green on the sides and middle abdomen. The Yellow Cheeked Conure (subspecies *chrysophrys*) actually has less yellow than the Margarita, Tortuga, Aruba, Bonaire, St. Thomas or Brazilian races. The Aruba Conure (subspecies *arubensis*) has a whitish tinge on the forehead and traces of yellow on the abdomen. St. Thomas' Conure (the nominate race *pertinax*) has some yellow on the abdomen, a dull brownish-olive on the chest, and bright orange-yellow over all the facial areas and the forehead. The upperparts are very bright green. The Bonaire Conure (subspecies *xanthogenia*) shows some yellow on the forehead, orange on the crown and cheeks, and a brownish-olive on the throat. The Brazilian race of the Brown Throated Conure (subspecies *chrysogenys* from the Rio Negro Yavanori district) has orange surrounding the eyes with a heavier concentration at the lower rear area. The olive-brown is smooth and evenly distributed on the rest of the face, throat, and chest shading into an orange-olive shade on the abdomen.

BROWN THROATED CONURE *(Aratinga pertinax aeruginosa) (25 cm).*
The Brown Throated Conure is a subspecies of the Brown Eared Conure. It is sometimes called the Chocolate Faced Conure. It is similar to the Brown eared, except for a lesser shade of brown on the cheeks and a whitish bill.

MARGARITA BROWN THROATED CONURE *(Aratinga pertinax margaritensis) (25 cm).*
This subspecies is the Brown Throated race from Margarita Island and the Paria Peninsula on the Venezuelan mainland.

TORTUGA CONURE *(Aratinga pertinax tortugensis) (25 cm).*
This subspecies is the Tortuga Island race of the Brown Throated, found off the northern coast of Venezuela.

YELLOW CHEEKED CONURE *(Aratinga pertinax chrysophrys) (25 cm)*
The Yellow Cheeked Conure resembles other members of the species, except for a few variations. There is some orange showing on the abdomen and on the face surrounding the eyes. The bare eye skin is bluish.
The Yellow Cheeked Conure is native to British Guiana, Cayenne, and Surinam.

ARUBA CONURE *(Aratinga pertinax arubensis) (25 cm)*
This Conure comes from the Island of Aruba. It is similar to the Yellow Cheeked.

Redrump Parrakeets. The dull colored female is at left. The male obligingly displays his red rump for the photographer. Owned by Kenneth Wyatt.

Bourke's and Redrump Parrakeets. These are among the most popular of Australian Parrakeets. Both species are very attractive and easily bred. Bourke's Parrakeet is almost extinct in its native habitat, but skilled aviculturists have successfully established it as an aviary breeder. There is no longer any real danger of the complete disappearance of this delightful and charming species. Owned by Kenneth Wyatt.

ST. THOMAS' CONURE *(Aratinga pertinax pertinax) (25 cm)*

St. Thomas' Conure is like the Yellow Cheeked Conure except that the orange is less vivid but more extensive. It covers the forehead, cheeks, throat, and part of the abdomen. The rear of the crown is slate blue, and the flights are bluish. The chest is pale brown shading to yellowish green on the lower part.

Its habitat is the Virgin Islands and the island of Curacao. On St. Thomas it was introduced.

BONAIRE CONURE *(Aratinga pertinax xanthogenia) (25 cm).*

This subspecies is the Yellow Cheeked from the Island of Bonaire.

CACTUS CONRE *(Aratinga cactorum cactorum) (25 cm).*

From Brazil comes this pleasant eleven-inch, long-tailed Conure.

The bill is whitish and the head brownish. The throat and chest are brown followed by yellowish olive. Flights and tail are grey-blue.

It is rare in the United States but there probably would not be a great demand due to its dull coloration. In Europe it is very popular.

A second race, *Aratinga cactorum caixana,* inhabits eastern Brazil.

GOLDEN CROWNED CONURE *(Aratinga aurea aurea) (26 cm).*

Ten inches long, half of which is a tapering tail, this is another Conure closely resembling Petz' Conure. It has a black beak, both upper and lower mandibles. The orange on the forehead is very bright and is a circular patch covering the entire forehead and crown.

This species comes from Brazil and north-western Argentina.

A second race, *Aratinga aurea major,* comes from the Paraguay River.

Genus: *Nandayus*

NANDAY CONURE *(Nandayus nenday) (30 cm).*

The popular Nanday Conure, from South America, has an attractive color scheme that shows up best in the company of the brighter and better known Janday Conure. In its own right, however, it is one of the most attractive members of the very large group of Conures.

The basic color scheme is black and green with a bright red accent. The bill and head are black. Many of the wing feathers are deep blue-black. The tail is black on the underside and bluish green on the upperside. The rest of the bird is a bright green which is darker on the uppersides and bluish on the chest. The ear coverts are green. Relief from the dignified and somber color

246

The Golden Crowned Conure is easily tamed and becomes docile and affectionate, although breeding pairs are spiteful with other birds.

scheme comes with the bright red thighs. We call it the bird with the red silk stockings. The black legs and feet highlight the red.

The Nanday is a well-proportioned bird of twelve inches, including the long tapering tail.

It is an ideal aviary bird and is a reasonably free breeder if given proper conditions. It is usually peaceful with other birds of similar size but a little aggressive during breeding operations. The only drawback to the Nanday, indeed with nearly all Conures, is the powerful voice, which can reach ear-splitting proportions in close quarters.

We have had pairs of adult Nandays take food from our fingers despite the fact that no concerted effort was given to training or taming. A single young Nanday could become a good pet with proper finger training; but, as a talking pet, its vocabulary would be somewhat limited.

The Nanday is the only member of its genus, but it is close in appearance to many members of the genus *Aratinga*.

247

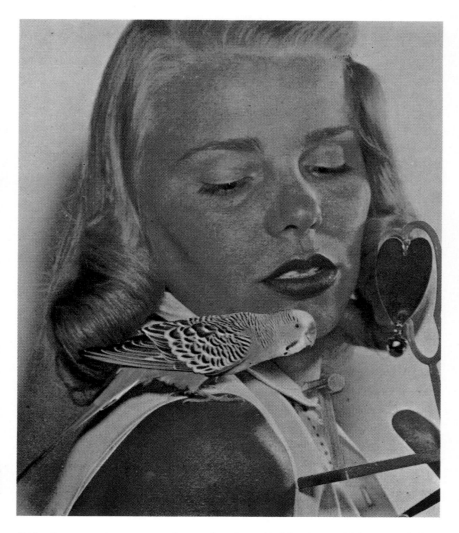

Budgerigars are the most popular species of pet bird in the world because of their adaptability to training and their ability to talk.

Female of Everett's Blue Backed Parrot (genus: *Tanygnathus*), a rare species from the Philippine Islands. This female is typical of all females of the genus in that the colors are far less vivid than in the male. Owned by Jerome Buteyn.

Genus: *Leptosittaca*

GOLDEN EARED or GOLDEN PLUMED CONURE *(Leptosittaca branickii) (35 cm).*

The long and slender Golden Eared Conure is from the humid temperate zone of the Andes Mountains from southern Ecuador to central Peru. It is thirteen inches long including the six and one-half inch tail. Bare skin surrounds the eyes, and the beak is horn colored. The main coloring is a bright shade of green which is duller and less glossy on the undersides. There are reddish-orange traces on the abdomen and dull reddish areas on the underside of the tail. The flights also have a bluish-black band on the outer tips. The most distinctive feature is a long yellow-orange wisp of feathers located above the ear and trailing beyond the eyes. A brownish-orange shade occasionally occurs on the lores. This distinctive species, the only known one in its genus, falls into place between the Nanday and Patagonian Conures.

Genus: *Cyanoliseus*

LESSER PATAGONIAN CONURE *(Cyanoliseus patagonus) (45 cm).*

The lesser Patagonian Conure is eighteen inches long, including a ten and a half inch tail. In its native habitat of Argentina it is called the Bank or Burrowing Parrot because it burrows up to five feet into the side of cliffs or banks to nest. Being sociable, these Conures live in colonies and nest closely together. Gradually, the Patagonian Conure is dying out. It is rare in captivity, but good numbers of this species should be made available to interested students of aviculture to keep it from becoming extinct.

The Patagonian Conure is attractive. The basic coloring is olive-green with a blackish cast, darker on the upper parts, almost black on the forehead and crown, and paler on the underparts. The throat has a greater concentration of olive coloring. There is a very narrow white band across the upper chest which ends in large white spots on the shoulders. The abdomen is yellow with red flecks concentrated in a solid area in the center. The lower ends of the thighs are red. The bill is black, and there is a very prominent white eye ring.

The species contains two other subspecies in addition to *C. patagonus patagonus: Cyanoliseus patagonus andinus* and *Cyanoliseus patagonus byroni.* The latter is called the Greater Patagonian Conure and comes from central Chile. It is similar to the Lesser Patagonian Conure except for its larger size of twenty inches. Also, the whitish chest band is slightly more prominent. The Lesser Patagonian Conure is from central and southern Argentina.

Greater Patagonian Conures are very rare and very unusual in color. This species is slowly dying out in South America. Unfortunately, very few are available to aviculturists who might succeed in domesticating them.

Top: Normal blue budgies. Budgies are available in a wide range of color varieties. *Right:* "Rare" parrakeets. These budgies showing various newer color combinations were very expensive only a few years ago. Now, through skilled handling by breeders, the so-called "rares" are as inexpensive as the older color varieties called "normals".

Genus:*Pyrrhura*

The numerous Conures of the genus *Pyrrhura* are unmistakably related to each other because of a basic pattern similarity. All are approximately the same size and have exposed nostrils, long tapering tails with a reddish shade on the underside, and an olive green coloring on the upperparts. The most prominent characteristic in all species is a scaled chest. In most cases, the colors of the chest are buffish or yellowish feathers with darker, usually brownish, outer margins. Usually, but not always, there is a bluish tinge to the wings and a variable, dull reddish abdominal patch matching the color of the underside of the tail. Most frequently, the bill is black, but in some species it is light horn in color. Highly variable in different species but always present is a prominent cheek patch covering a rather larger area than the ear coverts.

Members of the genus *Pyrrhura* are all rather small, ranging generally from eight to ten and a half inches in length, including the long tapering tail of four to five inches.

Their range extends from Costa Rica to southern Brazil and northern Argentina.

All are quite rare in captivity, and some have no records of domesticated life. Since many are quite similar in appearance, and since very little avicultural literature is dedicated to this genus, there has been much confusion properly identifying those which have been kept in captivity.

RED BELLIED CONURE *(Pyrrhura frontalis frontalis) (26 cm).*

From southeastern Brazil comes the Red Bellied Conure, the most typical species of the genus. Its general coloring is dark green with the following variations: some blue in the flights, dull reddish on the underside of the tail, red above the nostrils, prominent whitish bare eye ring, blackish bill, dull red on the abdomen between the legs, brown ear coverts with streaks of dull yellow in each feather, and a barred chest. The chest and sides have dull yellow feathers with dark brownish outer margins which give it the barred characteristic. Note the pale buffish tips on some of the feathers on the nape.

The Red Bellied Conure is nine inches long including the tail of nearly five inches.

AZARA'S CONURE *(Pyrrhura frontalis chiripepe) (26 cm).*

From eastern Salta and Paraguay comes this ten-inch subspecies, including a tail of four and three-fourths inches. Like other *Pyrrhura*, it has the scalloped chest area. The buff ear coverts are darker than those of most species. Red is scattered irregularly on the abdomen. The underside of the tail is reddish. There is also a fine band of brown above the beak.

Pyrrhura frontalis kriegi, from Brazil, is a ten-inch subspecies, including a four-inch tail. Typical of the genus, it has green upperparts with a bluish hue in the wings and reddish in the tail. The undertail is red. The red abdomen is present, and the chest is scaled with yellowish tips to the feathers. There is a thin brown line above the nostrils. The beak is blackish.

RED EARED CONURE *(Pyrrhura cruentata) (30 cm).*

The Red Eared Conure from the coastal states of Brazil is ten and a half inches long, including a tapering tail of five inches.

The overall coloring is a dull olive green with the following exceptions: bluish in the upper flights, deep maroon irregularly spread over the abdomen, undertail dull dusky red, bluish tinge to chest, bill black, maroon on lores, and a pale orange-brown following lores and up into the sides of the neck.

WHITE EARED CONURE *(Pyrrhura leucotis) (23 cm)*

Nine inches long, including the four-inch tail, the White Eared Conure is found in the Brazilian coastal states and northern Venezuela.

A basic dark green occurs on the upperwings, sides, and vent. There is a deep maroon above and through the rump with green at the sides. There is some brownish maroon on the tail which is darker on the upperside. The abdomen is a reddish brown surrounded by green. The head is brownish, the beak is black, and the collar is bluish. The lores and area under the lores are maroon. The ear coverts are whitish. The chest has green feathers scalloped with buff and a narrower fine line of black at the tips.

Sexes are alike.

With its brighter and more vivid color scheme, this is one of the most attractive members of the genus.

Recognized races are: *Pyrrhura leucotis griseipectus* from northeastern Brazil; *Pyrrhura leucotis pfrimeri* from Goyaz in north-eastern Brazil; *Pyrrhura leucotis emma* from the Caribbean coastal areas of Venezuela; and the nominate race from Bahia to Sao Paulo. The race *griseipectus* is slightly smaller, has grayish ear coverts, no blue on the head, and less red on the tail and abdomen. Emma's Conure (subspecies *emma*) has bright maroon on the lower cheeks, maroon in the center of the abdomen and lower chest, a bluish forehead and forecrown with a narrow maroon band above the nostrils extending to the lores. The ear covert coloring is reduced to a pearly buff rather than a prominent white. Red on the shoulders is bright. The small beak is black, and the total length is eight and one-half inches including the four inch tail. The subspecies *pfrimeri* is quite similar to Emma's Conure but has far more maroon on the face and above the eyes with less blue on the forehead. The scaled tips of the chest feathers are whitish, and the red starts higher on

Male Philippine Green Parrot (genus: *Tanygnathus*), a rare and attractive species from the Philippine Islands. Note the curious pattern of colors in the wing which is characteristic of all members of the genus. Owned by Jerome Buteyn.

Military Macaw (genus: *Ara*). This species has a longer tail than the one in the picture. It lacks the beautiful coloring and graceful proportions of the Scarlet and the Blue and Gold but has the advantage of being available at a lower price. Owned by Jerome Buteyn.

the chest. A reasonably new subspecies, *auricularis*, is slightly larger than Emma's conure and has yellowish tips on the scales of the lower chest area.

PEARLY CONURE *(Pyrrhura perlata perlata) (24 cm)*.

This nine and a half inch species is mainly green with the generic characteristics present: blue flights, reddish tail and abdomen, and scaled chest. Most of the head is dark, dull brown with a pale buffish patch on the ear coverts. Tinges of blue occur on the forehead, nape, cheeks, upper chest, and sides. A darker shade of blue occurs on the vent and tail coverts.

The range is northeastern Brazil.

Other races are *Pyrrhura perlata coerulescens* and *Pyrrhura perlata anerythra*.

The Pearly Conure has very prominent contrasts in the scaled chest because of the bright buff scalloped tips. Behind these scallops, the chest is very dark green with a blue wash. The lower facial area is tinged with dark bluish green, and a dark blue band occurs on the nape. The flights are very deep and bright blue. The beak is small and black. The subspecies *coerulescens* is slightly larger, and the race *anerythra* has a slight cast of orange-buff mingled on the throat scales. Another subspecies, usually called *lepida* but not finally settled when Peters' volume went to press, has more extensive and brighter blue on the wings and underparts.

BLAZE WINGED CONURE *(Pyrrhura devillei) (26 cm)*.

The Blaze Winged Conure from eastern Bolivia and the southern Matto Grosso is just under nine inches in length including the four inch tail. A narrow reddish-brown forehead merges into brown on the crown with the feathers edged in green. The cheeks are green, and the ear coverts are grayish-brown. The base color of the chest is olive-brown with each feather scaled on the tips with a narrow pale band preceded by a dusky blackish shade. Brownish-red dominates the abdomen, and crimson occurs prominently on the bend of the wing and smaller underwing coverts with black on the greater underwing coverts. Blue highlights the primary flights and primary coverts. Remaining upperparts are green. The tail is olive on the upperside and coppery reddish-brown on the underside with olive tips on each feather.

SANTA MARTA CONURE *(Pyrrhura viridicata) (25 cm)*.

The Santa Marta Conure from the Santa Marta Mountains of Colombia is nine inches long including the tail of four and one-half inches. Mostly green, this species has most of the scaled effect on the chest diminished to the point where only traces remain. The flights are bright blue; the rump is

Not all of the Conures are equally adaptable to training, but among those that are, patience and kindness and consistency must be used in the training program. Here a Halfmoon Conure (also called Petz' Conure) is being taught to eat food from its owner's hand as a first step in the taming process by which it will become a real pet.

Citron Crested Cockatoo with its owner, Dorothy Speed. In size and shape, the beautiful Citron Crested is a miniature of the Greater Sulphur Crested Cockatoo. A bright orange crest and a pale orange cheek patch are the other differences.

Gang Gang Cockatoo. This is a very rare and unusual species of Cockatoo with a strange and loose type of crest. It has a very pleasant disposition. This specimen is owned by Dorothy Speed.

green; the upperside of the tail is green and the underside dull red; and brownish-maroon covers the ear and throat. Traces of red occur above the nostrils, and a narrow band of bright red-orange crosses the lower chest. Bright reddish-orange also occurs at the bend of the wings, on the shoulders, and on the underwing coverts.

WHITE BREASTED CONURE *(Pyrrhura albipectus) (22 cm).*

The distinctively different White Breasted Conure from southern Ecuador is nine inches long including the four and one-half inch tail. The head is brownish gray with frosty tips on the feathers. A greenish eyebrow trails over an orange ear which has deep areas on the inner parts of the feathers. The sides of the face are greenish with indistinct scales of lighter and darker scallops. The throat and chest are grayish-white with faint bars of darker grayish-brown. Some creamy yellow invades the lower chest before turning into a dusky green. A few traces of red occur on the abdomen, and the underside of the tail is dull black.

The remaining upperparts are bright green with dark blue and black on the flights and black on the upperside of the tail. Bright red occurs on the bend of the wing and on the primary wing coverts.

FLAME WINGED CONURE *(Pyrrhura calliptera) (22 cm).*

The Flame Winged Conure from the subtropical zone of the western slope of the eastern Andes of Colombia is nine and three-fourths inches including the tail of four and three-fourths inches. It is similar to the species above except that it has a dark chestnut ear patch and red-orange and yellow instead of red on the wings with yellow especially prominent on the primary coverts. The chest has a basic dull reddish-brown color with faint traces of paler shadings on the tips of the feathers. The abdomen is dark maroon, and the tail is pale but dull reddish-chestnut on both sides.

ROSE HEADED CONURE *(Pyrrhura rhodocephala) (24 cm).*

The Rose Headed Conure of the mountains of western Venezuela is nine inches long including the four inch tail. The beak is pale horn in color. No scaling or barring occurs on the chest, and there is no red at all in the wings. The overall coloring is dark green with blue and black on the flights, dull reddish-chestnut in the tail, and dark, dull maroon on the abdomen. The bright feature is the colorful persimmon-red on the forehead and crown. The same coloring also appears on the ear coverts.

GREEN CHEEKED CONURE *(Pyrrhura molinae) (26 cm).*

The nominate subspecies *Pyrrhura molinae molinae* has a moderately dull scaled chest, dull wine-red on the abdomen, and a duller shade of wine-red on the five and one-half inch tail. Brownish-gray occurs on the ear with green on the lower cheeks. Flights are bluish-green and the back and wings are bright green. Green on the underparts is dull. The head is dark and dusky, and the bill is dark horn. Some individuals have paler areas on the chest, ears, and head and a less bright coloring on the tail. These variations may possibly be sexual. This race comes from Bolivia. The subspecies *australis* from southern Bolivia and northwestern Argentina is similar in most respects except the head is duskier, smoother, and darker. The race *phoenicura* is a distinctive subspecies having no red on the abdomen, but it has a more prominent dark red on both sides of the tail. This race from the west central Matto Grosso area is nine inches long including the four and one-half inch tail. *P. m. sordida* is from the Matto Grosso and eastern Bolivia; *P. m. restricta* is from Bolivia.

FIERY SHOULDERED CONURE *(Pyrrhura egregia) (25 cm)*.

The total length of this species from British Guiana is nine and one-fourth inches including the four and one-half inch tail. The basic coloring is dark and dull green, especially darker and dusky, almost blackish, on the head. The ear coverts are brighter green with underlying traces of hidden red. The chest is green with small scaled tips of buff. The abdomen shows traces of maroon-red. Flights are blue and black, and the tail is blackish. The brightest feature is the yellowish-orange blended with traces of red on the underwing coverts.

MAROON TAILED CONURE *(Pyrrhura melanura) (26 cm)*.

Three races of the Maroon Tailed Conure occur averaging nine and one-half inches including the tail of four and one-half inches. The race *melanura* from northwestern Amazonia and northwestern Peru is similar to the *Pyrrhura egregia*, but there is no bright coloring on the underwing coverts. Instead, a bright red-orange occurs in the primary wing coverts. The brownish head is mixed with green and has a fine line of maroon on the forehead. There is no blue in the green wings, but the blackish-maroon tail shows slight traces of red. The subspecies *pacifica* of southwestern Colombia has more extensive and brighter red on the primary coverts. The race *souancei* of Amazonian Ecuador has a bolder scalloped chest with broad white tips. The subspecies *chapmani* has less red on the primary coverts and broad scallops of ashy-white on the chest.

BERLEPSCH'S CONURE *(Pyrrhura berlepschi) (24 cm)*.

Berlepsch's Conure from eastern Peru is practically identical to the subspecies *souancei* of the species above.

Scarlet Macaw (genus: *Ara*). This one, named Red, is over 30 years of age and is a very good pet and talker. Macaws are among the largest and gaudiest members of the parrot family. The Scarlet Macaw is the most popular and readily available member of the family of Macaws. Owned by Palos Verdes Bird Farm.

Scarlet Macaw (genus: *Ara*). This picture shows the extent of the brilliant red on the underparts.

ROCK CONURE *(Pyrrhura rupicola) (25 cm).*

Totaling ten inches in length including the four and one-half inch tail, the Rock Conure is from the tropical zone of southeastern Peru and Bolivia. The beak is a dark horn color. The forehead is nearly black becoming slightly paler with a tinge of dusky brown on the crown and nape. There are buffish tipped scales on the lower nape and bluish tinges on the mantle. Facial areas are green. The chin, throat, and chest are mostly buffish-white because of the broad scaled tips. The inner areas of these feathers are dusky gray. The lower chest fades into pale yellowish-green tips changing into green on the abdomen. The back, rump, wings, and upper tail are bright green. The flights have some black, and the dull underside of the tail has a wash of dull red. The primary wing coverts and scapulars are bright red.

CRIMSON BELLIED CONURE *(Pyrrhura rhodogaster) (24 cm).*

The Crimson Bellied Conure of central Brazil is nine inches long including the tail of four and a half inches. The beak is a dark horn color, and the general appearance is similar to that of the Pearly Conure. However, the chest is more moderate and less contrasting than that of the Pearly Conure; and the red is brilliant from the lower chest through the abdomen. Lower facial area are tinged with green, and shades of red appear at the shoulders and on the underwing coverts.

BLUE WINGED CONURE *(Pyrrhura picta) (22 cm).*

There are seven races of the Blue Winged Conure. The nominate race *picta* from Venezuela through British and Dutch Guiana to Cayenne is described below. In addition to the characteristics described below, the following features are notable. The rump is dark red. The chest is more boldly scalloped rather than scaled, and this scalloping extends down to the lower chest in a bright accent. Pale red is washed over the scallops in the lower chest, and the feathers on the sides are bordered in pale red. The subspecies *amazonum* is more outstanding in the scalloped chest area, in the brighter blue of the wing, and in the brighter red on the rump. The race *subandina* is called the Painted Conure. It has more brown on the head. The race *caeruliceps* of eastern Colombia has more blue on the head. Lucian's Conure (subspecies *lucianii*) has a dull slate-blue cheek patch with buffish edges, and the scalloping on the underparts is less pronounced.

BLUE WINGED CONURE *(Pyrrhura picta picta) (22 cm).*

The main characteristics of this species are the blue primaries, red at the bend of the wing, blackish on the crown and nape, bluish on the forehead and on a faint band across the nape, greenish on the upper chest, and brown on the throat. The upper part of the cheeks is chestnut and the lower part bluish. The cheek patch is grey. The scaled chest, dull reddish abdomen, and reddish tail are present.

The size is nine and a half inches.

Six additional races exist: *Pyrrhura picta amazonum* from the Valley of the Lower Amazon; *Pyrrhura picta subandina* from north-western Colombia; and *Pyrrhura picta lucianii* from Upper Amazonia. The latter is called Lucian's Conure and differs from its relatives by having salmon red on the forehead and around the eyes. The cheek patch is slate blue with buffish edges. There is also some maroon on the abdomen.

Pyrrhura picta microtera from northern Brazil.

Pyrrhura picta roseifrons from north-western Brazil.

Pyrrhura picta caeruleiceps from Colombia.

The Blue Winged Conure is best kept in pairs in an outdoor flight where they may start breeding. A nest box 9 inches by 13 inches with an entrance hole of 3 inches in diameter, or a hollow log is essential. The three to four white eggs are incubated by the female. Next to corn-on-the-cob, oats, hemp and sunflower seeds should be part of their diet. Daily fresh twigs, preferably those of apple and pear trees, and young foliage is necessary as well as powdered egg shells, boiled potatoes, boiled maize, carrots, bread soaked in milk, hard-boiled egg, millet and canary seed. They will sometimes take pieces of apple and pear when these are offered.

The birds are shy at first but become very quickly accustomed to their new surroundings if they are placed in a large outdoor aviary, together with other parrakeets, as long as they are not species of the same genus. They usually become very friendly towards their owner.

The Blue Winged Conure is also called the Painted Conure. In the wild it is very common except in northern Colombia, although there are some data on its habits in the wild in this area. According to Haverschmidt (1968) the bird is often seen in Surinam, where it occurs in flocks in the forests near the sand ridges in the coastal region and in the interior. According to Forshaw (1973/77) the bird is common in Guyana (coastal rivers and forests in the interior). In Venezuela and northern Colombia the bird inhabits forests in the tropical zone.

Other species of *Pyrrhura* are:

Pyrrhura hoffmanni gaudens or Hoffman's Conure

A ten-inch Conure with a four-inch tail, this subspecies is long and slender and has bright red ear coverts with yellowish tinges in the green head. The red in the abdomen is absent, and there is yellowish in the wings. The beak is light horn. The characteristic reddish underside of the tail is present. From southern Costa Rica and western Panama.

Pyrrhura hoffmanni hoffmanni from southern Costa Rica, north to the hilly

267

Funereal or Yellow Tailed Black Cockatoo. This is a huge bird quite typical of the genus of very rare Black Cockatoos. The bird pictured is also a very affectionate pet.

Chattering Lories, brilliant and amusing members of the genus *Domicella*. Chattering Lories are very hardy and are delightful aviary birds. Their feathers have a high gloss and are always impeccable. These birds are owned by Jerome Buteyn.

Caribbean approaches to the central plateaus (Forshaw) but apparently does not quite reach the Cordillera Central.

Pyrrhura haematotis or Red-eared Conure

An eight-inch Conure from Venezuela, this species has the bronze face tinged with black and a few red and maroon feathers near the ear. There is also a maroon tinge to the ear coverts. Most of the head and neck are bronze. The beak is light horn in color. The flanks are red, as are the red sides under the wing. There is a bluish area on the wings. The underwings are bright green with a bluish tinge, and the flights are black.

Genus: *Ognorhynchus*

YELLOW EARED CONURE *(Ognorhynchus icterotis)*

The very pretty Yellow Eared Conure is sixteen inches long including the tail of eight inches. It has a large head and a large blackish beak with whitish tips. Bright yellow marks the forehead, lores, and a broad circular facial area surrounded by very dark and glossy green which also covers all the remaining underparts. Underparts are pale green with the underside of the tail dull reddish as is found in the tail of the Military Macaw. This distinctive species ranges through the subtropical zone of the Central Andes of Colombia through the Andes of northern Ecuador.

Genera: *Microsittace* and *Enicognathus*

CHILEAN CONURE *(Microsittace ferrugineus) (33 cm).*

Thirteen inches in length, the Chilean Conure is another bird whose main interest lies in its rarity. The coloring lacks inspiration. Mainly, it is dull green with dusky outer margins to the feathers. The forehead and lores are dull chestnut followed by a bluish tinge on the crown with black outer margins on each feather. The wings have a bluish tinge, and the chestnut brown of the head is repeated in the tail and an abdominal patch. The bill is dark horn color, and red occurs with the chestnut-brown in the tail and on an abdominal patch. The nominate race is thirteen inches long including the six inch tail. The subspecies *minor* is eleven inches long including the tail of five and one-half inches. This smaller race has a smaller and less noticeable abdominal patch.

The Chilean Conure is from western Argentina and south to Tierra del Fuego. A subspecies, *Microsittace ferrugineus minor*, is also found in Chile and in southwestern Argentina.

Wagler's (or Red Fronted) Conure has an intermediate amount of red on the head covering the crown and forehead. There is no red on the sides of the face. The body is much stockier than that of other "Red Headed" Conures.

SLENDER BILLED CONURE *(Enicognathus leptorhynchus) (40 cm).*

The Slender Billed Conure from Chile is fifteen and one-half inches long including the tail of seven and a half inches. It stands alone in its genus and is not particularly attractive. It is all bright green with blackish tips on many feathers and tinges of blue on the wings. A dark red occurs on the forehead, lores, and under and behind the eyes. Dull red occurs on the abdomen and tail, paler and duller on the underside. The brownish-horn beak is long and slender with no sharp curve. In some ways, this curious beak resembles that of the famed Kea Parrot.

Red Fronted Conure (genus: *Aratinga*). This is an excellent representation of a series of very similar large conures with only slight variations of red. Owned by Jerome Buteyn.

Conure of the genus *Pyrrhura*. The typical scaled chest is present but is not portrayed with enough prominence. The characteristic cheek patch does not show as prominently as it does in most species of the genus. Owned by Jerome Buteyn.

The African Grey Parrot, very seldom treacherous, has been bred at liberty, in aviaries, and in close confinement, although only on rare occasions. It is generally a brilliant talker.

14

PARROTS

Genus: *Psittacus*

AFRICAN GREY PARROT *(Psittacus erithacus erithacus) (33cm).*
The African Grey Parrot is the best known pet Parrot in Europe and is one of the ultimate goals for pet Parrot fanciers in America. It is much more expensive in America due to import regulations and the factor of distance. It is purported by many experts to be the best talking Parrot. Everyone would at least rank it in the top three. Competitors for top place are all in the family of Amazons: Mexican Double Yellow Head, Panama, Yellow Naped Amazon, and the often overlooked Blue Fronted Amazon. Most everyone will agree that the African Grey has voice inflections more human-like than Parrot-like.

African Greys are very lovely birds and present a wonderful contrast to the ever-present green of the more prevalent members of the Amazon family. The immediate color combination which one sees is black, grey, and red. The bill is shiny black, while the feet appear to be black dusted with grey powder which clings to the scale crevices. The tail is bright red. The rest of the bird is a soft pastel grey with various shadings to provide more of an interesting pattern. It is darker on the upper parts and wings and lighter on the lower parts. The breast feathers are tipped with whitish margins to give a scalloped effect. There is a large bare facial area, whitish in color, starting at the forehead and flaring backwards past the eye.

Sexual differences are slight. Males have a bulkier, more masculine appearance. Females have smaller heads, beaks, and feet. Females also have eyes which give a slight elliptical appearance.

Immature African Greys have dark grey eyes, while adults have pale, almost straw-colored, eyes.

African Greys have been bred on several occasions and are usually good parents. They require the same diet as other Parrots and similar aviary facilities.

About thirteen inches long, the African Grey is not the best-shaped Parrot. Its smaller head and longer neck make it somewhat less dignified than a

Blue and Gold Macaw (genus: *Ara*). This is the second most readily available member of the Macaw family. The black lines on the face are rows of tiny feathers. This picture is proof of the lengths a photographer will go to get a good picture. Mrs. Van der Meid was standing atop a 14 foot ladder when she took this picture. Owned by Jerome Buteyn.

Rose Breasted Cockatoos. The two birds obligingly showed a profile and a front view to illustrate their simple but strikingly beautiful color scheme. This print unfortunately does not show the full richness of their soft pastel colors.

Yellow Naped Amazon or a Mexican Double Yellow Head. Some people say it has a snaky appearance, but this is unfair and quite exaggerated.

They are alert and highly intelligent.

TIMNEH PARROT *(Psittacus erithacus timneh)*

A subspecies of the African Grey, the Timneh is one inch smaller, has darker grey, and has a brown tail. It is rare in America.

Another subspecies is questionable because of the doubtful distinction from the African Grey. Confined to certain islands in the Gulf of Guinea, it is identified as *Psittacus erithacus princeps.*

Genus: *Amazona*

AMAZON PARROTS

The Amazon family is one of the largest of the order of Parrots, consisting of over sixty different species and subspecies. Amazons range in length from eight to twenty-one inches. The predominant color of most members is green. They are well-proportioned birds of stocky build and with tails of approximately one-fourth the total length. All are New World birds and range from Mexico southward.

Most Amazons become excellent pets if they are trained while still young. They take most kindly to captivity and almost seem to prefer a household to an aviary. They thrive most on the standard diet.

There are many pet Amazons which are kept more or less at liberty on estates, farms, and other isolated places. The first Parrot the writers ever encountered in the semi-liberty state was a fine old Mexican Double Yellow Head who lived in a cage in a house on the edge of a river. Early each morning the Parrot was taken out to a large willow tree, which it regarded as its own private property. There was a feeding station, which was replenished every morning. All day long, the Parrot would play in the tree and would sing and laugh. Late in the afternoon, the bird would return to its feeding station and wait patiently for a short time to be returned to its cage. If the short wait went unnoticed, the bird would very impatiently call, laugh, and scream until someone returned it to its cage. Its owner insisted that this had been the happy bird's daily routine for twenty-eight years, and it had never wandered or flown out of sight of its willow tree.

At the time of this writing, there are at least three Amazons of individual species which have been living in a completely wild state for at least five years in the residential section of a town three miles away. When the reports first came to the writers, they shrugged them off in disbelief. However, twice in

A Yellow Naped Amazon Parrot being spoon-fed. Handfeeding is a chore not to be undertaken halfheartedly. Facial cleaning after feeding is usually necessary. Dried, hardened foods remaining on the beak can cause deformed beaks during the youngsters' rapid growth periods. The food should be 100°F, no more or less. Touching it to your lips is a satisfactory test. Food too hot will cause burns, and the birds sensibly reject it if it is too cold. Digestion is impaired by foods too low in temperature.

Blue Crowned Amazon and Mexican Double Yellow Head. Although the pose of the Blue Crowned hides the attractive shade of blue on top of the head, this is a good picture to show the ratio of size. Owned by Jerome Buteyn.

Blue Crowned Amazon showing the large white eye ring and blue shade of the head. This species is an excellent talker and is a very large bird. Owned by Dave Borgardt.

the last eighteen months the writers have witnessed one of the birds flying overhead. Its large head and heavy flight were startling to one used to nothing larger than a Mourning Dove or Sparrow Hawk flying above the neighborhood.

These parrots are in perfect health. No one owns them or apparently feeds them. They are wary and have escaped all types of attempted capture. They most certainly have captured the fancy of the town and have become quite the topic of conversation. Unfortunately, there have been many inconsiderate and unenlightened boys with air rifles trying their skill on the birds. There may have been some slight wounds because the birds are not agile enough to evade all the shots. Whether or not they can hold out against these predators is a matter of conjecture.

Amazons are not widely kept as aviary birds with breeding as the object. As a rule, overly tame birds have very little interest in breeding. When they do start breeding operations, most become very unfriendly or even savage. To achieve success in breeding, follow the suggestions set forth in the chapters on aviaries, equipment, breeding, and feeding, and fortify these with your own patience.

MEXICAN DOUBLE YELLOW HEAD *(Amazona ochrocephala oratrix)* *(35 cm)*

Also called Levaillant's Amazon or Yellow-headed Amazon, this is the most popular and one of the most prolific of Amazons.

It is about fifteen inches long and has a good talking reputation.

Mexican Double Yellow Head

282

When young, the Double Yellow Head has all the adult coloration except the yellow on the head, which is confined to the area extending from the forehead to the crown. As the bird grows older, flecks of yellow appear on the face and neck and gradually change to a complete yellow covering the entire head and neck. Other colors are red on the shoulders, wings, and tail feathers near the base. There is also some blue on the wings. The beak and feet are light horn in color, but there may be darker markings on the beak when the bird is very young. The rest of the coloring is bright green.

Slender when young, the Double Yellow Head becomes more massive as it matures.

Its native range extends from Mexico to Central America. It is hardy out-of-doors the year round if it is properly acclimated to outdoor conditions during the summer.

Some authorities rank this species' talking ability on a par with the African Grey. We have had dozens of Double Yellow Heads and have come to this conclusion: they are not always reliable. Some become extraordinary talkers; some become exceptionally affectionate pets. Others are the exact opposite. Some of our most affectionate Double Yellow Heads never uttered a word. Usually, if the bird is good, it is very good; but one should be certain of the personality and talking ability before he buys a Mexican Double Yellow Head.

YELLOW NAPED AMAZON *(Amazona ochrocephala auropalliata)* *35 cm).*

Somehow the Yellow Naped Amazon has mistakenly gained the popular name of Panama Parrot. The Yellow Naped, readily available in the United States, has no need to trade on another bird's name. If there is another species of parrot which is as consistently a good talker and good pet, the writers have never come across it. So far, they have never seen a young Yellow Naped which has not wanted to become an affectionate talking pet. An older bird may show a high degree of individual preference which may prevent it from being a good pet, but this is largely a matter of improper training and handling. For anyone wishing to have a parrot which is the most easily trained and a good performer, the writers unhesitatingly recommend a Yellow Naped Amazon.

This bird is usually a little more expensive than the Double Yellow Head; but, in the United States, it is far less expensive than an African Grey. In Europe, where the Yellow Naped is not so well known as the African Grey, the price structure may be reversed.

Slightly larger than and just as hardy as the Mexican Double Yellow Head, the Yellow Naped, also from Mexico, is a very attractive parrot. Its large head and massive body lend dignity to its more sedate coloring.

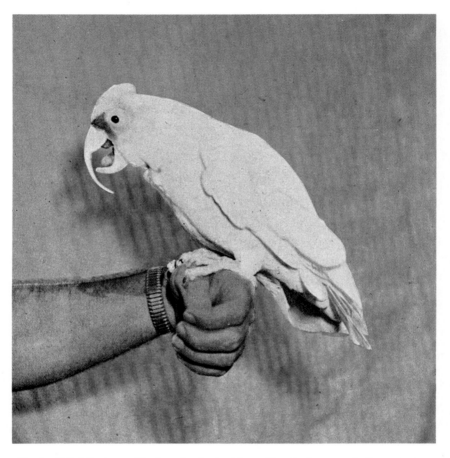

Slender Billed Cockatoo. The long slender beak is used for digging roots, bulbs, and tubers, which are used for food. This is a very rare species with caricaturistic proportions. This specimen is owned by Jerome Buteyn.

Moluccan Cockatoo. This is a large bird which appears even larger because of the luxurious nature of the long feathers. The especially large crest feathers add appreciably to the beautiful proportions of the bird.

Basically it is a deep green which appears to have a slight shading of blue. A band of yellow covers the nape of the neck, and a V-shaped yellow area occurs above the beak. This is absent in very young birds and develops slowly. The tail feathers are light yellowish green at the tips with a touch of red near the base of the outer feathers. There are also red and blue on the flight feathers. The beak is a very dark blackish-grey at the tip and a lighter grey at the base.

PANAMA AMAZON *(Amazona ochrocephala panamensis) (35 cm).*

This bird is an unexcelled talker.

The Panama, an inhabitant of Panama and northern South America, is much more rare in the United States than either the Mexican Double Yellow Head or the Yellow Naped Amazon. Since its name is synonymous with excellence, it is understandable that many people hopefully call their parrots Panamas.

In appearance the Panama is less distinguished than either the Mexican

A beautiful specimen of a Panama Parrot fanning its tail. The tail-fanning is usually accompanied by raised feathers around the neck and the wild screeching or call note of the Amazon.

Double Yellow Head or the Yellow Naped Amazon. Since it is frequently confused with the latter, the writers will point out the differences. Panamas are dark green but a little lighter in color and smaller than the Yellow Naped. There is no yellow nuchal collar, but both· have a yellow patch on the forehead. There is similar coloring on wings and tail, a red patch at the bend of the wing. The beak of the Panama is deeper horn color with a dark tip. There is also a bare eye ring.

YELLOW FRONTED AMAZON *(Amazona ochrocephala ochrocephala)* *(35 cm).*

This species is often confused with the Panama Parrot, which it closely resembles. The differences are a paler bill with a dark tip and a more extensive yellow which covers the forehead and extends slightly into the crown. The yellow of the Panama is confined to the center of the forehead. It is a somewhat lighter and brighter shade of green than the Panama. The eye is orange. The female is said to have paler eyes and less yellow on the crown. Like the Panama, it has red on the shoulders and a bare eye ring.

Its length is about fourteen inches.

The habitat is somewhat more southerly than that of the Panama Amazon, extending across the northern countries of South America.

The Yellow Fronted is frequently called the Colombian Amazon and the Single Yellow Head.

As a talking pet it is excellent, as are most of its close relatives. However, it is not regarded as highly as the Yellow Naped, Panama, or the Mexican Double Yellow Head.

Three other subspecies of *Amazona ochrocephala* occur. They do not figure highly in aviculture because they are not easily available.

TRES MARIAS AMAZON *(Amazona ochrocephala tresmariae) (35 cm).*

Restricted to Tres Marias Island, this subspecies can be distinguished from the Mexican Double Yellow Head by its larger bill and head, and a brighter, more extensive yellow head. A faint bluish tinge transforms it into a brighter green.

In America, they are mistakenly called Mexican Double Yellow Heads. The writers know of one whose toenails they have trimmed at regular intervals for several years. It is by far the most beautiful "Yellow Head" they have ever seen. The owner has no idea that it is a far more rare bird than the Mexican Double Yellow Head.

NATTERER'S AMAZON *(Amazona ochrocephala nattereri) (35 cm).*

Although an *ochrocephala*, this rare species more closely resembles the Plain Colored Amazon *(Amazona farinosa inornata)*. A large yellow area oc-

This hybrid macaw, the result of a mating between a Scarlet Macaw and a Blue and Gold Macaw, was reared from time of hatching to maturity by Mr. and Mrs. Ralph Small of Brookfield, Illinois. The youngster is shown here at an age of 73 days and weight of 975 grams. Photo by Ralph Small.

In this photograph, the Smalls' hybrid macaw shows characteristics of both of its parents, and the vivid sunset colors on the underparts are brighter and more attractive than on most other hybrids between Scarlet Macaws and Blue and Gold Macaws. At the time this photograph was taken the bird was 98 days old and weighed 869 grams, which is considerably less than its weight at 73 days of age. Photo by Ralph Small.

Tommy, the Greater Sulphur Crested Cockatoo belonging to the Palos Verdes Bird Farm, is particularly fond of women, especially Averil Powys, shown with him here. Tommy is usually not fond of men except when he is on television. He is an intelligent "ham" and never fails to be the stellar light regardless of who is handling him in front of the camera.

The Green Cheeked or Red Headed or Spectacled Amazon is well-known in captivity. The female has less red on the crown and a smaller beak.

curs on the forehead and crown followed by a bright border of green tinged with blue. The bird is about fifteen inches long. Its habitat is the interior parts of equatorial Peru and Ecuador.

MARAJO AMAZON *(Amazona ochrocephala xantholaema) (35 cm).*

The best description the writers have ever found of this bird is the one given by Karl Plath in *Parrots Exclusively.* He describes it as "like the Yellow-headed Amazon (Mexican Double Yellow Head) but yellow of more orange shade."

This description causes the writers to wonder if their pair of "cinnamon mutations" of Mexican Double Yellow Heads, mentioned in the chapter on Genetics and Hybrids, could possibly be this species. Their "mutants" have a bronzed shade overlying all of the green, a diluted red at the bend of the wing, and an apricot shade replacing the yellow.

At any rate, it is a very rare bird of fifteen inches which is confined to the Island of Marajo at the mouth of the Amazon River.

GREEN CHEEKED AMAZON *(Amazona viridigenalis) (33 cm).*

Also popularly called Mexican Red Head, the Green Cheeked Amazon is another of the medium sized (thirteen-inch) Mexican parrots which has been common in the United States but rare in Europe. Usually they are moderately priced.

A few years ago they had fallen out of favor because of the extremely noisy character of some specimens. The reputations of the bad ones had spread much faster than those of the good ones. But they are becoming fairly frequent again.

This little Amazon is certainly a pretty bird. Its red cap covers the crown down to the eyes and nearly down to the nape. Young have less red on the head. There is a hint of a lavender eyebrow above the eye which is also the lower rim of the red cap. The cheeks are bright green. This is supposed to be the only bird of the genus which has the red cap, bright green cheeks, and no yellow on the head. Th bill is yellowish horn color. The rest is the standard Amazon coloring of dominant green with red and blue in the wings.

FINSCH'S AMAZON *(Amazona finschi) (33 cm).*

Also called the Lilac Crowned Amazon, the little Finsch's Parrot is a somewhat readily available pet in the United States. It is not as common as the Green Cheeked Amazon, but it is a more reliable pet. Usually it is a slow-moving, but playfully active bird. It has such extreme confidence in its owner that it can be handled like an inanimate object.

Its voice is high-pitched, and it is a reasonably fair talker; but some individuals screech a lot.

Green Winged Macaw (genus: *Ara*). This is a very large Macaw which looks topheavy because of its huge head and bill and its proportionately shorter tail. The face of this species has red lines which is composed of tiny red feathers. Owned by Jerome Buteyn.

Severe Macaw (genus: *Ara*). This is one of the most popular and frequently available of the Dwarf Macaws. In appearance, it rather resembles a Military Macaw except it has better proportions and sharper color contrasts. It makes an excellent pet but is sometimes quite noisy. This specimen is a good talker and a very gentle pet owned by Dorothy Speed.

About twelve inches long, the Finsch's Amazon has a flatter head and a broad chest. With folded wings, many individuals present a squarish look from the front.

The coloring is somewhat subdued, yet very attractive. The forehead has a band of plum coloring connecting the eyes. As the color approaches the crown, it becomes paler and shades into a soft lavender. The cheeks are very bright green. The rest of the bird is duller and appreciably darker on the upper parts. The breast and abdomen have a pleasant scalloped effect caused by the darker margins on each feather.

SPECTACLED AMAZON *(Amazona albifrons albifrons) (26 cm).*

The little Spectacled Amazon is only ten to eleven inches long, but its vocal efforts are far from being pint-sized. Regarded as a fair talker, the Spectacled is more frequently a grating screecher. There are many which prove to be very satisfying pets, but these are definitely exceptions rather than the rule.

The Spectacled Amazon is an inexpensive, and common parrot in the United States and is regarded as a rather poor substitute for a higher priced Double Yellow Head or Yellow Naped Amazon.

Like most Mexican parrots, it is common in the United States though somewhat rare in Europe. The rarities in the United States are the South American parrots, which, conversely, are far more common in Europe.

The Spectacled Amazon is a very pretty little parrot. It is sometimes called the Red, White, and Blue Parrot because these colors appear prominently on the head. The forehead portion immediately above the beak has red which extends to, and surrounds, the eyes, giving a red masked effect. The main part of the forehead to the crown is white followed by a bright blue. Red and blue are repeated in the wing. Most of the green neck feathers have black borders. The rest of the bird is mainly bright green. The beak is a yellowish-white horn color.

Two subspecies of the Spectacled Amazon occur in Mexico. They are very much like the Spectacled and are undoubtedly sold as the same species in most instances.

LESSER WHITE FRONTED AMAZON *(Amazona albifrons nana)*

This bird is confined to southern Mexico. The only appreciable difference is that it is slightly smaller than the Spectacled Amazon.

SONORAN SPECTACLED AMAZON *(Amazona albifrons saltuensis)*

This bird is confined mostly to Sonora, a very arid section of northwestern Mexico. The appreciable differences are a paler red and deeper blue on the face and a bluish tinge to the green nape and chest. A very prominent

The Panama Parrot does much better in a flight cage, bird room or garden aviary than in a parrot cage.

Tommy, the Greater Sulphur Crested Cockatoo shows the effects of the molting period on his beautiful crest. Within a few weeks the small pin feathers will have blossomed.

Adult Swainson's Blue Mountain Lorikeets of the genus *Trichoglossus*. This is one of the most beautiful and entertaining of all members of the parrot family.

color variation, which we have noted in many Spectacled Amazons, is a yellow forehead replacing the white.

YELLOW LORED AMAZON *(Amazona xantholora) (26 cm)*.

A very rare species which is similar to the Spectacled Amazon, the Yellow Lored Amazon bears a patch of yellow between the eyes and beak. It is ten inches long and inhabits the Mexican state of Yucatan. The Yellow Lored Amazon has a yellow-horn colored beak, a black cheek patch, a large patch of bright yellow between the eyes and beak, and bright red surrounding the eyes.

YELLOW CHEEKED AMAZON *(Amazona autumnalis autumnalis)*
(34 cm)

The Yellow Cheeked Amazon, a native of Mexico and parts of Central America, is a very popular and abundant parrot in the United States, though apparently somewhat rare in Europe. It is an active bird and is far less sedate than the Yellow Naped. Usually the Yellow Cheeked, sometimes called Orange Cheeked, makes a good talking pet. It sometimes exhibits some of the undersirable characteristics found in some Mexican Double Yellow Heads, such as extreme devotion to one person with a resultant jealous hatred for all others, high-pitched screeches, and unreliability. For the most part, however, this species is a well-behaved and talented pet and is one of the writers' favorites. One should be certain of the individual habits before selecting a Yellow Cheeked Amazon, also called the Red-lored Amazon.

The Yellow Cheeked is a very attractive bird of thirteen to fourteen inches in length. The outstanding features are the colorful head and face, which have most of the colors of a beautiful desert sunset. There is nothing precise or clear-cut about the pattern. The very definite color changes are softly blended gradations rather than separations.

Basically, the color pattern is as follows: bright red forehead and lores, lilac-tinged violet crown, bright yellow cheeks with some red-orange shadings at the perimeter, especially where it blends into the red of the lores, crown, and under the beak. The beak is yellowish at the base and dark horn at the tip and outer margins. The iris is brownish orange. As the bird becomes older, the iris grows lighter and the yellow shows deeper tinges. The rest of the bird is typically Amazon in color with bright green predominant.

The price is comparable to that of a Yellow Head.

SALVIN'S AMAZON *(Amazonoa autumnalis salvini) (34 cm)*.

Similar to the Yellow Cheeked Amazon, of which it is a subspecies, Salvin's Amazon has a range extending from eastern Nicaragua, to eastern

Salvin's Amazon Parrot *(Amazona autumnalis salvini)* does well in captivity and is rather striking-looking. It does badly in a parrot cage but will live well in a large aviary. It would be unwise to expose this bird to a low temperature without great caution.

Jenday Conures (genus: *Aratinga*). This picture shows a considerable amount of the beauty of the Jenday but not all of it because the chest is a beautiful mixture of reddish orange. The Jenday is very popular and is quite readily available. Owned by Jerome Buteyn.

Two conures of the genus *Aratinga*. The brown-headed species is called the Brown Eared Conure, and the other is called Petz' Conure or Half Moon Parrot. The little fellow who sneaked into the background is a Harlequin Budgerigar which helps to show a ratio in size to the Budgerigar. Birds in this photograph owned by the Authors.

and southeastern Costa Rica, to northern Colombia, and including the Pearl Islands.

Its length is thirteen to fourteen inches.

The following differences separate Salvin's from the Yellow Cheeked: bright green cheeks instead of yellow and a narrower red band which has a rose tint.

DIADEMED AMAZON *(Amazona autumnalis diadema) (34 cm)*

Another subspecies of, but similar to, the Yellow Cheeked is the very rare Diademed Amazon. Its range is northwestern Brazil. It is very much like Salvin's Amazon except for the lilac tinge of the upper chest area and a purplish lilac hue on the nape of the neck. The beak is yellow above and black below.

LESSON'S AMAZON *(Amazona autumnalis lilacina) (34 cm).*

Also called Lilacine Amazon, this rare subspecies is similar to Salvin's Amazon except that it is very slightly smaller, has a black beak, and has more shading of lilac. The red in the wing is somewhat pinkish.

The habitat is tropical west Ecuador.

BLUE CROWNED AMAZON *(Amazona farinosa guatemalae) (38 cm).*

This large sixteen-inch, Amazon is very striking in appearance and makes a good talker and a fine pet. Some individuals show marked differences in personality and more often prefer one person than many. Some lavish an amazing amount of affection upon one person and allow the most indiscreet handling by that one person. As is often the case, a bird with this nature usually holds everyone else at bay. If one has the unusual opportunity of purchasing a Blue Crowned Amazon, he should be certain the bird is of a favorable disposition. Unfortunately, they are seldom available.

The Blue Crowned Amazon, sometimes called the Guatemalan Amazon and frequently erroneously called the Mealy Amazon, has a large head with dark bill and feet. The large dark orange eyes are surrounded by a prominent white naked ring. The head is blue, brightest on the forehead and crown and fading into a powdery blue tinge on the nape and shoulders. The basic green is dark with an almost bluish tinge. There is also red and blue in the flight feathers.

Its habitat is centered in Guatemala, extending into southern Mexico and Honduras.

MEALY AMAZON *(Amazona farinosa farinosa) (38 cm).*

This bird is a slightly smaller and a less colorful edition of the above. The blue on the head is less pronounced and there is the addition of some unattractive dull yellow-orange on the crown. The head, neck, and shoulders have the powdery appearance.

The Mealy Amazon is considerably less attractive than the Blue Crowned but is still a handsome bird. It makes a good pet and talented talker. Its habitat is Venezuela, Surinam, Peru, and parts of Brazil.

PLAIN COLORED AMAZON *(Amazona farinosa inornata) (38 cm).*

This sixteen-inch species is "plain colored" because it is the dullest of the four subspecies of the species *Amazona farinosa.* It is basically a dull green, brighter on the forehead and cheeks. The mealy tinge is present and the feathers on the nape are bordered with black and a slight purplish tinge. It is less bright than the Green Headed Amazon. The large eye is surrounded by the white eye ring.

The habitat is Panama and northwestern South America.

GREEN HEADED AMAZON *(Amazona farinosa virenticeps) (38 cm).*

This bird is similar to the Plain Colored except for a dull bluish-tinged forehead and scalloped neck feathers. There is a bright green forehead and eye area. There is red on the wings. It has a dark beak.

The habitat is Nicaragua, Costa Rica, and Western Panama.

Its size is fifteen inches.

BLUE FRONTED AMAZON *(Amazona aestiva aestiva) (37 cm).*

The Blue Fronted Amazon, like so many South American parrots, is common in Europe and somewhat rare in America. Fortunately, this bird is not as rare as many in that category; and the price is somewhat reasonable.

There are very few people in this country who fully appreciate, or know of, this bird's remarkable talent for mimicry; and it is, therefore, often overlooked as a suitable pet. As a talker, it easily rates a position in the top five species of good talking pets. In Europe it is very highly rated.

The Blue Fronted inhabits broad areas of Brazil and Argentina and is about fourteen inches long.

Basically, it is green in color. The bend of the wing may vary from reddish yellow to red. Some of this variation is said to be a sexual difference; hens are said to be all red at the bend of the wing. The feathers on the nape have dark borders, giving a scalloped effect. The bill is dark, nearly black.

The head is a variable mixture of blue and yellow with a definite blue forehead. The cheeks and crown are yellow. The red in the flights is rather extensive.

A curious mixup in popular names exists in the group of Amazons much the same as with Halfmoon Conures. As mentioned before, the Petz Conure

Red or Moluccan Lory (genus: *Eos*). This is an unusual picture of a very rare species because it is the only time the writers have ever seen a member of the Lory family with rough plumage. Usually they have an immaculate and glossy appearance.

Hyacinth Macaw (genus: *Anodorhynchus*). This is a huge macaw with an over-all deep, rich blue. It is a great rarity and is very expensive. Owned by Jerome Buteyn.

in the United States is called the Halfmoon while the Golden Crowned Con-ure is called the Halfmoon in Europe. The excellent reputation of the Blue Fronted Amazon as a pet came to the United States far more easily than did the birds which have always been very rare here. Eventually, another species which was more frequently available was popularly dubbed the Blue Fronted Amazon. In the United States the Orange Winged Amazon which to some extent has the same basic coloration of the true Blue Fronted Amazon became known as the Blue Fronted. The real Blue Fronted has far more bright blue above the nostrils, a slightly paler but more vivid shade of yellow surrounding the eyes, and a head contour which is less flat than that of the Orange Winged Amazon. The Blue Fronted Amazon is the most widely kept of all Amazons in Europe and fully deserves its popularity.

The subspecies *xanthopteryx* has a brighter yellow on the crown, particularly noticeable in adults.

YELLOW WINGED AMAZON *(Amazona aestiva xanthopteryx) (37 cm).*

Often sold under the name of Blue Fronted Amazon, a very close relative, this bird is confined to Bolivia, Paraguay, and northern Argentina. The only noticeable difference is the coloring at the bend of the wing, which is yellow with a few flecks of red. The bluish tinged forehead and crown are present. There are also scalloped feathers on the neck, back, and chest. The blue is a brighter turquoise. A yellow band follows the blue on the crown and surrounds the eyes, lores, and sides of the face.

ORANGE WINGED AMAZON *(Amazona amazonica amazonica) (31 cm)*

Recently the writers had the privilege of owning one of these very charming parrots. It had the best disposition they have ever seen, although this may be an individual characteristic rather than a trait of the species.

In appearance it resembled the Blue Fronted Amazon but had a much richer shade of blue on the forehead, a touch of orange in the yellow cheeks, and orange, instead of red, in the flights. Like the Blue Fronted, the yellow on the crown is present but it forms a circle on the adult and is somewhat variable in the young.

It is about thirteen inches long and occurs mainly in Colombia.

The attractive and more frequently available Orange Winged Amazon, erroneously but popularly called the Blue Fronted Amazon in the United States for reasons detailed in the preceding species, is equally as talented as a talking pet. It is a very attractive species.

TOBAGO ORANGE-WINGED AMAZON *(Amazona amazonica tobagensis) (31 cm)*.
This is a subspecies of the above, with very slight variations, that is confined to the islands of Trinidad and Tobago.

FESTIVE AMAZON *(Amazona festiva festiva) (34 cm)*.
If this bird could manage to keep its wings spread, it would be strikingly beautiful because of its brilliant red rump. There is also some rich dark blue on the flight feathers. When the wings are folded, these colors are all hidden. There is a narrow plum colored band across the forehead and a bluish tinge on the cheeks, throat, and crown.
Its range is eastern Ecuador and western Peru.
It measures fourteen and a half inches.

BODIN'S AMAZON *(Amazona festiva bodini) (34 cm)*.
The only differences that distinguish this bird from the Festive Amazon are a stronger shade of blue on the ear coverts, black on the back, and a red rump. A fine brownish band borders the lower red of the forehead and connects the eyes.

MERCENARY AMAZON *(Amazona mercenaria mercenaria) (34 cm)*.
Also called Tschudi's Amazon, this very rare bird's habitat is the Andes Mountains of Peru and northern Bolivia.
The Mercenary Amazon is basically like the Mealy Amazon except for the following variations: yellow at the bend of the wing and a greyish nape.

GREY NAPED AMAZON *(Amazona mercenaria canipalliata) (34 cm)*.
This equally rare Amazon is similar to the above. Its range is the temperate zones of the Andes mountains of Colombia. It has a paler nape which is grey rather than greyish-green.

IMPERIAL AMAZON *(Amazona imperialis) (45 cm)*.
Nineteen inches long, this royal purple Amazon is from the Island of Dominica and the Lesser Antilles. It is an extreme rarity.
The back and wings are green with the typical blue and red in the flights. The dominant feature of this extraordinary species is the deep purplish-red and violet covering the head, neck, chest, and tail. Pale pinkish-lilac scallops also occur on the chest feathers. The head also has dark blue and green. No purplish occurs on the broad nape or mantle. These areas are dark and dusky greyish-black.

Yellow Naped Amazon, a large parrot with a yellow patch above the nostrils and a broad yellow nape. The writers class this species as one of the top two or three talking parrots. Owned by Palos Verdes Bird Farm.

Tame, young Green Cheeked or Red Headed Amazon and its mistress Evelyn Quipp. The Green Cheeked Amazon is an affectionate pet, but it often is quite a noisy bird.

GUILDING'S AMAZON *(Amazona guildingi) (40 cm).*

Also called the St. Vincent's Amazon, this seventeen-inch Amazon is found only on St. Vincent Island and the Lesser Antilles.

The large and dignified Guilding's Amazon is a difficult bird to describe because of the rich and glowing shades of bronze which vary from golden -bronze to chestnut-bronze. Variations in shadings tend to appear in various areas. The soft white crown traced with lilac contrasts beautifully with the broad yellow on the end of the tail. Most of the tail is yellowish-green shaded with chestnut and orange. The underside of the tail is greenish with broad areas of yellow mixed with orange. The chestnut and orange are very bright on the rump. Large burnt-orange areas overlay the green and blue of the wings, and the cheeks have bright orange patches.

Altogether it is a magnificent bird, but it is rare.

SAN DOMINGO AMAZON *(Amazona ventralis) (28 cm).*

Also called Salle's or White Headed Amazon, this little Amazon is found on the islands of Hispaniola and Gonave.

It is about twelve inches long and is not particularly attractive. It has a white forehead, black ear coverts, and heavy dark borders on the neck feathers.

In addition ot the brief description given, Salle's Amazon has a slight addition of pink on the throat, a shade of bluish-black on the crown, bright blue in the flights, red in the tail, and extensive soft shades of burgundy on the abdomen.

VERSICOLOR or ST. LUCIA AMAZON *(Amazona versicolor) (43 cm).*

Inhabiting the Isle of St. Lucia and the Lesser Antilles, this large seventeen-inch parrot has a reddish pink chest with black bordered feathers, a dark blue face, and a black bead. It also has bronzed chestnut on the abdomen. Another important characteristic is the traces of reddish-pink on the chest.

It is very handsome but very rare.

VINACEOUS AMAZON *(Amazona vinacea) (30 cm).*

As the name implies, this bird has a vinous or burgundy tinge to the bluish grey breast and throat. There is a red forehead band and a pale red patch at the bend of the wings.

It is fourteen and a half inches long and inhabits southeastern Brazil and northeastern Argentina.

The red on the scapulars is particularly bright in the Vinaceous Amazon, and the black scalloped edges are prominent on the bright but pale blue nape. The most important color characteristics, of course, are the red forehead band and the burgundy on the chest and throat.

YELLOW CROWNED AMAZON *(Amazona xanthops) (27 cm)*.

Another rare ten-inch Amazon from eastern and central Brazil, the Yellow Crowned has extensive yellow on the head, also in the cheek area in the vicinity of the orange ear coverts, and occasionally on the abdomen and chest, with maybe a little red creeping out. The green feathers of the neck, nape, chest, and abdomen are heavily bordered with a dark shade preceded by a broad light band of green. The ear coverts are orange, and there is some red under the wings. The beak is mostly horn colored but has black extending from the nostrils to half the length of the beak.

PRETRE'S AMAZON *(Amazona pretrei)* (32 cm).

This rare Amazon is a native of southern Brazil.

It has red in the crown and forehead, under the eye, at the bend of the wing, and a red and yellow mixture in the thighs. There is a yellowish tinge from the mantle to the rump and on the wings. The beak is yellow. The rest of this bird, which measures from thirteen to fourteen inches, is green with black borders to many of the feathers, especially on the neck.

TUCUMAN AMAZON *(Amazona tucumana) (31 cm)*

This rare Amazon is similar to the above species in size and coloring. The differences are that it has less red and a duller green tinged with bronze.

It is a native of northern Argentina and southeastern Bolivia.

DUFRESNE'S AMAZON *(Amazona dufresniana dufresniana) (34 cm)*.

This fourteen- to fifteen-inch green parrot comes from British Guiana, Surinam, and Cayenne.

The main part of the green is somewhat dark with bright blue on the cheeks and bronzed orange on the crown and forehead. Orange instead of red is found in the flight feathers.

RED BROWED AMAZON *(Amazona dufresniana rhodocorytha) (34 cm)*.

If any main characteristic in shape can be applied to Amazons, it is that most Amazons are stocky and blocky, often rather flat headed, and to a great extent graceless compared to most members of the great parrot family. The Red Browed Amazon is an exception. It has a nicely rounded head, a slightly longer neck, and a pleasant shape to its body which is definitely not blocky or stocky. The length is twelve inches including the three inch tail. Slow to mature, a young Red Browed Amazon's first coloring is a bright shade of green with extensive blue areas on the cheeks, throat, and neck. When the coloring of the forehead and crown begins to appear, it is like a flower blossoming. Gradually a rich shade of fiery reddish-orange spreads over the forehead

Red Vented Cockatoo from the Philippines is a miniature with a recumbent crest like the Bare Eyed Cockatoo. This species is very rare in the United States. Owned by Dorothy Speed.

Bare Eyed Cockatoo. Probably the least attractive of the Cockatoo Family, the Bare Eyed is undoubtedly the most intelligent. This one from the Dorothy Speed collection was quick to strike a perfect pose for the photographer. This is a perfect illustration of the recumbent type of crest when it is raised. When lowered, it has the appearance of having no crest whatsoever.

The Cuban Amazon is noisy and an indifferent talker; it does better in an outdoor (large) aviary than in very close confinement. Hybrids with the Blue fronted Amazon are possible.

314

to the top of the crown producing a suprisingly attractive subspecies with bright, rich yellow traced with occasional flecks of red on the lores, sides of the face, chin, and part of the throat. The blue concentrates mainly on the hind part of the crown and stays to a lesser degree on the nape. It is also noticeable on the sides of the face and chin. The main green coloring is more attractive than the typical Amazon green because of a faint bluish cast overlying several areas. The female differs from the male in that her red brow has a predominance of orange rather than red, and the area of orange is far less extensive. The beak in both sexes has a fleshy pink dominating the grey on which the upper mandible occurs on the sides near the base. The lower mandible is dark grey with shadings of flesh pink. The immature specimen has red on the forehead and forecrown and a slight yellow on the lores. Though the size is similar to that of a Yellow Cheeked Amazon, the tail is longer and more slender.

YELLOW SHOULDERED AMAZON *(Amazona barbadensis barbadensis)* *(33 cm)*.

The distinguishing characteristics of this thirteen- to fourteen-inch green parrot are the yellow patches at the bend of the wing and the white frosting on the yellow forehead. More yellow is found on the crown, throat, cheeks, and on the thighs. The rest of the bird is mainly green with black borders on the neck feathers.

It is rare and is confined to the Island of Aruba off the coast of Venezuela.

ROTHSCHILD'S AMAZON *(Amazona barbadensis rothschildi)* *(33 cm)*.

This subspecies of the Yellow Shouldered Amazon is confined to the islands of Bonaire, Blanquilla, and Margarita off the coast of Venezuela.

It is similar to the Yellow Shouldered but has red suffusion on the yellow crown and red flecking on the yellow at the bend of the wing. It is said to be slightly smaller than the Yellow Shouldered and to have a bluish wash from the face through the breast.

CUBAN AMAZON *(Amazona leucocephala leucocephala)* *(32 cm)*.

This is the typical one of five subspecies which bears the name of *Amazona leucocephala*, and it is a great beauty among Amazons.

It is twelve to thirteen inches long and has the predominant characteristics of white on the forehead and pink on the throat and cheeks down to the chest. A dull slate blue follows the white on the crown. The neck feathers, chest, and abdomen are heavily bordered with a dark shading. The flanks have an extensive tinge of maroon forming a V to the vent.

It is found in Cuba and the Isle of Pines.

There are slight differences in the four subspecies which share the bright

315

A mutant **Blue Fronted Amazon**. The green coloring has been changed **to a yellowish-olive** and the blue is much paler. The red at the bend of the wing is prominent. **Owned by** Jerome Buteyn.

Blue Fronted Amazons, which are excellent talkers and are quite attractive. This pair is owned by Dorothy Speed.

white foreheads and rich pink of facial and throat area. The Cuban Amazon has been successfully bred in this country a few times since the publication of the first edition of this book, and it is a beautiful bird. The Cuban Amazon is the subspecies *leucocephala*. In addition to the characteristics described above it has bright blue in the wings. The Cayman Amazon (subspecies *caymanensis*) has a burgundy-red shade down to the lower chest. The Bahaman Amazon (subspecies *bahamensis*) is about an inch larger than the Cuban Amazon and has a particularly large white area on the crown. Another subspecies, *A. l. palmarum,* ranges over western Cuba and the Isle of Pines.

CAYMAN AMAZON *(Amazon leucocephala caymanensis) (32 cm)*

Confined to Grand Cayman Island in the West Indies, this bird is different from the Cuban Amazon because of the pinkish red tinge to the breast. The length is twelve inches.

CAYMAN BRAC AMAZON *(Amazona leucocephala hesterna)*

Like the Cayman Amazon, this species has a pinkish red tinge on the chest but it is about an inch shorter.

It inhabits Cayman Brac Island and Little Cayman Island.

BAHAMAN AMAZON *(Amazona leucocephala bahamensis)*

This subspecies inhabits the Bahamas and is similar to the Cuban Amazon.

RED THROATED or JAMAICAN AMAZON *(Amazona collaria) (28 cm).*

This rare eleven-inch Amazon from the Isle of Jamaica has a dull white forehead and an extensive area of dull pink extending from the beak about halfway down the neck and then extending back towards the nape. This gives a frame halfway around the cheeks which have the same dusky color as the crown.

JAMAICAN BLACK-BILLED AMAZON *(Amazona agilis) (25 cm).*

From the Island of Jamaica, this ten and a half inch parrot is practically all green except for red in the wings and tail and some blue in the wings. It has a black bill and is sometimes called the Active Parrot or the All Green Parrot.

PUERTO RICAN AMAZON *(Amazona vittata vittata) (29 cm).*

From Puerto Rico comes this small Amazon frequently called the Red Fronted Amazon. The forehead has a red band. The rest of the bird is green with a trace of red near the base of the outer tail feathers and blue on the wings. The green feathers of the head and neck are heavily bordered with black.

A subspecies, *Amazona vittata gracilipes,* from Culebra Island is now extinct.

DOMINICAN AMAZON *(Amazona arausiaca) (40 cm).*

This rare sixteen-inch Amazon has a bluish tinge to forehead, cheeks, and throat. There is a red band under the throat which extends up into the sides of the neck.

The dusky green on the Dominican Amazon is very dark but bright, and the bluish cast on most of the head is brightest on the crown. The red band under the throat is its most distinguishing feature.

RED TAILED AMAZON *(Amazona braziliensis) (37 cm).*

The very attractive Red Tailed Amazon of about fourteen inches is also called the Blue Faced Amazon, but this latter name is less appropriate because it could also be applied to *versicolor* and possibly other Amazons. The top of the head from forehead to rear of the crown is soft pink with a powderlike appearance. A dusky round cheek patch of purplish-blue is distinctly different from the dusty greyish-blue of the face and throat. The soft powdery appearance also extends through the green of the nape. Except for the tail, the remaining color is predominantly green, paler on the undersides. Bright red marks the bend of the wing. The undertail coverts fade to a greenish-yellow. The tail is multicolored, but the most prominent coloring is bright carmine -red on the outer part. This shading fades to bright yellowish with a trace of green on the outer tip. The carmine is very prominent on most of the underside. Subordinate colors nearer the base of the tail are purple, blue, and green.

This extremely rare parrot is about fourteen inches long and inhabits south-eastern Brazil.

Genus: *Pionus*

Of the twenty three races of the genus *Pionus,* fifteen are subspecies which are very similar to their basic species. Members of this genus are like Amazons in shape but do not have the wide range in size. Color similarities in all species are the peculiar dark, dusky bold coloring and the bronzed green of the wings. All are new world birds ranging from Mexico throughout tropical South America. Many of them come from mountainous areas.

Leadbeater's Cockatoos are rather small and rather expensive; but, with their soft pastel pinks against the white and a luxurious, brilliant crest, they are easily one of the loveliest birds in the world.

Hyacinth and Military Macaws. The good neighbor policy is a very workable arrangement among all the larger macaws, but the extent of friendship also depends upon individual differences. Here a Hyacinth from Brazil receives a friendly preening from the Mexican race of the Military Macaw.

The three races of the widespread Military show noticeable differences. The nominate race, *militaris* from Colombia, Ecuador, and Peru, has a darker shade of red on the forehead, a slightly smaller body, and black instead of black and red in the fine lines of feathers on the bare face. The subspecies *boliviana* has a slightly larger body than *mexicana*, a bright red on the forehead, and an extensive brownish shade on the chin. The Mexican race, *mexicana*, is about twenty-seven inches long with a body of ten to eleven inches. The forehead band of red is bright, but the most important variation occurs in the fine lined facial feathers which are red in the loreal area and, to a lesser extent, around the eyes. The lower facial feathers are black as in the other races.

RED VENTED PARROT *(Pionus menstruus).*

Called the Blue Headed Parrot with equal accuracy, this bird's two popular names describe its most outstanding features. A beautifully proportioned bird of eleven inches, the large head is a very rich shade of soft deep blue extending down the neck and onto the upper part of the breast. A charming accent is the blackish bill with a rather large area of rose-pink on each side. The other noticeably prominent feature is the bright red vent area and tail coverts. The tail is a mixture of blue and green. The rest of the bird is green, but a brassy tinge overlays the green of the wings. To top it all off there is a slight tinge of red on the throat.

Females have less pronounced blue heads which appear to be diluted with a greenish tinge.

Altogether, it is a very beautiful bird which makes a quiet and affectionate pet. However, it is not an excellent talker.

Red Venteds are rather rare and reasonably expensive in the United States. Those found in collections in the United States are usually housed in aviaries, with breeding as the ultimate goal.

SORDID PARROT *(Pionus sordidus) (28 cm).*

There is nothing sordid about this bird's habits. The unfortunate and deprecating name probably refers to the color scheme which, even so, is not sordid.

An eleven-inch bird from South America, its basic color is olive-green with a bronze tinge. The head is blue-green and buffish with a shade of lilac on the throat and upper breast. The underwings have red.

It is rare in the United States and Europe.

Pionus sordidus is divided into six subspecies: *Pionus sordidus saturatus* from Colombia; *Pionus sordidus mindoensis* from western Ecuador; *Pionus sordidus sordidus* from Venezuela; *Pionus sordidus corallinus,* which is described below; *Pionus sordidus antelius* from north-eastern Venezuela and *Pionus sordidus ponsi* from north-western Venezuela and northern Colombia.

CORAL BILLED PARROT *(Pionus sordidus corallinus) (28 cm).*

The outstanding feature of this rather somber garbed eleven and a half inch parrot from Colombia, Peru, and Ecuador, is the bright coral-red bill. The red is repeated in the undertail coverts and in outer tail feathers. The rest of the bird is dull dark green on top and dark blue underneath.

It is a subspecies of the Sordid Parrot.

It is also rare and unusual.

MAXIMILIAN'S PARROT *(Pionus maximiliani) (29 cm)*.

Another eleven-inch parrot, with four subspecies which are very similar, is Maximilian's Parrot. It is bronze green on the wings, chest, and abdomen, and has a dull dusky blue on the head. A wash of purple on the breast is attractive, but even more attractive is the red on the undertail coverts and vent. Brown and blue mark the tail. In many respects it resembles a duller edition of *Pionus menstruus* except that the head is very dusky instead of bright blue. There is no pink on the throat. The lower mandible is light. The upper mandible has a dark base which becomes lighter at the tip.

The three other races are *Pionus maximiliani siy* from eastern Bolivia, western and southern Brazil, Paraguay, and northern Argentina, *Pionus maximiliani lacerus* from northwestern Argentina and *Pionus maximiliani melanoblepharus* from Central Brazil, Paraguay and northeastern Argentina.

Pionus maximiliani lacerus has an olive chest, darker forehead, and black margins to the green feathers of the neck and facial areas. Otherwise, it is colored like Maximilian's Parrot.

It is ten and a half inches, with a tail of four inches.

MASSENA'S PARROT *(Pionus seniloides) (30 cm)*.

The only bright colors on this parrot are reddish undertail coverts and red on the outer tail feathers. The upper breast is a dusty brown with green bordering on the vinous lower breast. The wings are dark green. The dark blackish-blue head and neck are mixed with buff and pink tinged feathers.

Adult Massena's Parrots have a near white shade on the crown.

This is a somber-looking rare bird of eleven inches from northwestern South America in the Andes Mountains.

WHITE CROWNED PARROT *(Pionus senilis) (24 cm)*.

Another name for this bird is the White-Capped Parrot. Although from Central America and tropical Mexico, the White Crowned is nevertheless rare in the United States.

The basic colors are deep blue, bronzed green, and white. The cap, from the crown forward, and the throat are bright white. Both present a perfect contrast for the dull, deep blue chest. The bronzed green wings are an odd mixture with the dull blue escalloped over the green. There is some red mixed on the tail and in the bare skin around the eyes. The eyes are orange.

This is an unusual and rather attractive bird about nine and a half inches long. The few we have seen were mild and gentle even though they were being groomed for breeding.

323

Scarlet Chested Parrakeet. The small Scarlet Chested or Splendid Parrakeet, rare and expensive, has fortunately been increasing in numbers in the United States because of very good avicultural practices. This photograph by Kosmos Verlag shows the male in less than adult plumage. When fully colored the intensely vivid shade of red will solidly cover the chest and abdomen. The heavy, lustrous violet-blue and turquoise shades are already developed in this young male; but their full intensity, as with many iridescent or highly glossy colors, has not quite been captured by the camera. The female, though pleasantly and quietly attractive, cannot compare favorably to the beauty of the male.

The Bronze Winged Parrot is small and somberly colored. The wings are bronze-green and dominate the rest of the dull color scheme. These birds, because of the large eyes, can be denoted as immature.

BRONZE WINGED PARROT *(Pionus chalcopterus) (29 cm).*

An eleven-inch parrot from the Andes of Colombia, Ecuador, and north-western Peru, the name aptly describes its wings. The crown, cheeks, and back of the neck are dark blue-green. The tail and upper breast are dark blue, almost black; but the breast has pinkish red and buff in an irregular mixture. The red orange is repeated in the undertail coverts. The rump is blue black, the tail is dark blue, the abdomen is violet, and the bill is yellow. There is also some red on the vent area.

It is quite common and unusually attractive.

DUSKY or VIOLET PARROT *(Pionus fuscus) (27.5 cm).*

A slightly smaller (ten and a half inches) cousin of the Red Vented Parrot, this rare bird is a duller edition, though still very attractive.

The crown and cheeks are a deep, dull blue. The breast is dull burgundy. The mantle and rump are deep brown with   dusty pink borders on the

326

feather tips. The tail feathers are violet with bright red at their bases. The flight feathers are violet tinged with green. The bill is dusty black with yellowish replacing the rose-pink of the Red Vented. The eye area is unique: a black patch behind the eye radiates several brown feathers with streaks of pale buff. Its range is the Lower Amazon areas, Venezuela, and the Guianas.

RESTLESS PARROT *(Pionus tumultuosus) (27 cm).*

The Restless Parrot from Peru and Bolivia has a horn colored bill and is mostly green. The underside of the tail is pinkish-red. The head has an uneven reddish-plum shade changing to a greyish intermediate shading on the nape to separate the plum from the green. Ear coverts and cheeks are blackish with plum streaks on the centers of the feathers. The chest is dusky blue.

Genus: *Pionites*

CAIQUES

Possibly five species of this genus, *Pionites*, are recognized; but only two are given much notice from an avicultural standpoint.

Rare in this country, the Caiques usually command a premium price. If the price is based on acclimation efforts, we can assure the prospective buyer that almost any price would not be too exorbitant.

Without a doubt, these are the most stubborn, most interesting birds we have ever met in the parrot family. One must admire the tenacity and marvel at a stubbornness that means certain starvation, which they sometimes prefer, rather than compliance with man's dominance.

Our experience with Black Headed Caiques and White Bellied Caiques is limited to two of each and all in one group. An immature White Bellied Caique was always amenable and tame from the beginning. Though slow to change habits, this particular bird let it be known that he was not going to starve even though he preferred not to make any changes. Accepting only bananas at the beginning (a particularly dangerous diet), this bird led the others onto a mixture of bananas, peanut butter, and canned yams. (Emergencies call for drastic meaures.) Eventually, hulled sunflower seed, pablum, cod liver oil, fresh corn off the cob, hulled millet, nestling food, soaked raisins, and liquid vitamins were all acceptable if camouflaged into a goey mess by an electric blender. Gradually the mixture was thickened and hulled sunflower seed was sprinkled over the top. Corn on the cob was thereafter relished. Dried cobs led to sunflower seeds and eventually onto a normal diet of sunflower seed, parrakeet mix, and various fruits. This was a roundabout but still successful method of acclimation.

Green Winged Macaw. The Green Winged Macaw extends from Panama through the greater part of tropical South America to Bolivia, Paraguay, and parts of Argentina. This is a more southerly range than that of the Scarlet Macaw which extends from Mexico through Central America and a much smaller area in South America. Since exports to Europe more frequently emanate from Brazil than from Mexico and Central America, it is understandable that the Green Winged Macaw is far more frequently available in Europe than the Scarlet whereas the reverse is true in the United States.

Queen of Bavaria Conure. The brilliant and rare Queen of Bavaria Conure of north-eastern Brazil is the most vivid of all conures. The body is stocky and heavy and is shaped very much like those of several of the smaller Amazons. Though the slender tapering tail is nearly half the length of the entire bird, the appearance is that it is shorter. The large head and stocky body measures seven and a half inches from crown to beginning of the tail. The total length from crown to tip of the tail is fourteen inches. Sub-adult coloring shows irregular areas of green on the back. Youngsters are less attractive than adults because the coloring is neither vivid nor lustrous.

Adult White Breasted or White Bellied Caique. The apricot-colored head and green wings give this comic personality a striking color combination.

Only one holdout prevented complete success. This bird, a Black Headed Caique, decided it was fresh corn on the cob or nothing. After threee days on a starvation sit-down strike, while the others were happily cracking sunflower seeds, it was not the bird, but the keepers, who relented.

Once acclimated, Caiques are most interesting birds. Truly enigmatic, they are despised by almost as many as those who are charmed by their antics. Caiques are exceptionally intelligent and amusing comics and are very headstrong individuals.

Caiques form a small group of unusually colored, short-tailed parrots limited to South America. They range from nine to ten inches in overall length.

Sexing Caiques is difficult. The main difference seems to be in the beak. The male is said to have a broader and shorter beak than the female.

Breeding successes have been recorded, but they are rare. Gilbert Lee, of Los Angeles, is credited with the first breeding in the United States of the White Bellied Caique. Lady Poltimore, in Great Britain, reared a hybrid of Black Headed X White Bellied Caique.

WHITE BELLIED CAIQUE *(Pionites leucogaster leucogaster) (23 cm).*

This species is also called the White Breasted Caique and is the most common example of Caiques in captivity.

All upperparts from shoulders on down are bright green; chest and abdomen are off-white. The crown down to the shoulders is orange-apricot in color. The sides of the face and throat are yellow. Thighs are green, and undertail coverts are yellow. The beak is light horn color, and the naked eye ring and feet are pale flesh color. Immature birds have some black on the crown and on the beak.

BLACK HEADED CAIQUE *(Pionites melanocephala melanocephala) (32 cm).*

This bird is distinguished from the White Bellied Caique by an extensive black cap, eye ring, beak, and feet. There are some bluish-green feathers under the eye. Thighs and undertail coverts are a somewhat deeper shade of apricot-orange. Yellow areas on the face are less vivid and less extensive.

Black Headed Caique. The black cap and green loreal areas are a perfect contrast to the White Bellied species. These very tame birds are the special pets of Herb Melvin.

Swainson's Blue Mountain Lorikeets. Of the twenty-two races of *Trichoglossus haematod*, the most frequently available and easily one of the most colorful birds in the world is the subspecies *moluccanus* which is called Swainson's Blue Mountain Lorikeet. Several races are quite similar to the Blue Mountain and are sometimes confusing. The birds pictured here are not quite typical of most Blue Mountains, but then many individuals vary also. Swainson's Blue Mountain Lories are the most easily bred of all lories and lorikeets. They are very easily managed on a good diet, and have had very good success in raising youngsters. They have been excellent parents. By the time youngsters leave the nest at the age of one month, they are fully tame. Some of the tameness is lost in the next month while the fledglings are becoming weaned and fully self-sufficient, but the friendship is quickly regained after separating them from the parents. Photo by Kosmos Verlag.

PALLID CAIQUE *(Pionites melanocephala pallida) (32 cm)*.

The Pallid Caique very closely resembles the Black-Headed Caique except that the thighs and undertail are yellow instead of apricot-orange.

YELLOW THIGHED CAIQUE *(Pionites leucogaster xanthomeria) (23 cm)*.

This subspecies is very similar to the White Bellied Caique except that the thighs are yellow instead of green.

The fifth variety, *Pionites leucogaster xanthurus,* seems to have no popular name as yet and is not a fully recognized variety. It differs from the White Bellied Caique as follows: some yellow in the tail, some blue in the wings, an off-white breast tinged with a slight shade of yellow, and sides shaded with orange.

Genus: *Deroptyus*

HAWK-HEADED PARROT

The Hawk-Headed Parrot, usually grouped with Caiques, is sometimes called the Hawk-Headed Caique. It is an extremely unusual bird and has a very complicated color scheme which must be carefully inspected at close range to be fully appreciated. A description is really inadequate.

The total length is about fourteen inches, including the long, broad, square tail of approximately four inches. The long tail lends a rather slight appearance to the body.

The bill is black. The orange eye appears dominant because of the prevailing brown of the entire head. The forehead and crown are buffy brown and all the facial areas are dark brown with prominent streaks of a buffy shade radiating outwards from the lores.

The back of the neck and the sides of the lower neck have longer than normal feathers which are maroon with broad bands of bright blue at the tips. These feathers constitute a broad ruff which can be raised at will and which present a beautiful framework for the face. The ruff is erected during courting, for purposes of intimidation as well as vanity.

The wings and rump are bright, but dark green. The tail is a mixture of red, blue, green, and deep brown. The undertail coverts are green. The red forms a spot near the base of the feathers. Sexes are rather easily determined because the female lacks this red.

Hawk-Headed Parrots have good personalities and can become excellent pets. Also, they are ideal aviary birds and will breed if the situations are to their liking. Unfortunately, Hawk Heads are very rare in the United States and are usually very expensive. Purported to be delicate, Mrs. Speeds's birds winter outdoors even in the freezing weather.

The two races of the Hawk-Headed are as follows:

The GUIANA HAWK-HEADED PARROT *(Deroptyus . accipitrinus accipitrinus)*is from the tropical northern South America. *(35 cm).*

The BRAZILIAN HAWK-HEADED PARROT *(Deroptyus accipitrinus fuscifrons)* is from the Lower Amazon. *(35 cm).*

Genus: Pionopsitta

There are six species and four subspecies in this genus. All are confined to a range from southern Mexico to Brazil. *Pionopsitta* members are rather small, but otherwise they resemble those of the genus *Pionus* and *Pionites* in shape. The large heads, medium-sized bodies, short square tails, and large beaks are found in each species.

RED CAPPED or PILEATED PARROT *(Pionopsitta pileata) (22 cm).*

A nine-inch native to south-eastern Brazil, Paraguay and north-eastern Argentina, this rare little parrot has a vermilion crown which is lacking in the female. Mostly green, it has some deep blue in wings and tail.

BROWN HOODED PARROT *(Pionopsitta haematotis haematotis) (21 cm).*

The brownish hood is actually a dull olive on the crown and hind-neck. A red ear patch, another patch of red on the sides beneath the wings, and bright blue on the shoulder help to enliven the color scheme on this otherwise green bird.

The natural habitat is the southernmost areas lining the Gulf of Mexico.

A quiet, stocky, short-tailed bird, fairly abundant in its native land, it is not often found in captivity.

There are some differences in the subspecies of the Brown Hooded Parrot. The nominate race *haematotis* is eight and a half inches including the two and one-half inch tail. The chest is olive, and the bright blue of the shoulder also occurs under the wings. The race *coccinicollaris* from the Canal Zone is about eight inches long and also has an olive chest. There is less red under the wings, but there are flecks of red on the chest. The subspecies *pulchra*, also called the Beautiful Parrot, from Colombia and Ecuador has reddish-pink on the sides of the face surrounded on all sides by the darker brown of the crown. No red appears under the wings.

Jenday Conure. The Jenday Conure is a very brightly colored bird, but this photo does not show the vivid mixture of red-orange and yellow on the chest. The total length is ten to eleven inches including the five inch tail.

Two other species are closely related to the Jenday and are similar in all characteristics except coloring. The very rare Sun Conure has yellow replacing much of the green on the upperparts. Only the wings and tail remain green. Orange occurs in a fringe on the forehead, on a large and very bright cheek patch, and irregularly on the abdomen.

Nanday Conure. The very attractive Nanday Conure stands alone in its genus, but it mixes well with several conures of similar size and disposition. Because of the striking color contrasts, it can be attractively combined with Jenday Conures if individual personalities allow, which they usually do. Nandays and Jendays look well together, but they do not sound well together. Both species, in fact a great many species of conures, are particularly noisy. Both species can be tamed if hand-reared or if training is started just after weaning. In this manner, both species are usually quieter and are delightful as individual pets.

Halfmoon or Petz' Conure. The Petz' Conure is more popularly known in the United States as the Halfmoon Conure and is sold mainly as a pet "dwarf parrot." Of the two races, *eburnirostrum* is slightly larger than the nominate race. Sexes are particularly difficult to determine. A good pet Halfmoon is really a delightful bird, and youngsters are reasonably easy to train. A totally different species, the Golden Crowned Conure is known in Europe as the Halfmoon.

The beaks in all species and subspecies of the genus *Pionopsitta* are pale horn in color.

In addition, there are three very rare species of the genus *Pionopsitta* which at present do not figure importantly in aviculture. They are *Pionopsitta caica* from the Guianas; *Pionopsitta barrabandi* from Brazil, eastern Ecuador, and southern Venezuela; and *Pionopsitta pyrilia* from Panama and northern Colombia.

HOODED PARROT or CAICA PARROT *(Pionopsitta caica) (23 cm)*.

The Hooded Parrot from the Guianas, eight inches in total length including the two inch tail, has a black head and coppery-olive on the chest. There are also orange flecks on the brown nape. The rest of the plumage is bright but dark green with dull black in the flights.

ORANGE CHEEKED PARROT *(Pionopsitta barrabandi) (25 cm)*.

The Orange Cheeked Parrot from eastern Ecuador, southern Venezuela, parts of northwestern Brazil, to eastern Peru, is about eight and a half inches long including the two inch tail. The head is all black except for a large patch of bright orange extending from the lores and covering all the lower cheeks. A prominent bare eye ring is flesh colored. The shoulders are bright orange with traces of yellow. The main body color is bright green, glossy olive-green on the chest. Bright vermilion occurs on the scapulars and wing coverts with bright green on the inner areas of the flights. Leg feathers are tipped in yellow-orange, and the green tail is tipped in blue.

SAFFRON HEADED PARROT *(Pionopsitta pyrilia) (24 cm)*.

The sexes are similar in the Saffron Headed Parrot as they are in most species of this genus. This species ranges from Panama to northern areas of Colombia. The total length is seven to seven and a half inches including the two inch tail. The head is yellowish-orange with reddish ear coverts and a pale fleshy eye ring which has a dark outer rim. The chest is olive-green followed by a brighter green on the abdomen. Upperparts are green with dark shades of blue and black in the flights and a trace of red on the scapulars.

Genus: Poicephalus

The nine main species of the genus *Poicephalus* are supplemented by twenty three subspecies scattered throughout the genus. All are from Africa and range in size from eight and a half inches to thirteen inches in length. In

338

shape they somewhat resemble Amazons in miniature. There are wide variations in color. Many of the species were formerly grouped in the genus *Pionus*.

BROWN NECKED PARROT *(Poicephalus robustus fuscicollis) (33 cm)*.
Generally, this African parrot has varying shades of green with red on the thighs and outer edges of the wings starting from the shoulders and working down. The primary flights and tail feathers are brown. The head and neck are a silvery grey streaked with brown. The very large and powerful bill is greyish horn color. The female is brighter with a brick red forecrown. The male has grey brown on the same area.
The size is twelve inches.
Very rare, this parrot is not likely to gain a great deal of favor. It lacks attractive proportions and coloration.
Two similar subspecies are *Poicephalus robustus suahelicus,* from Mozambique, Rhodesia, northern Lesotho, northern South West Africa, southern Congo and central Tanzania; and *Poicephalus robustus robustus,* from southeastern Africa, western Zululand, western Swaziland and eastern Transvaal.

JARDINE'S PARROT *(Poicephalus gulielmi gulielmi) (33 cm)*
When the writers first encountered the Thick Billed Parrot from Mexico, they were very much bewildered. The only colored plate which came close to the characteristic red markings was in Greene's remarkable work on parrots. Jardine's, from Africa, is a far cry from the Thick Billed Parrot; but it does have red thighs, red shoulders, and the red crown. Wing feathers and tail have considerable dark, almost black, areas.
The overall length is twelve inches.
This rare bird is also called Red-Headed and Red-Crowned Parrot.

ORANGE CROWNED PARROT *(Poicephalus gulielmi fantiensis) (28 cm)*.
Another subspecies known on the African Gold Coast, this bird has orange replacing the red of the Jardine.
Another subspeces is called the Masai Red-Headed Parrot *(Poicephalus gulielmi massaicus).*
A fourth subspecies is *Poicephalus gulielmi permistus* from the highlands of Kenya.

YELLOW-FRONTED PARROT *(Poicephalus flavifrons flavifrons) (28 cm)*.
This common African parrot is about twelve and a half inches long and is basically green. The top of head and facial areas are bright yellow. The tail and flights are darker green with a bronze tinge. The eyes are orange-red; the

339

Blue and Gold Macaw. The Blue and Gold Macaw of tropical South America is often easily tamed even after it reaches adulthood; but, of course, that would require considerably more patience and skill. Along with the Scarlet Macaw, this is one of the most wonderful of all pet birds. Devotion to their masters is a strong characteristic of many pet birds, but a really friendly macaw is an incredibly gentle bird.

Hyacinthine Macaw. The Magnificent Hyacinth Macaw from Brazil is about thirty-four inches long and richly colored in a deep glossy hyacinth blue.

upper beak is blackish; and the lower beak is light grey. Altogether, this makes quite a pretty bird.

A second similar race is *Poicephalus flavifrons aurantiiceps*.

BROWN-HEADED PARROT *(Poicephalus cryptoxanthus) (22 cm)*.

This African species is a close cousin of the Senegal Parrot. The major difference is light green instead of yellow on the breast. The bright yellow under the wings gives it the name of *cryptoxanthus,* which means hidden yellow. It was formerly named *Pionus fuscicapillus*, a term descriptive of its dusky head. It has prominent yellow eyes.

There are three different forms that differ only slightly in color and size. The separations are also geographic and are as follows:

Poicephalus cryptoxanthus cryptoxanthus.
Poicephalus cryptoxanthus zanzibaricus.
Poicephalus cryptoxanthus tanganyikae.

The Brown-Headed Parrot is rarely seen in captivity.

NIAM-NIAM PARROT *(Poicephalus crassus) (25 cm)*.

This African parrot is similar to the Brown-Headed Parrot, but it is larger and has the dusky brown of the head extending down to the chest. The underwing coverts are green instead of yellow, and the eyes are red instead of yellow.

This bird is very rare.

SENEGAL PARROT *(Poicephalus senegalus) (23 cm)*.

This is a small, stocky, short, and square tailed parrot, of nine inches, from Africa.

It has a rich green tail and wings and a golden yellow breast which is cut into a V-shaped green area. However, this bright color scheme is interrupted by a brownish grey color which covers the entire head. The brownish grey head subdues the other colors, but it highlights a dominating yellow eye. The bill is dark.

Senegals are reasonably numerous and inexpensive in Europe, but in America they are far less numerous.

The Senegal Parrot has a reputation for being a charming pet and just about as docile as a parrot can be. Having read about these docile creatures for several years, we were delighted when we had the opportunity of taming one named Sambo. We were somewhat shaken to find the most obstreperous little keg of orneriness in all our experience with birds. We tried for weeks to tame it; and, after many savage onslaughts, lacerations, and spilled blood (ours, not his), we felt obliged to wear heavy gloves for self-preservation. This was the only instance in which we have ever used gloves.

Nothing worked. Sambo had the meanest eyes and the best biting technique of any bird we have met. We had to abandon the project. Even now, almost eight years later, Sambo gives us that mean glare which conveys a clear-cut message: "I conquered you before, and I can do it again." We treat him with the greatest respect and admiration.

We sould like to try taming one again someday. The whole trouble was those mean yellow eyes. Next time we will look for grey eyes; for grey eyes denote a young, immature bird which should respond to training in a much less exasperating manner.

There are three varieties of the Senegal Parrot:

SCARLET BELLIED SENEGAL PARROT *(Poicephalus senegalus versteri).* This subspecies, as the name suggests, has scarlet surrounding the "V" shaped green marking extending to the vent. The sides remain yellow.

ORANGE BELLIED SENEGAL *(Poicephalus senegalus mesotypus).* This subspecies has an orange belly and is paler above.

SENEGAL PARROT *(Poicephalus senegalus senegalus).* This subspecies is from Senegal and Gambia to Guinea.

BROWN PARROT *(Poicephalus meyeri) (21 cm).*

This African parrot, also called Meyer's Parrot, has a very unusual and beautiful color pattern. Head, neck, mantle, back, breast, tail, and wings are brown. Bright yellow appears on a headband, shoulder patch, and thighs. Blue is on the rump and uppertail coverts. The balance of underparts are pale grass green. Eyes are red; bill and feet are blackish.

Six known subspecies of *Poicephalus meyeri* show only such minor differences in coloration as a deeper or lighter brown, a brighter or duller blue rump mixed with green, or more or less blue around the vent.

There is also a very slight difference in size in some races, and each race inhabits a different part of Africa. Some are restricted to very small areas, and some seem to overlap the outer fringe areas of others.

The subspecies are as follows:

Poicephalus meyeri meyeri.

Poicephalus meyeri saturatus lacks blue on the rump and is green instead.

Poicephalus meyeri matschiei.

Poicephalus meyeri transvaalensis.

Poicephalus meyeri damarensis.

Poicephalus meyeri reichenowi.

ORANGE BELLIED PARROT *(Poicephalus rufiventris) (22 cm).*

Also identified as Abyssinian or Red-Breasted Parrot, this nine-inch African species is divided into two races: *Poicephalus rufiventris rufiventris* and *Poicephalus rufiventris pallidus.*

343

Golden Crowned Conure. Similar to the Petz' Conure but more attractive, the Golden Crowned Conure (*Aratinga aurea*) of Brazil is popularly known in Europe as the Half-moon and is quite well known there; but very little is known about it in the United States and very few are now in the United States. It is never available as a pet here such as is the Petz' Conure. Slightly larger and with a larger, more rounded head, the Golden Conure with its black beak, larger and circular orange patch on top of the head, and the bolder eye ring give it a much more dominant appearance than found in the Petz' Conure. There are two races: *major*, the larger of the two, and *aurea*. Photo by Horst Mueller.

Nanday Conures. Two very attractive features of Nanday Conures are not shown in this picture: the long graceful tail and the bright red thighs. This otherwise excellent photograph, much more than do most photographs, portrays two very alert, inquisitive, and intelligent birds. It does, in fact, nicely capture some of the better personality traits of this interesting species. Two possible drawbacks to this species from an avicultural standpoint are their fondness for chewing and an uncommon capacity for noise-making. The Nanday comes from southern Brazil, Paraguay, northern Argentina, and southeastern Bolivia. Photo by Horst Mueller.

The distinction between the two is doubtful. The male is ashy grey above with a blue-green wash on the wings. The rump is yellow, green, and blue. The grey throat is tinged with orange changing to deep orange on the chest, abdomen, and underwing coverts. The thighs and undertail coverts are green. The female lacks the orange and the feet and beak are black. Immatures lack the orange eyes, have a lighter shade on the upperparts, and, in the males, have a yellow and green mixture where the adult is orange.

RUPPEL'S PARROT *(Poicephalus rueppellii)* *(22 cm)*.

An eight and a half inch parrot from southwestern Africa, this rare bird is dark brown with grey tinged on the head and neck. A bluish tinge is on the rump. The thighs are yellowish orange. The underwing coverts and the bend of the wings are yellow. The female has more light blue on the rump, thighs, and abdomen.

Genus: *Coracopsis*

The nine members of the genus *Coracopsis* are all native to Madagascar and the surrounding islands. All are of somber appearance, being predominantly brown, but seem to make excellent and intelligent pets. They are very rare in the United States.

GREATER VASA PARROT *(Coracopsis vasa)* *(50 cm)*.

The greater length of this bird and its subspecies distinguishes the Greater Vasa Parrot from the other species and its subspecies. It is about twenty inches long.

The dull coloring is dusky brown with lustrous wings. The bill, black at birth, lightens as it matures.

Its habitat is eastern Madagascar.

A similar subspecies, *Coracopsis vasa drouhardi*, inhabits western Madagascar.

The second race is called COMORO ISLAND PARROT *(Coracopsis vasa cormorensis)*. It inhabits the Comoro Islands, is nineteen inches long, and has a greyish tinge to the flights. *Coracopsis vasa vasa* is confined to eastern Madagascar.

LESSER VASA PARROT *(Coracopsis nigra)* *(35 cm)*.

The Lesser Vasa Parrot is an exact counterpart of the Greater Vasa even to habitat; but it is smaller, being only fifteen and a half inches long.

There is also a similar subspecies from western Madagascar called *Cor-acopsis nigra libs.*

One of the three other subspecies is PRASLIN PARROT *(Coracopsis nigra barklyi)* from Praslin Island in the Seychelles. It is twelve inches long and is all brown with a brown bill. The other is the WHISTLING PARROT *(Coracopsis nigra sibilans)* from the Comoro Islands. This race is similar in size and appearance to the Praslin Parrot. *Coracopsis nigra nigra* is from Madagascar.

Genus: *Hapalopsittaca*

RUSTY FACED PARROT *(Hapalopsittaca amazonina)* (23 cm).

The Rusty Faced Parrot, with three subspecies from northern South America, is eight inches long including the two-inch tail. The beak is a horn color. The head is mostly chestnut with traces of yellow and orange in the centers of the feathers on the sides of the neck. Dull vermilion occurs beneath the lores and fades out on the chin. A large bright vermilion patch occurs on the shoulders followed by a smaller bright blue area below the shoulders. The major body coloring is green, brightest on the back and wings. The chest is olive with occasional flecks of dull red. The abdomen is bright green. A dusky red occurs on the center of the tail feathers with blue on the tips of the tail.

INDIGO WINGED PARROT *(Hapalopsittaca amazonina fuertesi) (23 cm).*

The Indigo Winged Parrot of Colombia is eight inches long including the three inch tail. It has a muddled appearance not only in colors but also in pattern. The coloring is mostly dull olive from the forehead through all the underparts. Blue occurs on the head and is mixed with green on the nape. Dull olive-green occurs on the back and becomes bright olive with traces of yellow on the rump. Black and blue darken the wings and tail. The shoulders have a bright patch of pale or vermilion red. The underside of the wings near the shoulders is pinkish-red mixed with blue. The remaining area on the underside of the wings is bluish-green. The female has crimson-maroon on the shoulders.

RED FACED PARROT *(Hapalopsittaca amazonina pyrrhops)*

The Red Faced Parrot, seven and a half inches long including the tail of two and a half inches, comes from Ecuador.˙It is now considered conspecific with *H. a. amazonina,* but there are variations in the appearance of the head and in size. Dark and dusky and mostly green, this race has traces of bright

347

Pileated Parrakeet. The brilliantly colored Pileated Parrakeet, approximately fourteen inches in length, is the only species in its genus. It is rare in the United States and highly prized. Upperparts of the male pictured here are bright green with dull bluish-black in the flights and a bright yellow rump. The female is similarly colored but in less vivid shades particularly on the cap and underparts.

Pair of Cockatiels. Cockatiels are usually very reliable breeders and are very good subjects for beginners in the avicultural fancy. The female is on the left. Both sexes are equal in pet potential and both will learn to talk. The male is usually preferred partly because it is more attractive and partly because of the persistent but erroneous belief that females do not learn to talk.
Youngsters resemble females, but the beaks are paler. Unfortunately, sexes are virtually impossible to determine at an early age. To wait until patches of yellow begin to appear on young males means losing months of valuable training time which, with some individuals, may never be fully reclaimed even with intensive taming and training.

yellowish-green on the ear coverts and red on the forehead, cheeks, and throat. A shoulder patch is pinkish-red. The underside of the wing is pinkish -red, blue, and green. Flights are blue and black.

BLACK EARED GREEN PARROT *(Hapalopsittaca melanotis) (23 cm).*

Two races of the Black Eared Parrot occur: *melanotis* from Bolivia and *peruviana* from Peru. The total length is nine inches including the three inch tail. The major coloring is dusky and powdery green changing gradually to a pale, dusky blue on the mantle and a brighter patch marks the ear coverts. A black bar crosses the wings from the shoulders through the scapulars and upper wing coverts. The flights are dark blue, and the tail is mostly green with black on the tips preceded by blue. The underparts are bright pale green on chest and abdomen and dusky bluish-green on the throat.

ECLECTUS PARROTS

Genus: *Eclectus*

Among the most beautiful of all parrots, the Eclecti cover a range which includes Australia, New Guinea, and most of the islands generally called Australasia, or the South Pacific Islands.

All ten members of the genus are regarded as subspecies of the Grand Eclectus *(Eclectus roratus)* and show only slight variations in size and coloring. A possible eleventh subspecies has not been fully confirmed. At one time the genus was called *Larius* and *Lorius*.

Eclectus Parrots are also called Sacred Temple Parrots because they have been the object of worship in native religious rites.

For quite some time ornithologists split the males from the females in their classifications and believed them to be totally different birds. It is no wonder, because there is no resemblance between the sexes. Males are brilliant green, brighter and lighter on the head, and have red patches at the sides of the chest. The underwing coverts are also red. The upper side of the tail is greenish with blue and white tips. The underside is bluish black with yellowish tips. The lower beak is black, and the strangely shaped upper mandible is yellowish with a pink orange base. The color pattern reminds one of the colors of candy corn of which children are so fond. The upper mandible is long and more rounded than the hooked appearance of most parrot bills.

Males are more slender than females but equal their twelve to fourteen inch length (35 cm).

Eclectus roratus polychloros, the Red Sided Eclectus Parrot, comes from New Guinea.

Female Eclecti have the most amazing color combinations and are perfect contrasts to the male's coloring. Starting with an all-black beak, the female has a brilliant red head and breast. The eye, in some races, is ringed with a very fine line of brilliant blue. There is a blue collar on the nape and a blue abdomen. The wings are deep maroon. The underwings are shaded with blue, maroon, and green at the upper end and extending to the black shading of the flight feathers. The vent is red. The underside of the tail is red, shading almost to orange at the tips. The upper side of the tail is maroon shading almost to orange at the tips. Variations show yellow on the tails and less vivid shades of blue on the chest.

Both female and male have peculiar body feather structure. In appearance, the feathers almost resemble fur which has been finely combed.

The Eclectus is a good breeder in a suitable sized aviary with the large parrot nestbox. Since they are often shy, they should have no interference during the breeding season. Females usually mar their appearance during the breeding season by plucking their chest feathers so badly that only the grey furry underdown remains. However, this condition bears no cause for alarm.

351

African Grey Parrot. The African Grey Parrot is noted for its exceptional talking ability and its bright red tail which is three and a half to four inches long. A good talking Grey can be exceptional, but there are many which are totally worthless as pets or as talkers. Many people, after a long search for an African Grey and a considerable cost, have been extremely disappointed in their Grey Parrots finding that a flawless reputation for the species as a whole does not necessarily mean flawless performances by individuals. The worthless ones, either trapped adults or adults which never received training while young, are frequently sought by aviculturists as potential breeding stock; but their value is considerably less than the high prices usually asked for good pet individuals. The legendary reputation of African Greys as the best of all pet parrots originally emanated from Europe. Since avicultural literature from England has nearly always surpassed American chronicles, it has for generations been transferred intact to America. Frequently American publishers have preferred British manuscripts to those of Americans. There is nothing wrong with this idea except that the species of parrots available in European countries have always been vastly different from those obtainable in America.

Cockatiel. The Cockatiel has one of the strongest pet potentials for everybody. Easily trained while young, reasonable in price, and attractive in appearance, the Cockatiel is outnumbered only by the Budgie and is usually even more highly regarded by its owners. It fully deserves its popularity.

The writers have seen several male Eclecti which have made affectionate pets and very good talkers, but they have never seen a female which might be called anything but shy.

Eclectus Parrots are rare and expensive but are far lower in price than some of the less desirable but highly expensive birds.

The varieties, many of which are Papuan forms, are listed below:

Eclectus roratus roratus is the GRAND ECLECTUS described above which comes from the southern Moluccas. The length is twelve and a half inches including the four inch tail. The female has dull blue on the chest compared to some of the races.

Eclectus roratus cornelia is from Sumba Island and is called CORNELIA'S ECLECTUS. The subspecies *cornelia* from Sumba Island, is fourteen inches long including the five inch tail; and so this race is a little larger than the Grand Eclectus. The female is particularly brilliant in the red, and the brightest shade of the red occurs on the chest. There is no blue on the lower chest or abdomen. The maroon on the back and wings is of a brighter and lighter shade. The male shows more red on the beak and bright blue on the wings.

Riedeli's Eclectus, subspecies *riedeli* from the northern Moluccas, is twelve inches long including the tail of three and a half to four inches long (slightly smaller than the Grand Eclectus). The female is less bright than Cornelia's but otherwise is similarly patterned with no blue on the abdomen. The reddish-maroon on the back is duller than on *roratus*. The male has less red on the sides which makes that accent far less visible than to be found on either Cornelia's or the Grand Eclectus. The yellow on the tip of the tail is dull.

The race *westermani*, not fully recognized, has a medium bright blue mantle on the female and dull maroon on the back and wings. The abdomen is dull and dark smoky blue. The male has less visible red on the sides.

The race *vosmaeri* of the northern Moluccas is thirteen and a half inches including the tail of five and a half inches. The males have extensive red on the sides in large roundish areas so that they are very prominently visible when the wings are folded. The green is paler but brighter than on most races. Females of this race show variations which may possibly be due to age difference. Some show brilliant blue on the abdomen while others show a dull and dark purplish-red. The flights are a dark bluish shade, and the mantle is bright lustrous blue. The back and wings are maroon varying from dull to bright.

The subspecies *aruensis*, a little smaller than the above, is thirteen and a half inches long including the tail of five inches. Additional red occurs on the sides of the male. On the female, the red goes to a lower area on the chest leaving less room for the blue below. The mantle is bright blue. All these colors

354

are rich, brilliant, and ideal for the bird fancier.

The race *macgillivrayi* is twelve to fourteen and a half inches with a tail of four and a half inches. The female is brilliant in all colors with a broad, bright blue mantle. She also has a prominent blue eye ring. The red ends at the middle chest followed by blue.

The Solomon Eclectus, subspecies *solomonensis*, is thirteen inches long including the tail of four inches. The male is quite typical of the best males in any race. The female has a bright blue mantle broader than in most races, and the maroon is of a good shade. The blue underparts starting at the middle of the lower chest has a slight purplish shade added on some individuals.

The *Eclectus roratus polychloros* from New Guinea is called the Redsided Eclectus Parrot. It is slightly smaller than the Grand Eclectus. The male has more extensive red sides, but the female has slightly less vivid red. The blue collar band and the blue band on the abdomen are smaller and also less vivid.

Genus: *Geoffroyus*

RED CHEEKED PARROT *(Geoffroyus geoffroyi) (21 cm).*

The Red Cheeked Parrot is a small green parrot with an attractive head. The length is eight and a half inches including the tail of two and a half inches. The tail is broad and squared. The green is soft and smooth, brighter above and shinier on the nape. Underwing coverts are bright turquoise, and in some species males have dark red on the rump. The head colors are soft and uniform, and changes to different shades are gradual blends. The males have violet on the crown and pinkish-red on the forehead, above the eyes, and on the chin and throat. The meeting place for the two shades leaves a plum coloring on the ear coverts. The males have red beaks. Females have black beaks and dull brown heads.

There are slight color variations in some of the nineteen subspecies. The race *cyanicollis* has a bright shade of dark turquoise blue on the nape and under the red throat. The female has blue on the nape and bronze on the mantle. The male of the subspecies *obiensis,* nine and a half inches including the three inch tail, has blue on the nape and lower throat or upper chest; but it is less bright than the blue on *cyanicollis.* The races *stresmanni* and *rhodops* are ten to ten and a half inches long including the tail of three to three and a half inches. The red is a darker shade but still pleasingly washed with a pinkish-rose. There is no blue on the mantle. The female has a bright chestnut-brown head in a smoother and uniform shade. The race *explorator* is just like the above two races but smaller, measuring eight and a half inches including the

Blossom Head Parrakeet. The beautiful male Blossom Head Parrakeet (*Psittacula roseata*) has a brighter and much richer coloring on the head than the Plumhead but is otherwise very similar. The male Plumhead (*Psittacula cyanocephala*) from India and Ceylon has a bright rose on the forehead fading only slightly around eyes, ear coverts, and upper crown. There is a gradual shading to a deep plum which is actually a blue blended with rose-red on the other areas of the head. Total length of twelve inches includes a long slender tail of seven inches. The tail has slightly enlarged, rounded tips in a much paler whitish-green shade. The subspecies *bengalus* shows more rose and less plum on the head than the nominate race.

Popular names are frequently interchanged, and scientific names have also changed. Peters (1937) lists the Plumhead as having three races which includes the Blossom Head. More recent work separates the two leaving two races of Plumheads (*cyanocephala* and *bengalensis*) and giving two races of Blossom Heads (*roseata* from northeastern India, southern China, and Burma, and *juneae* from Burma, Thailand, Cambodia, Laos, and North and South Vietnam. Whether grouped together or separated the aviculturist will be concerned only with the two extreme variations in head shading. The Blossom Head pictured here is the nominate race *roseata*. The total length is eleven and a half inches from crown to tip of the six and one half inch tail which has a pale tip as described for the Plumhead. This picture shows the narrow but bright plum colored band which cuts diagonally across the wing. The subspecies *juneae* has a less extensive bright rose-pink in a paler shade across the forehead, around the eyes, and on the cheeks. The female Blossom Head has a pale powdery blue-gray replacing the rose on the head.

Indian Ringneck Parrakeet. The Indian Ringneck Parrakeet (*Psittacula krameri manillensis*) is a beautiful and gracefully proportioned species of fourteen inches in total length, somewhat variable in individuals. This photograph by Horst Mueller fortunately shows the soft pastel shades of pink and blue on the sides and back of the neck ring of a mature male. Not shown is the long, slender eight inch tail.

two inch tail. The male of the race *timorlaoensis* has a paler shade of plum, and on *aruensis* the red on the male is a lighter shade. 'The race *tjindanae* is larger than *geoffroyi*. The race *keyensis* is one of the largest races, measuring eleven and a half inches including the four and a half inch tail. The race *orientalis* is much like *geoffroyi* but is an inch smaller in the body. The races *sudestianus* and *cyanicarpus* are also typical of *geoffroyi*, but they are larger measuring nine inches long including the tail of three and a half inches.

SONG PARROT *(Geoffroyus heteroclitus heteroclitus) (25 cm)*

This unusual parrot with a remarkably strange song comes from many islands, including the Solomons, New Britain, New Ireland, and the Lihir Group. It is a very rare parrot seldom found in captivity.

Its coloring is not spectacular. The male is mostly green with a dull yellow head and a pale blue-grey collar around the neck. The underwings are blue and the upper bill is yellowish. Females have blue-grey heads, bluish underwings, and black bills. The rest is green.

A subspecies, *Geoffroyus heteroclitus hyacinthinus*, is confined to Rennell Island in the Solomons. The blue-grey collar extends into the chest, back, and is found on the flanks.

Another species is *Geoffroyus simplex* with two races: *simplex* and *burgersi*. They are very rare and unknown in aviculture. The Lilac Collared Parrot *(Geoffroyus simplex)* is from New Guinea. The male is all green with a soft but not prominent purplish-lilac collar all around the neck, narrower but brighter on the throat. The female has no collar.

Genus: *Tanygnathus*

The members of this genus are all slender, long-tailed parrots. The general characteristics are large bills and broad but tapering tails which range from one-fourth to one-third of the total length of the bird. The main color is green, but the outstanding feature is the attractive variegated color patterns on the wings, and many of the scapular and covert feathers are brightly bordered in golden yellow.

All species are rare in Europe and America but are common cage birds in the Philippines. The range extends throughout the Philippine Islands and many islands in the general area extending to the Moluccan Islands.

PHILIPPINE GREEN PARROT *(Tanygnathus lucionensis lucionensis) (31 cm)*.

This is the most common of the genus and is a popular pet. It has a bright blue crown. The bill is red on the upper mandible with a dull yellow tip and dull yellow on the lower mandible.

There are eight subspecies of the Philippine Green Parrot, but the rank of some is questionable, and three are not from the Philippines. The nominate race is twelve inches long including the four inch tail. The variegation on the upper parts consists of blue feathers with light green scalloped edges and a broad area across the center with broader scallops of a bronze coloring. The mantle and back are pale green. The smaller subspecies *paraguensis* is ten inches long including the tail of four inches. The subspecies *koike* is ten and one-fourth inches long including the tail of three and a half inches. It has more olive on the mantle, and the dark centers of the variegated wing feathers are black. The shoulders are nearly all black. The Sulu Green Parrot (subspecies *moro*, covered in greater detail below) has a larger beak, black shoulders, and extensive bronze on the wings. Another race (*Tanygnathus lucionensis nigrogorum*, not listed in Peters' Checklist), is about the same. *Tanygnathus lucionensis salvadorii*, an island race coming from the Mantanani Islands near Borneo, is about twelve and a half inches long including the tail, which is five inches in length. *Tanygnathus lucionensis talautensis* comes from the Talaut Islands; like *T. l. salvadorii*, it also is about twelve and a half inches long and has a five-inch tail. Both *T. l. salvadorii* and *T. l. talautensis* are very similar in appearance to the Sulu Green Parrot. *T. l. horrisonus*, another subspecies, comes from Maratua Island off the east coast of Borneo.

Notable in the Philippine Green Parrot—and in fact in all members of the genus *Tanygnathus*—is the eye, which has a bright creamy iris.

SULU GREEN PARROT *(Tanygnathus lucionensis moro)* (33 cm).

This subspecies of *Tanygnathus lucionensis* is slightly larger than the Philippine Green Parrot and, in addition to its larger size and beak, can also be distinguished from the Philippine Green Parrot by virtue of having a paler shade of green on the upper parts.

EVERETT'S BLUE BACKED PARROT *(Tanygnathus mulleri everetti)* *(32 cm).*

This Philippine variety differs from other members of the genus by having the back and rump dark blue. The bill of the male is bright rose red, and the bill of the female is creamy white.

FREER'S BLUE BACKED PARROT *(Tanygnathus. mulleri freeri)*

This Philippine variety is larger than Everett's and has a lighter shade of blue on the back and a yellow collar on the hind neck.

359

Bourke's Parrakeets. Bourke's Parrakeets have plenty of charm and are now comparatively reasonable in price compared to many of the avicultural favorites. They are good breeders if not bullied by other birds and are gentle enough to be housed in aviaries containing finches. Still youngsters, these birds when mature will have brighter shades of blue and rose. The male will have a bright blue frontal band across the forehead and extending through the eyes. Photo by Horst Mueller.

Bee Bee or Tovi Parrakeet. Second to Halfmoons, the most popular of the so-called Dwarf Parrots are a few members of the genus *Brotogeris*. The most readily available is the Bee Bee or Tovi Parrakeet. Also called the Orange Chinned Parrakeet, an adult Bee Bee is identical to the birds pictured here except for the prominent patch of orange just beneath the beak. The four subspecies show slight variations in the shadings of brown on the wings and blue in the flights. A similar species lacking the orange patch under the chin is the All Green Parrakeet (*Brotogeris tirica*) from eastern and southern Brazil. It is seldom available in the United States. All other species in the genus have prominent distinguishing features which make identification easier.

BURBIDGE'S BLUE BACKED PARROT *(Tanygnathus mulleri burbidgii)*

Another Philippine subspecies, this bird is also larger than Everett's and is lighter on the head than on the body. It lacks the blue edgings to the feathers of the interscapular region.

Two subspecies not native to the Philippines are *Tanygnathus mulleri sangirensis* from the Sangir Islands and *Tanygnathus mulleri mulleri* from the Celebes and other nearby islands.

GREAT BILLED PARROT *(Tanygnathus megalorhynchos) (41 cm).*

The species *Tanygnathus megalorhynchos,* called the Great Billed Parrot and also sometimes referred to as the Large Billed Parrot, has a number of subspecies. The exact number of subspecies varies from authority to authority; listed below are eight subspecies and the range given for each subspecies. All of the subspecies listed have the bright red bill characteristic of the species, but the intensity of the red coloring varies somewhat from subspecies to subspecies. The eye in all of the subspecies is yellowish, and all of the subspecies show yellow under the wings and tail and an extensive bright blue area above the rump.

Tanygnathus megalorhynchos megalorhynchos is from the islands of Talaut, Sangir, Moluccas, and western Papuan

Tanygnathus megalorhynchos affinis is from the southern Moluccan Islands.

Tanygnathus megalorhynchos viridipennis is from the Tukang Besi Islands and other islands nearby.

Tanygnathus megalorhynchos djampeae is from the islands of Djampea and Kalao.

Tanygnathus megalorhynchos floris is from the island of Flores.

Tanygnathus megalorhynchos sumbensis is from the island of Sumba.

Tanygnathus megalorhynchos subaffinis is from the Tenimber Islands and the Isle of Babar.

Tanygnathus megalorhynchos helmayri is from the islands of Timor and Samao.

There are seven subspecies of the Great Billed Parrot listed in Peters' Checklist and further investigation has offered more races. Several of the races are much the same with subspecies rank given for geographical reasons rather than for individual differences in appearance. This is the most outstanding member of the genus. The huge beak is bright red, and the head is large. The wings have a more sharply contrasting scalloped pattern with the feathers on the scapulars mostly black with blue and green edges and a long area of orange prominent on the side margins of the individual feathers. To some extent these markings resemble the wing markings of Gold Mantled Rosellas. The race *affinis* has less orange showing up in the wings, and *sumbensis* has a beak larger than most races.

Two species exist in this genus about which little is known. One, *heterurus,* is known only from its type. Its true habitat and actual range is unknown. The other, *gramineus,* from the Buru Mountains is not outstandingly different from the other species. The upper part of the cheek is greyish-green, and the lower cheek area is greenish-yellow like the underparts. The primaries and primary coverts are blue edged with green. Secondary flights, median and greater wing coverts are green with yellow edges. The underwing coverts are greenish-yellow. The male has blue on the crown and a brighter shade of pink on the beak.

Genus: *Rhynchopsitta*

THICK BILLED PARROT *(Rhynchopsitta pachyrhyncha) (38 cm.)*

The only known examples of this rare parrot in captivity in this country are a pair in the San Diego Zoo. One of these birds formerly belonged to Dorothy Speed, and we had the privilege of taming it from a wild and frightened bird into a confident and docile pet.

This is a good-sized (fourteen inches), long and slender parrot closely resembling Macaws in many characteristics. It has a long, pointed six-inch tail and a very large black beak. The feet are also black. Its plumage is bright green with brilliant red on the thighs, on the crescent shaped crown extending back over the eyes, and on the bend of the wings. In flight the underwing coverts flash a bright yellow.

The Thick Billed inhabits desert areas of Mexico and is the only parrot which occasionally ranges into the United States. It frequently enters into Arizona and has been reported in New Mexico.

An interesting commentary on these birds is advanced by Bernard Roer. He states that these birds are kept from entering the avicultural field because of lack of interest in Mexico, inaccessibility of nests, and the hostile attitude of the birds themselves.

MAROON FRONTED PARROT *(Rhynchopsitta terrisi) (38 cm.)*

The Maroon Fronted Parrot is a close relative of the Thick Billed Parrot and resembles it in many respects. However, it is larger and has a darker green basic coloring. The red markings are replaced by a brownish maroon. The underwing coverts are brownish grey instead of yellow.

The Maroon Fronted is extremely rare and is not even listed by Peters.

The habitat is similar to that of the Thick Billed, except that it is more limited.

White Breasted Caique. The White Bellied Caique (*Pionites leucogaster*) has three subspecies with slight color differences: *leucogaster*, from the valley of the lower Amazon, with green thighs; *xanthomeria*, ranging from the eastern areas of Ecuador and Peru to western Brazil, with yellow thighs; and *xanthurus* which has a slight shade of yellow in the chest, orange shades on the sides, shades of blue mixed with the green on the wings, and some yellow in the tail. The latter race is not listed in Peters' Checklist. The subspecies *xanthomeria*, called the Yellow Thighed Caique, seems to be the most frequently available in the United States. The popular name seems to be shifting because of general usage to Apricot Headed Caique which is perhaps a little more distinctive than White Breasted Caique since both species have white underparts.

Both species of Caiques are exceptionally alert, intelligent, inquisitive, and headstrong. They are highly extroverted clowns almost rivaling lories and lorikeets in their acrobatic antics and extravagant poses. Fruits are a very important part of their diet, and they are happiest and prettiest when they can bathe often. Frequent bathing and a good diet give them a high plumage gloss.

Black Headed Caique. The brightly contrasting Black Headed Caique (*Pionites melanocephala*) has two subspecies: *melanocephala* from Eastern Venezuela, the Guianas, and parts of Brazil, and *pallida* from Eastern Colombia to Eastern Peru. The latter race, more correctly called the Pallid Caique, has yellow instead of apricot-orange on thighs and undertail coverts. This is the race pictured here and is the race most frequently available to fanciers in the United States, but individuals are rare with such bright blue between the beak and eyes. Usually it is much more subordinated. The bright green on the upperparts below the neck does not show in this picture.

Genus: *Gypopsitta*

VULTURE-HEADED PARROT *(Gypopsitta vulturina).*

From southern Venezuela comes the extremely rare and unusual nine-inch Vulture-Headed Parrot.

The Vulture-Headed is mainly green but has a yellow collar edged with a blackish tinge. There is some red on the undertail coverts and at the bend of the wing. The throat and chest are olive brown. Blue shades the tip of the tail and the flight feathers. The most unusual feature is the bare head, which sports a few hairlike feathers. The bare head is mostly dark with pale skin on the forehead and lores.

Genus: *Graydidascalus*

SHORT TAILED PARROT *(Graydidascalus brachyurus) (24 cm).*

This species, the only one of its genus, is green with paler scalloped edges to the feathers.

It inhabits eastern Ecuador, eastern Peru, and the Amazon Valley.

Short Tailed Parrots are a rare species and are sometimes given the popular name of Dwarf Panama. The bill is a shiny chestnut color; the plumage is dusty green.

It is somewhat less than nine inches and is a stocky bird with a short tail of one and a half to two inches.

It seems to have a pleasant personality and makes a good pet. It is very rare in avicultural or pet fields and shows little individuality. It is popularly called the Dwarf Panama.

Genus: *Triclaria*

PURPLE BELLIED PARROT or PURPLE BREASTED PARROT
(Triclaria malachitacea) (28 cm).

This unusual and charming bird from southeast Brazil is simply and effectively colored with a smooth bright green over the entire body except for a deep violet abdomen. The beak is a light horn color. The female lacks the violet abdomen.

Except for the shorter tail, this rare bird has a shape similar to that of the King Parrakeet from Australia. It is ten and a half inches long, including the broad four-inch tail.

The popular name of Purple Bellied Parrot is more appropriate than Purple Breasted Parrot.

This species is the only member of the genus and has been listed by some authorities as *Triclaria cynogaster.*

Genus: *Psittinus*

Members of the genus *Psittinus* number three, and all are subspecies of the Blue Rumped Parrot. Their range extends generally around Sumatra, the Malayan Peninsula, and a few neighboring islands.

All are small, short-tailed parrots of elusive and erratic habits about which little is known. The writers have never heard of any of them in captivity.

BLUE RUMPED PARROT *(Psittinus cyanurus cyanurus) (18 cm).*

The coloring is variable but not particularly bright. The bill is red on the upper mandible and green on the lower mandible. The entire head is blue, shading to an irregular grey mantle. The back and rump are blue. There are two dull red bands on the shoulder. The wing coverts are dark green with yellow borders. The rest of the wings are mainly blue with some black and green on the flights. The underparts are greyish green. Females have a brownish grey head and green on the mantle and back. The nominate race *cyanurus* from Burma, Thailand, Malaysia, and parts of Indonesia and

Peach Faced Love Birds. Very few parrot family birds build nests, and none go through such elaborate and amusing preparations with the nesting materials as do Peach Faced Love Birds. They first cut it into long strips and then soften it with their beaks before tucking it between feathers on sides and rump for the flight to the nest box. Much of the material becomes dislodged during the flight to the nest and falls to the ground. There are other Love Birds which tuck nesting material between feathers for transportation, but they usually work with small pieces. Madagascar, Abyssinian, Red Faced, and possibly Swindern's Love Birds are the other species with this unusual characteristic. Their nests are primitive compared to nests of Peach Faces. On the other hand, the nest of the Peach Face is far less elaborately constructed than nests of the white eye-ringed species which carry nesting material in their beaks.

Golden Cherry Love Bird. The most beautiful mutation yet to occur in Peach Faced Love Birds was established and developed by Masaru Iwata of Nagoya, Japan. Mr. Iwata calls his achievement the Golden Cherry Love Bird. In Japan the Peach Face is called *Kozakura* which means "Little Cherry" Love Bird.

Borneo, is five and three-fourths inches including the tail of one and a half inches. The two other races, *Psittinus cyanurus pontius* and *Psittinus cyanurus abbotti,* are similar but larger. The race *pontius* comes from the Mentawi Islands, and the race *abbotti* is confined to Simalur Siumat off the western coast of Sumatra.

Genus: *Psittrichas*

PESQUET'S PARROT *(Psittichas fulgidus) (46 cm).*

This very rare and unusual parrot from the forested mountains of New Guinea was formerly called *Dasyptilus pesqueti.* It is a large and bulky parrot with a small hawklike head.

It is seventeen inches long, including a square five and a half inch tail.

The basic colors are black and red. The flights, abdomen, and vent area are a deep red which is lighter on the flights. The rest of the bird is basically black, including the feet and the long narrow beak; but there are light greyish brown shadings at the tips of the feathers.

Its diet, said to be similar to that of lories, includes nectar, milk, and a variety of fruits. It is reputed to eat no seed, a fact which adds to the strangeness of this unique bird.

Genus: *Psittacella*

The three species of Ground Parrots are all from New Guinea. They resemble overgrown Love Birds in shape. They are rather heavy for their sizes, have large heads, short necks, broad tails with blunt tapered tips. Sexes are like, but immatures have varying degrees of pattern which may even be completely absent on the chest.

BREHM'S GROUND PARROT *(Psittacella brehmii* with six subspecies*) (24 cm).*

The total size of the nominate race is nine inches including the four inch tail. The head is completely brown, and the wings are uniformly dark green. The lower abdomen is a uniform brighter green. The upperside of the tail is bright green, and the underside is dull black. Undertail coverts are bright red. All the other areas are evenly barred with zebra markings. The upperparts are finer bars of alternating green and black. Underparts have bolder bars of yellow and black. There is a yellow patch on the sides just near where the bend of the wing lies when folded, but this is apparently on the male only. The beak is dark with a paler tip. This is indeed a very striking bird. The

370

subspecies *intermixta* is half an inch shorter and has a larger and longer yellow patch which extends onto the sides of the neck. The race *pallida* is eight and a half inches long including the tail of three inches. Another race, *harteri*, is even smaller, totaling seven inches including the tail of two and three-fourths inches.

PAINTED GROUND PARROT *(Psittacella picta) (19 cm)*

The nominate race *picta* is seven and one-fourths inches long including the tail of two inches. The brown on the head is brighter and more of a chestnut shade. Cheeks and lower facial areas are covered in blue, and this seems to be variable. It sometimes appears on juveniles which are totally lacking in the zebra markings. In the subspecies *lorentzi* the cheek patch is more of an orange shade with less brown in the head and green on the lower face, chin, and throat. The size is also about half an inch shorter. Males, at least in some instances, have blue on the chest.

MODEST PARROT *(Psittacela modesta) (14 cm)*.

There are four races of this smaller species with some variations in size. The nominate race *modesta* is six inches long including the two inch tail. The zebra markings on the chest are orange and black instead of yellow and black, and they are totally absent from the back. The smaller head is all brown. The subspecies *madaraszi*, often listed as a separate species, has no bars on the chest and only traces of the zebra markings on the rump of mature birds. They do appear on the nape of immature birds. The head is brown with paler centers on each feather.

Leadbeater's Cockatoo. There are four races of the lovely Leadbeater's Cockatoo, but the reasons for the subspecies rank appear to be geographical more than anything else. There are very slight variations in size and in the depth of pink shading. Those which are most common had deeper shades of pink on the head and underparts than the birds pictured here. They measure thirteen inches in length from the crown to the tip of the four and one-half inch tail.

This is a delightful picture which illustrates the affectionate personalities of these birds. However it does not show the broad band of bright yellow which bisects the vivid pinkish-red in the crest. For some reason many reproductions of color photographs fail to depict this very attractive color feature.

Barnard's Parrakeet. The handsome, broad tailed Barnard's Parrakeet from Australia is an avicultural favorite but is not often available. The upperparts on males are brighter and a lighter shade of green than indicated here.

Barnard's is one of four parrakeets which, though considerably different in color, are obviously closely related. Peters lists all four parrakeets plus four other races as belonging to a single species of the genus *Platycercus* (Rosella Parrakeets). Several authorities disagree and cling to the previous separation listing the four as species of the genus *Barnardius* with the other races given subspecies rank.

The Indian Ringneck Parrakeet has a very amusing courtship. The male slightly spreads his wings, draws his plumage close and hops and bows around his bride, or as the Duke of Bedford states: "he may sit by her side and rock himself backwards and forwards, letting go the perch with one foot and pawing the air, and at regular intervals imprinting an impassioned kiss on the back of her neck."

15

PARRAKEETS

Genus: *Psittacula*

Birds of this genus are some of the most popular in aviculture. All are confined to a large area, including India, China, Ceylon, Africa. All have a ring of color which starts at the throat and flares outwards and downwards around the neck. The colors are almost all pastels, with the predominant color being soft green in most species. The males all have red bills, and most species of both sexes have long pointed tails.

INDIAN RINGNECK PARRAKEET *(Psittacula krameri manillensis)* *(42 cm).*

The Indian Ringneck Parrakeet is one of the loveliest of all the larger parrakeets and is one of the most plentiful. In America, it is reasonably inexpensive. In Europe, it is very inexpensive and plentiful. In India, Ringnecks are everywhere. The writers became enthralled with the perfect beauty of the Ringneck when they first saw a pair. The graceful and slender proportions of the birds seemed to be in perfect harmony with the simple design and pastel colors. There have been many Ringnecks since then, but the first thrill of its beauty has never faded.

The male is a long, slender bird of seventeen inches. Half the length is devoted to a long tapering tail. The two central blue feathers give the length. All the other tail feathers become progressively shorter to the outer tail feathers. The flights also have some blue on the upper side, but the undersides of both tail and flights are yellowish green. The bill is a lovely soft shade of red. There is a fine black line across the forehead which touches the bill and connects the eyes. A faint ring of orange flesh surrounds the eyes. Starting from the base of the lower mandible on the throat, a fine black line flares outwards and downwards towards the back of the neck. It doesn't quite connect. After the black ring are two pastel rings, one pale rose and the other powder blue. The blue is carefully blended above the black ring. These colors add just the right accents to the otherwise all over pastel green, which is slightly lighter in shade on the underparts graduating to pale yellowish green around the vent.

Abyssinian Love Bird. The Abyssinian Love Bird (male with red on the forehead and forecrown) is rare in this country. It is one of three species in which colors differ in the sexes. The other two species showing such differences are the Madagascar and the Red Faced Love Birds. The nests are less elaborate and less well constructed than those of the Peach Face and the white eye-ringed species.

Peach Faced Love Birds. The ever popular Peach Faced Love Bird is the largest and most aggressive of the Love Birds and should not be housed with the other species. It is also the most easily bred and the lowest in price. Youngsters with grayish faces and black tips on the beaks are the most likely prospects for taming and training. Peach Faces and all the white eye-ringed species are social birds in that they breed well in colonies of reasonable size. Madagascar, Abyssinian, and Red Faced Love Birds are more successful if housed one pair per aviary. "Colonies," by the way, does not mean mixing species. These birds hybridize freely which tends to destroy the beauty of the individual species.

The Pied Peach Face which first appeared in California has, after a prolonged slow start, become well established in aviculture. Through selective breeding the amount of yellow has been slowly increased so that there are now many individuals available in which the amount of yellow equals or exceeds the amount of green. It is at this point that the Pied Peach Face becomes a very attractive color variety. Photo by Horst Mueller.

Indian Ringneck Parrakeet. The male has the ring around the neck, and the female lacks this ring. This perfect specimen is a blue mutation owned by Harold Rudkin.

Females and young are duller in coloration and lack the blue and rose coloring on the neck. The black ring is absent also. There is an area of paler green which seems to be waiting for the other colors to appear. The only drawback to Ringnecks is that the young take a long time to mature. At least a two-year wait is necessary to determine sex; and, apparently, some do not mature until they are three years old. This means that many young birds are sold as females only to mature into males about the time the new owners are hopeful of breeding success. Females are in shorter supply than males. The mistake is a common one.

Like Budgies, the Ringneck has shown a penchant for mutations. Blue and Lutino Ringnecks have been captured in the wild state and have successfully been established in aviculture, but their prices are very high, and they are seldom available.

Ringnecks are good breeders and can successfully be mixed with a few varieties of other birds. The writers have kept them in complete harmony with Cockatiels and Australian Crested Doves during the breeding season.

AFRICAN RINGNECK *(Psittacula krameri krameri) (40 cm)*

This distinctive subspecies of the Indian Ringneck is from Afica and is less plentiful than the Indian Ringneck. The African variety is slightly smaller and lacks the pink around the ring. The blue, if present, is greatly reduced. Because of the reduced coloring, the African variety has less popular acceptance. Those which the writers have had showed exactly the same personalities as the Indian variety.

Other races of *Psittacula krameri* are from Africa, *Psittacula krameri parvirostris* from Eritrea and northern Ethiopia, and *Psittacula krameri borealis* from West Pakistan, northern India and from Nepal through to central Burma.

ALEXANDER RINGNECK PARRAKEET *(Psittacula eupatria nipalensis) (58 cm)*

Also called Alexandrine Parrakeet, this is the largest member of the genus. It is about twenty inches long and is one of the most outstanding specimens of the genus. This subspecies inhabits India; but similar species also occur in Ceylon, Burma, Cachar, and the Andaman Islands.

At first sight, the writers must confess that they did not think this a beautiful bird. Compared to the Indian Ringneck, it seemed a top-heavy and ungainly bird. The large head and huge bill seem out of proportion. All in all,

Princess Alexandra Parrakeet. Softly colored, the male Princess Alexandra Parrakeet is very attractive in a quiet but variable color scheme. Not shown in this photograph are the blue crown, chartreuse wing coverts, and violet rump which add variation to the subordinate shades of green and olive shades which cover the remaining areas of the upper parts. The female is considerably duller and has a shorter tail. Photo by Horst Mueller.

Barraband Parrakeet. The very beautiful Barraband Parrakeet is quite a prize for bird fanciers. Not shown in this photograph by Horst Mueller is the long tapering tail which is also green with some pink and black. The female lacks the distinctive red and yellow areas and has the green generally more subdued.

it appeared to be a gross caricature of the beautiful Ringneck. Then the writers saw an Alexander Ringneck with a full length tail and realized how wrong they were. The extra length in the tail made all the difference. The bird no longer seemed out of proportion and held an attitude of majesty which the Ringneck does not possess.

In appearance, the Alexander Ringneck is a larger version of the Ringneck. Its bill and head are larger in proportion than those of the Ringneck. There is more rose to the hindneck and a patch of deep red on the wings. Females lack the pink and black on the neck.

The Alexander Ringneck is a popular favorite and a fair breeder. It is more expensive than the Indian Ringneck due to its greater rarity.

Other races are as follows:

Psittacula eupatria eupatria inhabits Ceylon and parts of India and is slightly smaller and duller.

Psittacula eupatria siamensis inhabits Siam and Cochin-China.

Psittacula eupatria avensis inhabits Burma and Cachar.

Psittacula eupatria magnirostris, the large ANDAMAN ISLAND PARRAKEET, inhabits the Andaman Islands. It has a larger beak and a narrow bluish band above the rose collar.

Psittacula eupatria wardi is possibly extinct and inhabits the Island of Silhouette.

MOUSTACHE PARRAKEET *(Psittacula alexandri fasciata) (33 cm)*

A very attractive parrakeet of thirteen to fifteen inches from India, the Moustache, or Banded Parrakeet, has a large black moustache and a black band across the forehead connecting the eyes. The entire head is bluish grey and is bordered on the nape by a brighter green than the rest of the green on the upper sides. There is a bright and light green patch on the wings. The chest is a rufous (brownish-red) color with a violet tinge.

The bill of the male is red. The female has a black bill and is somewhat duller in color.

This species is not known as a free breeder, but it is very attractive and worth a try. It is quite similar to the Derbyan but has a smaller head and body. The dividing line on the head is less distinct than that of the Derbyan and the blue is less extensive.

Other races of this species are listed below with their habitats:

Psittacula alexandri abbotti is from the Andaman Islands.

Psittacula alexandri cala is from Simeulue Island.

Psittacula alexandri major is from the Lasia and Babi Islands.

Psittacula alexandri alexandri is from Java, Bali, southern Borneo, and the Kangean Islands.

Male Moustache Parrakeet, a rare and beautiful species with a large black moustache similar to that of the Derbyan.

Psittacula alexandri perionca is from Nias Island.
Psittacula alexandri dammermani is from Karimon, Java Island.
Psittacula alexandri kangeanensis is from the Kangean Islands.

DERBYAN *(Psittacula derbiana) (50 cm)*.

The Derbyan comes from remote areas of southeastern Tibet and southwestern China and is similar to the Moustache Parrakeet except for a larger body and head. The head is bluish grey, and the black forehead band covers the lores and extends to the eyes. There is a sky-blue area adjacent to this band. The large moustache covers most of the throat. The back is green, and the chest is mauve. The pale green or chartreuse wing patch is duplicated in the thighs and vent area.

This is a beautiful but rare species which needs more serious attention from aviculturists to establish it as a successful breeder. Unfortunately, it does not readily cooperate in such a project. The total length is eighteen

Black Cheeked Love Bird.

Blue Masked Love Bird. The Blue Masked Love Bird is a beautiful mutation of the
Black Masked Love Bird. It has long been established in the United States.

Scarlet Macaw. The Scarlet Macaw, also called Red and Yellow Macaw, is offered for sale more frequently than any other Macaw. This large bird makes a good pet but requires a very roomy aviary strong enough to stand up to its destructive beak. Photo by Horst Mueller.

inches including the nine and a half inch tail, and the male has a reddish upper mandible with a pale tip while the female has a black beak. The mantle is particularly glosssy.

LONG-TAILED PARRAKEET *(Psittacula longicauda longicauda)*

The beautiful Long-Tailed Parrakeet, like so many other birds from Malaysia, is rare in captivity. This species comes from the Malay Peninsula and neighboring islands. It frequents heavily forested area. In captivity, Long Tailed Parrakeets are not the most ideal birds because of their characteristic wildness.

The male is about sixteen inches long, including the long tapering tail of ten inches. The two central feathers give the greatest length. All the other feathers in the tail taper from short feathers on the outside to about four inches on the inside. The two central tail feathers, which are soft deep blue, extend about six inches longer than this point. The basic coloring of the bird is a soft shade of green which is darker on the uppersides and lighter on the undersides. As the green approaches the abdomen, it becomes progressively lighter in color until it reaches the underside of the tail, which has a soft yellow tinge. There are tinges of blue on the mantle and a more pronounced blue on the back. The flights are mainly dark blue with some green.

The head has an outstanding coloration. The bill has a rose-red upper mandible and a black lower mandible. A dark green crown is followed by a lovely pastel rose-pink covering the hind neck and the sides of the face. The throat has a bold, black walrus type of moustache flaring outwards and downwards and tapering to a point near the shoulders. All in all, it has a soft pastel loveliness with just the right dark accents.

Females have brown replacing the red bill; and, with the two long tail feathers missing, she is less shapely. The walrus moustache is absent and is replaced by a yellowish green with a suggestion of a green moustache. The pink on the face is also duller.

There are four other races of the Long-Tailed Parrakeet:

Psittacula longicauda defontainei is a paler form from Natuna Islands, Rhio, and neighboring islands.

Psittacula longicauda modesta called the LUCIAN PARRAKEET, is another paler form from Engano Island.

Psittacula longicauda nicobarica is from the Nicobar Islands. This subspecies is called the NICOBAR PARRAKEET.

Psittacula longicauda tytleri is from the Islands of Andaman.

BLOSSOM-HEADED PARRAKEET *(Psittacula rosa) (30 cm)*.

This lovely slender parrakeet from India is eleven inches, with a five and a half inch tail. The beautiful head of the male is a rose color with a bluish tinge. There is a narrow black neck ring connected to a black throat. The basic body color is a soft shade of green with a bright maroon shoulder patch which is usually hidden when the wings are folded. The flights are a darker shade of green, and the tail is blue with whitish tips on the upperside and is a yellowish on the underside. The beak is horn-colored on the upper mandible and darker on the lower side.

Females and immatures have a lavender-grey color on the head. Females are rare, and it is not uncommon to have a "female" change its head color and blossom into a mature male at three years of age. It is always wise to check into the age of the female before making a purchase.

These parrakeets are common in Europe but not in America. More attention should be given to their firm establishment as good breeders in captivity. They are beautiful and are ideal aviary birds.

PLUM HEAD PARRAKEET *(Psittacula cyanocephala) (30 cm).*

These beautiful birds are very tolerant towards other parrakeets, even towards little finches, although for breeding purposes a pair should be given a large garden aviary to themselves. A nest box of 8 x 12 in. must be hung in a light spot; room must be available on top of this box, as the birds love to perch on it.

SLATY-HEADED PARRAKEET *(Psittacula himalayana himalayana)* *(40 cm).*

The Slaty-Headed Parrakeet of the Himalayas of northern India resembles a female Plum Headed Parrakeet except that it is larger. In size, it comes closer to the Ringneck Parrakeet. This species is also rare in captivity.

The male has a red bill, a slate colored head, wine red shoulder patches, and white tips to the tail feathers. Otherwise, it is the same green of the Ringneck and Plum Head.

Females lack the wine red shoulder patches and are a paler shade of grey on the head.

Another race, *Psittacula himalayana finschii*, is native to Burma and India and is called the BURMESE SLATY-HEADED PARRAKEET.

LAYARD'S or EMERALD COLLARED PARRAKEET *(Psittacula calthorpae) (29 cm).*

Layard's Parrakeet is a little smaller than the Ringneck and lacks the added tail length which gives the Ringneck so much more shapeliness. It comes from the forests of Ceylon and is a rarity in captivity.

Top to bottom: yellow variety of Redrump Parrakeet; lutino variety of Nyassaland Love Bird; blue variety of Masked Love Bird. Drawing by R. A. Vowles.

Fischer's Love Bird. The delicate beauty of Fischer's Love Bird has made the species one of the most popular Love Birds in the United States. Photo by Horst Mueller.

The male has a red bill and a grey head with soft green tinges in the area of the eyes and lores. The black ring extending rather broadly from the throat circles around the back of the neck in a diminishing line which disappears before it connects. A bright soft green area follows on the nape of the neck. The pale grey back gradually deepens to a cobalt shade on the rump, which continues into the tail, where it becomes pale again. There is a broad area of pastel olive green on the wings which deepens to a dark green on the outer rim of the wings. Flights are dark but still soft, bluish green. The underparts are a soft pastel green.

Females have black bills and are duller in coloration.

MALABAR or BLUE WINGED PARRAKEET (Psittacula columboides) (38 cm).

Rare in its native southwestern India, the Blue Winged Parrakeet is a highly prized rarity in captivity. It is shaped like a Ringneck and is about the same size.

The male has a red bill and a slightly rose-tinted grey head which has a tinge of powder blue on the forehead and a tinge of pale green around the eyes. The black ring is bold and meets on the back of the neck. A pale blue collar follows and graduates to a paler green below the throat. The chest, abdomen, and mantle are soft grey with the rose cast again present. The wings and tail are blue and are darker on the flights. The wing feathers have paler edges giving them a scalloped effect, and the tail has yellowish tips. The vent, tail coverts, and underside of the tail are a yellowish green which becomes less yellow on the tail.

Females have black bills and lack the collar. The rose cast seems absent from the grey areas. The wings are also duller.

The scientific name was formerly Psittacula peristerodes.

There are three other members of the genus Psittacula which are very rare and about which little is known.

Psittacula intermedia has an uncertain status and an unknown distribution.

Psittacula exsul, believed by some to be extinct, inhabits the Island of Rodriquez.

Psittacula caniceps inhabits the Nicobar Islands. It is called BLYTH'S NICOBAR PARRAKEET. It is large-bodied and long-tailed like the Alexander Ringneck. The total length is twenty-two inches, including the fourteen-inch tail. The greyish head is accented by the reddish bill, a black forehead band, and a filled-in triangular moustache.

Genus: *Aprosmictus*

CRIMSON WINGED PARRAKEET *(Aprosmictus erythropterus erythropterus) (32 cm).*

The beautiful Crimson Winged Parrakeet is an Australian bird inhabiting eastern Australia from southern Queensland to New South Wales. It is slightly over twelve inches long, including the broad five and a half inch tail. It is beautifully proportioned and has a good sized body and head.

The male has a reddish bill shading to a light horn color at the tips. The head, neck, and all underparts through the tail coverts are bright grass green with a turquoise tinge to the crown. The underside of the tail is black, lighter at the tips. The upperside of the tail is dark green. The rump is a brilliant dark blue shading to a chartreuse at the lower part. The back is black. The upper parts of the wings are brilliant red surrounded by a dark, dull green area. The flights are bright green.

Crimson Winged Parrakeet, a handsome parrakeet rivaling the majestic King Parrakeet.

Red-Fronted Parrakeet.
Photo by Horst Mueller.

Stanley Rosella, male. Photo
by Horst Mueller.

Gold Mantled Rosella.
Photo by Horst Mueller.

Albino Cockatiel. Photo by
Horst Mueller.

The female is a duller edition of the male. It lacks the turquoise in the crown, has no black on the back, and the red in the wings is restricted to tinges of color. The overall green coloring is lighter on the chest, abdomen, vent area, and the undertail coverts. The underside of the tail is blackish tinged with a dull red. The underwings are green at the shoulder and are slate color on the flights. There is a bright turquoise blue area just above the rump and a chartreuse area behind. The wings have a band of red on the median and lesser coverts and on the scapular area. The flights are blackish with a greenish tinge. The beak is a horn color with an orange tint.

A close relative from southern New Guinea is *Aprosmictus erythropterus coccineopterus*. This lovely subspecies from New Guinea differs from *Aprosmictus erythropterus erythropterus* in size and coloring. It is ten inches long, including the five-inch tail. The red in the wings is darker, and the reddish color of the beak is lighter. The female is similar to the female of the aforementioned subspecies except that it has more red in the wings.

TIMOR ISLAND CRIMSON WINGED PARRAKEET *(Aprosmictus jonquillaceus).*

The nominate race of this species has no black on the back. In its place is dark green with pale green on the rest of the wing except in the crimson bar. The crimson bar is less extensive than in *erythropterus.* The rump is brilliant turquoise-blue. The subspecies *wetterensis* from Wetar Island has the brilliant crimson in an even less extensive area.

Genus: *Alisterus*

AUSTRALIAN KING PARRAKEET *(Alisterus scapularis scapularis) (43 cm).*

The most majestic of all the parrakeets is the beautiful King Parrakeet from southern Queensland, New South Wales, and Victoria.

The male is the brilliant one of the species. It is fourteen to fourteen and a half inches in length, including the broad seven-inch tail. The beak is reddish orange with black tips on the upper and lower mandibles. A brilliant red covers the entire head down to the shoulders on the upper side and, on the underside, down through the vent, becoming deeper on the abdomen and vent. The undertail coverts are black with red borders of nearly a half inch on each feather. The tail is black on both sides. The wings and back are brilliant green with a dull, deep blue starting at the lower half of the back and shading into the black tail. There is a bright pale green patch on the bend of the shoulders of each wing. An irregular, narrow, bluish collar follows the red neck.

Kings are ideal aviary inhabitants but are not particularly good breeders. They are rather sluggish and, at times, clumsy. They should be kept in a large aviary.

A subspecies, *Alisterus scapularis minor*, comes from northern Queensland. It is smaller with a darker shade of red.

GREEN WINGED KING PARRAKEET *(Alisterus chloropterus chloropterus) (36 cm)*.

This beautiful Green Winged Parrakeet has a very bright and light green wing bar which gives it even more brilliance than the Australian King. But it has a little less majesty than the latter.

There are three other subspecies of this wonderful bird:

Alisterus chloropterus callopterus from the Upper Fly River in New Guinea. This subspecies shows blue flecks on the mantle.

Alisterus chloropterus wilhelminae from the mountains of New Guinea.

Alisterus chloropterus moszkowskii from northern New Guinea.

Their deeper shade of green and more brilliant red are vivid contrasts for the bold light green wing bar. In the nominate race, bright blue on the lower part of the crown extends to the mantle. The sides of the cheeks and neck are still bright red. The back and nearly all of the wings are black except for the bright pale wing bar and the dark green surrounding this area. The length is twelve and a half inches including the tail of seven inches. The subspecies *wilhelminae* has less blue on the mantle and none on the nape. In the subspecies *callopterus* only traces of blue occur on the nape. The subspecies *moszkowskii* is a little larger totaling fourteen inches including the seven to seven and one-half inch tail.

Other species of the King Parrakeets are very rare and show only slight variations. Mainly there is more blue on the wing and the pale wing bar is missing.

Breeding results of the Green Winged King Parrakeet are usually obtained in a large outdoor aviary with quiet surroundings. It is recommended to keep a pair all by themselves. The hen usually refuses to use a nest box and rather will lay her eggs in a depression made in the aviary floor. A 14 x 14 x 45 in. nestbox in the open air must be offered, either hung up or set on the aviary floor, with a 6-in.-deep layer of rotten wood chips. Note that the males are extremely ferocious during nesting and rearing-time. Hybrids with the Crimson Winged Parrakeet and the Barraband Parrakeet are known.

1. Greater Sulphur Crested Cockatoo; 2. African Grey Parrot; 3. Finsch's Amazon Parrot; 4. Yellow-Naped Amazon Parrot; 5. Blue and Yellow Macaw; 6. Blue-Headed Parrot; 7. Blue Fronted Amazon Parrot; 8. Roseate or Rose Breasted Cockatoo; Scale: $\frac{1}{4}$ actual size. Drawing by R. A. Vowles.

9. Blue Wing Parrotlet; 10. Lineolated Parrakeet; 11. Tovi Parrakeet; 12. Petz' Conure; 13. Yellow Fronted Amazon Parrot; 14. Green Cheeked Amazon Parrot; 15. Spectacled Amazon Parrot; 16. Golden Crowned Conure. Scale: $\frac{1}{4}$ actual size. Drawing by R. A. Vowles.

This pair of Green winged King Parrots *(Alisterus c. chloropterus)* needs a deep and roomy nest box (14 x 14" and 34 to 50" deep) and a good layer of rotted wood chips on the bottom (6" deep).

AMBOINA KING PARRAKEET *(Alisterus amboinensis) (35 cm).*

The nominate race of the Amboina King Parrakeet, *amboinensis,* does not have pinkish margins on the wing feathers; but the dark blue is more extensive covering the bend of the wing and shoulders and all of the back. The rump is especially brighter; the red is lighter; and the tail is black. The Buru Island King Parrakeet, subspecies *buruensis,* is sixteen and a half inches long including the tail of nine to nine and a half inches. The head is large; the red is very bright; the tail is black; upperparts are dark green; and the rump is deep cobalt blue. The Salwattee King Parrakeet, subspecies *dorsalis,* has a bright shade of blue, a deep shade of red, and the all black lower mandible. The Halmahera King Parrakeet, subspecies *hypophonius,* is fourteen inches long including the seven and one-half inch tail. The red is very rich and dark on the head and all underparts. Underwing areas are black, and all remaining upperparts back from the mantle are black except for the dark blue on the rump. The Sula Island King Parrakeet, *sulaensis,* is twelve and a half inches long including a seven and one-half inch tail. The head is smaller and darker red. Dark blue occurs on the lower back and rump, and traces of blue also occur on the upper back. The tail is black.

MUSK PARROTS

Genus: *Prosopeia*

There are two species of the genus *Prosopeia* with one of the species divided into four subspecies which mostly denote geographical differences. All are confined to the many small Fiji Islands and feed upon the abundant fruitful vegetation. Their plumage has a musky odor. In many repects, members of this genus resemble the King Parrakeets of the genus *Alisterus.* In fact, they were once classified under that genus.

Their size is eighteen inches, including the broad tail of eight and a half inches. They are very rare in aviculture, as are all birds from these areas. From most reports, however, they are common in the wild state and are popular as talking pets in their native habitats.

RED BREASTED MUSK PARROT *(Prosopeia tabuensis tabuensis)* *(45 cm).*

The gorgeous Red Breasted Musk Parrot (or Parrakeet) is a very large parrakeet shaped in almost every respect like a King Parrakeet.

It has a black beak, deep maroon head, red chest and abdomen, and green wings and rump. There is some blue in the long broad tail, on the flights, and on the nape. Eyes are bright yellow.

Scarlet Macaw. Photo by Albert Gommi. Reproduced with permission of the copyright owner, the Champion Paper and Fibre Company.

It is found in the Fiji Islands on Vanua Levu.

Seventeen inches long including the broad eight and a half inch tail, the Red Breasted Musk Parrot has maroon covering the head, chest, abdomen, and undertail coverts. The rump and wings are brilliant dark green. Sexes are alike. Another subspecies, *atrogularis*, not listed by Peters, is very similar. The Koro Island Parrakeet (subspecies *koroensis*) is from Koro and Kagu in the Fiji Islands. This race has the blue collar greatly reduced and has darker maroon. The Taviuni Parrakeet (subspecies *taviunensis*) has a duller maroon, and the blue collar is missing in some individuals but not all.

Another race, the RED SHINING PARRAKEET *(Prosopeia tabuensis splendens)* is from Viti Levu, Kandavu, and Mbau, in the Fiji Islands. This species has bright crimson instead of maroon coloring and a more conspicuous blue collar.

YELLOW BREASTED MUSK PARROT *(Prosopeia personata) (47 cm)*.

From the Fiji Islands, but probably confined to Viti Levu, comes the striking Yellow Breasted Musk Parrot, sometimes called Masked Parrakeet. It is similar in shape but an inch longer than the Red Breasted Musk Parrot.

The bill, face, and underside of the tail are black. The outer tail feathers on the upperside are bluish. The yellow chest shades into a deep orange on the abdomen. The sides of the chest and abdomen are flanked with green, as are all other parts not already mentioned. Flights and outer rim of the wing as well as primary coverts and scapulars are blue. Dark bluish shadings occur on the upperside of the outer tail feathers.

Genus: *Polytelis*

Polytelines have long, narrow tails, small heads, and rather plumpish bodies; but they exhibit a grace and charm far above most other parrakeets. All are Australian birds and are sedately rather than gaudily colored. All are popular but expensive in America.

The Barraband and Rock Pebbler are of the subgenus *Polytelis*, and the Princess Alexandra is of the subgenus *Spathopterus*.

BARRABAND PARRAKEET *(Polytelis swainsonii) (40 cm)*.

This lovely Australian parrakeet is neither gaudy nor pretentious; it possesses more grace, charm, and dignity than nearly any other parrakeet. The nearest similar demeanor in a parrakeet is that of the King Parrakeet, which displays more of a proud, regal bearing.

This demeanor accounts for the Barraband's apt synonym, Superb Parrakeet. It is a highly desirable bird and is somewhat rare and expensive.

402

This cock Barraband Parrakeet and Budgerigar are great friends. The Barraband is a very peaceful bird and may therefore be kept with other birds (Budgies, Cockatiels, Bourke's, etc.) Skirmishes are likely to occur only at mating time.

Rock Pebbler. Judging from the greater depth of yellow in its coloration, this bird probably comes from that part (Victoria) of the species' range in which the population shows the brightest yellow. Photo by Horst Mueller.

A pair of Golden Shouldered Parrakeets, male at left. Photo by Horst Mueller.

Cloncurry Parrakeets.
Photo by Horst Mueller.

Lutino Indian Ringneck Parrakeets. Photo by Horst
Mueller.

The slender shape and long tapering tail are predominantly a soft shade of bright green. Males have a rich shade of yellow on the forehead and crown which is repeated in a large area covering the cheeks and throat. A flaring, broad crescent of light but bright red frames the lower boundaries of yellow on the throat. The bill is a slightly duller shade of red.

The female and immature birds lack the yellow and red markings. Females are less numerous than males, and many "females" mature into males just about the time when the proud possessor dreams of possible nesting successes. When purchasing a female make sure it is two years old to be certain of its sex.

Barrabands are peaceful with other congenial birds. They are hardy and long-lived. They cannot be too highly recommended.

ROCK PEBBLER *(Polytelis anthopeplus) (40 cm).*

The unusually colored Rock Pebbler from southern Australia is seventeen inches long, including the long slender tail. The dark reddish maroon bill contrasts with the dull, olive-yellow underparts. The upperparts are basically a darker shade of olive coloring.

Color variations add a pleasant, though subdued, pattern to the overall effect. There is a chartreuse wing patch and a reddish coloring in the secondary flights. The primaries are dark blue-green. The olive rump is a lighter shade than the back. The upper side of the tail is dark olive, blue, and black with a reddish tint underneath.

Females combine a duller shade of olive with a rose color in the outer tail feathers.

PRINCESS ALEXANDRA PARRAKEET *(Polytelis alexandrae) (45 cm).*

The popular names of this beautiful Australian parrakeet follow the pattern of a princess's ascension to the throne. It is known as Princess Parrakeet, Princess Alexandra Parrakeet, Princess of Wales Parrakeet, and Queen Alexandra's Parrakeet. It should never be called Alexandra Parrakeet because it could become too easily confused with the Alexander Ringneck Parrakeet.

The Princess Alexandra Parrakeet is, like others of the genus, a long-tailed slender parrakeet of almost regal bearing. Its coloring is one of soft pastels. The male has a blue crown, coral beak, olive mantle, chartreuse wing coverts, pink throat, greyish green chest and abdomen, pinkish thighs, olive green undertail coverts, olive green tail, violet rump, deep olive green wings (other than the chartreuse wing coverts), and a brighter shade of green on top of the head.

The female has a shorter tail and duller colors, particularly on the head and rump. Immatures resembles females in coloring, but young males have

The Princess Alexandra Parrakeet is most graceful in a large outdoor aviary. A true pair is worth watching during the mating-period; they seem to embrace one another with their wings and sit cheek to cheek.

larger, flatter heads and brighter crowns. They mature between twelve and fifteen months.

The reason for the subgenus is a peculiar elongation of the third primaries which is lost prior to the moult.

Princess Alexandras are rare and highly desirable, but they are rather expensive.

Genus: *Platycercus*

The genus *Platycercus* features some of the most popular and most beautiful parrakeets in aviculture. All species have long, broad tails and are within the size range of ten and a half inches to sixteen inches. All are well-proportioned, slender birds with a reputation for aggressiveness with other parrot-like birds.

The genus is sharply divided in characteristics. Most of the species are Rosellas and have a characteristic black shoulder patch and scalloped feathers on the back, or mantle. The centers of these feathers are black, but the colors

Indian Ringneck Parrakeets. Blue variety above, lutino variety below. Drawing by R. A. Vowles.

Yellow Fronted Amazon Parrot. Photo by Horst Mueller.

of the outer margins vary with individual species. Most Rosellas also have low cheek patches which are broad and tend to rest almost on the jaw line.

Several species, starting with Barnard's Parrakeet, were originally classed in a genus named *Barnardius*. Some authorities still class them under that name, but Peters maintains that all of them should be members of a single species: *Platycercus zonarius*. These species have the same general shapeliness and broad tail, but they lack the scalloped mantles and cheek patches. Instead they have a "ringneck" collar.

CRIMSON ROSELLA *(Platycercus elegans elegans) (36 cm)*.

The Crimson Rosella is larger and heavier than most of the more popular members of the genus. It is thirteen inches long, including the six and a half inch tail.

All the head, neck, and underparts are deep crimson red except for blue cheek patches and a pale blue on the underside of the tail. The upper side of the tail is dark blue and green. The rump is red. The scalloped back area has some dull green and red on the outer margins of the black feathers. The upper wing coverts have a pale violet-blue coloring.

Immatures have considerably more green. Much of the crimson is replaced by it.

The Crimson Rosella is a popular aviary bird but not readily available.

Another race of the Crimson is *Platycercus elegans nigrescens,* found in the coastal areas of northern Queensland. It is slightly smaller and darker than the Crimson.

Another subspecies, *Platycercus elegans melanoptera*, is similar to and also called by the same name as the Crimson Rosella. It is, however, larger and brighter: fourteen inches, including the seven-inch tail, is its length. The scalloped area has red margins, and all the red is more vivid. It is confined to Kangaroo Island and northeastern Australia.

There is some question as to the validity of the latter subspecies. It has been disclaimed by some authorities as being doubtfully distinct from *Platycercus elegans elegans.*

ADELAIDE ROSELLA *(Platycercus adelaidae) (36 cm)*.

This rare and desirable subspecies is from Southern Australia in the Adelaide region. It is like the Crimson Rosella except for an orange-red coloring infringing on much of the crimson areas. The sides of the breast fade to a yellowish tone. There is considerable variation.

The Adelaide is common in its wild state but rather rare in captivity. Strong attempts have been made to establish it in aviaries in southern California. David West has been the most successful to date.

YELLOW ROSELLA *(Platycercus flaveolus) (33 cm).*

Also called the Yellow-Rumped Parrakeet, the Yellow Rosella is confined to the area of the Murray River and its tributaries in southern Australia. Therefore, it is sometimes called Murray Rosella.

The Yellow Rosella is slightly smaller than the Crimson Rosella. There is a red frontal band. The cheeks are blue. The rest of the head, chest, and abdomen are pale yellow. The back, or mantle, has the black feathers scalloped in yellow. The rump is yellow, the tail is blue, and there is blue in the wings. The black shoulder patch is present.

Sexes are determined by the brighter coloration and larger head and beak of the male. Females also have a few reddish flecks on the yellow throat and breast. The pale yellow takes on a greenish cast in the immatures.

The Yellow Rosella is a very rare species, but it makes a very desirable aviary bird and is a fair breeder.

GREEN ROSELLA *(Platycercus caledonicus) (36 cm).*

Sometimes called the Yellow Bellied Rosella, this very rare species is found in Tasmania and the islands of Bass Straits.

It is the largest of the Rosellas and, despite its name, has little of a true green in its coloring. The black mantle feathers have dark green margins. The same shade of green is repeated in the rump. The head and underparts are yellowish olive. A red frontal band, blue cheek patches, and blue on the wings are present.

Females have smaller and more feminine looking heads and bills. Immature birds, which reach the adult stage in fifteen months, have a brighter shade of green on the underparts and head.

The Green Rosella has been bred in captivity, but it is unfortunate that a good supply of aviary birds is not available to help establish sound breeding stocks as has been done with several other Rosellas.

RED ROSELLA *(Platycercus eximius eximius) (30 cm).*

Eleven to twelve inches long and inhabiting the Victoria and eastern New South Wales area of Australia, the Red Rosella sports one of the brightest and most cheerful color schemes of all parrakeets.

The brilliant red head and chest are accented by a white patch on the lower cheek area. The yellow chest band is made up of feathers with very fine dark margins. The red chest area is V-shaped and flanked by yellow on each side. The yellow chest shades into a green abdomen. The vent is red, and the underside of the tail is sky blue. The upperside of the tail is dark greenish blue bordered by a light green rump. The scallops covering the area of the back and wings are black in the center with bright yellow outer margins

411

A pair of Australian King Parrakeets. The male is the upper
bird. Drawing by R. A. Vowles.

Crimson Rosellas. Photo by Horst Mueller.

which become greener on the lower areas. The upper wing coverts are bright blue; and the flights are deep, dull blue-black. The undersides of the wings are black.

Hens are duller in color and have some white spots on the flight feathers. Immatures have green replacing some of the red coloring.

The Red Rosella is one of the most popular of the larger parrakeets and is well established in aviculture.

There are two subspecies of Red Rosella.

One, *Platycercus eximius diemenensis*, inhabits Tasmania and is larger with more extensive white cheek patches.

The other is called the GOLDEN MANTLED ROSELLA and inhabits southern Queensland and the interior of New South Wales. Its Latin name is *Platycercus eximius cecilae*, but it is sometimes also called *Platycercus eximius splendidus*. All of the mantle feathers have bright yellow margins. The rump is a deeper shade of green.

STANLEY or WESTERN ROSELLA *(Platycercus icterotis icterotis)* (25 cm).

The rather rare Stanley Rosella is about ten and a half inches long and inhabits southwestern Australia. Compared to other Rosellas, it is less colorful; but it is still an attractive bird.

The head of the male and all underparts are red. The cheeks are greenish yellow. The scalloped feathers of the back and wings have black centers with green outer margins. The flights are blue and black. The uppertail is green with a bluish tinge and a paler blue on the underside.

The Stanley is the smallest of the Rosellas and is the only Rosella in which the sexes have a different coloration. The female has a duller shade of red with olive green intermixed. Immature birds lack the yellowish cheek patches and have more green than red in the plumage.

Unlike other Rosellas, the Stanley has little difference in size of head and bill between the sexes. Most bird fanciers prefer to wait until a fourteen month period has elapsed before trying to sex them.

Stanleys are ideal aviary birds and are easier to breed than most Rosellas. They are also less pugnacious than their larger cousins.

There is a questionable subspecies called *Platycercus icterotis xanthogenys* which ranges inland from the above. Variations from the true Stanley show a duller shade of red, have paler yellow cheeks, and have mantle feathers with red margins instead of green and red ones. Females are more like the males. They are said to resemble Adelaide Rosellas, but they have yellowish cheeks instead of blue.

BLUE ROSELLA or MEALY ROSELLA *(Platycercus adscitus adscitus)* *(30 cm)*.

The twelve-inch Blue Rosella comes from the northern Queensland area of Australia. The six-inch tail is broad.

The whitish head has a yellowish tinge. The general color is blue, the blue irregular on the chest. The vent is red. The black shoulder patch is present. The wings and back have yellow scallops on the black feathers like the Red Rosella. The cheek patch is white and would be overlooked except for a trace of pale blue on the lower margin.

Males have a brighter blue chest. Females have a grey tinted blue.

A few years ago, Blue Rosellas were the lowest priced of all the Broadtailed Parrakeets, but its availability has waned, and prices are rather high at the time of this writing. They are ideal birds but should be kept by themselves because of their aggressiveness toward other birds.

An apparent mutation of the Blue Rosella has occurred in the wild. It would, however, seldom be found. It has a white chest and back with no black or scalloping on the back. Some yellow tinges occur on the back.

A second race, *Platycercus adscitus elseyi*, is reported in the interior of the Queensland. However, it has not fully achieved its rank of subspecies and is doubtfully distinct from the Blue Rosella described above.

A third race has achieved the rank of subspecies. It is named *Platycercus adscitus palliceps*, and it shows minor variations from the Blue Rosella. It is smaller, has more blue on the cheeks, and has a pale yellow area across the chest.

BROWN'S ROSELLA *(Platycercus venustus) (28 cm)*.

The members of the Rosella family show many contrasts, and a remarkably contrasting color scheme is that of Brown's Rosella, sometimes called the Northern Rosella. It is a ten and a half inch species from the Northern Territory of Australia and Melville Island.

The black head contrasts with the light horn-colored beak. The pale blue ear coverts shade to a darker shade of blue on the lower part. An irregular deep blue patch follows farther back. The yellowish chest and abdomen are scalloped by faint black tips. The vent area is red, and the underside of the tail is light sky blue. The upper side of the tail is greenish blue. The scalloped area of the back and wings starts with black shoulders with whitish yellow marginal scallops. A yellowish white area forms a "V" to separate the back and wings. The wings are blue and are darker on the flights. There is also a black shoulder patch.

Sexes are difficult to distinguish, but often the size of head and bill are smaller in the female. Immatures are duller editions of the parents.

415

African Grey Parrot. Although the configuration of the African Grey Parrot is less pleasing than that of other good talkers, the alertly curious expression of a good African Grey makes it look especially intelligent. Photo by Horst Mueller.

Cactus Conures. The Cactus Conure, from southeastern Brazil, makes up for its lack of gaudy color by its friendly, outgoing personality. Kept with other Conures, it is reasonably peaceful. Cactus Conures reach a length of about eleven inches. Photo by Horst Mueller.

Bee Bee Parrot. The Bee Parrot, also known as Tovi Parrakeet and Orange Chinned Parrakeet, is a peaceful and sociable dwarf parrot; some individuals become proficient at talking, but most Bee Bees are not good talkers. This common and inexpensive species reaches a length of about six and a half inches.

Although there is considerable variation among individuals, only one other race has been validated. It is confined to northwestern Australia and is called *Platycercus venustus hilli.*

BARNARD'S PARRAKEET *(Platycercus zonarius barnardi) (38 cm).*

A lovely Australian Broadtail, Barnard's is from a portion of Victoria, southwestern Queensland, and the interior of New South Wales. It is one of the most popular of the parrakeets in aviculture, and this is rightly so because it is a great beauty and an ideal aviary bird. It is also known as the Mallee or Ringneck Parrakeet.

Many individuals become quite tame, and a few have been taught to talk. The natural voice is pleasant and is often accompanied by a song.

The Barnard is twelve and a half inches long, including the six and a half inch tail.

The male has an overall basic turquoise-green coloring with several contrasting touches: a red forehead band connects the eyes; a bluish tinge is under the beak; an irregular band of rusty yellowish-orange separates the chest and abdomen; a turquoise blue tinge is on the underside of the tail; and the underwings are bright turquoise blue at the bend with the rest black. The upper sides show the nape as a greyish-blue dull color leading into the basic green, the green covering part of a yellow collar that extends down into the sides of the shoulder area. The wings are brilliant turquoise-green with a deep blue surrounding the area. The flights are blue shading to black in the lengthened areas. The upper tail is deep bluish-green.

The female is like the male, but it has less of a bright forehead. The crown is more of a greyish-green and the overall green coloring is somewhat duller.

Another race, *Platycercus zonarius whitei,* inhabits the Flinders range in southern Australia and is reported to be smaller, with a darker head and a smaller orange, rather than yellow, band on the abdomen.

CLONCURRY PARRAKEET *(Platycercus zonarius macgillivrayi) (33 cm).*

Very rare both in captivity and the wild state, the Cloncurry has habits and an appearance which more closely link it to Barnard's Parrakeet. It comes from the interior of central Queensland.

The prevailing color is light green. There is yellow on the abdomen and on a neck ring. There is also blue on the cheeks and wing margins like the Rosellas.

Sexes are similar, but the hens are slightly less vivid and have a smaller head and bill. Immatures have an orange frontal band, which dissappears after a time.

Although practically nonexistent in the aviaries of most countries, there are hopes of establishing the Cloncurry aviculturally. Some serious-minded aviculturists in Australia have been very successful in breeding it.

As mentioned earlier, some authorities consider that Barnard's Parrakeet and the Cloncurry Parrakeet are in the genus *Barnardius*.

BAUER'S or PORT LINCOLN PARRAKEET *(Platycercus zonarius zonarius) (38 cm)*.

Not too much attention has been given this somewhat rare South Australian bird. The writers feel this is a definite mistake because it is a beautifully proportioned and handsomely colored species of stately bearing and of rather large size. Its voice has a musical quality that is quite pleasant.

The basic coloring is deep green with several noteworthy colorful features. The dull black head is framed by a bright yellow collar sourrounding the sides and back of the neck. The same yellow is repeated on the abdomen. The cheeks are bluish.

Sexes are difficult to distinguish, but the male is said to have a larger and flatter head than the female. The beak is supposed to be larger and more masculine in appearance.

Young specimens have a less intense black area on the head. In many instances, the heads are almost a brownish color that takes a full year to develop.

A variation of the Port Lincoln is given rank of subspecies. It is called *Platycercus zonarius occidentalis*, and it comes from western Australia. It is purported to be smaller and to have a paler shade of green, a greyer black head, and paler blue cheeks.

TWENTY-EIGHT PARRAKEET *(Platycercus zonarius semitorquatus) (38 cm)*.

This beautiful Australian species is similar to Bauer's or Port Lincoln Parrakeet except that it is larger (sixteen inches), has yellow on the shoulders of the wings, and a red band on the forehead.

Females are duller and smaller than the males, have smaller beaks, rounder heads, and a duller shade of red on the forehead. Immature specimens resemble the female except for the size of the beak, which determines the sexes.

The Twenty-Eight often becomes a good pet and is an ideal aviary bird. It is rare and expensive in America; but, in Australia, there is a continual war waged against it by farmers, who maintain that it destroys crops and is unpleasant in other ways.

A second race exists in southwestern Australia around Lake Dundas. It is called *Platycercus zonarius dundasi*. It is smaller, has a definite, though variable, yellow abdomen, and a more variable red frontal band.

A pair of Abyssinian Love Birds. The male is at left. Drawing by R. A. Vowles.

Ivory Conures, very similar to Petz' Conure. Photo by Horst Mueller.

A pair of Manycolor Parrakeets, male at left. Photo by Horst Mueller.

Genus: *Purpureicephalus*

PILEATED PARRAKEET *(Purpureicephalus spurius) (36 cm).*

Also called Red Capped Parrakeet, this well-known, but rare, species hails from southwestern Australia and is the only member of its genus.

The Pileated Parrakeet is a slender, broad-tailed parrakeet of medium size with a deep purplish red cap on the head extending down through the nape. The cheeks, wings, and tail are green. A yellowish green covers an extensive area under the cheeks. The breast and part of the abdomen are purplish blue. The rest of the abdomen and tail coverts are a mixture of red, yellow, and green. The rump is yellow. The beak has a curious shape, which is less curved and far narrower than those of most parrakeets.

The female is less vividly colored, especially on the cap and breast. Immatures have the cap mostly green. They mature in twelve to fifteen months. Young cocks have larger and flatter heads than females.

The Pileated Parrakeet is a very desirable aviary bird but is expensive and seldom available.

Genus: *Psephotus*

Some species of the genus *Psephotus* were originally classified under the genus *Northiella*. All are from Australia and are very rare in aviculture. They are smooth colored and somberly attractive. They are pugnacious toward other parrot-like birds and should not to trusted as companions to other species.

RED VENTED BLUE BONNET *(Psephotus haematogaster haematorrhous)* *(27 cm).*

· This slender and dainty-looking Australian parrakeet from southern Queensland and eastern and northern New South Wales is twelve inches long, including the long, pointed tail of six and a half inches. It is also known as the Crimson Bellied Parrakeet.

The male of this species has a bright blue forehead with some blue below the eyes down to the chin. The brownish-grey on the chest, neck, back, rump, and tail is offset by a metallic turquoise green at the bend of the wing, followed by some red and then light blue. The flights and three inches of the tail end are deep blue. The undersides of the wings are bright, deep blue at the bend and greyish black over the remaining area. The grey chest is followed by a yellow band separating chest from abdomen and swerving down the sides. The main part of the abdomen, vent and undertail coverts are red. The tail is black on the upper side, and black frames the whitish undertail feathers.

The female has a smaller and less bright red area on the abdomen and a smaller bill. Immatures have duller coloration and a smaller red abdominal patch.

YELLOW VENTED BLUE BONNET *(Psephotus haematogaster haematogaster) (28 cm).*

This species is from the interior of New South Wales and adjacent portions of Victoria and South Australia. It differs from the Red Vented Blue Bonnet in that it has a yellow vent and an olive-toned band next to the blue wing margins.

A subspecies, called *Psephotus haematogaster pallescens,* inhabits the interior of South Australia. It is regarded by some authorities as a pale mutation and not deserving of the rank of subspecies.

LITTLE BLUE BONNET *(Psephotus haematogaster narethae) (28 cm).*

The full range of this Australian species is not determined, but it is known to inhabit deserts or plains in and around Narethea.

The Little Blue Bonnet is smaller than other members of the genus and shows more obvious sexual differences.

The male has a turquoise shade on the forehead, and the abdomen is a pale orange with no red. The undertail coverts are bright scarlet. There is some scarlet below the bend of the wing. The back, rump, and chest are a pale olive.

The female has a smaller head and beak. It has duller turquoise on the forehead and a yellow abdomen. The young are like the female, but they are of duller coloring. They can be sexed by the size of head and beak.

REDRUMP PARRAKEET *(Psephotus haematonotus) (27 cm).*

The Redrump is one of the first subjects for the novice parrot fancier, the next step upwards from Love Birds and Cockatiels, along with the Indian Ringneck Parrakeet.

Unlike the Indian Ringneck, sex is easily determined in Redrumps within a very short time. Often, the Redrump will be ready for breeding at one year of age; but the greatest success will be achieved after it is two years old. It is a prolific species in captivity as well as in its native Australian habitat, where it is very common.

Though lacking in particularly brilliant colors, the Redrump has great charm and an attractively melodious whistle. Sometimes pugnacious toward other similar sized or slightly smaller parrot family birds, the Redrump is very frequently housed with small finches in perfect harmony, even during the breeding season.

Male Crimson Winged Par-
rakeet. Photo by Horst
Mueller.

Chattering Lory. Photo by
Horst Mueller.

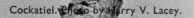
Cockatiel. Photo by Harry V. Lacey.

Most notable features of the males are red rumps and yellow lower chest and abdomen. The small beak is dark. The main part of the back is a brownish-tinged green. The entire head and a patch on the wings are bright green with a tinge of turquoise for added brightness. The flights are dull bluish, and the upper side of the broad tail is greenish and bluish with whitish tips. The underside is whitish and blackish grey. The vent and tail coverts are yellow cast white.

The female lacks the bright head coloring and has a trace of blue in the wing patch. The rump is green instead of red, and the abdomen has only a dull tint of yellow. Immature birds are duller editions of both sexes.

The color scheme of Redrumps lacks the precise separation or the smooth blending of color notable in many other parrakeets. A trace of dark scalloping to their feathers makes an accurate description difficult. There are touches of greys and browns in the color scheme that occur almost haphazardly and the coloring lacks brilliance. Nevertheless, the Redrump is still very attractive and is highly recommended to all bird fanciers.

MANYCOLOR PARRAKEET *(Psephotus varius) (27 cm)*.

This lovely ten and a half inch Australian parrakeet is one of the favorites of the medium price range. It is a high-class cousin of the popular and charming Redrump Parrakeet and more diversified in color.

The yellowish forehead is followed by a reddish patch on the nape. A yellowish shoulder patch is offset by blue upper wing coverts. There is a light yellow cast green band on the upper part of the rump, followed by a darker green band and a red band on the lower rump. The tail is greenish blue on the upperside and a light but dull bluish white on the underside. The tail coverts are dull yellowish with red-tinged feather tips. There are red splashes on the abdomen. The chest is a brilliant turquoise green similar to that on the neck and throat.

The female has a brownish tinge to the green, a dull red shoulder patch, a dull yellow frontal band, and an occasional red flecking to the green abdomen. Young females are like the adults, and young males are like adults but are duller.

This parrakeet deserves the popular name of Manycolor and is a delightful aviary subject.

There are three slightly different races of this species:

Psephotus varius exsul comes from the west central portion of western Australia.

Psephotus varius ethelae comes from the middle part of Australia.

Psephotus varius varius is extensive in southwest Queensland, the interior of New South Wales, the mallee of Victoria, and southeast and southern Australia.

426

HOODED PARRAKEET *(Psephotus chrysopterygius dissimilis) (26 cm)*.

A lovely ten-inch northern Australian parrakeet, the Hooded has a remarkable color scheme. The forehead, crown, and nape are a rich black color. The back is a dull blackish tone. Yellow is extensive on the wing area, and the flights are dark or blackish. The rump is turquoise; the upperside of the tail is blackish green; the lower side of the tail is lighter than the upperside; and the vent area is a dull buffish orange. The ear coverts, sides of neck, throat, and all under parts to the vent are brilliant turquoise.

The female and the young are yellowish green with a paler blue shade here and there. The young have yellowish beaks. Young males can be sexed by brighter blue cheeks.

Rare and beautiful, the Hooded Parrakeet exhibits a quality of daintiness and is always expensive in America. It is a reasonably free breeder in captivity but is pugnacious toward other birds.

GOLDEN SHOULDERED PARRAKEET *(Psephotus chrysopterygius chrysopterygius) (26 cm)*.

This very rare species seems to be confined to the western shores of Cape York Peninsula and the coasts of the southeast part of the Gulf of Carpenteria. It is sometimes called the Golden Winged Parrakeet and is well known as the Antbed Parrot because it burrows its nest into the tremendous termite anthills.

It is similar to the Hooded Parrakeet but slightly smaller. It has a yellow frontal band, a less extensive black cap, a less extensive yellow wing patch, and pinkish feathers with white tips in the vent and under tail covert areas.

The female has a pale cream frontal band. Immature birds are like females except for the bright blue cheek patches of the male.

PARADISE PARRAKEET *(Psephotus pulcherrimus) (27 cm)*.

This species, though greatly reduced in numbers, is confined to southeast Queensland and northern New South Wales. Sexes are well differentiated.

The male has a red forehead and wing bar. The crown is black and the mantle grey with a tinge of brown. The rump is pale blue. The facial areas and breast are bright green, the green shading to blue on the sides of the abdomen. The center of the abdomen and undertail coverts are red.

The female has a yellow forehead with some red feathers. The crown is brownish instead of black. The abdomen replaces red with pale blue and the red wing patches are duller toned. The young are like females except that the males have brighter red wing patches.

The Paradise Parrakeet is extremely rare in captivity. At one time it was

427

Australian King Parrakeet.
Photo by Horst Mueller.

A pair of Stanley, or Western, Rosellas. The male is at right. Photo by Horst Mueller.

A Black-Capped Lory of the genus *Domicella*. Photo by Horst Mueller.

Senegal Parrot, Photo by Horst Mueller.

thought to be extinct, but it was rediscovered in the middle of the 1920's. Its reputation of delicacy possibly means that it will never be prominent in aviculture.

Genus: *Neophema*

All species of the genus *Neophema* are smaller than Cockatiels and are called Grass Parrakeets because of their feeding habits. All have rather small bills and a frontal band which is blue. With their small bills, small heads, well-proportioned bodies, and long narrow tails, the species of *Neophema* exhibit a pleasant air of daintiness. Some members are among the most brilliant and attractive of the parrot family, while others have a very dull coloration.

Several of these species are in danger of extinction in their native habitats; but, fortunately, all except the Rock Grass Parrakeet and the Orange Breasted are being successfully perpetuated by aviary breeding.

ELEGANT PARRAKEET *(Neophema elegans elegans) (23 cm)*.

Also called the Grass Parrakeet in Australia, this somber colored parrakeet inhabits southern Australia and the adjacent parts of New South Wales and Victoria.

The Elegant is widely known and favored in aviculture. Though not colorful in appearance, its charming demeanor is enough to give it its name.

The basic coloring is a vivid shade of olive with gently shaded yellow on the face, abdomen, and undertail coverts. Two shade of blue show up in the frontal band: dark blue in front and light blue at back. These colors are repeated in the wings. A small orange patch is centered on the abdomen.

Females are duller, lack the vivid yellowish tint, and have no orange abdominal spot. Immatures are like adults but have only a trace of the frontal band.

The western race, which is very similar in appearance, is called *Neophema elegans carteri* and is from southwestern Australia.

BLUE WINGED GRASS PARRAKEET *(Neophema chrysostomus) (20 cm)*.

This species comes from Tasmania. It is rare in captivity and is not known as a free breeder.

The male is basically olive-green with yellow on the face, abdomen, and undertail coverts. The wings are bright blue. There is a frontal band similar to that of the Elegant.

Females are duller, and the blue of the wing has a tinge of green. The young are duller and similar to the females.

A second race, *Neophema chrysostomus cyanopterus*, is doubtfully distinct from the above. The rank of subspecies is questionable. Its range is Victoria and the adjacent parts of southern Australia.

ORANGE BREASTED PARRAKEET *(Neophema chrysogaster) (20 cm).*

Tasmania is the stronghold of this rarest species of the *Neophema* genus.

In many respects, the Orange Breasted Parrakeet is similar to the Elegant except that the green is brighter and the chest and abdomen have more yellow. The abdominal patch is bright red-orange. The blue frontal band is lighter.

The female is duller and has less of a blue frontal band. The young are similar to females.

A second race, *Neophema chrysogaster mab,* inhabits southeastern Australia, New South Wales, and Victoria. Its rank of subspecies is questionable since it is doubtfully distinct from the above.

ROCK GRASS PARRAKEET *(Neophema petrophila) (22 cm).*

The Rock Grass Parrakeet is not considered a good aviary subject, and there are several reasons for its lack of popularity. It is of dull coloration and lacks the beauty exhibited by so many other species. In overall appearance it is a very dull and plumpish edition of the Elegant, which in itself is not a bright species. It is also difficult to breed and is apparently short-lived in captivity. The Rock Parrakeet, as it is sometimes called, is a heavy and bulky bird compared to its cousins; and it has a further tendency to become overly fat in captivity.

The male is olive brown on top and olive yellow at bottom. The blue frontal band is present as in other members of the genus. The face is dull blue, and a rim following the edges of the wings starts off as dark blue and shades into a paler blue.

Females are duller than males and often have a narrower frontal band. The young lack the frontal band and are difficult to sex; but they attain adult plumage only three months after leaving the nest.

This species inhabits the coastal areas and islands of southwestern Australia.

A second race, which shows no outward variation, inhabits similar areas of southern Australia. Its name is *Neophema petrophila zietzi.*

431

Blue, or Mealy, Rosellas. Photo by Horst Mueller.

Leadbeater's Cockatoo.
Photo by Horst Mueller.

Rose Breasted Cockatoo.
Photo by Horst Mueller.

TURQUOISINE *(Neophema pulchella) (20 cm).*

The lovely Turquoisine is one of the most colorful and desirable of all parrakeets. At one time it was thought to be extinct. It had disappeared from its normal haunts due to man's encroachment upon its natural breeding grounds, but it reappeared in another area. It is still not plentiful; but, fortunately, it is well established as a good breeder in aviculture. This establishment will probably save the Turquoisine from extinction.

Turquoisines are expensive and rather rare, but their charm and beauty make any investment in a pair worthwhile. In order to increase the numbers of Turquoisines, they should be placed only in the hands of serious-minded aviculturists who are interested in breeding. By now Turquoisines are considered as thoroughly domesticated.

The male has a bright shade of turquoise on the forehead and face sides that is also repeated on the broad wing band. There is some deep reddish brown on the shoulder. The rest of the upper parts, such as head, neck, back, rump, and uppertail, are bright green. The underparts, starting with the chest and going through the tail coverts, are bright yellow. Sometimes the abdomen shows a concentration of orange.

Females have less turquoise in the face and either lack or show only a trace of the reddish brown on the shoulder.

Immatures acquire adult plumage about four months after leaving the nest. Until then they look like females. They can usually be sexed even at this age because young males have a brighter turquoise on the face.

SPLENDID or SCARLET CHESTED PARRAKEET *(Neophema splendida) (19 cm).*

Certainly the most beautiful member of the genus, the Splendid Parrakeet is also one of the most striking of all parrakeets. It is rare and quite expensive in America.

The Splendid is a small, slender, and long-tailed parrakeet measuring seven to seven and a half inches in length.

In the male, the forehead, throat, and lower cheek area are brilliant violet-blue, this color shading into turquoise on the crown and sides of the head. The chest and abdomen are brilliant red, the red shading into yellow near the vent and extending through the undersides of the tail. The sides of the red chest are dull green. The back and rump are green. There is a brilliant turquoise wing bar starting at the bend of the wings. The flight feathers are black. Descriptions are far too inadequate to give an idea of this bird's beauty.

The female lacks the red chest and has less extensive areas of turquoise and violet. The chest is bright turquoise-shaded green.

The Splendid Parrakeet is now confined to a rather small area of southern Australia.

BOURKE'S PARRAKEET *(Neophema bourkii) (19 cm).*

The lovely and charming Bourke comes from western and southern Australia and New South Wales. Though not far from extinction in its native habitat, it is, fortunately, well established and a good breeder in captivity.

Bourke's Parrakeets are the largest of the Grass Parrakeets and are held to be a genus of their own by some experts. They are rather small, with small beaks, and have a lovely pastel coloring that is mainly soft rose with blue accents.

The male has a brownish shade on the upper parts with pale buffish margins on the feathers of the mantle. The abdomen, chest, and face are a rose color. Wing margins are a blue violet, and the sides of rump and undertail coverts are blue. There is also a frontal band of blue extending through the eyes.

Females lack the blue frontal band and have a tinge of white shading. The breast has a scaly appearance with pink scallops. The young have less pink on the abdomen but can be easily sexed; young males have larger and flatter heads. They mature in about four months after leaving the nest.

Bourke's Parrakeets are good breeders and are relatively inexpensive. For anyone who contemplates an addition to his aviaries and is looking for a dependable and good performance, the writers unhesitatingly recommend a pair of Bourke's.

Genus: *Myiopsitta*

QUAKER PARRAKEET *(Myiopsitta monachus) (29 cm).*

Although it lacks brilliant colors, the Quaker Parrakeet still gets its share of attention by being lively and boisterous. Very prevalent in its native South America, it is prolific and gregarious, preferring to live communally in flocks.

The Quaker is one of the few species of parrot-like birds which builds a nest. The nest itself may be a gigantic affair composed of large and small twigs, grasses, and anything else at hand. It usually resembles an apartment dwelling with its many nesting cavities, each cavity housing a different pair.

In captivity, the Quaker is also a very free breeder and a pleasant aviary inhabitant. It lacks great popularity because, though attractive, it is not as glamorous as many members of the parrot family.

It is a well-proportioned, slender bird of nine and a half inches, with a long pointed tail of four and a half inches.

The beak is horn color. The forehead, crown, and all the underparts to the vent are grey. The green loreal area extends around the eyes and connects to a bright green nape. The vent, thighs, tail, rump, and wings are green. The underwings are greenish grey with a slight bluish tint. The flights are dark,

435

Upper: Nyassaland Love Bird. *Lower:* Black-Cheeked Love Bird. Drawing by R. A. Vowles.

Male Blossom Head, or Plum Head, Parrakeet. Photo by Horst Mueller.

Blue variety of Alexander Ringneck Parrakeet. Photo by Horst Mueller.

almost black, with some green and a bluish tint. The grey chest has lighter grey scallops on the ends of the feathers. The grey shoulder and crown areas also have faint traces of grey scalloping.

There are four races of this bird with only slight variations:

Myiopsitta monachus luchsi.
Myiopsitta monachus cotorra.
Myiopsitta monachus calita.
Myiopsitta monachus monachus.

Genus: *Brotogeris*

The twenty two members of the genus *Brotogeris* make southern Mexico through central South America their habitat. All are small and slender, but are shaped like standard parrots rather than parrakeets. By far the most plentiful species is the well-known Bee Bee or Tovi Parrakeet.

BEE BEE PARROT or TOVI PARRAKEET *(Brotogeris jugularis)* *(18 cm).*

Also called the Orange Chinned Parrakeet, this well-known and rather popular species is normally termed a dwarf parrot and is usually sold as a moderately priced individual pet. It becomes reasonably tame and, occasionally, a good talker. The Bee Bee is six and a half inches long.

The basic coloring is green, lighter underneath. There is some dull blue in the flights and a bright orange spot under the chin. Its body is slender and well proportioned.

The subspecies *cyanoptera* had a brighter blue on the wings but no brown on the shoulders. The race *exsul* has more brown on the shoulders.

There are four races of the Tovi Parrakeet: *Brotogeris jugularis cyanoptera* from the rivers of the Amazonian drainage; *Brotogeris jugularis jugularis* from the arid tropical zone of southwestern Mexico to northern Colombia; *Brotogeris jugularis exsul* from northern Venezuela; and *Brotogeris jugularis apurensis* from western central Venezuela. The latter is called the Apure Tovi Parrakeet.

GOLDEN WINGED PARRAKEET *(Brotogeris chrysopterus chrysopterus)* *(16 cm).*

From eastern Venezuela and the Guianas comes this rare species, slightly less than seven inches long.

It is mostly all green and resembles the Bee Bee in shape. The only color variations are orange on the upper parts of the flights, followed by a less noticeable blue. There is a bare eye ring.

TUIPARA or GOLDEN FRONTED PARRAKEET *(Brotogeris chrysopterus tuipara) (16 cm).*

The Tuipara Parrakeet is from the lower Amazon and shows yellow orange in a band above the nostrils and on the chin.

This is a very pretty species and would surely replace the Bee Bee in popularity if it were not considerably rarer.

GOLDEN PARRAKEET *(Brotogeris chrysopterus chrysosema) (16 cm).*

The writers believe that the names of these last subspecies are not descriptive but are used mainly to denote differences between the birds. The Golden Parrakeet, for instance, is not golden in color, but has bright yellow scapulars as well as a more extensive orange area under the chin.

It comes from the Rio Madiera in Brazil.

TUI PARRAKEET *(Brotogeris sanctithomae sanctitomae) (16 cm).*

This is probably the prettiest of the genus. The bright green coloring is accented by a shiny chestnut beak and a large patch of yellow on the forehead. The wings have shadings of blue. The total length is six and three fourths inches.

The Tui is from eastern Ecuador and northeastern Peru.

A subspecies, *Brotogeris sanctithomae takatsukasae,* is found in the lower Amazon and has more yellow on the head extending to the crown.

Tui Parrakeet *(left)*, White Winged Parrakeet or White Winged Beebee *(right)*. The attractive Tui has a shiny chestnut-colored beak topped by a yellow forehead. The White Winged is dull by comparison. Note the bill on the Tui. Slightly deformed, this is a good example of a beak that will normally need trimming at regular intervals.

A male of one of the many subspecies of *Trichoglossus haemotod* bearing a great resemblance to Swainson's Blue Mountain Lorikeet. Photo by Horst Mueller.

Lesser Sulphur Crested Cockatoo. Photo by Horst Mueller.

Male (right) and female Crimson Winged Parrakeets. Drawing
by R. A. Vowles.

CANARY WINGED PARRAKEET *(Brotogeris versicolorus chiriri) (20 cm).*

This eight and three-fourths inches long species resembling the Bee Bee has a tail of four and one-fourth inches.

The beak is a light horn color. The overall green, which is lighter underneath and darker on the flights, is broken only by a bright yellow wing bar and some blue on the wings.

A second and similar race, *Brotogeris versicolorus behni,* comes from southern Bolivia.

BLUE MARGINED PARRAKEET *(Brotogeris gustavi) (18 cm).*

The Blue Margined Parrakeet has bright orange on the chin with yellow on the shoulders and the outer rim of the wings. De Schauensee's recent reclassification places this species as an intermediate of *cyanoptera,* a subspecies of the Bee Bee.

WHITE WINGED PARRAKEET *(Brotogeris versicolorus versicolorus) (22 cm).*

The White Winged Parrakeet is from the Amazon Valley. It has a whitish wing bar with a yellow tinge.

ALL GREEN PARRAKEET *(Brotogeris tirica) (23 cm).*

A long, slender bird like the Bee Bee, the All Green Parrakeet comes from eastern and southern Brazil. It is slightly over ten inches, with a tail less than four inches.

Its overall coloring is bright green, lighter underneath. The flights are blue, and the beak is horn color.

ORANGE FLANKED PARRAKEET *(Brotogeris pyrrhopterus) (20 cm).*

The eight-inch Orange Flanked Parrakeet is bright green, paler underneath. There is a tinge of blue to the crown and a tinge of grey on the chin, forehead, and face sides. The flight feathers are blue. A bright feature of this species is the orange coloring on the underwing coverts and sides.

The habitat is the arid tropical zone of Peru and Ecuador in western South America.

Genus: *Touit*

Members of this genus resemble those of *Brotogeris* in size and shape. They all come from South America; most likely, any members in America are thought to be of the genus *Brotogeris* because of the similarity. They were formerly grouped under the generic name of *Urochroma,* no longer in use.

There are eight species and two subspecies of the genus. All are very rare in the United States and are of little importance in aviculture.

LILAC TAILED PARROT *(Touit batavica) (14 cm).*

The most important feature of this very different species is the pale but very noticeable lilac tail of about one and three-fourths inches. The wings and back are black with a pale bright green wing bar across the secondary coverts. The underside of the tail has traces of pale pink. The head is yellowish-green with dark margins on the mantle feathers. The chest is pale blue-grey shading into dull, pale greenish-grey on the abdomen.

Six inches in length, this little parrot comes from Venezuela, British Guiana, Surinam, and the islands of Tobago and Trinidad. It is characterized by different tinges of blue on the body and a lilac tail.

BLACK EARED PARROTLET *(Touit melanonotus) (15 cm).*

This species from southeastern Brazil has dull black on the shoulders and back and blackish primary coverts. Most of the coloring is green, paler and dusty on the abdomen. Bright red is mostly hidden on the inner parts of the outer tail feathers which have broad black margins. The central tail feathers are green. The green tail coverts are very long and nearly cover the tail.

SAPPHIRE RUMPED PARROTLET *(Touit purpurata) (17 cm).*

There are two races of the Sapphire Rumped Parrotlet. The nominate race *purpurata* is from the Guianas and northwestern Brazil. It is five and one-half inches long including the tail of one and one-fourth inches. Most of the coloring is bright green except for a violet-blue rump and blackish-blue crown. A blackish bar across the inner scapulars forms a noticeable V-pattern when the wings are folded. The tail has magenta and purple mostly hidden as the red is hidden in the species above. The subspecies *viridiceps* from southern Venezuela and parts of Colombia is similar but smaller, and the crown is green. Olive-green occurs on the sides.

SCARLET SHOULDERED PARROTLET *(Touit huetii) (15.5 cm).*

The Scarlet Shouldered Parrotlet has a wider range in northwestern South America than do most species of this genus. The size is five and a half inches including the one and one-half inch tail. It is also a beautiful and distinctive species. There are brilliant color flashes of bright red on the undersides of the wings from the sides and underwing coverts, of brilliant cobalt on the scapulars, and from a reddish-pink spot on the outer reaches of the shoulders. The tail is especially different. The rump and two central tail feathers are bright green, but the other feathers have a vivid pinkish-lilac with

443

Mexican Double Yellow Head Amazon Parrot, also known as
Levaillant's Amazon. Drawing by R. A. Vowles.

Blue Eared Lorikeet. Photo
by Horst Mueller.

African Grey Parrots make
very friendly and affectionate pets if they are handled
properly. Photo by Sam
Fehrenz.

outer black margins of one-eighth of an inch. The underside of the tail is the same but in a paler shade. Yellow occurs with the green in the long undertail coverts.

The flights are mostly black with dark turquoise-green on the outer edges of the feathers. The black and inner wing areas are bright green. Underparts are also green. The head is mostly dark and dull green with blackish-blue on the forehead and dark blue below the lores and eyes. The top of the crown is dusky greyish-green. There is also an orange fleshy eye-ring.

RED WINGED PARROTLET *(Touit dilectissima) (17 cm)*.

The nominate race *dilectissima* from eastern Panama to western Venezuela is six and a half inches including the one and one-half inch tail. Mostly green, this species has bright red traces on the lores and under the eyes on an otherwise dull head which is dark showing traces of dusky blue. The wings are brightly marked with a dark red bar with black preceding it on a shoulder patch and following it on the primaries. The flights are both black and green. The undersides of the wings and the sides under the wings are bright yellow with bright red on the bend of the wings. The tail pattern is similar to the species above but has bright yellow replacing the pinkish-lilac. The female lacks the scarlet on the wing coverts. The subspecies *costaricensis* from Costa Rica has red also on the forehead and crown.

SPOTTED WINGED PARROTLET *(Touit stictoptera) (17 cm)*.

The Spotted Winged Parrotlet from Colombia and Ecuador is slightly over five and a half inches including the tail of two inches. The flights are especially long on this species. This species is all green with a large and extensive brownish-black bar extending from the shoulders through primary scapulars and secondary flights showing a prominent "V" when the wings are folded. This feature is apparently variable among individuals which may have the inner parts of the shoulder feathers merely dark which deteriorates the prominent V-pattern. Females are said to be different from males by having green wing coverts with black centers on the feathers instead of brown.

The species listed by Peters as *Touit emmae* has now been proven to be the female of this speces.

GOLDEN TAILED PARROTLET *(Touit surda) (16 cm)*.

This species has a reddish tinge on the underside of the tail and a brownish-grey wing bar to add the V-shaped pattern when the wings are folded. It is duller than most species with dull olive-green on the face and throat and the dark flights. The other areas of green are bright but somewhat paler on the underparts.

Genus: *Nannopsittaca*

TEPUI PARROTLET *(Nannopsittaca panychloris)*

The Tepui Parrotlet from Guiana is rather a nondescript bird with a very small beak and all dark green coloring. It is five and one-fourth inches long including the tail.

Genus: *Bolborhynchus*

LINEOLATED PARRAKEET *(Bolborhynchus lineola lineola) (16 cm)*.

The Lineolated Parrakeet from Mexico to Panama is an all-green bird, darker on the upper parts and paler and brighter on the underparts. The rump has an olive tinge. The head and cheeks have the brightest and richest green coloring of this otherwise dull bird. Starting on the nape of the neck, many feathers have fine black scallops, giving a barred effect. On the wings, rump, legs, and sides the black edges are more pronounced. The bend of the wing is particularly dark.

Lineolateds have a total length of seven inches, including the two-inch tail.

The bill is small and horn colored, darker at the tips. The feet are flesh colored. The tail is broad and all the feathers are pointed.

The tail is one of the most interesting and expressive features of the bird. Whenever the bird shows emotion, the tail fans outward in an unusual gesture.

The stealthy movements of the Lineolated are fascinating to watch. With his head held low and outstretched, the bird crouches and creeps along a branch like a cat stalking its prey. A group of Lineolateds on a tree play an amusing rough and tumble sort of game.

Determining the sex of Lineolateds is accomplished by examining the pelvic bones. If the pelvic bones are close, the bird is a male; if they are far apart, the bird is a female.

Lineolateds are good breeders in captivity and are usually very inexpensive.

Two other races of the species occur in South America, one of which is questionable. These subspecies have only slight differences in appearance.

Bolborhynchus lineola tigrinus is from the Andes of Colombia.

Bolborhynchus lineola maculatus is a questionable subspecies from eastern Peru.

The other two species which complete the genus are very rare in avicultural fields and probably would command very little attention from bird fanciers.

Top: Fischer's Love Bird. Bottom: Peach Face Love Bird. Drawing by R. A. Vowles.

The Rufous Fronted Parrakeet *(Bolborhynchus ferrugineifrons)* from Colombia is more than an inch longer than the Lineolated and has a rusty rufous coloring on the forehead, lores, and upper throat. The black bars on tips of the feathers are missing, and most of the green is duller with a shade of olive added to the chest.

The Andean Parrakeet *(Bolborhynchus andicolus)* from Peru is seven inches long including the three inch tail. The total coloring is very dark green with a bluish cast in the flights. There is no black on the shoulders, and the black linear bars which distinguish the Lineolated Parrakeet are also missing. De Schauensee has listed this species as *orbygnesius.*

Genus: *Psilopsiagon*

Members of this genus are all from South America and are no bigger than a Budgerigar. They are often placed in the genus *Bolborhynchus.* They have orange colored bills. Their basic color is green with orange or yellow area in various parts, distinguishing the subspecies. Both sexes have blue in the primaries, but the orange is missing in the female.

They are extremely rare in captivity and have, unfortunately, a tremendous voice which could be a drawback if they ever became plentiful.

In one subspecies, the GOLDEN FRONTED PARRAKEET *(Psilopsiagon aurifrons aurifrons)*, the yellow is on the forepart of the head and extends down into the chest.

Another subspecies, ORANGE—FLANKED PARRAKEET *(Psilopsiagon aurifrons orbygnesius)* has orange on the sides and legs.

A third subspecies, *Psilipsiagon aurifrons robertsi,* has yellow on the forehead, cheeks, and throat.

A fourth subspecies is *Psilopsiagon aurifrons rubrirostris.*

Genus: *Amoropsittaca* and *Psilopsiagon*

AYMARA PARRAKEET *(Amoropsittaca aymara) (20 cm).*

Also called the Sierra or Grey Headed Parrakeet, the Aymara Parrakeet comes from Bolivia and Argentina and is the only member of its genus. Previously rare, this species has been available to Europeans in recent years. Long and slender, the total length is seven and a half inches including the narrow tail of three inches. The head and the beak are small. Quietly attractive, the major coloring is smooth and bright green, deeper above and paler below. Bright blue occurs on the wings, margined on the fine line edges in pale

449

bluish-white. Black also occurs on the wings. There are variations in individuals. Some have sooty grey on the upper part of the head and pale pearl grey on the lower sides of the face, chin, and throat changing softly to green on the lower chest. Some of the blackish accents are sharp and attractive. They are quiet and rather retiring birds and gentle enough to be housed with several of the smaller Australian Grass Parrakeets.

In a recent reclassification, De Schauensee groups the Aymara Parrakeet with the genus *Bolborhynchus*.

Many of the parrotlike birds in South America are called parrakeets. To the average person in South America, anything not a macaw or an Amazon-type parrot is a parrakeet; and this includes all conures, the Bee Bees, and all other diverse forms. We have all perhaps been remiss in trying to be slightly more specific especially in that large group we call conures. The only real conure was the Carolina Parrakeet. Not only is it extinct, but it was popularly called a parrakeet. Such a distinctive group should be called something other than a parrakeet, and the persistent usage of the term conure has prevailed on most bird fanciers. To think of a parrakeet in a less diverse form, most people's thoughts would quickly tend towards the Ringneck family or the lovely Australian species rather than to some of the short tailed species to be found in South America or in the long tailed conures.

The Aymara Parrakeet is a parrakeet in the purest sense. Dr. Brereton in his paper "Evolution Within Psittaciformes" devotes attention to the similarities of *Amoropsittaca* and *Neophema*. In a paragraph headlined "The Enigma of 'Platycercines' in South America" he states "that two hypotheses are tenable: Either the platycercine type has arisen twice (a remarkable case of parallel evolution) or platycercines have made their way to South America comparatively recently." In his proposed rearrangement of the genera, Dr. Brereton includes far more Australian birds in his superfamily Platycercoidea than the Rosellas or the birds generally called Platycercines.

In his family of Amoropsittidae, he includes four known genera which he did not name. Undoubtedly he is also including the genus *Psilopsiagon*.

Genus: *Prioniturus*

Rare and unusual, these thirteen-inch pastel-shaded birds have a curious tail of normal size except for two central feathers, with feathered rounded tips, which extend webless twice the tail's length.

The colors are mainly green, blue, and greenish yellow. Individuals have lilac, turquoise, and red markings.

In captivity they have the reputation of being delicate.

Three main species come from the Philippines: one is composed of six subspecies, and another is composed of three subspecies. Altogether there are nine different forms in the Philippines.

LUZON RACKET-TAILED PARRAKEET *(Prioniturus luconensis) (29 cm).*

The synonym for this species is Green Headed Racket-Tailed Parrakeet. The name is aptly descriptive. It is the least embellished species. It has a body length of six inches from the crown to the base of the tail. The tail itself is two and a half inches long, and the two central extensions with the two black racket tips are two and a half inches longer. The coloring is smooth and pale green, darker on the wings, darker still on the flights, and paler on the undersides.

PHILIPPINE RACKET-TAILED PARRAKEET *(Prioniturus discurus discurus) (27 cm).*

Also aptly called Blue Headed Racket-Tailed Parrakeet. There is a light blue wash on the head.

The Philippine Racket Tailed Parrakeet has six subspecies with slight variations. The nominate race *discurus* has a body of seven to seven and a half inches plus the normal tail of two and a half inches. The spatulated tips extend two and one-half inches further. It is more attractive than the species above because of a bright light blue wash on the head and a bright lustrous green on the facial areas. The subspecies *platenae* has bright but light lustrous blue on all of the head, neck and underparts. The race *mindorensis* has a larger head and body and a violet tinged blue crown patch. The subspecies *waterstradti* has less blue on the head, but greenish-brown is added to the rump as well as a brownish cast on the back and scapulars.

MALINDANG RACKET-TAILED PARRAKEET *(Prioniturus discurus malindangensis) (30 cm)*

Distinguishing features are the yellow coloring of the underside, less brown on the back and scapulars, and a longer tail with shorter naked shafts.

SULU RACKET-TAILED PARRAKEET *(Prioniurus discurus suluensis)*

This bird has more blue on the crown and an olive patch centering between the nape and upper back. It is also larger.

LUZON CRIMSON SPOTTED RACKET-TAILED PARRAKEET *(Prioniturus flavicans montanus) (30 cm).*

As the name implies, this bird has a large red spot on the crown, which is lacking in the female. The patch is surrounded by blue which extends over most of the face.

The Crimson Spotted Racket-Tailed Parrakeet has three subspecies. The nominate race *flavicans* from the northern Celebes and Tongian Islands has a body of eight inches and a tail of one and three fourths inches. The tail extensions extend three to three and a half inches longer. The male has a bright cobalt crown and nape with a brighter red patch on the crown. The female lacks the red patch. The rest of the head is bright lustrous green. A broad collar around the mantle through the upper chest is dull olive. Remaining upperparts are dark green, and underparts are pale green. The two subspecies, both from the Philippines, are *montanus* (Luzon Crimson Spotted Racket-Tail) and *verticalis* (Everett's Racket-Tail). The Luzon subspecies is slightly smaller, has less cobalt on the head and cheeks, less olive, and more blue-green. Everett's subspecies has a smaller head patch.

The Celebes Racket-Tailed Parrakeet *(Prioniturus platurus)* has two races: *platurus* from the Celebes Islands and *talautensis* from the Talaut Islands. The body length is six and a half inches on the subspecies *platurus* plus three inches on the tail with three inches more for the tail extensions. The male has a grayish-lavender crescent-shaped patch straight across the center of the crown and curving out to the rear of the nape. A bright coral accent is splashed across the center of the crown. The rest of the head feathers are bright and lustrous green. The mantle is dull rust-orange. The wings are greyish with a faint olive cast. Underparts are bright light green. The female is all green. The subspecies *talautensis* has more coral on the crown and brighter orange in the mantle.

The last species in this genus, *Prioniturus mada*, is a rare high elevation species from the mountains of Buru. None were available for description.

NEW ZEALAND PARRAKEETS

Genus: *Cyanoramphus*

This group of beautiful small parrakeets has the native name of Kakariki in its habitat of New Zealand and neighboring islands. Three members are already extinct and others are believed to be extinct. Nearly all face extinction, their numbers being greatly reduced by farmers who protect their crops from flocks of these birds.

An alternative to the almost certain extinction of the entire genus, which has four species, one with nine subspecies and another with two races, is to breed them in captivity. However, there does not seem to be much opportunity to establish them in aviaries due to the present shackling import restrictions in Britain and the United States and the unavailability of the birds themselves. Few have ever been kept in captivity, but avicultural records show them to be hardy and pleasant. In Holland they are very popular!

They are reported to be very good breeders and to have delightful personalities. All those the writers have seen have been less attractive than their bright aviary companions but far more shapely than most. In New Zealand they are strictly protected, but in recent years they have become more frequently available to aviculturists there and are becoming quite well established.

The members of the genus *Cyanoramphus* are well-proportioned, long tailed, and attractive birds of nine to thirteen inches in size. The basic coloring is green, which is lighter on the chest. There are variations of colors on wings, foreheads, and crowns, which distinguish different species. The bills are silver with black tips.

Some of the members of the genus are listed below:

Cyanoramphus unicolor, the ANTIPODES ISLAND PARRAKEET, is from the Antipodes Islands. The coloring of this, the largest of the genus, is all green with a brighter head. There are some shadings of yellow and blue in the tail and wings. The bird is eleven inches long including the tail of five inches. The greenish beak has a black tip.

Cyanoramphus novazelandiae, the RED-FRONTED PARRAKEET, has many subspecies, one of which is extinct and at least one other believed to be extinct. Some of these members are confined to very barren islands which have very little vegetation. Variations from the green coloring are a crimson red forehead and crown, a red patch behind the eye, blue on the wings, and yellowish-green below. The bird is eleven inches long including the six inch tail.

Cyanoramphus auriceps, with two subspecies, is referred to as the YELLOW-FRONTED PARRAKEET or GOLDEN-HEADED PARRAKEET. It has yellow-orange on the crown as the only difference which distinguishes it from the Red-Fronted. The outer webs of the primaries are slate blue. The bird is smaller with a length of nine inches including the four inch tail. It has a small amount of bright red on the forehead.

Cyanoramphus malherbi, the ORANGE-FRONTED or ALPINE PARRAKEET, shows an orange forehead and yellow crown. The bird is nine inches in length including the four and one-half inch tail. It is like the Yellow Fronted; but orange occurs on the forehead and crown.

Two other species are extinct: *Cyanoramphus zealandicus* and *Cyanoramphus ulietanus.*

There are two members of this genus. Both have spare crests and live in tall forests. They are quiet and wary and usually travel in pairs. Very little is known about them, and it is doubtful that they have ever been kept really successfully in captivity. They are related to the genus *Cyanoramphus* but have a distinct notch in the upper mandible. They have unusual crests, and the feathering of the loreal region is less dense.

CRESTED PARRAKEET *(Eunymphicus cornutus cornutus) (32 cm)*.

The New Caledonian race has only two long black feathers on the crest. Both have red tips and trail backwards over the head. The forehead and crown are red, followed by yellow on the hind neck and ear covert. The rest of the face is dull black. Beyond that, the plumage is green with blue on the tail and wings.

The subspecies *Eunymphicus cornutus uvaeensis,* from the Loyalty Islands, is called the UVEAN PARRAKEET. It has a crest of six green feathers. The yellow hind neck and ear coverts are replaced by green. There is just a little red in the center of the forehead. The black face is tinged with green. The bill is blue with black on the tip.

Genus: *Melopsittacus*

BUDGERIGAR *(Melopsittacus undulatus) (18 cm)*.

No description is needed for this small Australian grass parrakeet, the most popular pet of the bird world. It is known by many names: Shell Parrakeet, Budgie, Australian Love Bird, Undulating Grass Parrakeet, and others. It is what springs into the mind of most people when they hear the word "Parrakeet."

Many books have been written on the breeding, diseases, feeding, mutations and color variations of the Budgerigar. (See the "Recommended Reading List" at the back of the book.) Therefore, it would be pointless to go into any details concerning this wonderful and talented little bird.

In the wild state, its natural color is green. It migrates whenever depletion of food and water becomes evident. It is the only member of its genus.

Genus: *Pezoporus*

GROUND PARRAKEET *(Pezoporus wallicus) (30 cm)*.

Also called the Swamp Parrakeet, this diminishing and now rare Australian species holds no status in aviculture because it is never available. It

A baby lutino Budgie—only a few weeks old. During the breeding-season, daily inspection of the nest boxes is in order. Check to see whether the young are being fed properly, that hens are not egg-bound, that the nest boxes are not wet or require cleaning, and that hens are not feather-plucking their young. Don't disturb the hen by too much cleaning!

455

has a reputation for being shy and is not too well suited to aviary life. It spends nearly all its time on the ground except when alarmed into flight.

In color, the bird is bright grass green with black and yellow flecks. The breast is duller green with smaller black flecks. The abdomen is yellowish with black barring. The long tail has the same coloration with a darker shade above and a duller shade below. An orange frontal band on the forehead is found on adults but is absent in young specimens.

The three subspecies of this bird are:

Pezoporus wallicus flaviventris from the coastal districts of southwest Australia; *Pezoporus wallicus wallicus* from the coastal districts of New South Wales, Victoria, and southern Australia; and *Pezoporus wallicus leachi* from Tasmania.

16

LOVE BIRDS AND PARROTLETS

LOVE BIRDS

Genus: *Agapornis*

All true Love Birds come from Africa and belong to the genus *Agapornis*. There are nine species which are scattered over a wide area. A few species are very rare and localized in habitat.

Love Birds are duplicates in minature of the larger, more standardized parrots. In size they range from the small Nyassaland, which is four to five inches in length, to the Peach Faced, which is five and a half to six inches in overall length. All have very engaging personalities, and most are highly colorful.

Love Birds are very hardy and long lived, and some species are very free breeders in this country. Therefore, they are excellent for beginners.

Love Birds are best kept to themselves because of their aggressions against other kinds of birds. Some are downright mean. Each species should be kept by itself to prevent hybridizing. Love Bird hybrids are less attractive than the original species.

Love Birds can become excellent pets if a concerted effort at taming is made right after they are weaned. They do not tame as easily as Budgies or Cockatiels, but a good job of taming results in a much more talented pet. The unlimited number of tricks which they very readily learn provide endless amusement. They also learn to talk if lessons are conscientiously provided.

Love Birds nest in a standard-sized budgie nest-box in which is built a very fancy nest with a spiralling tunnel from the entrance to the base of the nest. Palm leaves, bamboo leaves, green bark stripped from trees, and sometimes feathers are used in nest construction.

Plenty of nesting material should be provided because constant additions are made during the nesting period. Love Birds pulverize and soften the material by running it back and forth in their beaks, biting it just enough to achieve the right texture. They often tuck the material into the feathers on the rump before flying to the nest. More often than not, the material falls to the ground. Non-plussed, they quickly retrieve it or start on a new piece. The

Fischer's Love Bird, *Agapornis fischeri*, is among the Love Bird species that are commonly available.

material should be green and fresh rather than dried. Green leaves, especially palm leaves which dry slowly, provide a certain amount of moisture, which keeps the thick-shelled eggs soft enough for the baby chick to peck its way out at hatching time. Lack of moisture results in very hard eggshells and a higher percentage of dead young imprisoned in the egg. Of course, improper diet for parents can produce the same result.

The breeding aviary can be reasonably small. Even a good-sized breeding cage is sufficient. For some unaccountable reason, our Love Birds have always done better in small aviaries less than twelve feet in length.

Breeding seasons are not exact. Some will prefer late summer and fall breeding, while others do better in springtime. This preference has nothing to do with different species. Instead, it seems to hinge more on different climates and availability of nesting material.

Being hardy, Love Birds can be kept in outdoor flights the year around in most climates. They like to use nest-boxes for sleeping quarters. This is a good plan, since it will keep them out of drafts during cold weather. They should not be allowed to breed in very cold weather because of the danger of egg-binding and a higher rate of infertile eggs. Withholding nesting material and removing some of the old is usually enough to discourage them from breeding.

An average clutch is three or four young per nest. Usually there are two nests per season. Third clutches should be discouraged to maintain strong stock.

Sexing Love Birds is not easy. Some varieties show differences in coloration between the sexes, but the species available in the United States are alike in outward appearance.

The most reliable method of sexing Love Birds is the pelvic bone test, and even this method is to be suspected. Young birds particulary seem to have movable pelvic bones which may seem like those of a hen at one moment and like those of a cock a few moments later. The odds, however, are in favor of the pelvic bone test. If the two pointed pelvic bones are so close that they nearly touch, the bird is most likely to be a male. If they are separated by a distance of more than an eighth of an inch, the bird is likely to be a female.

Our first Love Birds were a guaranteed "mated pair." They went to nest very readily and worked assiduously to perfect their nest. Both birds spent a great deal of time in the nest. We were immensely pleased when we peeked in and discovered eight eggs. Later, we were disappointed when none hatched; but they dutifully went back to work. Soon there were eight more eggs. This procedure continued for over a year before we finally realized that both birds were hens. This illustration is given to demonstrate that two hens will nest readily as a pair. They even spend considerable time in what appears to be copulation. Two males will go through the same procedure but will not spend much time in the nest-box once the construction work is completed.

Like those of budgies, eggs are laid every other day. If the hen sits closely from the beginning, the first egg will hatch in twenty-one days. Every other day another will hatch.

Babies venture from the nest after about five weeks but return upon the slightest disturbance and at night. Two weeks later should find them weaned and spending most of their time outside the nest while the hen prepares for another clutch.

Mentioned before is the fact that Love Birds are mean to other types of birds. They can also be mean to each other. Sometimes the result is feather plucking, which can be traced to two causes: improper diet or an acquired vice. Many baby Love Birds are plucked by their own parents. This is a difficult problem to overcome. Suggestions are made in the chapter on diseases under the heading Feather Plucking. The addition of new branches containing plenty of bark will probably provide a distraction if the vice is an acquired habit.

The diet consists of parrakeet mix, sunflower seed, health grit, cuttlebone, green food, and a dietary supplement. See the chapter on Diet.

Some people object to the somewhat shrill voices of Love Birds; but, if kept at a reasonable distance, the voice becomes less harsh and, therefore, less objectionable.

PEACH-FACED LOVE BIRDS *(Agapornis roseicollis) (15 cm)*.

Sometimes called Rosy-Faced Love Bird, this is the largest of the Love Bird tribe and the most pugnacious. It is primarily a softly shaded green with a soft rose-colored face and deeper shaded rose crown of crescent shape. The beak is horn colored, and no eye ring is present. The upper tail coverts are bright, lustrous blue. The tail is very beautiful when spread, as in flying, because of the orange-pink and blackish bands.

The Peach-Faced is very easily bred and is the most popular of the Love Birds in the United States.

Immature birds have greyish faces; they acquire the rose-colored face when they are about six months old. Very young birds have black bases of the beak for a few weeks.

There is a pied mutation of the Peach Face in existence. We have had several examples of this mutation, and we do not think it particularly attractive unless the bird shows yellow predominantly. We once saw one completely rose-colored bird. It was truly a beautiful specimen.

BLACK MASKED LOVE BIRD *(Agapornis personata) (14.5 cm)*.

Rivaling the Peach-Faced Love Bird in numbers and popularity is the beautiful Black Masked Love Bird, formerly called Masked Love Bird. The

A Black Masked Love Bird (left) and a Peach-Faced Love Bird pose together here peaceably enough—but keeping them caged together could result in an entirely different situation.

name has been changed to designate the difference from the blue variety, which is a mutant form of this variety.

The Black Masked is slightly smaller than the Peach Faced, is less pugnacious, and is somewhat quieter; but it still is not safe with other types of birds. It is a beautiful bird with startling color combinations. The black head is offset by a brilliant red beak and large white eye rings. A yellow, sometimes greenish-yellow, collar and broad, bright yellow chest contrast vividly with a bright green wings and abdomen. There is a much fainter trace of similar coloring in the tail, as in the Peach-Faced Love Bird, but this is far less noticeable.

Immature birds have the same colors as adults, but there is less vividness. Very few young birds often show traces of black on the beaks for a few weeks.

Black Masks are easily bred and highly popular. Because this is one variety with which most beginners start this fascinating hobby of aviculture, Black Masks are often more or less forgotten as new and rarer birds are added to the collection. Regardless of what the new variety may be, it would be difficult to surpass this Love Bird in appearance and personality.

BLUE MASKED LOVE BIRD

This variety, a mutation from the Black Masked Love Bird, is so well established in America that it is only slightly higher in price than the Black Masked and is just as good a breeder. In England, the variety never became really well established until after World War II. Serious British aviculturists, concentrating upon this variety, have bred them in sufficient numbers to insure prevalence from now on.

Francis Rudkin, Sr., who was one of the most charming and most distinguished aviculturists in the world and who was loved by all, was the champion of the Blue Masked Love Bird in this country and was largely responsible for its successful establishment. He reared many hundreds of Blue Masks at his ranch in Fillmore, California. As a result of his selective breeding, Mr. Rudkin's flock of blues, which started with a single blue bird cropping up in a clutch of Black Masks, were larger and of better type than most Black Masks.

The Blue Masked is the same species as the Black Masked. The pattern is the same, but all the yellow has been deleted in the bird, leaving blue where the Black Masked is green and an off-white where the Black Masked is yellow. The only other color variation is the beak, which is a faded pink instead of the bright red of the Black Masked.

FISCHER'S LOVE BIRD *(Agapornis fischeri) (15 cm).*

The Fischer's Love Bird is fourth in popularity in the American Love Bird population. Once reasonably common, there was a severe scarcity of these birds a few years ago. Fortunately, there are greater numbers of good strong stock again. For some unknown reason, the Fischer's is not as reliable a breeder in America as the Black Masked; whereas, in Europe the situation seems to be the opposite.

Fischer's Love Bird possesses a remarkable beauty. Similar in size to the Black Masked, it has the same bright red beak and white eye ring. The head is a fiery orange-red, and the rest of the plumage is a very pleasing shade of green except the rump, which is dusky blue, and the flight feathers, which are tinged with blue-grey, and the tail feathers, which are more lightly tinged with blue.

NYASSALAND LOVE BIRD *(Agapornis lilianae) (13.5 cm).*

Fifth in popularity, but still of considerable rarity, is the small and lovely Nyassaland. In appearance it more closely resembles the Fischer's, except that it is smaller, has a less extensive area of the red-orange on the head, and has chin and nape areas shading into a definite yellow. The red beak and eye rings are smaller than in other Love Birds.

The correct identification of this bird is important because many hybrids have been sold as Nyassalands. Particularly persistent is the dusty-faced hybrid of Peach-Faced and Black Masked represented as Nyassaland. This is possible because the Nyassaland is known in name only by many people who have never seen it.

Nyassalands are very pleasant little birds. Their voices are less harsh than other Love Birds. They do not harm other birds their own size; and, even with frequent handling, we have never had one try to bite.

Although breeding reports from abroad are most encouraging, Nyasslands do not seem to flourish in America. Their constant scarcity and high price tend to substantiate this fact. They have the reputation of being hardy but not interested in reproduction. Possibly we need fresh stocks in this country to strengthen existing numbers and to provide good foundation breeding stock.

RARE LOVE BIRDS

In America, at least, the other members of the Love Bird family are very rare.

None of these rarer Love Birds is as flashy in color as the ones which have been established here and which have already been described.

RED-FACED LOVE BIRD *(Agapornis pullaria pullaria) (15 cm).*

Sometimes called the Red-Headed Love Bird, this bird has entered this country from time to time. Though rather common in Europe, it has never become established in America. The coloring is attractive, but less so than that of the well-established favorites. The face is a particularly attractive shade of bright coral red; the rump is a good shade of bright blue; and the beak is red. The breast has an orange-red tinge. There is green around the eyes. It is four and a half inches. The rest of the bird is very bright green. Sexes can be determined by the underwing coverts, which are green on the hen and black on the male.

A little known but similar subspecies is *Agapornis pullaria ugandae.*

463

BLACK-CHEEKED LOVE BIRD *(Agapornis nigrigensis) (13.5 cm).*

Reasonably common in Europe, we have seldom seen this species. It resembles the Black Masked except that the breast is green instead of yellow, the crown is brown instead of black, and the throat is pinkish. The darker area on the head is less extensive than that of the Black Masked.

MADAGASCAR LOVE BIRD *(Agapornis cana cana) (14 cm).*

This is another rare species which we have very seldom seen.

Sexes are different in coloration. The male has lavender-grey head, neck and throat, and green on the body and wings. The hen is dull green.

An equally rare but similar subspecies is *Agapornis cana ablectanea.*

ABYSSINIAN LOVE BIRD *(Agapornis taranta) (16.5 cm).*

This species is sometimes called Black-Winged Love Bird.

The sexes are easily discernible because the male carries a red band on the crown. Otherwise, both male and female are green with red beaks and a black bar across the tails.

There is also a subspecies of this bird called *Agapornis taranta nana.*

The Abyssinian Love Bird *(Agapornis taranta)* has been bred in captivity on a number of occasions, but it can not be considered to be a free breeder. It is perhaps for this reason that comparatively few fanciers who are interested in Love Birds have bothered with the species.

BLACK-COLLARED LOVE BIRD *(Agapornis swinderniana swinderniana)* *(14 cm)*.

This species is sometimes referred to as Swindern's Love Bird.

The Black-Collared, and the following two subspecies of Love Birds, will most likely never be plentiful because of their extreme rarity even in their natural habitat. They are described as being mainly green with a light yellow throat and a black half-collar at the back of the neck bordered with yellow underneath. The tail has a red band bordered with black, and the rump is bright blue.

CAMEROON BLACK-COLLARED LOVE BIRD *(Agapornis swinderniana zenkeri)* *(14 cm)*.

This bird is similar to the above except for a reddish collar beneath the black collar at the back of the neck. The red extends in a narrower band around to the throat.

The other subspecies is *Agapornis swinderniana emini*.

PARROTLETS

Genus: *Forpus*

The South American counterpart of the African Love Bird is the Parrotlet. The Parrotlet is a miniature of the Love Bird in every respect except the bill, which is even smaller. The coloring is much less diversified, but the colors that are present are quite vivid. The varying shades of blue are especially bright and glossy. The main coloring in all species is bright, smooth green. The small bills are usually whitish.

Parrotlets are not highly popular as pets or as avicultural subjects in America because there are many other birds that are more colorful and more easily tamed. Even so, there are plenty around which are highly regarded by their owners. Several species have been successfully bred in captivity.

Most Parrotlets are easily sexed because the females usally lack the additional colors to the basic green.

There are five species of Parrotlets in the genus *Forpus*. One of the species, *passerinus*, has nine races with considerable variations in the blue accents, in shadings and extent, and in sizes. Spengel's Parrotlet (subspecies *spengeli*) has traces of yellow on the forehead as well as brilliant turquoise on rump and scapulars. The races *vividus* and *flavescens* have brilliant cobalt on the rump and wings. Another race, *deliciosus*, has turquoise green on the

465

rump and cobalt and turquoise-green in the wings. Confusion is therefore understandable when trying to pinpoint exact identification.

GREEN RUMPED or VENEZUELAN PARROTLET *(Forpus passerinus viridissimus) (12 cm).*

All green, brighter on the face and forehead and lighter on the undersides, this species has a particularly bright green rump. On the wing there is a faint turquoise tint. The beak is light horn color.

The habitat is Venezuela, Trinidad and Curacao.

GREEN RUMPED or GUIANA PARROTLET *(Forpus passerinus passerinus) (12 cm).*

The Guiana Parrotlet is like the Green Rumped Parrotlet except for the addition of a greyish tinge on the hind neck, pale blue on the wings, and brilliant dark blue on the underwing coverts. Females lack the blue.

The length is five and a half inches.

The habitat is British Guiana, Surinam, and Cayenne.

BLUE RUMPED PARROTLET *(Forpus passerinus flavissimus) (12 cm).*

From northeastern Brazil comes this species, which is similar to the Blue-Winged Parrotlet.

It has the cobalt blue in the wings and repeats it on the rump. The nape of the neck has a very slightly deeper bluish tinge and pale green on the throat. The female lacks the blue.

BLUE-WINGED PARROTLET *(Forpus passerinus vividus) (12 cm).*

This is a small bright green parrotlet only four and a half inches long, including the one and a half inch pointed tail.

The underside is a paler shade of green, and the head has a deeper and richer shade of green. The bill is greyish. The male has a large brilliant cobalt patch on the wings, which is missing in the female. The green shading of the female is also less vivid.

The native habitat of this very pretty little bird is eastern Brazil to Paraguay and northeastern Argentina.

There are several other subspecies of *Forpus passerinus* that differ but slightly from the above varieties. Consequently, most are difficult to detect. Just to keep the record straight, however, we are listing these subspecies and their habitats below.

Spengel's Parrotlet, *Forpus passerinus spengeli,* from Colombia.

Forpus passerinus cyanophanes from Colombia.

Forpus passerinus cyanochlorus from northwestern Brazil.

Forpus passerinus deliciosus from the lower Amazon River.
Forpus passerinus crassirostris from Peru and western Brazil.
Forpus passerinus flavescens from Bolivia.

TURQUOISE RUMPED PARROTLET *(Forpus cyanopygius cyanopygius)*
(13 cm).
The lovely Turquoise Rumped Parrotlet is a Mexican species with turquoise blue on the rump, lower back, greater wing coverts, and underwing coverts. The female has no blue. A bright yellowish green appears on the forehead and face of both sexes.

The range of this subspecies is western Mexico.

Two other subspecies are *Forpus cyanopygius pallidus* of northwestern Mexico and *Forpus cyanopygius insularis* from the Tres Marias Islands off western Mexico.

Mexican or Turquoise Rumped Parrotlet. Attractive green is highlighted by a bright turquoise blue on the rump, greater wing coverts and under the wings. Females lack the blue. Parrotlets are the South American counterpart of African Love Birds.

Celestial Parrotlets. The green on this bird is accented by a vivid blue on the wings and rump. The underwing coverts are brilliant cobalt blue. It is usually regarded as the most attractive member of the genus.

SPECTACLED PARROTLET *(Forpus conspicillatus caucae)* *(12 cm).*

Five inches long, including an inch and a half tail, this species is a little larger than most parrotlets.

There is a bright deep cobalt coloring on the rump and wing area. The rest of the bird is green, lighter underneath, and brighter under the eyes and on the lores. The female has no blue on rump and wings.

The habitat of this subspecies is western Colombia.

A second race, *Forpus conspicillatus conspicillatus,* is from Colombia.

CELESTIAL PARROTLET *(Forpus coelestis coelestis)*

This small parrotlet comes from the arid tropical zones of western South America. It ranges from four to four and a half inches in total length.

The underwing coverts are brilliant cobalt blue. There is also a vivid blue on the wings and rump. A faint line of blue follows the eye, and the back is greyish green. The rest of the bird is bright green.

The Celestial is distinct and different and is usually regarded very highly among admirers of Parrotlets.

A subspecies, *xanthops,* is different enough in appearance to be a separate species. It is five and one-fourth inches in length including the tail of one and one-half inches. The male's body coloring is basically bluish-grey, paler and more blue on the mantle. Underparts have a yellowish cast added to the powdery blue-grey. The rump and primary coverts are brilliant cobalt blue. The scapulars are lavender-violet. The forehead and crown cap as well as the throat and sides of the face are bright yellow with a greyish case. The ventral area and undertail coverts are pale yellow-grey with a cast of blue. The same brilliant blue which occurs on the upperside also occurs under the wings. This is easily the prettiest of all the parrotlets in this genus. The female is similar, but the blue is paler on the rump and absent on the wings on both the upperside and underside.

Sclater's Parrotlet *(Forpus sclateri* with two very similar races) is very dark green with brilliant dark cobalt on the rump and on a broad wing bar. The scapulars are paler. The underwing coverts are the same dark cobalt. The female lacks the blue.

The two similar races are:

> *eidos* from eastern Venezuela, the Guianas, and western Brazil.
> *sclateri* from eastern Ecuador and eastern Peru.

17

HANGING PARRAKEETS AND GUAIABERO

HANGING PARRAKEETS

Genus: *Loriculus*

All birds of this genus are agile, small, and basically vibrant green in color with various bright markings that are usually red, scarlet, or blue. Differences in coloration usually account for the differences in species and subspecies.

These are lovely little birds and have aptly been described as tiny living jewels of the tropics. They range in size from five inches to slightly over six inches. All have short tails, stocky bodies, small enlongated beaks, and a generally delicate appearance.

Hanging Parrots or Parrakeets (either name is acceptable) are also called Loriquets and do not roost in a normal manner. They hang upside down from a small branch, with their long claws interlocked to keep them from falling while asleep.

In their tropical habitats they are very abundant. They are kept as caged pets on a very wide scale and natives feed them the local fruits and nectar which make up their normal diet. Adaptation to an avicultural life has been successful in Europe, but they are not often seen in America. If the ban on psittacine birds is ever lifted, we, too, may have some of these highly desirable little birds.

In captivity, they should be fed the same diet as Lories, with plenty of fruit.

They have several avicultural advantages. They have weak, pleasant voices, an ability to get along with small finches, and do not destroy shrubs or plants.

There are ten species and numerous subspecies among the Hanging Parrakeets ranging from the India and Ceylon through much of Southeast Asia and the Philippines to New Guinea, New Britain, and New Ireland. Though they are closely related to Love Birds, in most respects, the aviculturist will regard them as members of the group of lories because of their diet. A total hummingbird diet will suit them quite well along with plenty of fruit, but a standard lory diet is more frequently used. Hanging Parrakeets have become available from time to time in the United States in recent years, but they really are too expensive. Unfortunately exporters in their countries of origin are generally not aware of the requirements of these birds, or else they totally disregard them. Those the writers have seen in foreign export markets in the Orient have always been in exceptionally overcrowded conditions. Mortality rates are very high under such circumstances. and the original very low cost understandably climbs incredibly to the point of ultimate delivery. When attention and care are given to these charming birds in collecting and export areas the current prices may be considerably reduced to the ultimate hobbyist in many other parts of the world.

Mostly green in color, the various species have several bright color accents in vivid colors; and they are delightful birds. Differences in coloring occur between the sexes. Usually the male has an additional color on the side of the face or sometimes on the throat which the female lacks.

Two races of *Loriculus vernalis,* called INDIAN LORIKEET or VERNAL HANGING PARRAKEET, are found in India. The green is relieved only by a blue throat patch in the male. The female is completely green. *Loriculus berylinus,* called CEYLONESE HANGING PARRAKEET, is found in Ceylon, and *Loriculus pusillus,* called JAVANESE HANGING PARRAKEET, is found in Java and Bali.

The Vernal Hanging Parrakeet *(Loriculus vernalis)* has two races. Red occurs on the beaks and rumps of both sexes, and a bright blue throat patch distinguishes the male. The Ceylonese Hanging Parrakeet *(Loriculus berylinus)* is five inches long including the one inch tail. Bright but deep red highlights the forehead, crown, and rump with olive-bronze added to the nape and back. The lower part of the face is blue on the male, but this color is absent on the female. The beak is red. The rest of the coloring is bright green. The Javanese Lorikeet or Hanging Parrakeet *(Loriculus pusillus),* also about five inches in length, has bright red on a large area covering the rump and tail coverts and a yellow throat patch. The green is even brighter on the head. Blue appears under the wings. The female has the yellow on the throat either reduced or absent.

PHILIPPINE HANGING PARRAKEETS *(Loriculus philippensis) (14 cm).*

There are eleven subspecies of this abundant bird, all showing slight differences in color patterns. Kept widely as cage birds in the Philippines, these would be ideal for aviculture. They are hardy, highly colorful, and have bright beaks ranging from orange to scarlet. Their basic colors are green, but there are several brilliant red accents and sometimes deep blues.

The Philippine Hanging Parrakeet is five inches long including the one and one-fourth inch tail. The beak is red. Bright red occurs on the forehead and a large area covering the rump and uppertail coverts. Blue on the underside of the wings and tail is vivid. The male shows a large area of red mixed with orange on the chin, throat, and upper chest. The female lacks this last feature but has a pale yellowish-green on the upper chest area and some blue on the facial areas. The different races show minor variations mostly in yellow or orange additions to the above pattern and coloring. The nominate race *philippensis* has a yellow line behind the red forehead and a yellow-orange band on the nape. A small yellow patch next to the red on the head distinguishes the race *bournsi* and *panayensis* is the same with slightly more yellow. The race *regulus* has much more yellow in a bright golden shade covering the entire hindcrown. On *chrysonotus* the golden-yellow extends from the hindcrown down through the upper back. The race *worcesteri* has more scarlet red covering the entire crown and changing to orange on the nape and then fading back to green on the mantle. The blue on the face of the female is much more extensive. The subspecies *siquijorensis* has the red restricted to the forehead, and the throat patch is smaller. Green returns to the nape and hindcrown. The race *apicalis* has scarlet red on the crown changing to orange on the nape and fading out on the mantle. The race *dohertyi* is like *apicalis*, but the orange extends down into the mantle. The race *bonapartei* has more orange on the nape and hindcrown, and the beak is black.

The Red Throated Hanging Parrakeet (*Loriculus amabilis* with four subspecies) is four to four and a half inches long including the one and one-fourth inch tail. The beak is black. Bright red appears on a patch on the head and on a small patch under the throat. The rump and uppertail coverts are dull red, and the mantle is olive-brown. This species is less colorful than any of the previous and is also less likely to become available. Their habitats range through the Sula Islands, Great Sangir Islands, and the islands of Pelling, Banggai, Halmahera, and Batjan.

The Red Capped Hanging Parrakeet (*Loriculus stigmatus* with two subspecies) has a bright red cap, a dark red chin patch, and a dark red rump. The bird has one subspecies on the Celebes Islands and another on the Togian Islands.

The Blue Crowned Hanging Parrakeet (*Loriculus galgalus* with two subspecies) is among the most likely species to become available since it occurs in a wide range from Thailand, through Malaysia, much of Indonesia, and parts of Borneo. It is four and one-half inches long including the tail of one and one-fourth inches. The beak is black, and a small but bright blue patch highlights the crown. A large red patch covers the rump and uppertail coverts. The male has a large circular throat patch of red and yellow on the shoulders, both of which are missing in the female.

The Celebes Hanging Parrakeet (*Loriculus exilis*) is very tiny, measuring only three and one-fourth inches from crown to tip of the half inch tail. Its on-

472

ly coloring beside the basic bright green is a bright red on the rump and uppertail coverts. The Flores Hanging Parrakeet (*Loriculus flosculus*) is very
similar.

Loriculus exilis inhabits the Celebes Islands. *Loriculus flosculus* inhabits
the island of Flores.

The Orange Fronted Hanging Parrakeet (*Loriculus aurantiifrons* with
four races) is three and three-fourths inches including the one inch tail. The
beak and cere are black. A trace of pale yellow crosses the forehead. The eyes
are straw-colored with large black pupils. A bright red throat patch is small,
and a large patch covering the rump and uppertail coverts is darker and duller
red. The habitats for the different races are Misol, Fergusson and
Goodenough Islands, the Bismarck Archipelago, New Guinea, and Waigeu.

GUAIABERO

Genus: *Bolbopsittacus*

There are three subspecies of the Guaiabero. All are very small and are
peculiar to the Philippines. There is no record of any of these species in captivity outside the Philippines. Occasionally they are kept as cage birds in the
Philippines and are fed on guavas.

They are stocky little birds with a broad short bill, short wings and tail,
and have colorings limited to green, blue, and yellow. Males are more
definitely patterned and have blue collars and yellowish rumps. Females have
collars of light greenish yellow. They seem to feed on berries and fruit,
especially guavas, from which the native name, Guaiabero, is derived.

LUZON GUAIABERO *(Bolbopsittacus lunulatus lunulatus)*
This species has face and collar prominently and attractively marked with
sky blue.

INTERMEDIATE GUAIABERO *(Bolbopsittacus lunulatus intermedius)*
This species is similar to the Luzon Guaiabero, but the blue areas of the
face have a deeper shade of blue tinged with purple.

MINDANAO GUAIABERO *(Bolbopsittacus lunulatus mindanensis)*
This species is also similar to the Luzon Guaiabero. The difference is the
green cheeks, which gives the male a triangular blue pattern around the eyes
that reaches down to the chin and connects with the blue collar.

Baby Cockatiels, as is the case with all other species of parrots, have very large crops and therefore need feeding about five times a day. Later, when they are beginning to feather, they need to be fed only three times a day. Admittedly they might benefit if the meals came slightly more frequently than this. Apart from food, the very young chicks need to be kept warm until they are three weeks old. If too cold, they will not feed with any enthusiasm nor can they digest their food efficiently; they could pine away and die or, at best, grow slowly. For the first week the chicks might be kept at about 95°-100°F (35°-38°C), dropping to 80°F (27°C) at two weeks. When too warm the chicks will pant and take on a rich pink color. In this case, drop the temperature by 5°F (3°C).

474

18

ADDITIONAL DATA ON SEX DETERMINATION, BREEDING, AND HAND FEEDING

The several subjects of this chapter include material which, judging from the preponderance of letters, the writers feel will be helpful to bird fanciers everywhere. It includes formulae for hand-rearing parrots, cockatoos, macaws, lories, and various species of valuable parrakeets. There is also a documentation of changes in diet and behavior of growing chicks being fostered.

Much progress in aviculture has been accomplished since the first edition of this book appeared in 1959. It is impossible to detail the accomplishments or even to evaluate them in this chapter. In fact, it is impossible for two people even as intensely interested in birds or as inquisitive as are the writers to be fully informed on all the studies, the experiments, and the results which are occurring right now.

An incredible amount of misinformation exists on all the subjects in this chapter. Since nearly all aviculturists are lay people rather than scientists or avian veterinarians, it is understandable that many inconsistencies and errors have been perpetuated in standard avicultural practices both in print as well as by word of mouth. Also, too often it is true that a bird fancier establishes as a set rule a theory that seemed to be successful on a one-time basis. This is a very poor practice to follow. A rule cannot be established on the basis of a singular success with the premise that it will be successful on all other similar problems with all other birds. Each individual is different; each species is different; and requirements vary accordingly. However, since there has always been a great lack of good scientific information available to aviculturists in the fields of behavior, diet, and illnesses, it is necessary for bird fanciers to use the trial and error method of solving problems. When coupled with a good share of common sense, successful solutions are often a reality. Fortunately findings of extensive scientific research in avicultural diets have begun to appear in print with the promise of more to follow.

In the chapters of this book concerning feeding, the caged household pet, and diseases, the writers have been most gratified to realize from the widespread response of readers that many of the suggestions based on experience and common sense have saved many birds' lives and that improved diets have eliminated many recurring problems. Furthermore, many readers seemed grateful that the suggestions and instructions were easy to put into effect. The writers feel that many changes will be forthcoming in the future, and all the information in this book can eventually be expanded or improved. Some parts will eventually be superseded by newer findings.

SEX DETERMINATION

One of the many problems facing aviculturists is accurately attempting to sex those species in which both sexes have the same pattern and coloring. This is particularly a problem with a species that has several subspecies showing slight variations in coloring or pattern. Often these slight variations have been interpreted by aviculturists as sexual differences. Wherever possible, even slight sexual differences in shape or body structure have previously been indicated; but this is still a haphazard affair. The Amazons are among the most difficult to sex, but the writers have mentioned before that the female usually has a rather smaller skull and a less bold look. Often the beak is less massive. The same is true of macaws.

After the publication of this book's first edition, the writers received a very nice letter from Miss E. Maud Knobel regarding sexing of parrots. Miss Knobel not only worked at the London Zoo but has also for many years served as an officer of the Avicultural Society in Great Britain. She was, by doing post mortem work at the zoo on parrots, able to ascertain sex definitely. Miss Knobel states that the pelvic method of determining sex in parrots the size of Amazons and African Greys is very satisfactory and accurate. The pelvic method of sexing birds is described on page 459 for Love Birds. The writers, even before receiving Miss Knobel's letter, had been applying the pelvic test to other smaller parrot members, particularly to Lorikeets since they were raising Swainson's Blue Mountain Lorikeets on a regular basis at that time. To date, the writers have never known of an error they have made by using this test on these lorikeets. Several pelvic tests on other birds were not definitive because few of the other species of birds tested show such an eagerness to breed at an early age as do the lorikeets. Since receiving Miss Knobel's letters, the writers have extended the pelvic tests to many other parrots, particularly to macaws.

There are drawbacks to this method. Immature birds do not have their pelvic bones "set" at consistent spacing. Females in particular have very movable pelvic bones. At one moment they may be very close together and very far apart the next. Adult males have pelvic bones only slightly separated, and they are usually not movable. Fully mature females have these bones placed far apart so that eggs can pass between them, and this may amount to a very considerable spacing.

Because muscular exertion is particularly important in laying eggs, these pelvic bones are still to some extent movable. The writers therefore add an

476

additional step to this process. They try to maintain the muscular exertion at its most consistent level by having each bird being tested gripping a perch and standing at as natural an angle as possible. Of course, some birds can be held easily; and many struggle inordinately during this process. Pictures showing handling of parrots appear on pages 42 and 92. It is understandable that the bird on page 92 is using its leg muscles in a very different manner from the bird on page 42. Variations in muscular contractions exert a remarkable influence on pelvic bones. If all birds being tested can firmly grip a standard parrot perch, most of the variables and chances for error are removed. Stresses and pressures are equalized as much as possible. This added step removes many adult birds from the ranks of the "in-between" questionables. Even so, there will be adults which, like juveniles, will remain indeterminate because the pelvic bones will be neither close nor widely spaced. With such birds, behavior, often over a prolonged period, must be the determining factor.

BREEDING

Generalized notes on breeding are very brief in this text; and, unfortunately, in the original manuscript, that short section was misplaced at the time of printing so that it appears in the wrong chapter. That information is to be found on pages 52 and 53. More detailed information wherever possible has been given in the chapters covering the different groups of birds as well as in the chapter on aviaries and equipment. More detailed information cannot be given in a volume covering the entire family, but perhaps a few additional suggestions can be given here along with simple restatements of previously cited principles.

With few exceptions parrots of all types stand better chances for breeding success if each pair is given an aviary to themselves. The primary social unit is the pair and its immature offspring. Every other bird, including mature offspring, represents a possible intrusion or distraction. The exceptions to this rule are Budgerigars, Quaker Parrakeets, and certain species of Love Birds, notably Peach-Faced, Masked, Fischer's, and Nyassaland. These birds actually seem to prefer colony breeding. Other birds may accept colony conditions and breed successfully, but that fact represents acceptance of a condition rather than a preference. Some birds such as Cockatiels, Bourke's, Redrump, and other closely related parrakeets do not object to other species of birds being present if all are congenial. Finches are therefore often included successfully in aviaries containing these birds.

Many species of *Aratinga* conures, despite easy maintenance and rapid adjustment to aviary life, have been consistently slow to start nesting activities. In studies of behavior in the wild state, Dr. John William Hardy of Occidental College in Los Angeles has conducted experiments in trying to simulate the territaries which many of these birds select for nesting sites. Reports of

Bourke's Parrakeet *(Neophema bourkii)* from New South Wales, southern, central and western Australia is bred extensively and is therefore usually obtainable. Pairs become inseparable and do everything together, even drinking, eating and roosting. Nest boxes of 8 in. by 8 in. with a depth of 16 in. should be hung outside, and rotted wood chips should be placed inside.

Extensive flights with natural cover for nesting. Ideal for all species of Australian parrakeets! (Steyn's aviaries, Pretoria, Transvaal, South Africa).

This is a very suitable design to provide separate breeding accommodation for four pairs of Australian Parrakeets. This aviary is entered by a main door at the rear of the shelters. There is also a low connecting little door between each shelter and flight.

these studies appeared in Volume 67 of the Condor, 1965, pages 140 to 156. The writers have not referred to this article, but Dr. Hardy's experiments seem to have stimulated through this technique a higher degree of interest than is usually experienced. It is true that many of those who have nested in conventional nestboxes quite possibly did so because the nesting instincts overcame their reluctance to wait until their native accommodations became available.

A correct diet is the most important principle in successfully raising parrots. It is true that the natural instincts to breed and to rear a family occur in most birds, even those whose nutrition has been deficient. It is also true that many birds successfully rear youngsters even though they are not properly fed. Another sad truth is that many youngsters appear to be fit and to mature successfully on poor, deficient diets. For the most part such successes are exceptions or are short-lived. Problems do begin to appear. Diet is a huge and complicated subject, very frequently not understood and unfortunately clouded by incredible misinformation, incorrect beliefs, and incomplete concepts. To make the subject even more difficult, the birds frequently will not accept all the items in a complete diet. Birds are creatures of habit, and they accept foods to which they have become accustomed. They do not, as is frequently believed, select the correct items out of a large variety of foods served cafeteria style to form a balanced diet. They may do so in the wild state, but they do not do so in captivity. Domestic foods are completely different from their natural foods, and so "instincts" and "inherited memories" cannot be relied upon to aid a bird's judgment in selecting for himself. A bird selects the wrong foods just as frequently as do his owners. Most of the mysterious and perplexing problems can be avoided and greater assurances of success can be expected if diets are sound and balanced long before the breeding season arrives.

A young Swainson's Blue Mountain Lorikeet in its nest shows the bottom of this box designed especially for Lories. This box is described in the text on page 40 and is shown from below on page 37. After this youngster fledges and before the parents lay their next clutch of eggs, more charcoal must be added so that the eggs will not rest directly on the wire mesh which breaks the eggs.

Already very brightly colored but incompletely feathered, this nestling Swainson's Blue Mountain Lorikeet is receiving daily handling by one of the authors so that when it fledges it will already be accustomed to human companionship. Not all parrot parents permit this freedom with their youngsters.

Exercise is also important for breeding birds. The most important problem to develop as a result of inadequate exercise is egg-binding, although part of this problem can also be malnutrition. Muscular strength is necessary to expel the eggs at nesting time, and there is no better method of insuring good muscular tone than to provide enough space in which to fly and to remain active. It is true that some of the larger birds have successfully nested in cages or in very small aviaries, but this is usually due to the over-powering desire of the birds to rear families despite all obstacles. More youngsters are raised in suitable aviaries than in cages.

Interference is an important factor in desertions of eggs or youngsters, although again inadequate diet causing nervousness or instability is frequently a contributing factor. Aside from diet, however, curiosity of humans can be a serious disturbance to birds when nesting. The savage protectiveness of many parrots, even in very tame parrots, is a natural instinct which develops to prevent interference; but very often this offensive technique is not effective against intrusion. Deserting the nest and abandoning the natural instincts to rear a family is a natural outcome of too much interference. There are exceptions to this rule also.

The most notable exception the writers have ever experienced was the regular nesting of Swainson's Blue Mountain Lories who produced many youngsters in several seasons of repeated breedings in an aviary which was exposed to close contact with countless numbers of visitors nearly every day of the year. This, however, was not an accident. It was the result of prolonged and careful conditioning to the point that such activity ceased to be inter-ferences, becoming instead an accepted part of the regular routine. The writers went even further in this conditioning by handling the youngsters every day after they hatched. By waiting until the eggs hatched when the desire not to desert was strongest, the writers, already familiar with the birds

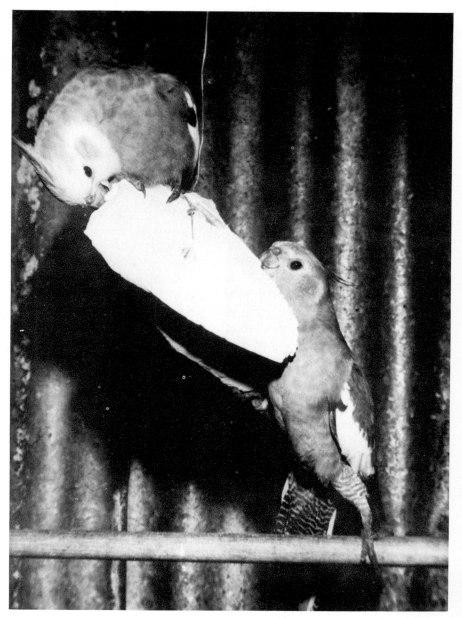

Cuttlefish bone contains about eighty percent lime, and this is present in a readily digestible form. Therefore it should always be available. The great thing to bear in mind with regard to cuttlefish bone, however, is that what is found on the seashore has to be thoroughly cleaned before it is given to any birds. It is much safer to purchase comparatively inexpensive supplies at your pet shop than to use makeshift substitutes.

in non-nesting periods, entered the aviary with no disturbance. The parents gradually allowed and even accepted this routine handling of the chicks. Both parents and some of the youngsters are pictured in this book. Conditioning of this nature is slow, gentle, and carefully accomplished; and it can be considered as companionship rather than intrusion. Frequently the most important aspect of conditioning in this manner is recognizing whether or not any particular pair of birds will allow this type of companionship during nesting.

Patience is another very important factor in successful breeding results. Too many people feel that a male and a female and a nestbox automatically add up to instant nesting preparations. Patience is required for a mutual acceptance before the birds may become a pair. "Proven breeders" or "mated pairs" are magic selling words, but they may mean absolutely nothing to you in production results. Because a pair of birds may have successfully nested and reared youngsters in one location does not mean they will repeat the accomplishment when they are sold and transferred to a totally different environment and possibly different foods as well. It only means that they *have* produced. They could successfully repeat if you provide the necessary foods, satisfactory environment, lack of interference, and have the patience till the birds become adequately settled in their new surroundings. "Mated pairs" means far less than "breeding pairs". Many birds easily and satisfactorily select mates and breed frequently for prolonged periods but never enter into an actual nesting cycle even though everything conducive to nesting has been supplied.

Many birds are sold with the comforting phrase "breeding age". This phrase is even more nebulous than the other two. It merely means that one bird is capable of laying eggs and that another is capable of fertilizing them. Patience must be added to all the aforementioned requisites. Instant success is rarely attainable. Many unmated females produce eggs at regular breeding seasons. One would think that the introduction of an available male might quickly solve all problems. Usually it does not. Given patience and time, a satisfactory union may result; but the birds themselves must make the decision.

Successful nesting and rearing of families are not all instinctive traits. Much of the procedure is the result of learning, and this is sometimes a slow and haphazard process. Many people regard a nesting failure as a total loss; but, more often than not, a pair of birds failing in a first attempt will learn something of value. The writers seldom expect success during the first breeding season of a pair of birds. With this approach to raising birds, many unexpected successes can be registered over disappointing failures. With many species of birds dismal failures may occur two or three times per season for two years before the learning processes can be successfully instilled.

483

COMPARATIVE NESTING PERIODS

	Incubation Period	Fledging Age	Weaning Period	Age at Independence
Budgerigar	18 days	5 weeks	1 week	6 weeks
Cockatiel	18–21 days	5 weeks	2 weeks	7 weeks
Love Bird	22–25 days	6–7 weeks	2 weeks	8–9 weeks
Parrakeets (Elegants and close relatives)	18 days	5 weeks	2 weeks	7 weeks
Parrakeets (Ringneck family)	18 days	5 weeks	4–5 weeks	9–10 weeks
Parrots (Amazons, Caiques, African Greys, etc.)	28 days	8 weeks (longer for African Grey)	5–6 weeks	13–14 weeks
Lories and Lorikeets	28 days	4–5 weeks	4 weeks	8–9 weeks
Cockatoos	28 days	8 weeks	5–6 weeks	13–14 weeks
Macaws	28 days	12–13 weeks	8–10 weeks	20–23 weeks

There are considerable variations in the larger birds particularly in fledging periods and in the weaning periods. In some instances, even incubation periods differ. Rose Breasted Cockatoos, for example, hatch in 24 days instead of 28. Eggs are nearly always laid every other day; and, if incubation starts right away as is the general practice, the eggs hatch every other day.

HANDFEEDING

The writers have received many letters regarding handfeeding. This subject was only slightly mentioned in the first edition because the writers have had very little experience in handfeeding baby parrots. They have weaned many parrots and transferred them to seed diets. Even that is a difficult and time consuming task.

For help on this subject the writers have turned to three friends who have had extensive experience in this aspect of raising birds. Mrs. Velma Hart of Long Beach, California, has developed her own routine of feeding and diet with necessary changes for different ages of the babies. Starting with Love Birds, she has raised babies from hatching to weaning and has offered far more information on the care during this procedure than on diet alone. The writers consider her contribution invaluable to this volume. She has raised more than one hundred birds on this diet including various species of Amazons and African Greys as well as Leadbeater and Rose Breasted Cockatoos. Mrs. Hart developed her diet carefully making adjustments whenever problems became evident and studying dietary needs as a lay student with an inquiring mind and an intense interest. Her accomplishment is notable indeed.

Hybrid offspring of male Rosella x female Red-rumped Parrakeet. The first Rosellas were bred in Spain in 1862, the first Red-Rumped in Britain (1857) and Germany (1863).

Mr. Kenneth Wyatt of San Pedro, California, has a great interest in Australian birds, notably Australian Parrakeets. When he was faced with an emergency condition which meant handfeeding nestlings to prevent losing valuable birds, he referred to Mrs. Hart's experience with the larger parrots. Using her diet as a basis but with changes appropriate to his own routines and his birds' needs, he developed an additional diet and routine which is also presented along with additional information by Mr. Wyatt and the writers.

Ralph Small of Brookfield, Illinois, has successfully handreared baby macaws on a separate diet and has maintained an account showing comparisons with babies who were reared by their own parents. This statistical report is particularly interesting because it points up the differences in the development of chicks reared by human foster parents and those reared by natural parents.

HANDFEEDING PARROTS

Mrs. Hart writes:

"When someone says 'How do you handfeed a bird?', the question could fill a book, I'm sure. I ask them 'What age is the bird?' There are different food requirements at various stages of growth of all living things.

"I have learned over the years that getting food into those little mouths at the right times is of course very important, but there are a great many other factors and details to be considered. There seems to be very little information in print about many important incidentals such as digestion, for example, and what to do in case things go wrong. If all the food agrees and the baby grows properly, then all is fine; but here are a few of the problems I have faced and my solutions to them.

"Most often the problem human foster parents face in handfeeding is that the baby formula digests very slowly. It may just stay there in the crop, a lump, moist or dry, depending on what is being fed. Dry cereal with hot water poured over it and fed before the cereal really has a chance to absorb the moisture can be very harmful. The digestive system uses the moisture; and the dry mass of cereal remains as a hard lump in the crop going nowhere and offering little, if any, nourishment. For this situation, a very moist, thin cooked cereal with a drop or two (no more) of black strap molasses usually gives relief. This must be continued till the hard, dry lump lodged in the crop has been absorbed.

"Another cause of this impacted crop condition is food that has been fed while too cool and formulated without enough vegetable or fruit for proper elimination. Sometimes it is caused by too much food intake. Regardless of the moisture content, the food usually gets no further than the crop where it becomes sour causing considerable discomfort for the bird as evidenced by the whining sounds it makes. Fast relief is necessary. One-fourth to one-half teaspoon of plain unflavored milk of magnesia in the crop nearly always sweetens the crop and relieves the blockage. This dosage will vary in amount with the size and age of the baby. Very young babies could not possibly take one-fourth of a teaspoon, but this problem seldom develops in the tiny youngsters. An additional very important cause of this condition is that the baby itself is not kept warm enough for digestive processes to function properly.

"A very damaging accident, by no means infrequent, in handling baby birds during the handfeeding processes can easily be avoided. We all think we know how to handle birds, but we get too confident sometimes. There are times when it is impossible to keep your eyes on all the babies at once and also times when it is necessary to turn away even if only for a moment. There is always that unguarded moment. The most heartbreaking thing I ever did was to turn my eyes away from a month-old baby for just a moment's distraction. He gave a push with one little foot, and his fat little body tumbled off balance and rolled off the edge of the table. He was on a turkish towel, but there were no barriers to stop the roll. Since then I have always put the babies in a wicker basket during feeding times. The basket may have dangerously sharp wicker edges; so check for any danger areas. This very same accident has happened to a good many other people.

"Another accident in handling babies which happens more frequently than is generally supposed can easily be avoided. If you lift a baby bird by its body, notice how the legs stretch down and stiffen in an instinctive grasp for a solid footing. This is a very insecure moment for the bird. Chicks with soft bone structures hardly more than cartilege at this stage have more muscular power than bone strength. Legs and even other bones can easily be broken in this manner especially since he will grasp at anything for a foothold, even the top of the box from which he is being removed. The grip is powerful enough for quite a tug-of-war for those soft bones. The best method for handling a baby chick is to lift with one hand and slip the upturned palm of the other hand under him. Let the little feet become secure in your hand. He will be safe and comfortable and will snuggle down into the palm showing a sense of security and almost a sense of appreciation for the considerate handling.

"Warmth between feedings should be approximately the same as would emanate from his real mother's hovering body. It is said that the mother's body temperature is 105° to 107° Fahrenheit. If you reach into a nest of growing babies you feel a positive, warm, moist heat which emanates from the mother and permeates the babies, the nestbox, and any nesting material maintaining a fairly constant temperature. When the hen is off the nest, the chill comes on quickly; and, if she is off for any extended period, really young unfeathered chicks cannot generate or hold their own heat. Losses in youngsters can occur very rapidly. Therefore it is important to remember when you accept the responsibility of handfeeding that you must maintain the mother's body warmth at all times. For young babies at least 85° Fahrenheit is necessary, but 90° is better. You can soon tell how content and comfortable they are. If they settle into a regular routine of eating and then sleeping till they become empty again with frequent repetition, then all is well.

"Someone once told me to 'remember the little things and the big things will take care of themselves', but I was not informed about just how many 'little' things I would have to learn before the big ones began helping. Handfeeding is a big job requiring attention to a great many small details, and that attention must be frequent. I began handfeeding several years ago by feeding Black Masked Love Birds on a prepared product which is no longer manufactured. I graduated to the larger birds first by rearing Mexican Double Yellow Headed Amazons. After that came Panamas, Cuban Amazons, African Greys, Rose Breasted Cockatoos, and Leadbeater Cockatoos. My recipes have been successful on all these species, and I feel they will be satisfactory with many others as well. These recipes are not given with any implication that they are the *only* handfeeding formulas. Each human foster parent has his or her own ideas, and many other procedures give satisfactory results. I use these procedures because I have found them to be the easiest and best for my needs and because they fulfill all my babies' needs.

"First of all, cooking the food assures me that the babies will absorb all the food and not just the liquid which would leave a packed crop as mentioned above when a dry mix is used merely with hot water. If a baby hatches in an incubator, I wait until at least twelve hours and sometimes a little longer before giving it anything at all. The first feeding is only a drop or two of very warm gruel. Each time the tiny crop empties, the chick is fed again, usually about every two hours for the first three days and nights. With each feeding the chick is able to take a tiny bit more; and, within a week, it will be sleeping longer between feedings. The temperature should be 90°F. to 95°F., and the bed should be kept dry. A wet spot may wake the youngster and cause loud complaints.

"The food formula for the first ten to twelve days is as follows:
One half cup boiling water
One tablespoon wheathearts (This is a hot, cooked cereal composed of hearts of wheat. There may be differences in brand names in different areas, and surely the names will be different in other countries, but the composition should not be different whatever the name may be.)
Cook three to five minutes
Add one egg yolk
one rounded teaspoon powdered milk (furnishes calcium as well as other nutrients)

$2\frac{1}{4}$ ounces (one half of a $4\frac{1}{2}$ ounce jar) of strained oatmeal with apple sauce and bananas, a human baby cereal preparation.

one teaspoon honey (optional)

"At this stage it is almost impossible to add vitamins since even a tiny amount would be too much, and the cereals are adequately fortified. The added applesauce and banana in the baby cereal preparation are for a gentle but beneficial laxative effect as well as food value. This food should be fed thin and warm. Test against your lip. If it is warm against your lip, it is the right temperature. A single egg poacher or similar receptacle is a satisfactory size for heating small amounts. Excess amounts must be refrigerated.

"Most parrot babies open their eyes between the tenth and fourteenth day, and the quantity of food and nutritional requirements have increased tremendously by this time. The formula is changed to the following:

Two cups boiling water

Two teaspoons corn oil (as used in salads or for cooking)

A slight dash of salt

One-half cup Wheathearts

Cook three to five minutes; remove from stove and add the following:

One-half cup powdered milk

Four and one-half ounces (the standard sized jar) of the human baby cereal as in the first formula (oatmeal with applesauce and bananas)

One tablespoon honey

One-third to one-half cup fine sunflower meal (this is usually available at stores specializing in health or special foods)

"Some of this can be sealed into jars and frozen if you are feeding only one small baby. You may need to add a few drops of water to make a better consistency for spoonfeeding. Add vitamins of your own choosing. The best ones are available in pet shops because they are formulated especially for birds and other pets. They are compounded so that evaporation is extremely slow even when exposed to air. Most liquid vitamins prepared for infants are meant to be used straight from the eyedropper, and they lose potency very rapidly when exposed to air or when mixed in preparations such as this formula. Be conservative with vitamins though. Too much can make a jittery, nervous wreck of your bird.

"Brooder temperature by this age is gradually reduced to about 85°F. Feed when the crop is empty. The babies will overeat if given the chance; so do not stuff the crop. You can see the food as it goes down into the crop. Stop when the crop is rounded which will give a plump appearance.

"Between the third and fourth week, tremendous changes in size and appearance have occurred. The babies seem to grow noticeably even between feedings. Intake increases greatly after the end of the third week. When you run out of the formula prepared above, another change takes place as follows:

Five cups water

One cup quick oatmeal (Note: not the 'instant' oats)

One half cup Wheathearts

One tablespoon corn oil

One-half teaspoon salt

When the cereal is cooked, remove from stove and add:

One $4\frac{1}{2}$ ounce jar of baby vegetables labeled 'Garden Vegetables' (a combination of peas, carrots, and spinach). Note: for cockatoos and Cockatiels increase this amount by $\frac{1}{3}$ to $\frac{1}{2}$ to keep the formula moving through the bird at a satisfactory digestive rate. If this is not increased, a slowdown in digestion and feeding could occur with these birds. An acceleration in absorption and feeding periods could also occur, but this is good because it means faster growth.

One cup powdered milk

Two cups sunflower meal

"As before food can be stored in jars and frozen. Sunflower meal is most safely kept in jars stored in the refrigerator or frozen since it otherwise quickly becomes rancid and therefore presents a danger. If you wish to grind your own sunflower meal, buy hulled sunflower seed. Break up about two slices of very dry whole wheat bread to be mixed with one and one-half to two cups of hulled seed and grind it in a blender. The hulled sunflower seed ground alone would become soggy and sticky. The bread adds only nourishment when used in the soft food.

"Temperature can be lowered once the baby has feathered. After the sixth week, the mother would most likely be letting the chicks sleep in the box alone; and so very little heat is needed toward the final days in the nestbox.

"The next step is very important and one which usually causes worries among foster parents. As the birds begin to exercise their wings in the box, they try to climb to any ledge they can reach trying to perch. They enter a seemingly ungrateful period regarding the patient and seemingly endless day and night handfeeding which has taken so much of your time and effort. They clamp their beaks shut so that feeding is very difficult. If you do get their mouths full, they may very well, with one shake of the head, throw the food in all directions. You are about to mutter something about ingratitude, but the bird is going into a slimming phase before being able to fly. The crop shrinks from the soft food diet, and the youngster is old enough to begin picking at seeds (preferably softened by soaking), strips of carrot, pieces of apple, a piece of dry whole wheat bread, or other good dietary selections to start him on his mature diet. As soon as the first seeds are given, a good health grit also becomes necessary.

"A light feeding in the mornings should still be continued until the bird

490

becomes really self sufficient. At night another feeding prevents the baby from going to bed hungry. The amount will vary as he learns to eat more and more on his own. The adult foods should be placed within easy reach wherever the bird turns since this will encourage him to sample these new foods frequently. By now he should be housed in a deep open-top box or a flat-bottomed cage.

"Each bird and each species gains its independence in its own time which is always variable. Each baby has a different personality with no two alike. Still, you will remember them all and will feel a real sense of accomplishment when you put him into a parrot cage with cups on the side. Watching him holding a piece of sweet corn or an apple wedge in his foot just like other grownup birds, you think back over all the time and concern you have lavished on this project and quite simply realize that it was worth it after all."

Mrs. Hart adds some additional helpful comparative information. Most youngsters are trying to fly in eight weeks, but African Greys take longer. Handfeeding finally is finished at about ninety days. In the Mexican Double Yellow Head, the egg at hatching time weighs fourteen grams. The baby at three weeks of age weighs 240 grams and 464 grams at seven and a half weeks. After this age the slimming process starts as the birds take less soft food and begin picking at seed on their own. The Cuban Amazon egg at hatching time weighs twelve grams, and the baby at ten days of age weighs sixty grams.

In the event that the cereal of wheat hearts is not available by brand name, the cereal is composed of "selected portions of toasted wheat berry, toasted wheat germ with added iron, niacin, thiamin, and riboflavin". By checking ingredients on other packages, a satisfactory substitute may be found.

Mrs. Hart also adds a light sprinkling of poultry powdered Vitamin A and D on the food. The amount, though not actually measured, is conservative. She also discovered early in her formula development that too high a protein content in the formulas overworks the kidneys. Admittedly there are different kinds of proteins, but the addition of any protein added above and beyond the amounts furnished in the components of the formulas may bring on the same problem.

If a youngster must be removed from the parents for handfeeding, all the food which the parents have fed must be absorbed before handfeeding starts. One other hint Mrs. Hart offered is not necessarily confined to handling baby parrots any more than it does to handling adult parrots which as mentioned before usually become quite savage during the nesting periods. She says if she ever receives a bite or any injury from any of her birds she merely applies household peroxide right away. It acts as a disinfectant and promotes healing quickly with no swelling.

Mrs. Hart also adds a small portion of a supplement which is available on a local basis only. Though it is an optional addition, it is beneficial. Mrs. Hart indicates that some of the additional value of it can be supplied if a trace of kelp and an average-sized pinch of alfalfa meal be added to the $4\frac{1}{2}$ ounce size jar of the formula beginning at the second stage in her diet. A trace in this instance is difficult to describe and, in fact, so is a pinch; but few kitchens have any other method of weighing amounts this small. The trace is less than the pinch described above, rather more like a light sprinkling of salt. The addition of too much of these two items will cause more harm than benefit.

HANDFEEDING PARRAKEETS

Mr. Kenneth Wyatt's experiences in the parrot family apply mostly to Australian Parrakeets. His experiences are somewhat different from Mrs. Hart's, and they are therefore of importance to aviculturists who face the problems of non-feeding parents or any of the other reasons by which they become the owners of fertile eggs or newly hatched chicks with no satisfactory parents to take over the job of rearing valuable youngsters. Mr. Wyatt usually has several species of other parrakeets; and, if it is possible, he fosters the eggs or youngsters with other species. Many times this cannot be.

Other birds, to take over this job, must be in a similar cycle at approximately the same time. Since the physiological changes of birds during the nesting cycle change according to the stage of the cycle, it is impossible to put chicks in another nest where eggs have not yet hatched. The foster parents would not be physiologically equipped to feed them, nor would the instinctive desire to feed yet be present. Also, to put young chicks in another nest with older chicks nearing fledging age would again upset the orderly physiological stages. Parents with noticeably older chicks cannot properly feed newly hatched babies; and, even if they did, that instinctive desire in most instances is depleted before the foster chicks would be reared. There are exceptions to this, but they are somewhat rare.

Several species, such as Elegants or Bourke's Parrakeets, even Budgerigars, are good tight setters which can be used to incubate other birds' eggs; but they cannot successfully feed Rosellas, Manycolors, and most of the other larger parrakeets because the seed content is higher and the fruit intake is low in comparison. Compacted crops are the usual result. The food will not digest or pass through, and so these valuable youngsters die from starvation as a result. They can be safely left with these foster parents for two or three days, or they can be brought in for handfeeding the minute they hatch.

There are many species which will incubate and hatch other birds' eggs, and some which will even be able to rear the youngsters. A good rule of thumb method for anyone attempting to do so would be to put the eggs under birds of the same genus. This is not always possible unfortunately. Certain species of Love Birds, as an example, will refuse to feed other species of Love Birds after hatching them if the coloring of the down on the chicks is different

492

from what they are accustomed to rearing. Variation of down coloring occurs in some species.

Eggs can be incubated if no foster parents are available. The temperature for the eggs must be 100°F., or to be exact, 99¾°F. A precise, good quality incubator will maintain this temperature as well as the necessary humidity of 60% to 80%. Humidity lower than this point may hatch certain types of eggs but not parrots.

A brooder of some sort is necessary to maintain heat at all times, but this can be variable according to what is available. Mr. Wyatt keeps his chicks in a sizeable box and uses a fifteen watt bulb for heat. The bulb must be closed off from the birds so that they will not sustain a burn when snuggling up close. Mr. Wyatt puts the light bulb down inside a wooden finch box which is then wrapped with a cloth. The wood offers just the right insulation. Metal is very dangerous and must be avoided. Some plastics are all right as a cover for the bulb with this small a wattage but should be checked carefully before putting the chicks next to it. As a general rule, the finch box with the cloth cover works out best for Mr. Wyatt. Those birds needing 100°F. will snuggle right up to the box, and those a little older which need only about 85° will stay back from the box. They are very sensitive to temperature and will move to the location giving the temperature needed. Mr. Wyatt uses wood shavings in the bottom of the brooder to absorb the droppings and changes them as often as necessary.

Some birds do better feeding from a plunger type feeder, but some people and some birds still work more easily with a small spoon with the sides turned up into a narrow funnel outlet. It should be turned to as narrow an opening as will allow easy feeding into the beak without allowing the food to run down the sides. The food should be of a thickness so that it will run slowly off a spoon. The first day or two the bird will not understand the feeding routine, and it will probably be necessary to force the beak open at first. During the natural feeding process, the mother usually does a considerable amount of vigorous pumping up and down not only to regurgitate the food she has ingested and partially digested but also to be certain that the food is pumped down into the crop of the youngster. This behavior is less pronounced in the beginning becoming stronger as the chick gets older. The instinctive odd jerky movements even with newborn chicks may be a slight problem in keeping the food off the faces; but, in most instances, the birds adapt very quickly to handfeeding. Facial cleaning after feeding is usually necessary. Dried, hardened foods remaining on the beak can cause deformed beaks during those rapid growth periods.

The food should be 100°F., no more or less. As with Mrs. Hart's instructions, touching it to your lip is a satisfactory test. Food too hot will cause burns, and the birds sensibly reject it if it is too cold. Digestion is impaired by foods too low in temperature.

Mr. Wyatt's feeding schedule is every two hours around the clock gradually changing to every four hours when the chicks reach the age of two weeks. This means getting up nights, of course, for the first two weeks. At that age, the chicks can go eight hours without food during the night. At the sixth week, the babies are already flying; and Mr. Wyatt removes them to an outside aviary (possible only in mild climates) and continues the handfeeding in the aviary as long as is necessary which is about another week for Rosellas and three or four for Ringneck Parrakeets.

For newly hatched chicks, Mr. Wyatt feeds straight pablum moistened with water for two or sometimes three days. For the next two days, a similar baby cereal is used, one manufactured from seven grains with a protein content of 35% compared to 16% for regular pablum. The formula starts on the fourth or fifth day.

Mr. Wyatt uses a one pound coffee can as a receptacle, and all these ingredients and measurements are based on filling that can with the total wet food formula. The formula can be stored in a refrigerator for as long as a week. If he does not use all of this quantity in a week's time, he discards it because there is too much danger of souring after that point.

The basis of the formula is cooked oatmeal. He uses the one-minute kind instead of the longer one which Mrs. Hart uses but avoids the instant variety which does not require cooking. The total quantity of oatmeal is one-third of the coffee can contents which includes the water used in preparation.

To the cooked oatmeal, Mr. Wyatt adds one heaping tablespoon strained carrots, a heaping tablespoon strained peas, and two heaping tablespoons of strained applesauce. All three of these ingredients are standard infant foods. The juice from half an orange is also added along with four heaping tablespoons of ground millet meal, two heaping tablespoons of a good standard wheat germ meal, two heaping tablespoons powdered milk, one level teaspoon standard liquid vitamin preparation for birds and pets, and two hard boiled egg yolks. The seven grain cereal with the 35% protein is then added along with enough water to make a thick porridge texture till the can is full. The storage in the refrigerator allows complete absorption of the moisture so that the problem Mrs. Hart mentioned will not happen. After a day in the refrigerator, it is unlikely that the moisture alone could be absorbed by the chick's system leaving a heavy lump of undigested food to give problems. As much as is needed is warmed before each feeding.

On the tenth day the formula undergoes a slight but important change. To the total formula above add four heaping tablespoons of sunflower meal. This is a rich addition to the formula; and, if used too soon, it will contribute to compacted crop problems. The millet meal will also contribute to the same problem if fed before the fifth day.

494

Mr. Wyatt adds the same supplement that Mrs. Hart uses. In this instance, the reader has a little easier task in the measurements—or perhaps four traces of kelp and four pinches of alfalfa leaf meal is still the easiest addition.

Mr. Wyatt mentions that other bird fanciers also use his basic formula but with minor changes. Some people use raw eggs instead of hard boiling them, and others substitute half the quantity of oatmeal for an equal portion of wheat heart cereal. Many people have their own preferences and slightly varying methods in this routine, and it seems to be human nature for bird fanciers to want to improve upon proven formulas. This is perfectly acceptable and commendable.

The main objective is to avoid shortcuts which would reduce nutritional values. Attempted shortcuts in the work load by stretching the intervals between feedings is as hazardous as using an incomplete formula. Handfeeding, as mentioned before, is a chore not to be undertaken half heartedly. It would be better to let the newly hatched chick die in the beginning than to do a haphazard job on handfeeding. A minute error in the early stages, even missing a single feeding, will be magnified many times by the time the chick is grown. Many weaknesses to be found in birds can be attributed to small early events or deprivations. Mrs. Hart correctly calls it cheating when inadequate diets and shortcuts are employed. The most visible result of deprivation is poor feather development which is sometimes corrected after the first moult but may never be overcome. Other results of this cheating are less difficult to detect. Parent fed nestlings often face the same deprivations which can be brought about by overworked, overbred, and undernourished parents.

Handreared birds are, of course, much tamer than parent raised babies; and Mr. Wyatt has noted that his and other handreared birds also have become good breeders. Parent raised babies go through a more natural set of circumstances during which quite a lot of learning occurs. A good portion of a bird's supposed natural instincts are actually acquired behavior traits, and many of these are acquired from the parents during the nestling stage. Even more are acquired between the age of fledging and weaning. Handrearing represents an interruption in these orderly processes of learning. The interruption can be made up in later stages of life. Slow starters, errors, patterns of behavior which prevent successful nesting, and many other problems can sometimes be traced to the interruption of these orderly processes.

Of course, aviculture itself is also an interruption of these orderly processes of nature. With some birds under certain favorable conditions, it is a considerable improvement over nature's sometimes harsh ways; but domestic aviary life still represents an adjustment. Nesting problems and behavior problems can as a result occur latently even with parent raised chicks in aviary life. There are also notable exceptions which defy all accepted theories and conclusions in behavior. Mr. Wyatt has noted that handreared birds proved themselves to be good breeders. He cited a handreared male Blue Ringneck Parrakeet, not owned by him, which fathered three youngsters at the age of one year. This is notable for any Ringneck. Rarely do they breed successfully even at two years, and a few males do not even show their colors until they are three years old.

Behavior of birds is an intensely interesting subject not only in a domestic situation but also in the wild state. It is a virtually untapped field and will hopefully receive an increasingly greater attention judging from some of the impetus given in recent years by notable ornithologists who are urging aviculturists to cooperate in their studies.

The writers are indebted to Mr. Wyatt for the addition of another subject which could prove helpful to bird fanciers during emergencies and which could save the lives of valuable birds. Occasions arise at hatching times when the chicks just cannot get out of the eggshell. There is a general belief that any chick which cannot hatch is a weakling to begin with. This is not necessarily true because many times the eggshell is too thick or too tough or lacking in sufficient moisture for a normal breakthrough.

The normal breakthrough takes the imprisoned chick forty-eight hours of hard labor from the first peck till the final release which is quite an exhausting ordeal. If, at any time after twenty-four hours of regular pecking, the baby can be heard crying with the pain of each peck, it is in trouble and needs help from the outside. The imprisoned chick will soon die under such circumstances. If it is not crying, it is not in pain or trouble; and so this sound is of particular importance to any would-be rescuer. An overzealous helping hand can also kill a youngster by releasing it too soon. Moreover, a chick too weak to cry at hatching time will probably not be strong enough to survive under even the best of conditions to follow.

However, if the youngster is crying within the egg, outside help can save its life. Using a small toothpick, start breaking the shell where it has already been pecked or cracked. The usual pattern is a line following the circumference of the egg. This is a tense, slow job requiring the greatest care so as not to injure the baby. The shell must come off in little pieces meticulously worked away. When the egg finally opens and the exhausted chick is released, it should be placed under the mother so that she can properly dry it. A fair share of excrement can be observed inside the eggshell. If outside help had not been given, the amount of excrement would have rapidly increased and poisoned the exhausted prisoner.

HANDFEEDING MACAWS

Mr. and Mrs. Ralph Small have taken over the task of handrearing baby macaws when a breeding pair at the Brookfield Zoo refused to feed them.

These macaws, a Scarlet mated to a Blue and Gold, produce variable and colorful offspring; but they have not always taken care of them. Mr. and Mrs. Small keep their young macaws in a thermostatically controlled box which is maintained at 95°F. for the first two weeks, 90°F. for the next two, and 85°F. from then till the pinfeathers are fairly well opened. Paper handkerchiefs are used for lining the box and changed after each feeding or when necessary. Babies are fed outside the box and cleaned after each feeding.

The baby, usually one at a time, is fed with an eyedropper for the first fourteen days and then with a small spoon which has turned up ends to make a funnel. As the bird increased in size, a larger spoon was substituted until eventually a tablespoon was used. Food was mixed once a day and refrigerated until warmed for use. Mr. and Mrs. Small's routine in many ways paralleled Mrs. Hart's and Mr. Wyatt's, and their findings were similar. They noted that the birds do not take food not sufficiently warmed, that it is unwise to fill the crop too full, and that the baby should not be fed too fast. They also never let the crop become really empty, and diet changes are brought about gradually. The food was kept warmed by floating the dish in hot water.

They feed the baby macaws every two hours around the clock for the first three weeks and every three hours for the next week. After this the intervals between feedings are gradually lengthened until the bird is finally on its own. They sprinkle a little gravel in the food about every ten days. If the birds for any reason go off their food, they put them on oatmeal which usually helps to relieve the trouble. They feel that a lack of gravel also occasionally will put youngsters off their foods even though the foods at this time are soft. The only other problems which have occurred have been respiratory disorders which were cleared up by the use of terramycin, but such disorders are rare.

The diet itself was considerably different from Mrs. Hart's and Mr. Wyatt's which only indicates that there are different routes to the same goal. Mrs. Hart's diet would surely do as well for macaws as it does for Amazons, African Greys, and Cockatoos. Mr. and Mrs. Small's diet has also worked on smaller parrots, the most notable being a Hawk Headed Parrot in 1966.

The first two days oatmeal pablum was fed with two drops of liquid vitamins and a pinch of vitamin-minerals added daily. After the second day the seven grain mixed baby cereal was gradually substituted for the pablum. On the fourteenth day ground millet and ground sunflower meal were gradually added and thereafter increased over a period of time.

Starting on the twenty-fourth day, the formula listed below gradually replaced the simple mixture above. The gradual shift was not completed until the forty-eighth day. Measurements are by volume rather than weight: one part pablum, one part seven grain mixed baby cereal, one part ground hulled millet, one part hulled ground sunflower, one part mynah bird pellets, one part dry meal dog food. To this mixture is added a small dosage of liquid vitamins and a light sprinkling of a powdered vitamin-mineral supplement. The food is mixed with hot water to about the same consistency as Mrs. Hart's formula. Shortly after the forty-eighth day the bird began taking small quantities of fresh fruits and cooked vegetables which gradually increased.

Actual development of parent fed babies was about the same as for handreared babies, but the parent fed babies were much heavier. Mr. Small provided a daily weight chart on one of the baby hybrid macaws and noted significant physical changes. It is understandable that Mr. Small ends his information over the 134 day fostering project with this advice: "If parent birds can take care of the babies, let them do so because they can do a much better job with less effort."

At one day of age, the weight of the baby macaw is 24 grams. Using an eyedropper, Mr. and Mrs. Ralph Small feed every two hours. All the photos in this series are by Ralph Small.

The writers have condensed Mr. Small's daily weight chart showing significant changes and omitting the information already given above.

When first hatched, the baby macaw weighed 24 grams which increased at an accelerated rate to 40 grams on the seventh day. By the fifth day, the toenails, beak, and tongue started to change to a darker shade. By the end of the second week, it had doubled in weight to 80 grams. On the next day feeding started with a spoon, and the eye slits were noticeable. On the sixteenth day, the eye slits were prominent. Pinfeathers were beginning to show under the skin of the wings and tail on the seventeenth day. From the end of the second to the end of the third week the weight had more than doubled again from 80 grams to 165.5 grams. At that time intervals between feedings were stretched to three hours. On the 23rd day the eye slits were watering in the morning, and by 4:00 p.m., eyes were visible through the slits. The next day

498

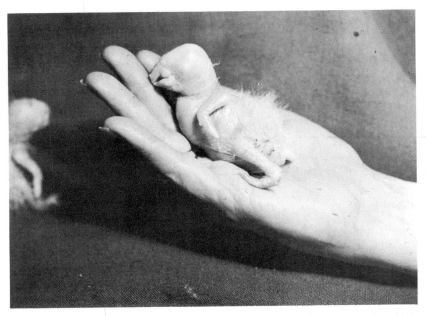

At seven days, the baby's weight has increased to 40 grams. Temperature is held at 95°F for the first two weeks.

At nine days old, the weight is 49.5 grams, which shows a steady growth.

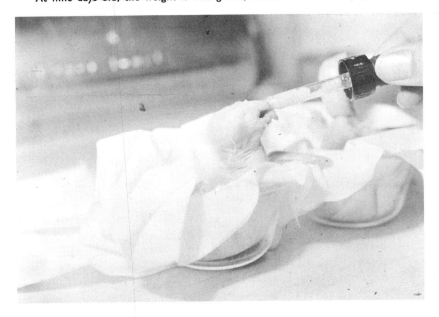

At fifteen days, the weight is 85 grams. The fast-growing chick has graduated from an eyedropper to a funnelled spoon for feeding, and the diet is also different.

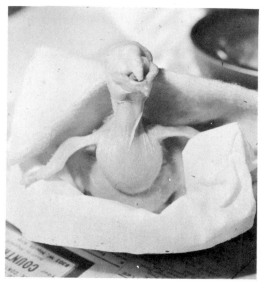

The unlovely and helpless chick at fifteen days can manage at times to sit up.

The 150-gram weight at twenty days shows a sudden upsurge in growth.

the gradual changeover to the full formula was started. At the end of the fourth week, the weight was 253 grams compared to the 165.5 grams a week earlier.

On the 30th day the eyes were wide open, and the bird indicated that he could see movement. The next day the ears were open. On the 33rd day, the bird went five hours twice between feedings. At the end of the fifth week, pinfeathers had started to break through on the wing, and the weight had increased to 401 grams.

On the 36th day, Mr. Small noted that the body and wings were turning dark with pinfeathers, and the wingspan was already fourteen inches. The egg tooth was nearly gone, and the baby was eating about one-third of a cup of food at each feeding. During the next week, the baby was developing blue pinfeathers all over with those on the secondary flights beginning to open. The interval between feedings was stretched to six hours on the 40th and 41st days.

At the beginning of the seventh week, the weight was 609 grams. On the 44th day, the tail quills were about an inch long. Gray downy feathers were prominent on the back and nape. The tips of the wing quills were noticeably blue. The chest and underparts were still bare, but pinfeathers were forming under the skin. By the end of the seventh week opening pinfeathers showed blue, green, and orange. The full strength formula listed above was started.

At twenty-four days, the weight has increased to 194 grams, a phenomenal growth distributed mostly in bulbous baby fat. The diet begins a gradual change to a different formula, and by now feedings are three hours apart.

At twenty-four days, the fast growing youngster is approximately the same size as a Cockatiel.

At thirty-two days, the beak is beginning to show macaw-like characteristics. The weight is now 321 grams, and the eyes are now open.

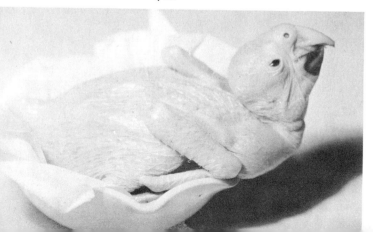

At thirty-nine days, the weight is 491 grams. Pinfeathers are beginning to develop, and intervals between feedings become longer.

At the beginning of the eighth week, the weight was 820 grams. The day after that the body was thirteen inches long with a wingspan of twenty inches. The baby was playfully chewing on its toes and wings. During this week daily weight increases fluctuated from six to 37 grams; and, on the 56th and 57th days, the weight remained at 950 grams which was the first time no gain was recorded and possibly the beginning of the slimming process. On the 57th day the parent fed babies still in the nest weighed 1,620 grams and 1,470 grams respectively which is a very noticeable difference. The handreared baby was observed scratching his neck for the first time. Pinfeathers measured three and one-fourth inches in the tail and two and one-eighth inches in the primary flights. During the ninth week the baby started to pick up things nearby, and the iris was getting lighter. On the 60th and 61st days no gain was registered, and no night feeding was given on the 61st day. The interval between feedings stretched from 10:00 p.m. till 5:00 a.m., but this was an exception. Afterwards the 3:00 a.m. feedings were resumed.

At the beginning of the tenth week, the handreared baby weighed his greatest at 1,000 grams compared to the two parent fed babies which weighed 1,440 grams and 1,470 grams. The tail feathers measured four and one-half inches on the foster chick, and the flight feathers measured four and one-fourth inches. The wingspan was twenty-eight inches, and the total length was sixteen inches. He also began to regurgitate food right after feedings in what seemed to be a definite attempt to lose weight. At times he became quite active and could scratch his head while standing.

503

By the time the baby macaw is forty-nine days old and 820 grams in weight, pinfeathers are sprouting in most body areas. The head, like the beak, resembles that of a macaw.

At fifty-seven days, the baby macaw weighs 950 grams. At this stage, weight gains are small just before the slimming phase starts. The ever more adult youngster by now is playfully nibbling on its toes.

The slimming process has started by the 65th day. In seven days, the bird's weight has increased only seven grams. Wing and tail feathers are not fully grown, but the development is rapid indeed. Facial feathers in their fine lines are very prominent.

On the 69th day, at a weight of 968 grams, a new feeding schedule went into effect. The 3:00 a.m. feeding ceased; and regular feedings were given at 6:00 a.m., noon, 5:00 p.m., and 10:00 p.m. During the eleventh week, the baby's balance improved noticeably, and he walked efficiently. Up to this point he had walked off the table twice but quickly learned to stop as soon as the toes went over the edge. At the end of the week, the overall length was nineteen inches including a wingspan of thirty-two inches. The tail was eight and a half inches long, and the baby was completely feathered except on the sides of the back, rump, and under the wings.

At the beginning of the twelfth week (78th day), the weight was 952 grams, and he started picking up things by his feet. During the week he began eating oranges, grapes, apples, and peaches. At the beginning of the thirteenth week, the weight was 925 grams, and it was during this week that he started to fly off low perches for the first time. On the 95th day he said "hello" for the first time, and he said it very clearly. By the 104th day, he flew very well but did not know how to come down from his high landing points.

As will be noticed, the weight is consistently less than at the beginning of the tenth week; and it continued to drop for sometime thereafter with variable fluctuations until the end of the handfeeding.

92nd day — 900 grams   113th day — 844 grams
99th day — 867 grams   120th day — 858 grams
106th day — 830 grams

Now fully grown and in magnificent plumage at 98 days, the hybrid macaw weighs 869 grams. The colors are attractively mixed and blended in this individual. Color results in this hybrid mating are not fully predictable. Variations in individuals may be extensive. This is one of the most beautiful the writers have yet seen.

At this age, the bird is eating some foods on his own but is also still being handfed. It is already starting to talk and can fly with rather clumsy inefficiency.

At 136 days, the delightfully tame hybrid baby, reared and still owned by Mr. and Mrs. Ralph Small of Brookfield, Illinois, is essentially the same in appearance and weight as it was at 98 days.

At this point handfeeding was reduced to once daily in the evenings. On the 115th day, the baby weighed 823 grams compared to 1,440 grams and 1,470 grams for the parent fed babies.

On the 134th day, handfeeding stopped entirely. The baby voluntarily ate soft foods *ad lib* and was cracking sunflower seed. On the 180th day, the weight was 930 grams. Parent fed babies did not start eating on their own till the 150th day. The total weaning of the parent fed babies was accomplished slowly but totally. They were finally removed from their parents on the 250th day because the parents were too aggressive towards them.

HANDFEEDING LORIES

The handfeeding of baby Swainson's Blue Mountain Lorikeets (and presumably other lories as well) is accomplished perhaps more easily. Mr. and Mrs. Edward Dimitri of Long Beach, California, have handreared several starting as early as hatching age. The diet is, of course, considerably different from other types of birds because the adult diet is different; but certain principles are the same. The food must be warm, and two hour feedings are necessary at first. Occasional lapses of three hours occur at night with no apparent harm. Gradually the intervals between feedings lengthen until at the pinfeather stage the youngsters receive three or four feedings daily as needed. Mrs. Dimitri advises that the crop should be empty before feeding the youngsters.

Mrs. Dimitri's formula starts with a teaspoon of honey. This is a full teaspoon dipped into the honey and includes whatever clings to the spoon after several turns. This is heated to thin it down so that the other ingredients can be easily added. Two teaspoons of cooked Wheathearts, full but not heaping, are added along with a level teaspoon of powdered milk and one rounded-heaping teaspoon of each of the following strained baby foods: mixed green vegetables, applesauce, and creamed corn. This is a satisfactory thickness so that it easily runs off the spoon when feeding with no addition of water. However, the mixture must be quite thin in the beginning; and water may be necessary for thinning at first. Usually it is not. Mrs. Dimitri's proportions are small because she does not make an advance supply.

Mrs. Dimitri varies the strained fruits at times for variety and sometimes uses a rice cereal similar to the heart of wheat cereal. Some people, she says, use oatmeal. Mrs. Dimitri feeds her adult birds rice, fresh corn on the cob, as well as romaine lettuce as part of the regular adult feeding routine in addition to honey and powdered milk in the honey nectar. This is somewhat different from the feeding regimen offered as standard fare for lories and lorikeets by the writers.

Another diet for handrearing lorikeets was used by Bill Wilson, Dick Clarkson, and Erling Kjelland, all from Chicago. Their routine of feeding was also every two hours in the beginning, and the formula had to be warm as in the other formulas. The thickness also was important or else the birds would refuse it. Their experience was that the formula became thinner as the birds matured till weaning age at eight weeks. The regular diet for the adults was used, and the only difference is the addition of pablum. This nectar diet is as follows: for a pint mixture, add six teaspoons honey, six teaspoons Mellins Food, nine teaspoons evaporated milk, a pinch of table salt, a pinch of a powdered vitamin-mineral supplement for pets (as sold in pet shops). Fill the remainder of the pint jar with water. Pablum is added for the youngsters to thicken it up. The amount was not specified and is probably variable.

Judging from these two formulas, it seems evident that some leeway is permissible. The writers feel fortunate in not having had to resort to hand-feeding any of theirs. The diet and the carefully developed composure of the birds under all conditions of interruptions or distractions have never resulted in desertions or other problems.

DISEASES, MEDICATIONS, AND EMERGENCY DIET

Illnesses and accidents have been the subjects of many of the letters received since the first edition was issued. Many people complained that no one in their particular areas were concerned or informed about birds, particularly the veterinarians. It is true that the bird practice in the field of veterinary medicine has been very limited in the past, but greater interest and considerable work has been accomplished within the past few years. Hopefully, professional interest will continue to expand in all dimensions.

Most of the real progress has come about with veterinarians and medical doctors who have gained an interest in aviculture. There have been many problems with medications, knowledgeable diagnoses, and difficulties in administering efficient dosages. Administration of medications through foods or water or both is lacking in efficiency because of variation in amounts consumed not only in species and in individuals but also because a bird usually consumes less when it is sick than when it is well. Unfortunately, it has been the only easy way to administer internal medications. The use of microliter syringes radically changes all previous modes of administering medicine. Accurate dosage is now possible, and the best intramuscular injection site in most birds is in the heavy pectoral muscles. Subcutaneous injections can be given in the loose skin of the neck or in the web of the wing. Not likely to be settled for some time yet to come, of course, will be recommended dosages and selections of medications. There are too many specific problems, a varied range of medications, and a huge variety of birds involved.

There is still heavy reliance upon the "doctor of experience" whose knowledge is often haphazardly compiled partly as a result of trial and error but often based on sincere interest and practical experiment. It is all too true that most doctors do not know about birds and most people who know about

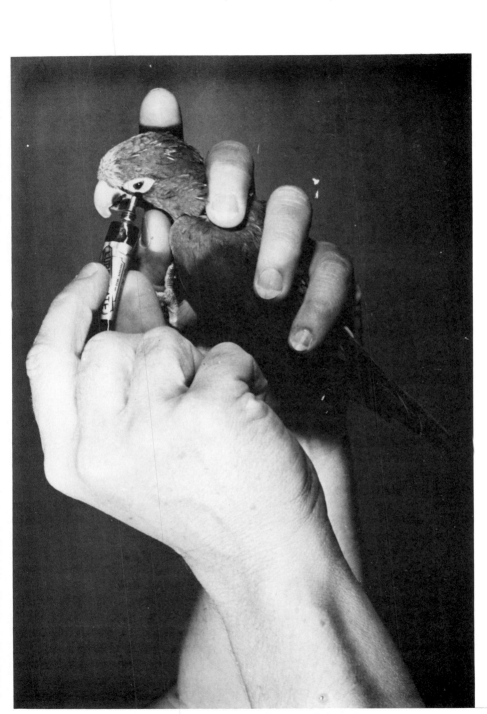

Apply an antibiotic if your bird's eye should become infected.

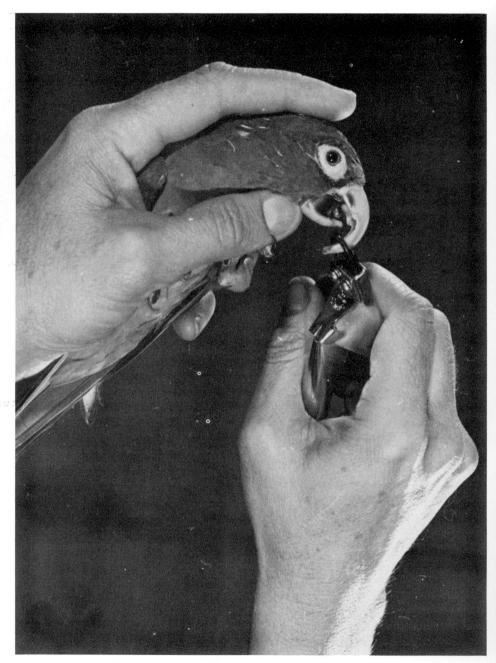

Be conservative in cutting away the overgrowth on a too-long beak. Cutting too deeply into the beak can result in serious injury to your pet.

birds know nothing about medicine. Judging from the many letters, the chapter on diseases and ailments in this book has solved many problems; readers interested in a truly comprehensive treatment of bird diseases are referred to *Bird Diseases,* by Arnall and Keymer. (T.F.H. Publications).

Perhaps the most frequent problem encountered with home treatment has resulted from the overuse of wonder drugs and antibiotics. They still are used repeatedly on totally unnecessary treatments and for problems which could not possibly be solved by such medications. As mentioned on page 81, overuse and prolonged use cause problems of a different nature. Overuse and prolonged dosage destroy the vitally necessary bacteria as well as those which are harmful. Digestive disorders usually accompanied by chronic diarrhea are the most frequent and persistent complaints.

In order to restore the necessary bacteria, some of which synthesize certain vitamins, to the digestive tract, one local veterinarian suggested a simple solution which worked quite well. Upon checking more extensively, the writers have found it to be a reasonably common and effective practice to correct this situation in many types of animals. The doctor suggested taking a portion of the droppings of another bird of the same species, crushing them to a fine texture, and adding the powder to the food of the bird afflicted. Perhaps once would be enough. Of course, the bird furnishing the droppings must be in very good health. The droppings furnish a satisfactory culture of the beneficial bacteria; and, after they have become re-established in the digestive tract, the condition gradually is corrected. This corrective treatment is not related to the occasional problem of a bird which eats droppings. A bird eating feces usually needs a mineral supplement, but it can also be an attempt to obtain vitamins manufactured in the intestine.

The letters and telephone calls of desperation frequently come too late for help. Birds in their last stages rarely can be helped, but unfortunately many people do not recognize symptoms of illness until too late when the birds are totally off their food. The writers have frequently recommended, to very good effect, that a simple emergency liquid diet usually acceptable to most birds is a mixture of peanut butter, honey, and water. Warmed to insure easier mixing, the three items blend very well. Honey supplies quick energy, and peanut butter gives abundant food value both of which can help sustain life at its low ebbs. The writers use equal parts of honey and peanut butter and twice the total in water content. When the rallying point occurs, the sick bird may voluntarily return to its regular diet; but the emergency honey and peanut butter liquid should be continued until the bird has regained some of its weight and is really eating enough of its regular diet to assist in complete recovery. Usually the recuperation is gradual.

The writers once saved a macaw's life on hummingbird nectar. This macaw had a heavy infestation of worms and had deteriorated so slowly that the owners had not realized the problem. The hummingbird nectar, incidentally, was a total formula rather than a partial formula as is usually given to hummingbirds. This was an exception, however.

If recovery is prolonged and the sick bird is reluctant to return to its regular diet, the writers gradually thicken the peanut butter and honey by adding ground or strained vegetables, hulled sunflower, and small chunks of fruit. The hulled sunflower, because of its size and texture, may be the transition needed for a gradual return to the regular diet.

Another excellent emergency diet which the writers can strongly recommend is Mrs. Hart's handfeeding formula diluted or thickened to any texture required for acceptance. Of course, adult birds rarely cooperate in force feeding or handfeeding as readily as will babies being handreared. Those which will not allow handfeeding must be given a liquid diet which they will drink. A bird under heat will drink more readily than one not given warmth. This diet ties in with all the principles covered under First Aid on pages 79 and 80.

It is still an important maxim that prevention of problems is far easier and more effective than treatment. It would be a good plan for the reader to review periodically the chapters on diet and general care as well as many of the principles in this chapter.

APPENDIX

The following species listed below are protected by law and therefore cannot be kept in cage and aviary, nor can they be captured or sold.

PARROTS *(Psittaciformes)*

Palm Cockatoo - *Probosciger aterrimus*
Slender Billed Cockatoo - *Cacatua tenuirostris*
All Ground Parrots from New Guinea - *Genus Psittacella*
Pesquet's Parrot - *Psittrichas fulgidus*
All Musk Parrots - *Genus Prosopeia*
Crested Parrakeet - *Eunymphicus cornutus*
Swamp or Ground Parrakeet (from Australia) - *Pezoporus wallicus*
Night Parrot - *Geopsittacus occidentalis*
All Vasa Parrots - *Genus Coracopsis*
Cape Parrot - *Poicephalus robustus*
Black-Collared Love Bird - *Agapornis swinderniana*
Mauritius Parrakeet - *Psittacula echo*
Genus Anodorhynchus - all species
Spinx's Macaw - *Cyanopsitta spixi*
Scarlet Macaw - *Ara macao*
Military Macaw - *Ara militaris*
Red-Fronted Macaw - *Ara rubrogenys*
Buffon's Macaw - *Ara ambigua*
Golden Conure - *Aratinga guarouba*
Yellow-Eared Conure - *Ognorhynchus icterotis*
Thick-Billed Parrot - **Rhynchopsitta pachrhyncha**
Blue-Throated Conure - *Pyrrhura cruentata*
Genus Touit - all species
Pileated Parrot - *Pionopsitta pileata*
Genus Hapalopsittaca - all species
Yellow-Billed Amazon - *Amazona collaria*
Cuban Amazon - *Amazona leucocephala*
Hispaniolan Amazon - *Amazona ventralis*
Black-Billed Amazon - *Amazona agilis*
Puerto Rican Amazon - *Amazona vittata*
Tucuman Amazon - *Amazona tucumana*
Red-Spectacled Amazon - *Amazona pretrei*

Red-Tailed Amazon - *Amazona brasiliensis*
Blue-Cheeked Amazon - *Amazona dufresniana*
Yellow-Shouldered Amazon - *Amazona barbadensis*
Scaly-Naped Amazon - *Amazona mercenaria*
Vinaceous Amazon - *Amazona vinacea*
St. Lucia Amazon - *Amazona versicolor*
Red-Necked Amazon - *Amazona arausiaca*
St. Vincent Amazon - *Amazona guildingii*
Imperial Amazon - *Amazona imperialis*
Kakapo -*Strigops habroptilus*
Patagonian Conure - *Cyanoliseus patagonus*

SELECTED BIBLIOGRAPHY

Allen, Gerald and Connie J. Allen (1977). *All about Cockatiels*, TFH Publ. Neptune, N.J.

Allen, William (1967). *Halfmoons and Dwarf Parrots*, TFH Publ. Neptune, N.J.

Allen, William H. Jr. (1959). *How to raise and train Budgerigars*, TFH Publ. Neptune, N.J.

Arnall, L. and I.F. Keymer (1975). *Bird Diseases*, TFH Publ. Neptune, N.J.

Austin, O.L. Jr. (1961). *Birds of the World*, Golden Press, New York.

Duke of Bedford, The (1969). *Parrots and Parrot-like Birds*, TFH Publ. Neptune, N.J.

Forshaw, J.M. (1969). *Australian Parrots*, Lansdowne Press, Melbourne.

Forshaw, J.M. (1977). *Parrots of the World*, TFH Publ. Neptune, N.J.

Hart, Ernest H. (1970). *Budgerigar Handbook*, TFH Publ. Neptune, N.J.

Plath, K. and Malcolm Davis (1971). *This is the Parrot*, TFH Publ. Neptune, N.J.

Soderberg, P.M. (1977). *All about Lovebirds*, TFH Publ. Neptune, N.J.

Stroud, Robert (1964). *Diseases of Birds*, TFH Publ. Neptune, N.J.

Vane, E.N.T. (1957). *Guide to Lovebirds and Parrotlets*, Cage Birds, London.

Vriends, T. (1977). *Agapornissen en andere Dwergpapegaaien*, Veen, Wageningen.

Vriends, T. (1976). *Das grosse Buch der Vögel in Käfig und Voliere*, Mosaik Verlag, Meunchen.

Vriends, T. (1975).*Groot Volière Boek*, Amsterdam Boek, Amsterdam.

Vriends, T. (1974). *Het Sierparkietenboek*, Kessing, Amsterdam.

Vriends, T. (1977). *Prisma Papegaaienboek*, Het Spectrum, Utrecht.

Watmough, W. (1967). *The cult of the Budgerigar*, Cage Birds, London.

Index

The following is a subject index only. An index of illustrations begins on page 541.

A

Abscesses, 25
Abyssinian Love Bird, 464
Abyssinian Parrot, 343
Achromycin, 81, 83
Active Parrot, 318
Adelaide Rosella, 410, 414
African Grey Parrot, 54, 75, 275, 278, 283, 484
African Ringneck, 379
Agapornis
 cana ablectanea, 464
 cana cana, 464
 fischeri, 462
 lilianae, 463
 nigrigensis, 464
 personata, 460
 pullaria pullaria, 463
 pullaria ugandae, 463
 roseicollis, 460
 swinderniana emini, 464
 swinderniana swinderniana, 465
 swinderniana zenkeri, 465
 taranta, 464
 taranta nana, 464
Age, for training, 41
Ailments, and diseases, 79 ff, 486, 491
 prevention of, 80
Albinos, 72 ff.
Alexander Ringneck Parrakeet, 379, 390, 406
Alexandra Parrakeet, 406
Alexandrine Parrakeet, 379

Alisterus, 104, 394
 amboinensis buruensis, 399
 amboinensis dorsalis, 399
 amboinensis hypophonius, 399
 amboinensis sulaensis, 399
 chloropterus callopterus, 399
 chloropterus chloropterus, 399
 chloropterus moszkowskii, 395
 chloropterus wilhelminae, 395
 scapularis minor, 395
 scapularis scapularis, 394
All Green Parrakeet, 318, 442
Alpine Lorikeet, 154
Alpine Parrakeet, 453
Amazon Parrots, 19, 39, 278
Amazona, 104, 278, 484
 aestiva aestiva, 303
 aestiva xanthopteryx, 306
 agilis, *318*
 albifrons albifrons, 294
 albifrons nana, 294
 albifrons saltuensis, 294
 amazonica amazonica, 306
 amazonica tobagensis, 307, 306
 arausiaca, *319*
 autumnalis autumnalis, 298
 autumnalis diadema, 302
 autumnalis lilacina, 302
 autumnalis salvini, 298
 barbadensis barbadensis, 315
 barbadensis rothschildi, 315
 braziliensis, *319*
 collaria, *318*
 dufresniana dufresniana, 311

dufresniana rhodocorytha, 311
farinosa farinosa, 302
farinosa guatemalae, 302
farinosa inornata, 287, 302
farinosa virenticeps, 303
festiva bodini, 307
festiva festiva, 307
finschii, 291
guildingi, 310
imperialis, 307
leucocephala bahamensis, 318
leucocephala caymanensis, 318
leucocephala hesterna, 318
leucocephala leucocephala, 315
leucocephala palmarum, 318
mercenaria canipalliata, 307
mercenaria mercenaria, 307
ochrocephala auropalliata, 283
ochrocephala nattereri, 287
ochrocephala oratrix, 282
ochrocephala panamensis, 286
ochrocephala tresmariae, 287
ochrocephala xantholaema, 291
pretrei, 311
ventralis, 310
versicolor, 310
vinacea, 310
viridigenalis, 291
vittata gracilipes, 319
vittata vittata, 318
xantholora, 298
xanthops, 311
Amboina King Parrakeet, 399
American Museum of Natural
    History, 214
Amoropsittaca aymara, 102, 449
Amoropsittidae, 452
Andaman Island Parrakeet, 382
Andean Parrakeet, 449
Anodorhynchus, 102, 109
  glaucus, 222
  hyacinthus, 222
  leari, 222

Antbed Parrot, 427
Antibiotics, 81
Antipodes Island Parrakeet, 453
Aprosmictus, 104
  erythropterus coccineopterus, 391
  erythropterus erythropterus, 391
  jonquillaceus, 394
  jonquillaceus wetternsis, 394
Apure Tovi Parrakeet, 438
Ara, 102, 199, 214
  ambigua, 218
  amgibigua ambigua, 218
  ambigua guayaquilensis, 222
  ararauna, 206
  auricollis, 210
  caninde, 222
  chloroptera, 206
  couloni, 222, 218
  macao, 206
  manilata, 214
  maracana, 214
  militaris boliviana, 206
  militaris mexicana, 206
  militaris militaris, 206
  nobilis cumanensis, 215
  nobilis longipennis, 215
  nobilis nobilis, 215
  rubrogenys, 218, 222
  severa, 214
  severa castaneifrons, 218
  severa severa, 218
  tricolor, 222
Aratinga, 102, 222, 226, 247
  acuticaudata, 226
  acuticaudata haemorrhous, 226
  acuticaudata neumanni, 226
  aurea aurea, 246
  aurea major, 246
  auricapilla auricapilla, 242
  auricapilla aurifrons, 242
  cactorum cactorum, 246
  cactorum caixana, 246
  canicularis canicularis, 239

canicularis claroe, 239
canicularis eburnirostrum, 239
chloroptera chloroptera, 234
chloroptera maugei, 234
erythrogenys, 234
euops, 234
finschi, 231
guarouba, 226
holochlora brevipes, 231
holochlora brewsteri, 231
holochlora holochlora, 230, 231
holochlora rubritorquis, 231
holochlora strenua, 230
jandaya, 226
leucophthalmus, 230, 231, 234
leucophthalmus callogenys, 234
mitrata, 231
mitrata alticola, 231
nana, 239
nana astec, 239
nana vincinalis, 239
pertinax aeruginosa, 242, 243
pertinax arubensis, 243
pertinax chrysogenys, 242
pertinax chrysophrys, 243
pertinax margaritensis, 242, 243
pertinax ocularis, 242
pertinax pertinax, 243, 246
pertinax tortugensis, 243
pertinax xanthogenia, 243, 246
solstitialis, 230
wagleri, 231
wagleri frontata, 231
wagleri minor, 231
wagleri transilis, 231
wagleri wagleri, 231
weddellii, 238
Aratinga Conures, 477
Arfak Lory, 147
Arthritis, 29
Arteriosclerosis, 29
Asthma, 26

Aruba Conure, 243
Australian Broadtail, 418
Australian Crested Dove, 198, 379
Australian Grass Parrakeet, 450,
    454
Australian Love Bird, 454
Australian King Parrakeet, 394
Australian Parrakeet, 486
Aviculture, definition of, 11
    history of, 12
    rewards of, 13
Aviculturist, 11, 12
Avian Bacterial Diseases, 82
Aviary, construction of, 24ff
    equipment for, 35ff
    planning of, 24ff
Aymara Parrakeet, 449
Azara's Conure, 254
Aztec Conure, 239

B
Bacteria, 21-22, 88
Bahaman Amazon, 318
Banded Parrakeet, 382
Bank Parrot, 250
Banksian Cockatoo, 167
Bare-Eyed Cockatoo, 178, 182, 186
Barnardius, 100, 410, 419
Barnard's Parrakeet, 410, 418, 419
Barrabond Parrakeet, 395, 402
Bathing, 64-65
    habits, 65-66
Baudin's Black Cockatoo, 170
Bauer's Parrakeet, 419
Beaks, 91-92
    deformed, 510
    overgrown, 91
    trimming, 91
Beautiful Parrot, 335
Beccari's Pigmy Parrot, 111
Beford, Duke of, 134
Bee Bee Parrot, 438, 439, 442

Berlepsch's Conure, 263
Bernstein's Lory, 113
Bird Pox, 82
Biting, in training, 44ff
Black-capped Lory, 126
Black Cheeked Fig Parrot, 147
Black Cheeked Love Bird, 464
Black Cockatoos, 163
Black Collared Love Bird, 465
Black Eared Green Parrot, 350
Black Eared Parrotlet, 443
Black Headed Caique, 327, 330, 331
Black Headed Macaw, 214
Black Headed x White Bellied Caique, 330
Black Lory, 113
Black Masked Love Bird, 460, 462, 463, 464
Black Winged Lory, 115
Black Winged Love Bird, 464
Blaze Winged Conure, 258
Blossum Headed Conure, 386
Blue and Gold Macaw, 199, 206, 218, 222
Blue and Yellow Macaw, 206
Blue-Browed Lorilet, 151
Blue Cheeked Lory, 115
Blue Crowned Amazon, 302, 303
Blue Crowned Conure, 215, 226
Blue Crowned Hanging Parrakeet 472
Blue Crowned Lory, 131, 134
Blue Eared Lorikeet, 139
Blue Eared Lory, 117
Blue Eyed Cockatoo, 174
Blue Faced Lorikeet, 120, 121, 122
Blue Faced Lorilet, 150
Blue Fronted Amazon, 275, 303, 306
Blue Headed Parrot, 322

Blue Headed Racket-Tailed Parrakeet, 451
Blue Margined Parrakeet, 442
Blue Masked Love Bird, 462
Blue Ringneck Parrakeet, 379
Blue Rosella, 415
Blue Rumped Parrot, 367
Blue Rumped Parrotlet, 466
Blue Streaked Lory, 115
Blue Tailed Lory, 116
Blue Thighed Lory, 131
Blue Winged Conure, 266, 267, 270
Blue Winged Grass Parrakeet, 430
Blue Winged Parrakeet, 390
Blue Winged Parrotlet, 466
Blyth's Nicobar Parrakeet, 390
Bodin's Amazon, 307
Bolbopstittacus, 104, 473
  lunulatus intermedius, 473
  lunulatus lunulatus, 473
  lunulatus mindanensis, 473

Bolborhynchus, 102, 447, 450
  andicolus, 449
  ferrugineifrons, 449
  lineola lineola, 447
  lineola maculatus, 447
  lineola tigrinus, 447

Bonaire Conure, 243, 246
Boric acid ointments, 86
Botulism, 89
Bourke's Parrakeet, 435, 492, 477
Brazilian Hawk Headed Parrot, 335
Breeding, 52-53, 475, 477
  inbreeding, 76
  line, 76, 77
  selective, 76
Brehm's Ground Parrot, 370
Brereton, Dr. J. LeGay, 450
Broadtailed Parrakeets, 415

Broken bones, 95-96
Bronchitis, 82
"Bronchos," 60
Bronze Winged Parrot, 326
Brooks Lorikeet, 122
Brotogeris, 102, 438
  chrysopterus chrysopterus, 438
  chrysopterus chrysosmea, 439
  chrysopterus taipara, 439
  gustavi, 442
  jugularis, 438
  jugularis apurensis, 438
  jugularis cyanoptera, 438
  jugularis exsul, 438
  jugularis jugularis, 438
  pyrrhopterus, 442
  sanctithomae sanctithomae, 439
  sanctithomae takatsukasae, 439
  tirica, 442
  versicolorus behni, 442
  versicolorus chiriri, 442
  versicolorus chiriri, 442
  versicolorus versicolorus, 442
Brown Eared Conure, 242, 243
Brown Parrot, 107, 343
Brown Headed Parrot, 342
Brown Hooded Parrot, 335
Brown Necked Parrot, 339
Brown Throated Conure, 242, 243
Brown's Rosella, 78, 415
Budgerigar, 11, 12, 21, 27, 29, 39,
  45, 54, 72, 74, 77, 104, 454,
477, 484, 492
Budgie, 454
Bumblefoot, 93
Burbridge's Blue Backed Parrot,
  362
Buru Lorikeet, 146
Burmese Slaty-headed Parrakeet,
  387
Burrowing Parrot, 250
Buteyn, Jerome, 186

C

Cacatua, 100, 102, 159, 171
  alba, 175
  ducorps, 182
  galerita, 174
  galerita eleonora, 174
  galerita fitzroyi, 174
  galerita galerita, 171
  galerita ophthalmica, 174
  galerita trobiandi, 174
  goffini, 182
  haematuropygia haematuropygia,
    178
  haematuropygia mcgregori, 178
  leadbeateri, 179
  leadbeateri leadbeateri, 179
  leadbeateri mollis, 179
  moluccensis, 178
  sanguinea, 182
  sulphurea abbotti, 175
  sulphurea citrinocristata, 175
  sulphurea djampeana, 175
  sulphurea occidentalis, 175
  sulphurea parvula, 175
  sulphurea sulphurea, 174
  tenuirostris pastinator, 186
  tenuirostris tenvirostris, 186
Cacatuinae, 159
Cactus Conure, 246
Caica Parrots, 338
Caiques, 327
Callocephalon, 102, 159, 170
  fimbriatum, 170
  fimbriatum fimbriatum, 171
  fimbriatum superior, 171
Calyptorhynchus, 102, 163, 159
  baudinii, 170
  funereus, 170
  lathami, 167
  magnificus, 167
  magnificus macrorhynchus, 167
  magnifucus magnificus, 167

magnificus naso, 167
magnificus samueli, 167
Cameroon Black-Collared Love Bird, 465
Canary Winged Parrakeet, 442
Cancer, 84
Candida albicans, 87
Canker, mouth, 87
"Captivity" definition of, 13
  diet in, 15 ff, 62, 63
Cardinal Lory, 114
Carolina Conure, 104, 105
Carolina Parrakeet, 450
Cataracts of the eye, 93
Cayman Amazon, 318
Cayman Brac Amazon, 318
Celebes Hanging Parrakeet, 472
Celebes Racket Tailed Parrakeet, 452
Celestial Parrotlet, 469
Ceram Lory, 117
Ceylonese Hanging Parrakeet, 471
Chalcopsitta, 101, 113, 115
  atra atra, 115
  atra bernsteini, 115
  atra insignis, 113
  cardinalis, 114
  duivenbodei duivenbodei, 114
  duivenbodei syringanuchalis, 114
  insignis spectabilis, 113
  sintillata chloroptera, 114
  sintillata rubrifrons, 114
  sintillata sintillata, 114
Charmosyna, 101
  diadema, 139
  josefinae, 146
  josefinae cyclopum, 146
  josefinae sepikiano, 146
  margarethae, 139
  meeki, 138
  multistrata, 146
  palmarum, 138

placentis, 139
placentis intensior, 42
placentis ornata, 142
placentis pallidor, 142
placentis placentis, 142
placentis subplacens, 142
papou goliathina, 142
papou papou, 142
papou stellae, 142
papou wahnesi, 142
pulchella bella, 143
pulchella pulchella, 143
pulchella rothschildi, 143
rubrigularis rubrigularis, 143
rubronotata kordona, 146
rubronotata rubronotata, 146
toxopei, 146
wilhelminae, 142
Chattering Lory, 125, 126
Check List of Birds of the World, 99
Cherry Headed Conure, 234
Cherry Red Lorikeet, 118
Chilean Conure, 270
Chocolate Faced Conure, 243
Citron Crested Cockatoo, 175
Cholera, 82
Chromosomes, 70 ff
Cleanliness, as a preventive measure (see Diseases and Ailments) 79 ff
Cloncurry Parrakeet, 418, 419
Clostridium botulinus, 89
Coccidia (see Coccidiosis), 84
Coccidiosis, 84, 88
Cockatiel, 12, 14, 16, 18, 21, 27, 29, 36, 37, 39, 40, 41, 45, 55, 64, 75, 93, 102, 159, 190, 198, 194, 379, 484, 477
Cockatoos, 12, 19, 28, 31, 39, 64, 101, 159, 167, 171, 190, 484
Coconut Lorikeet, 120, 122

Colds, 82
Collared Lory, 131
Colombian Amazon, 287
Comoro Island Parrot, 346
Conditioned response, 58, 59
Condor, The, Vol. 67, 1965, 480
Constipation, 88-89
Construction of aviary, 24 ff
Conures, 18, 27, 37, 77, 102, 199, 203, 215, 222, 226, 247, 250, 254, 450
Conuropis, 102, 104
Coracopsis, 104, 346
  nigra barklyi, 347
  nigra libs, 347
  nigra nigra, 347
  nigra sibilans, 347
  vasa cormorensis, 346
  vasa drouhardi, 346
  vasa vasa, 346
Coral Billed Parrot, 332
Cornelia's Eclectus, 354
Coulon's Macaw, 218, 222
Crested Parrakeèt, 454
Crimson Bellied Conure, 266
Crimson Bellied Parrakeet, 422
Crimson Rosella, 410, 411
Crimson Winged Parrakeet, 391, 395
Crop, impacted, 87
  sour, 87
Cropworms, 94
Cuban Amazon, 315, 318
Cuban Conure, 234
Cuttlebone, 17
Cyanistic phase, 74
Cyanoliseus, 102, 250
  patagonus andinus, 250
  patagonus byroni, 250
  patagonus patagonus, 250
Cyanopsitta spixii, 222

Cyanoramphus, 104, 452, 454
  auriceps, 453
  malherbi, 453
  novazelandiae, 453
  ulietanus, 453
  unicolor, 453
  zealandicus, 453

D

Dark Throated Lorikeet, 121
Dasyptilus pesqueti, 370
Derbyan Parrakeet, 382, 383
Deplanch's Lorikeet, 122
Deroptyus, 104, 334
  accipitrinus accipitrinus, 335
  accipitrinus fuscifrons, 335
Desertion, of eggs, 481
  youngsters, 481
Diademed Amazon, 302
Diarrhea, 88, 511
Diet, 15 ff, 62-64, 480
  (See Diseases and Ailments, 79, 502)
Dietary supplement, 18
Dilger, William C., 99
Dimitri, Edward, 507
Diseases and ailments, 79 ff
  digestive disorders, 511
  prevention of, 80
  worms, 512
"Domesticity," definition of, 13
Domicella, 101, 125
Dominican Amazon, 319
Double Eyed Fig Parrot, 150
Drafts, 66
Duchess Lorikeet, 139
Ducorp's Cockatoo, 182
Ducorpsius, 102
Dufresne's Amazon, 311
Dusky Lory, 124
Dusky Parrot, 326

Duyvenboide's Lory, 114
Dwarf Macaws, 203, 210, 222
Dwarf Panama Parrot, 367

E

Eclectus Parrots, 350
Eclectus roratus, 350
  roratus cornelia, 354
  roratus polychloros, 355
  roratus roratus, 354
Ecuadorian All-Green Conure,
  234
Edward's Lory, 116, 121
Elegant Parrakeet, 27, 430, 492
Egg-binding, 89-90, 481
Egg sac rupture, 90
Emerald Collared Parrakeet, 387
Emergency Diet, 508, 511
Emma's Conure, 255, 258
Enicognathus leptorhynchus, 102,
  271
Eolophus, 102, 187
  roseicapillus assimilis, 190
  roseicapillus kuhli, 190
  roseicapillus roseicapillus, 190
Eos, 101, 113, 115
  bornea, 117
  bornea bersteini, 117
  bornea bornea, 117
  bornea cyanonothus, 117
  bornea rothschildi, 117
  cyanogenia, 115
  goodfellowi, 117
  histrio, 116
  histrio challengeri, 117
  histrio histrio, 116
  histrio talautensis, 116
  reticulata, 115
  semilarvata, 117
  squamata, 115
  squamata atrocaerulea, 116

squamata obiensis, 116
squamata riciniata, 116
squamata squamata, 116
Epidemics, 81, 82
Equipment, for aviary, 34ff.
Eunymphicus, 104, 454
  cornutus cornutus, 454
  cornutus uvaeensis, 454
Euop's Conure, 234
Everett's Blue Backed Parrot, 359
Everett's Racket-Tailed Parrakeet,
  452
Exercise, 16, 61, 481
Eye, cataracts of, 93
  treatment for, 81
  worm, 94

F

Fair Lorikeet, 143
Fanciers of birds, history of, 12
Fatworms, 94
Feather mites, 95
Feather plucking, 90
Feeders, 35
Feeding, 15ff.
Feed, 92, 93, 95
Festive Amazon, 307
Fiery Shouldered Conure, 263
Fig Parrots, 147
Finches, 477
Finsch's Amazon, 291
Finsch's Conure, 231
Finsch's Pigmy Parrot, 111
First Aid, 79-80
Fischer's Love Bird, 462, 477
Flame Winged Conure, 262
Flores Hanging Parrakeet, 473
Forpus, 102, 465
  coelestis coelestis, 469
  coelestis xanthops, 469
  conspicillatus caucae 469
  conspicillatus conspicillatus, 469

cyanopygius cyanopygius, 467
cyanopygius insularis, 469
cyanopygius pallidus, 467
passerinus crassirostris, 467
passerinus cyanochlorus, 466
passerinus cyanophanes, 466
passerinus deliciosus, 465-466
passerinus flavescens, 465-466
passerinus flavissimus, 466
passerinus passerinus, 466
passerinus spengeli, 465-466
passerinus viridissimus, 466
sclateri eidos, 469
sclateri sclateri, 469
sclateri xanthops, 469
Forsten's Lorikeet, 100, 120
Fowl cholera, 82
Freer's Blue Backed Parrot, 359
French Molt, 93
Funereal Cockatoo, 167, 170

G
Galah, 187
Gang-Gang Cockatoo, 170
Gaudy Macaws, 218
Geelvink Pigmy Parrot, 111
Genes, 70ff
Geoffroyus, 104, 355
  geoffroyi arusensis, 358
  geoffroyi cyanicarpus, 358
  geoffroyi cyanicollis, 355
  geoffroyi explorator, 355
  geoffroyi geoffroyi, 355
  geoffroyi keyensis, 358
  geoffroyi obiensis, 355
  geoffroyi orientalis, 358
  geoffroyi rhodops, 355
  geoffroyi stresmanni, 355
  geoffroyi sudestianus, 358
  geoffroyi timorlaoensis, 358
  geoffroyi tjinoanae, 358

  heteroclitus heteroclitus, 358
  heteroclitus hyacinthinus, 358
  simplex buergersi, 358
  simplex simplex 358
Glaucous Macaw, 203
Glossopsitta, 101, 135
  concinna, 135
  porphyrocephala, 135
  pusilla, 138
Glossy Black Cockatoo, 167
Goffin's Cockatoo, 182
"Going light", 88
Golden Conure, 226
Golden Crowned Conure, 246,
  306
Golden Eared Conure, 250
Golden Fronted Parrakeet, 439,
  449
Golden Headed Conure, 242
Golden Headed Parrakeet, 253
Golden Mantled Rosella, 414
Golden Parrakeet, 439
Golden Plumed Conure, 250
Golden Shouldered Parrakeet, 427
Golden Tailed Parrotlet, 446
Golden Winged Parrotlet, 427,
  438
Goldie's Lorikeet, 123-124
Gout, 89
Grand Eclectus, 350
Grass Parrakeet, 430, 435
Graydidascalus brachyurus, 102,
  366
Great Billed Parrot, 362
Greater Patagonian Conure, 250
Greater Sulphur Crested Conure,
  159, 171, 174
Greater Vasa Parrot, 346
Greater White Crested Cockatoo,
  175
Great Green Macaw, 218

Green Cheeked Amazon, 291
Green Cheeked Conure, 262
Green Conure, 230, 234
Green food, 17
Green Headed Amazon, 303
Green Headed Racket-Tailed
  Parrakeet, 451
Green Naped Lorikeet, 121
Green Palm Lorikeet, 138
Green Parrakeet, 230
Green Rosella, 411
Green Rumped Parrotlet, 466
Green Tailed Lory, 128
Green Winged King Parrakeet,
  395
Green Winged Macaw, 206, 210
Grey Headed Parrakeet, 449
Grey Naped Amazon, 307
Grit, 16
Ground Parrakeet, 454
Ground Parrots, 370
Guaiabero, 104, 470, 473
Guatemalan Amazon, 302
Guiana Hawk-Headed Parrot, 335
Guiana Parrotlet, 466
Guilding's Amazon 310
Gypopsitta vulturina, 102, 366

H
Haitian Conure, 234
Halfmoon Conure, 239, 242, 303,
  306
Halfmoon Parrot, 14, 51, 55
Halmahera King Parrakeet, 399
Handfeeding, 16, 23, 475, 484,
  486, 488, 492, 507
Handrearing, 496, 497, 507
Hanging Parrakeets, 470
Hanging Parrots, 470
Hapalopsittaca, 102, 347
  amazonina amazonina, 347
  amazonina fuertesi, 347

amazonina pyrrhops, 347
melanotis melanotis, 350
melanotis peruviana, 350
Hardening of the arteries, 89
Hardy, Dr. John William, 477
Hart, Mrs. Vilma, 484, 486
Hawk-Headed Caique, 334
Hawk-Headed Parrot, 334
Head injuries, 96
Heart Attack, 89
Helmeted Cockatoo, 170
Hemp Seed, 19-20
Heterozygous mutations, 73
Hoffman's Conure, 267
Homozygous mutations, 73
Hooded Parrakeet, 427
Hooded Parrot, 338
Hospital cage, 79-80
Hyacinth Macaw, 203
Hybridizing, 70ff., 77-78
Hybrids, 77-78
Hydrogen peroxide, 80, 92, 93

I
Illiger's Macaw, 214, 218
Immelmann, Karl, 99
Imperial Amazon, 307
Inbreeding, 76
Indian Lorikeet, 471
Indian Ringneck Parrakeet, 74,
  375, 379, 387
Indigo Winged Parrot, 347
Individualism, in parrots, 50ff.
Infections, 81-82
Intermediate Guaiabero 473
Iris Lorikeet, 124
Iron sulfate, 80

J
Jamaican Amazon, 318

Jamaican Black Billed Amazon, 318
Jamaican Conure, 239
Jardine's Parrot, 339
Javanese Hanging Parrakeet, 471
Javanese Lorikeet, 471
Jenday Conure, 226, 230, 242, 246
Jobi Lory, 126, 128
Josephine's Lorikeet, 146

K
Kaha, 107
Kakapo, 107
Kakarki, 452
Kakatoe, 100
Kakatoeinae, 101
Kea Parrots, 101, 109, 271
Key's Pigmy Parrot, 111
Kidney Disease, 89
King Parrakeet, 367, 394, 395, 399, 402
Knobel, E. Maud, 476
Kordo Lorikeet, 146
Koro Island Parrakeet, 402
Kuhl's Ruffed Lory, 134, 135

L
Large Billed Parrot, 362
Larius, 350
Lathamus, 101
   discolor, 151
Layard's Parrakeet, 387
Leadbeater, 484
Leadbeater Cockatoo, 179
Leadbeater's Lorilet, 150
Lear's Macaw, 203
Lee, Gilbert, 330
Leg mites, 95

LeGay, Brereton, J., 99
Leptosittaca branickii, 102, 250
Lesser Patagonian Conure, 250
Lesser Pigmy Parrot, 111
Lesser Sulphur Crested Cockatoo, 174, 175
Lesser Vasa Parrot, 346
Lesser White Fronted Amazon, 294
Lesson's Amazon, 302
Lethal factors in mutations, 70ff.
Levaillent's Amazon, 282
Leukosis, 82
Licometis, 102
Lignum vitae, 203
Lilac Collared Parrot, 358
Lilac Crowned Amazon, 291
Lilac Tailed Parrot, 443
Lilacine Amazon, 302
Limberneck, 89
Line Breding, 76-77
Lineolated Parrakeet, 18, 27, 37, 74, 447
Lipomas (see tumors, 84-85)
Little Blue Bonnet, 423
Little Corell
Little Lorikeet, 138
Liver disease, 89
Long Tailed Parrakeet, 386
Lophochroa, 102
Loriculus, 470
   amabilis, 472
   aurantiifrons, 473
   berylinus, 471
   exilis, 472
   flosculus, 473
   galgalus, 472
   philippensis apicalis, 472
   philippensis bonapartei, 472
   philippensis bournsi, 472
   philippensis chrysonotus, 472
   philippensis dohertyi, 472

philippensis philippensis, 471
philippensis regulus, 472
philippensis siquijorensis, 472
philippensis worcesteri, 472
pusillus, 471
stigmatus, 472
vernalis, 471
Lories, 40, 101, 112, 470, 484
Loriinae, 101, 112
Lorikeet, 101, 112, 484
Loriquets, 470
Lorius, 100, 125, 350
  albidinucha, 131
  chlorocerus, 128
  domicella, 128, 131
  garrulus, 126
  hypoinochrous devittatus, 126
  hypoinochrous hypoinochrous, 126
  hypoinochrous rosseliana, 126
  lory cyanauchen, 126
  lory erythrothorax, 128
  lory jobiensis, 126
  lory lory, 126
  lory rubiensis, 128
  lory salvadorii, 128
  lory somu, 128
  lory viridicrissalis, 128
  tibialis, 131
Louisade Lory, 126
Love Birds, 14, 16, 18, 21, 27,
  29, 37, 41, 47, 53, 64, 74, 77,
  78, 93, 147, 198, 457, 465,
  484
Lucian's Conure, 266
Lucian Parrakeet, 386
Lutino, 73, 74
Lutino Ringneck Parrakeet, 379
Luzon Guaiabero, 473
Luzon Crimson Spotted Racket-
  Tailed Parrakeet, 451
Luzon Racket-Tailed Parraket,
  451

M

Macaws, 11, 19, 31, 40, 41, 102,
  199, 486
Madasgascar Love Bird, 464
Major Mitchell's Cockatoo, 179
Malabar Parrakeet, 390
Malindang Racket-Tailed
  Parrakeet, 451
Malee Parrakeet, 418
Mange mites, 95
Manycolor Parrakeet, 426
Many Striated Lorikeet, 146
Margarita Brown Throated
  Conure, 243
Maroon Fronted Parrot, 363
Maroon Macaw, 206
Maroon Tailed Conure, 263
Marquesas Blue Lory, 134
Marshall's Lorilet, 150
Mascarinus, 140
Masked Love Birds, 74, 460, 477
Masked Parrakeet, 402
Massena's Lorikeet, 120
Massena's Parrot, 323
Mauge's Conure, 234
Maximilian's Parrot, 323
Mealy Amazon, 302, 303, 307
Mealy Rosella, 415
Medications, 80 ff., 508, 511
Meek's Lorikeet, 138
Meek's Pigmy Parrot, 111
Melopsittacus, 104
  undulatus, 454
Mendel's Laws, 72 ff.
Mercenary Amazon, 307
Mercury oxide ointment, 86
Mesh, wire, 29
Mexican Double Yellow Head, 54,
  75, 275, 278, 282, 283, 286,
  287, 291, 294
Mexican Red Head, 291
Meyer's Lorikeet, 123

Meyer's Parrot, 343
Micropsitta, 101
  bruijnii, 110
  finschii, 111
  geelvinkiana, 111
  keinensis chloroxantha, 111
  keinensis keinensis, 111
  meeki, 111
  proxima, 111
  pusio beccarii, 111
  pusio pusio, 111
Micropsittinae, 101, 102, 109
Microsittace, 102
  ferrugineus, 270
  ferrugineus ferrugineus, 270
  ferrugineus minor, 270
Military Macaw, 206, 210, 214, 218, 222, 270
Mindanao Guiaiabero, 473
Mirrors, 59
Misori's Pigmy Parrot, 111
Mitchell's Lorikeet, 120
Mites, red, 68-69, 94-95
Mitred Conure, 231
Miyagawanella psittaci, 83
Modest Parrot, 371
Modifiers, 75-76
Molds, 86
  (see External molds, 86-87. See Internal molds, 87; mold pneumonia, 87)
Moluccan Cockatoo, 162, 175, 178
Moluccan Lory, 117
Monsel's salts, 80, 92, 93
Moult, 67, 68, 93
Mount Apo Lorikeet, 123
Mountain Pigmy Parrot, 110
Mourning Dove, 282
Moustache Parrakeet, 382-383
Mouth Canker, 87, 88
Mrs. Johnstone's Lorikeet, 123
Mules, 77

Murray Rosella, 411
Musk Lorikeet, 135
Musk Parrots, 104, 399
Musschenbroek's Lory, 154
Mutations, 70 ff.
Mycobacterium avium, 83
Myiopsitta, 101, 435
  monachus, 435
  monachus calerita, 438
  monachus cotorra, 438
  monachus luchsi, 438
  monachus monachus, 438

N
Nanday Conure, 246, 250
Nandayus nenday, 102, 246
Nannopsittaca panychloris, 102, 447
Natterer's Amazon, 287
Neophema, 104, 430
  bourkii, 435
  chrysostomus· chrysogaster, 431
  chrysostomus chrysostomus, 430
  chrysostomus cyanopterus, 431
  chyrsostomus mab, 431
  elegans carteri, 430
  elegans elegans, 430
  petrophila petrophila, 431
  petrophila zietzi, 431
  pulchella, 434
  splendida, 434
Neopsittacus, 101, 154
  musschenbroekii major, 154
  musschenbroekii musschenbroekii, 154
  pullicauda alpinus, 154
  pullicauda pullicauda, 154
  pullicauda socialis, 154
Nest boxes, 37 ff.
Nesting failures, 483

Nesting periods, chart of comparative, 484
Nestor, 101
   meridionalis meridionalis, 107, 108
   meridionalis septentrionalis, 108
   notabilis, 109
   productus, 109
Nestorinae, 101, 107
New Caledonian Lorikeet, 139
Newcastle's Disease, 82
New Zealand's Parrakeets, 452
Niam-Niam Parrot, 342
Nicobar Parrakeet, 386
Noble Macaw, 214, 215, 226
Northern Rosella, 415
Nyassaland Love Bird, 457, 463, 477
Northiella, 104, 422
Nymphicus hollandicus, 102, 159, 190

O

Ognorhynchus icterotis, 102, 270
Oil gland, treatment of swelling, 84
Old age, 89
Olive Green Lorikeet, 122
Olive Throated Conure, 239
Oocysts, 84
Opopsitta, 101, 147
   diophthalma aruensis, 150
   diophthalma coccineifrons, 151
   diophthalma coxeni, 151
   diophthalma diophthalma, 150
   diophthalma inseperabilis, 151
   diophthalma macleayana, 150
   diophthalma marshalli, 150
   diophthalma virago, 151
   gulielmiterti, 147
   gulielmiterti amabilis, 150
   gulielmiterti fuscifrons, 150
   gulielmiterti melanogenia, 150

gulielmiterti nigrifrons, 150
gulielmiterti ramuensis, 150
gulielmiterti suavissima, 150
Orange Bellied Parrot, 343
Orange Bellied Senegal Parrot, 343
Orange Breasted Parrakeet, 430, 431
Orange Cheeked Amazon, 298
Orange Cheeked Parrot, 338
Orange Chinned Parrakeet, 438
Orange Crowned Parrot, 339
Orange Flanked Parrakeet, 442, 449
Orange Fronted Hanging Parrakeet, 473
Orange Fronted Parrakeet, 453
Orange Naped Lorikeet, 119
Orange Winged Amazon, 306
Oreopsittacus, 101, 147
   arfaki àrfaki, 147
   arfaki grandis, 147
   arfaki major, 147
Ornate Lory, 118
Ornithologist, contributions of, 11
Ornithosis, 83-84
Outcrossing, 76
Overgrown beaks, 91-92
Overgrown toenails, 92-93
Owl Parrots, 101, 107

P

Painted Conure, 270
Painted Ground Parrot, 371
Pallid Caique, 334
Palm Cockatoo, 159, 162
Panama, 275
Panama Amazon, 54, 286, 287
Panama Parrot, 283, 287
Papuan Lory, 142
Paradise Parrot, 427
Paralysis, 89

Parasitic worms, 93
Paratyphoid, 82
Parrakeets, 102, 375, 454
Parrakeets, (Elegants and close
    relatives), 484
Parrakeets (Ringneck group), 484
Parrot family, definition of, 98
Parrot fever, 83
Parrotlets, 102, 457, 465
Parrots, 275
Parrots (Amazons, Caiques, African
    Grey, etc.), 484
Parrots Exclusively, 291
Pasteurellosis, 82
Patagonian Conure, 250
Peach Faced Love Bird, 74, 457,
    460, 463, 477
Peanut Butter, 22-23
Pearly Conure, 258, 266
Penicillin, 81
Perches, 34-35, 61-62, 95
Perfect Lorikeets, 117
Peroxide, 81
Pesquet's Parrot, 370
Peters, James Lee, 99
Petz' Conure, 14, 214, 239, 242,
    246, 303
Pezoporus, 104, 454
  wallicus, 454
  wallicus flaviventris, 456
  wallicus leachi, 456
  wallicus wallicus, 456
Phigys, 101, 131
  solitarius, 131
Philippine Cockatoo, 178
Philippine Green Parrot, 358
Philippine Hanging Parrakeet, 471
Philippine Racket-Tailed
    Parrakeet, 451
Pied factor, 74
Pigmy Parrot, 101, 109
Pileated Parrakeet, 422

Pileated Parrot, 335
Pink Cockatoo, 179
Pionites, 102, 327
  leucogaster leucosgaster, 331
  leucogaster xanthomeria, 334
  leucogaster xanthurus, 334
  melanocephala melanocephala, 331
  melanocephala pallida, 334
Pionopsitta, 102, 335
  barrabandi, 338
  caica, 338
  haematotis coccinocollaris, 335
  haematotis haematotis, 335
  haematotis pulchra, 335
  pileata, 335
  pyrilia, 338
Pionus, 102, 319
  chalcopterus, 326
  fuscicapillus, 342
  fuscus, 326
  maximiliani lacerus, 323
  maximiliani maximiliani, 323
  maximiliani melanoblepharus, 323
  maximiliani siy, 323
  menstruus, 322
  senilis, 323
  seniloides, 323
  sordidus antelius, 322
  sordidus corallinus, 322
  sordidus mindoensis, 322
  sordidus ponsi, 322
  sordidus saturatus, 322
  sordidus sordidus, 322
  tumultuosus, 327
Plain Colored Amazon, 287, 303
Plath, Karl, 291
Platycercidae, 151
Platycercus, 100, 104, 407
  adelaide, 410
  adscitus adscitus, 415
  adscitus elseyi, 415
  adscitus palliceps, 415

barnardius macgillivrayi, 418
caledonicus, 411
elegans elegans, 410
elegans melanoptera, 410
elegans nigrescens, 410
eximius cecilae, 414
eximius splendidus, 414
flaveolus, 411
icterotis icterotis, 414
icterotis xanthogenys, 414
venustus hilli, 418
venustus venustus, 415
zonarius barnardi, 418
zonarius dundasi, 419
zonarius occidentalis, 419
zonarius semitorquatus, 419
zonarius zonarius, 410, 419
Playpens, 61-62
Pleasing Lorikeet, 139
Plum Head Parrakeet, 387
Pneumonia, 82
 mold, 87, 88
Poicephalus, 104, 338
 crassus, 342
 cryptoxanthus, 342
 cryptoxanthus cyrptoxanthus, 342
 cryptoxanthus tanganyikae, 342
 cryptoxanthus zanzibaricus, 342
 flavifrons aurantiiceps, 342
 flavifrons flavifrons, 339
 gulielmi fantiensis, 339
 gulielmi gulielmi, 339
 gulielmi massaicus, 339
 gulielmi permistus, 339
 meyeri damarensis, 343
 meyeri matschiei, 343
 meyeri reichenowi, 343
 meyeri saturatus, 343
 meyeri transvaalensis, 343
 robustus fuscicollis, 339
 robustus robustus, 339
 robustus suahelicus, 339

rueppellii, 346
rufiventris pallidus, 343
rufiventris rufiventris, 343
senegalus, 342
senegalus mesotypus, 343
senegalus senegalus, 343
senegalus versteri, 343
Polytelines, 402
Polytelis, 104, 402
 alexandrae, 406
 anthopeplus, 406
 spathopterus, 402
 swainsonii, 402
Port Lincoln Parrakeet, 419
Pox (bird), 82
Praslin Parrot, 347
Pretre's Amazon, 311
Prevention of diseases and
 disorders, 80
 (See Diseases and Ailments,
 79ff.)
Princess Alexandra Parrakeet, 74,
 402, 406
Princess of Wales Parrakeet, 406
Princess Parrakeet, 406
Prioniturus, 104, 450
 discurus discurus, 451
 discurus mindorensis, 451
 discurus platenae, 451
 discurus suluensis, 451
 discurus waterstradti, 451
 flavicans flavicans, 451
 flavicans montanus, 451
 flavicans verticalis, 452
 luconensis, 451
 mada, 452
 malindangensis, 451
 platurus platurus, 452
 platurus talautensis, 452
Prosciger, 102, 159, 163
 aterrimus aterrimus, 163
 aterrimus goliath, 163

aterrimus stenolophus, 163
Prosopeia, 104, 399
  personata, 402
  tabuensis atrogularis, 402
  tabuensis koroensis, 402
  tabuensis splendens, 402
  tabuensis tabuensis, 399
  tabuensis taviunensis, 402
Protozoan, diseases, 84, 88
Proventriculus, 94
Psephotus, 104, 422
  chrysopterygius chrysopteryguis,
    427
  chrysopterygius dissimilis, 427
  haematogaster haematogaster, 423
  haematogaster haematorrhous, 422
  haematogaster narethae, 423
  haematogaster pallescens, 423
  haematonotus, 423
  pulcherrimus, 427
  varius ethelae, 426
  varius exsul, 426
  varius varius, 426
Pseudeos, 101, 124
  fuscata fuscata, 124
  fuscata incondita, 125
Psilopsiagon, 102, 449
  aurifrons aurifrons, 449
  aurifrons orbygnesius, 449
  aurifrons robertsi, 449
  aurifrons rubrirostris, 449
Psittacella, 104, 370
  brehmii brehmii, 370
  brehmii harteri, 371
  brehmii intermixta, 371
  brehmii pallida, 371
  modesta madarazzi, 371
  modesta modesta, 371
  picta lorentzi, 371
  picta picta, 371
Psittacidae, 98, 101
Psittaciformes, 98-101

Psittacinae, 102
Psittacula, 104, 375
  alexandri abbotti, 382
  alexandri alexandri, 382
  alexandri cala, 382
  alexandri dammermani, 383
  alexandri fasciata, 382
  alexandri kangeanennsis, 383
  alexandri major, 382
  alexandri perionca, 383
  calthorpae, 287
  columboides caniceps, 390
  columboides columboides, 390
  columboides exsul, 390
  columboides intermedia, 390
  cyanocephala, 387
  derbiana, 383
  eupatria avensis, 382
  eupatria eupatria, 382
  eupatria magnirostris, 382
  eupatria nidalensis, 379
  eupatria siamensis, 382
  eupatria wardi, 382
  himalayana finschii, 387
  himalayana himalayana, 387
  krameri borealis, 379
  krameri krameri, 379
  krameri manillensis, 375
  krameri parvirostris, 379
  longicauda defontainei, 386
  longicauda longicauda, 386
  longicauda modesta, 386
  longicauda nicobarica, 386
  longicauda tytleri, 386
  peristerodes, 390
  roseata, 386
Psittaculirostris, 101
  desmarestii blythi, 155
  desmarestii cervacalis, 155
  desmarestii desmarestii, 154
  desmarestii godmani, 155
  desmarestii occidentalis, 155

salvadorii edwardsii, 155
salvadorii salvadorii, 155
Psittacus, 104, 275
  erithacus erithacus, 275
  erithacus princeps, 278
  erithacus timneh, 278
Psitteuteles, 101
Psittinus, 104, 367
  cyanurus abbotti, 370
  cyanurus cyanurus, 367
  cyanurus pontius, 370
Psittrichas, 104, 370
  fulgidus, 370
Puerto Rican Amazon, 318
Pullorum, 82
Purple Bellied Lory, 126
Purple Bellied Parrot, 367
Purple Breasted Parrot, 367
Purple Crowned Lorikeet, 135
Purple Naped Lory, 128, 131
"Putting to sleep", 97
Purpureicephalus, 104, 422
  spurius, 422
Pyrrhura, 102, 254
  albipectus, 262
  berlepschi, 263
  calliptera, 262
  cruentata, 255
  devillei, 258
  egregia, 263
  frontalis chiripepe, 254
  frontalis frontalis, 254
  frontalis kriegi, 254
  haematotis, 267
  hoffmani gaudens, 267
  hoffmani hoffmani, 267
  leucotis auricularis, 258
  leucotis emma, 255
  leucotis griseipectus, 255
  leucotis leucotis, 255
  leucotis pfrimeri, 255
  melanura chapmani, 263

  melanura souancei, 263
  molinae molinae, 263
  molinae phoenicura, 262
  molinae restricta, 262
  molinae sordida, 263
  perlata anerythra, 258
  perlata coerulescens, 258
  perlata lepida, 258
  perlata perlata, 258
  picta amazonum, 266, 267
  picta caeruliceps, 266, 267
  picta lucianii, 266, 267
  picta microptera, 267
  picta picta, 266
  picta roseifrons, 267
  picta subandina, 266, 267
  rhodocephala, 262
  rupicola, 266
  viridicata, 258

Q
Quaker Parrakeet, 435, 477
Quarrion bird, 198
Queen Alexandra's Parrakeet, 406
Queen of Bavaria Conure, 226, 230

R
Raja Lory, 115
Rare Love Birds, 463
Red and Blue Lory, 116
Red and Blue Macaw, 206, 219
Red and Green Macaw, 206
Red and Yellow Macaw, 210
Red and Bellied Conure, 254
Red Bellied Macaw, 214
Red Breasted Lorikeet, 120
Red Breasted Musk Parrot, 399, 402
Red Breasted Parrot, 343
Red Breasted Pigmy Parrot, 110
Red Browed Amazon, 311
Red Browed Lorilet, 150

Red Capped Hanging Parrakeets, 472
Red Capped Parrakeet, 422
Red Capped Parrot, 335
Red Cheeked Parrot, 355
Red Collared Lorikeet, 119
Red Crowned Cockatoo, 170
Red Crowned Lorikeet, 124
Red Crowned Macaw, 218
Red Crowned Parrot, 339
Red Eared Conure, 267
Red Faced Lorilet, 157
Red Faced Love Bird, 463
Red Faced Parrot, 347
Red Flanked Lorikeet, 139
Red Fronted Amazon, 318
Red Fronted Conure, 231
Red Fronted Lory, 114
Red Fronted Macaw, 218
Red Fronted Parrakeet, 453
Red Headed Conure, 234
Red Headed Love Bird, 463
Red Headed Parrot, 339
Red Lored Amazon, 294
Red Lorikeet, 118
Red Lory, 117, 118
Red Marked Lorikeet, 146
Red Masked Conure, 234
Red mites, 68-69, 94-95
Red Quilled Lory, 113
Red Rosella, 411, 415
Redrump Parrakeet, 14, 423, 426, 477
Red Shining Parrakeet, 402
Redsided Eclectus Parrot, 355
Red Speckled Conure, 234
Red Tailed Amazon, 319
Red Tailed Black Cockatoo, 167
Red Throated Amazon, 318
Red Throated Hanging Parrakeet, 472
Red Throated Lorikeet, 143

Red Vented Blue Bonnet, 422, 423
Red Vented Cockatoo, 178, 182
Red Vented Parrot, 322
Red, White and Blue Parrot, 294
Red Winged Parrotlet, 446
Regurgitation, 89
Restless Parrot, 327
Rhynchopsitta, 102, 363
  pachyrhyncha, 363
  terrisi, 363
Riedeli's Eclectus, 354
Ringneck Parrakeets, 12, 14, 37, 53, 198, 418
Rock Conure, 266
Rock Grass Parrakeet, 430, 431
Rock Parrakeet, 431
Rock Pebbler, 402, 406
Roseate Cockatoo, 187
Rose Breasted Cockatoos, 11, 75, 187, 190, 484
Rose Crested Cockatoo, 178
Rose Headed Conure, 262
Rosellas, 37, 407, 410
Rosenberg's Lorikeet, 121, 122
Rosy-Faced Love Bird, 460
Rothschild's Amazon, 315
Rothschild's Lorikeet, 143
Ruby Lory, 134
Rudkin, Sr., Francis, 462
Rufous Fronted Parrakeet, 449
Ruppel's Parrot, 346
Ruptured egg sac, 90
Rusty Faced Parrot, 347

S

Sacred Temple Parrot, 350
Saffron Headed Parrot, 338
St. Lucia Amazon, 310
St. Thomas Conure, 243, 246
St. Vincent's Amazon, 310
Salle's Amazon, 298, 302

Salmon Crested Cockatoo, 178
Salvador's Lory, 155
Salvin's Amazon, 298, 302
Salwatte King Parrakeet, 399
San Domingo Amazon, 310
Santa Marta Conure, 258
Sapphire Rumped Parrotlet, 443
Scaly Breasted Lorikeet, 118
Scaly leg mites, 95
Scarlet Bellied Senegal Parrot, 343
Scarlet Chested Parrakeet, 434
Scarlet Macaw, 56, 206, 210
Scarlet Shouldered Parrotlet, 443
Sclater's Lorikeet, 142
Sclater's Parrotlet, 469
Selective Breeding, 76
Senegal Parrot, 342, 343
Severe Macaw, 210, 214
Sex Determination, 475, 476
Sex-linked mutations, 72
  definition of, 72
  description of, 72
  varieties, 72, 73
Sharp Tailed Conure, 226
Shell Parrakeet, 454
Shock, 89
Short-Tailed Parrot, 366
Sierra Parrakeet, 449
Single Yellow Head, 287
Sinus, 85-86
Skin, 96
Slaty Headed Parrakeet, 387
Slender Billed Cockatoo, 186
Slender Billed Conure, 271
Small, Mr. and Mrs. Ralph, 486, 496
Soft Shelled eggs, 90
Solitary Lory, 131
Solomon Electus, 355
Song Parrot, 358
Sonoran Spectacled Amazon, 294
Sordid Parrot, 322

Sour Crop, 87
Sparrow Hawk, 282
Spathopterus, 104
Spectacled Amazon, 21, 294, 298
Spectacled Parrotlet, 469
Speed, Dorothy, 167
Spengel's Parrotlet, 465
Sphaerophorous, 85
Spiral worms, 94
Spix Macaw, 222
Splendid Parrakeet, 434
Split tongues, 60
Sports, 72
Spotted Winged Parrotlet, 446
Spray, 64
Stanley Rosella, 414
Staphylococcosis, 82
Stella's Lorikeet, 142, 146
Stella's Lory, 142
Stephen's Lory, 135
Strigopinae, 101, 107
Strigops, 101, 107
  habroptilus, 107
Sula Island King Parrakeet, 399.
Sulfamethazine, 81, 88
Sulphur Crested Cockatoo, 52
Sulu Green Parrot, 359
Sulu Racket-Tailed Parrakeet, 451
Sun Conure, 230
Sunshine, 66-67
Superb Parrakeet, 402
Supplement, to diet, 18
Swainson's Blue Mountain
  Lorikeets, 100, 112, 119, 120,
    121, 122, 476, 481
Swamp Parrakeets, 454
Swift Lorikeet, 151
Swift Parrakeets, 151
Swindern's Love Bird, 465
Symptoms, (see Diseases and
  Ailments, 79ff.)

T

Table snacks, 15
Tahiti Blue Lory, 134
Talking, 54 ff.
Taming, 41 ff.
Tanygnathus, 104, 358
  lucionensis horrisonus, 359
  lucionensis koike, 359
  lucionensis lucionensis, 358
  lucionensis moro, 359
  lucionensis nigrogorum, 359
  lucionensis paraguensis, 359
  lucionensis salvadorii, 359
  lucionensis talautensis, 359
  megalorhynchos affinis, 362, 363
  megalorhynchos djampeae, 362
  megalorhynchos floris, 362
  megalorhynchos helmayri, 362
  megalorhynchos megalorhynchos,
    362
  megalorhynchos subaffinis, 362
  megalorhynchos sumbensis, 362,
    363
  megalorhynchos viridipennis
  mulleri, 359
  mulleri burbidgii, 362
  mulleri freeri, 359
  mulleri mulleri, 362
  mulleri sangirensis, 362
  sumatranus, 359
Tapeworm, 94
Taviuni Parrakeet, 402
Techniques for speech training,
  59-60
Temperatures, brooders, 487, 488,
  489, 493
Tepui Parrotlet, 447
Terramycin, 81, 83
Thick-Billed Parrot, 339, 363
Thrush, 87
Timneh Parrot, 278
Timor Cockatoo, 159, 175

Timor Island Crimson Winged
  Parrakeet, 394
Tobago Orange Winged Amazon,
  307
Toenails, 92, 93
Tortuga Conure, 243
Touit, 102, 442
  batavica, 443
  dilectissima costaricensis, 446
  dilectissima dilectissima, 446
  huetii, 443
  melanonotus, 443
  purpurata purpurata, 443
  purpurata viridiceps, 443
  stictoptera, 446
  surda, 446
Tovi Parrakeet, 438
Toys, 62
Training techniques, 59 ff.
Treat seed, 21
Tres Marias Amazon, 287
Trichoglossus, 101, 117, 138
  chlorolepidosus, 118
  euteles, 117
  flavoviridis flavoviridis, 123
  flaviviridis meyeri, 123
  forsteni, 100, 120
  goldei, 123
  haematodus, 110, 122, 138
  haematodus aberrans, 122
  haematodus brooki, 122
  haematodus caeruliceps, 121
  haematodus capistratus, 121
  haematodus deplanchii, 122, 123
  haematodus djampeanus, 120
  haematodus flavicans, 122
  haematodus flavotectus, 122, 123
  haematodus forsteni, 100, 120
  haematodus fortis, 122
  haematodus haematodus, 121
  haematodus intermedius, 120-121,
    122

haematodus massena, 120
haematodus micropteryx, 122, 123
haematodus mitchelli, 120
haematodus moluccanus, 100
haematodus nesophilus, 122, 123
haematodus nigrogularis, 121
haematodus rosenbergii, 122
haematodus rubritorquis, 119
haematodus stresemanni, 122
haematodus weberi, 122
iris, 124
johnstoniae, 123
ornatus, 118
rubriginosus, 118
rubripileum, 124
versicolor, 124
wetterensis, 124
Triclaria, 104, 367
  cyanogaster, 367
  malachitacea, 367
Tri-Colored Lory, 126
Triton Cockatoo, 174
Tschudi's Amazon, 307
Tuberculosis, 82-83
Tucuman Amazon, 311
Tui Parrakeet, 439
Tuipara Parrakeet, 439
Tumors, 84-85
Turquoise Rumped Parrotlet, 467
Turquoise Parrakeet, 434
Twenty-eight Parrakeet, 419
Typhoid, 82

U
Ultramarine Lory, 134-135
Umbrella Crested Cockatoo, 175
Undulating Grass Parrakeet, 454
Urochroma, 442
Uvean Parrakeet, 454

V
Varied Lorikeet, 124

Vegetables, 21, 22
Vernal Hanging Parrakeet, 471
Versicolor Amazon, 310
Victoria Lory, 147
Vinaceous Amazon, 310
Vini, 101, 131
  australis, 131
  kuhli, 134
  peruviana, 134
  stephani, 135
  ultramarina, 134
Violet Necked Lory, 115, 116
Violet Parrot, 326
Virus infections, 81-82
Voices, of parrot, 55-56
  natural call, 55 ff.
  talking, 55 ff.
Vulture Headed Parrot, 366

W
Wagler's Conure, 231
Wagler's Macaw, 222
Wallace's Lory, 116
Water, 117
Waterers, 36
Webby seed, 20
Weber's Lorikeet, 121, 122
Weddell's Conure, 238
West, David, 410
Western Rosella, 414
White Bellied Caiques, 327, 331
White Breasted Conure, 262
White Capped Parrot, 323
White Crested Conure, 175
White Cockatoo, 159
White Crowned Parrot, 323
White Eared Conure, 255
White Headed Amazon, 310
White Necked Lory, 131
White Rumped Lory, 125
White Tailed Black Cockatoo, 170
White Winged Parrakeet, 442

Whistling Parrot, 347
Wilhelmina's Lorikeet, 142
Wings, broken, 95-96
  clipping of, 41-42
Wire mesh, 29
Wire-worm, 94
Wonder drugs, 81, 83
Worms, 93, 94
Wyatt, Kenneth, 486, 492
Woodpecker parrots, 109

Y
Yellow and Green Lorikeet, 123
Yellow Backed Lory, 126
Yellow Bellied Rosella, 411
Yellow Bibbed Lory, 128
Yellow Breasted Musk Parrakeet, 402
Yellow Cheeked Amazon, 298, 302, 315
Yellow Cheeked Conure, 243, 246
Yellow Collared Lory, 128
Yellow Conure, 226, 230

Yellow Crowned Amazon, 311
Yellow Eared Conure, 270
Yellow Fronted Amazon, 287
Yellow Fronted Parrakeet, 453
Yellow Fronted Parrot, 339
Yellow and Green Lorikeet, 123
Yellow Headed Amazon, 282
Yellow Lored Amazon, 298
Yellow Naped Amazon, 54, 75, 275, 278, 283, 286, 287, 294, 298
Yellow Naped Macaw, 210
Yellow Rosella, 411
Yellow Rumped Parrakeet, 411
Yellow Shouldered Amazon, 315
Yellow Streaked Lory, 114, 146
Yellow Tailed Black Cockatoo, 170
Yellow Thighed Caique, 334
Yellow Vented Blue Bonnet, 423
Yellow Winged Amazon, 306

Z
Zanda, 102, 163

Illustrations Index

Abyssinian Love Bird, 376, 420, 464

African Grey Parrot, 221, 274, 352, 396, 416, 445

Alexander Ringneck Parrakeet, 212, 437

Amazon Parrot (lutino), 71

Australian Finches, 34, 35

Australian King Parrakeet, 412, 428

Aviaries
 for Cockatoos, 25
 for Macaws, 25, 30
 for Parrakeets, 34
 with pipe framework, 26
 tall flights, 26
 wooden framework, 27, 29

Aviary feeding, 23

Aztec Conure, 238

Banksian Cockatoo, 166

Bare Eyed Cockatoo, 36, 183, 313

Barnard's Parrakeet, 208, 373

Barraband Parrakeet, 200, 381, 403

Bee Bee Parrakeet, 361

Bee Bee Parrot, 417

Black Capped Lory, 429

Black Cheeked Love Bird, 384, 436

Black Headed Caique, 331, 365

Black Masked Love Bird, 129, 384, 461

Blossom Head Parrakeet, 356, 437

Blue and Gold Macaw, 103, 207, 276, 340

Blue and Yellow Macaw, 396

Blue Crowned Amazon, 280, 281

Blue Eared Lorikeet, 445

Blue Fronted Amazon, 316, 317, 396

Blue Headed Parrot, 225, 396

Blue Masked Love Bird, 388

Blue Rosella, 201, 432

Blue Winged Parrotlet, 397

Bourke's Parrakeet, 245, 360, 478

Bronze Winged Parrot, 149, 326

Brown Eared Conure, 301

Brown Parrot, 157

Budgerigar, 161, 164, 165, 168, 169, 172, 173, 176, 177, 180, 181, 184, 185, 188, 189, 192, 248, 252, 253, 403, 455

Cactus Conure, 417

Cages, 62, 63

Canary, 188

Carolina Parrakeet, 105

Celestial Parrotlet, 469

Chattering Lory, 157, 268, 424

Cherry Headed Conure, 235

Citron Crested Cockatoo, 260

Cloncurry Parrakeet, 405

Cockatiel, 55, 137, 140, 191, 194, 195, 205, 349, 353, 393, 425, 474

Cockatoo hybrid, 78
Crimson Rosella, 413
Crimson Winged Parrakeet, 391, 424, 441
Cuban Amazon, 314

Derbyan Parrakeet, 193
Dwarf Panama Parrot, 366

Elegant Parrakeet, 209
Everett's Blue Backed Parrot, 249

Feeding station, 30
Festive Amazon Parrot, 233
Finsch's Amazon Parrot, 396
Finsch's Conure, 227
Fischer's Love Bird, 224, 389, 448, 458
Funeral Cockatoo, 268

Gang Gang Cockatoo, 261
Gold Mantled Rosella, 393
Golden Cherry Love Bird, 369
Golden Crowned Conure, 247, 344, 397
Golden Shouldered Parrakeet, 404
Grand Eclectus Parrot, 196, 221
Greater Patagonian Conure, 251
Greater Sulphur Crested Cockatoo, 46, 50, 171, 289, 296, 396
Green Cheeked Amazon, 141, 290, 309, 397
Green Conure, 227, 235
Green Winged King Parrot, 398
Green Winged Macaw, 219, 292, 328

Half Moon Conure, 49, 51, 67, 301, 337
Hawk Headed Parrot, 232
Hyacinth Macaw, 202, 305, 321, 341

Indian Ringneck Parrakeet, 241, 347, 374, 379, 405, 408
Ivory Conure, 421

Jardine's Parrot, 133
Janday Conure, 300, 336

Kakapo, 106
Kea Parrot, 109
King Parrot, 216

Leadbeater's Cockatoo, 179, 320, 372, 433
Lear's Macaw, 25, 202
Lesser Sulphur Crested Cockatoo, 440
Levaillant's Amazon, 444
Lineolated Parrakeet, 397

Macaw, growth stages of, 498-506
Macaw, hybrid, 288
Malabar Parrakeet, 157
Manycolor Parrakeet, 421
Mealy Rosella, 201, 432
Mexican Double Yellow Head Parrot, 17, 33, 44, 280, 282, 444
Mexican Parrotlet, 467
Meyer's Parrot, 157
Military Macaw, 211, 257, 321
Moluccan Cockatoo, 39, 162, 285
Moluccan Lory, 304
Moustache Parrakeet, 383

Nanday Conure, 336, 345
Nestboxes
  for Cockatiels, 32
  for Cockatoos, 28
  for Conures, 34, 38
  for Lories and Lorikeets, 37

for Macaws, 30
for Parrakeets, 34, 38
for Parrots, 38
Grandfather clock, 40
Metal, 31, 36
Tree trunk, 40
Wooden barrel, 39
Noble Macaw, 215
Nyassaland Love Bird, 388, 436

Panama Parrot, 286, 295
Peach Faced Love Bird, 368, 369, 377, 461
Petz' Conure, 49, 51, 67, 301, 337, 397
Philippine Green Parrot, 256
Pileated Parrakeet, 349
Plumhead Parrakeet, 228
Princess Alexandra Parrakeet, 380, 407

Quaker Parrakeet, 149
Queen of Bavaria Conure, 329

Record training, 57
Red and Blue Macaw, 219
Red Bellied Conure, 136
Red Fronted Conure, 271, 272
Red Fronted Parrakeet, 392
Red Headed Amazon, 290, 309
Red Headed Conure, 235
Red Lory, 304
Red Rosella Parrakeet, 236
Redrump Parrakeet, 34, 35, 209, 244, 246, 388, 485
Red Sided Eclectus Parrot, 351
Red Tailed Black Cockatoo, 166
Red Vented Cockatoo, 312
Red Vented Parrot, 225
Rock Pebbler, 229, 404
Roseate Cockatoo, 396

Rose Breasted Cockatoo, 158, 187, 277, 396, 433
Rosella hybrid, 237, 485

Salvin's Amazon Parrot, 299
Scarlet Chested Parrakeet, 325
Scarlet Macaw, 132, 264, 385, 400, 401
Senegal Parrot, 145, 213, 429
Severe Macaw, 293
Short Tailed Parrot, 366
Slender Billed Cockatoo, 186, 284
Spectacled Parrot, 152, 290, 397
Spix Macaw, 223
Stanley Rosella, 392, 428
Swainson's Blue Mountain Lorikeet, 130, 297, 480, 481

Thick Billed Parrot, 99
Tovi Parrakeet, 361, 397
Tui Parrakeet, 439
Turquoise Rumped Parrakeet, 467

Vinaceous Amazon, 153

Wagler's Conure, 270
Western Rosella, 428
White Bellied Caique, 240, 330
White Breasted Caique, 330, 364
White Cockatoo, 160
White Crowned Parrot, 197, 204
White Winged Beebee, 439
White Winged Parrakeet, 439

Yellow Backed Lory, 127
Yellow Cheeked Amazon, 217
Yellow Fronted Amazon Parrot, 397, 409
Yellow Naped Amazon Parrot, 44, 53, 279, 308, 396
Yellow Tailed Black Cockatoo, 268